The Convergence of Mathematics and AI:

A New Paradigm in Education

Ali Mazı
https://orcid.org/0000-0001-9188-8583
Ministry of National Education, Turkey

IGI Global
Scientific Publishing
Publishing Tomorrow's Research Today

Vice President of Editorial	Melissa Wagner
Director of Acquisitions	Mikaela Felty
Director of Book Development	Jocelynn Hessler
Production Manager	Mike Brehm
Cover Design	Jose Rosado

Published in the United States of America by
IGI Global Scientific Publishing
701 East Chocolate Avenue
Hershey, PA, 17033, USA
Tel: 717-533-8845 | Fax: 717-533-7115
Website: https://www.igi-global.com E-mail: cust@igi-global.com

Library of Congress Cataloging-in-Publication Data

Names: Mazı, Ali, 1992- editor
Title: The convergence of mathematics and AI : a new paradigm in education / edited by Ali Mazı.
Description: Hershey, PA : IGI Global Scientific Publishing, [2026] | Includes bibliographical references and index. | Summary: "This book provides a comprehensive guide to the ongoing technological transformations in the field of education by addressing the intersection of mathematics education and AI"-- Provided by publisher.
Identifiers: LCCN 2025024592 (print) | LCCN 2025024593 (ebook) | ISBN 9798337319988 h/c | ISBN 9798337319995 s/c | ISBN 9798337320007 ebook
Subjects: LCSH: Mathematics--Study and teaching--Data processing | Artificial intelligence--Educational applications | Educational technology
Classification: LCC QA16 .C66 2026 (print) | LCC QA16 (ebook)
LC record available at https://lccn.loc.gov/2025024592
LC ebook record available at https://lccn.loc.gov/2025024593

British Cataloguing in Publication Data
A Cataloguing in Publication record for this book is available from the British Library.

Table of Contents

Detailed Table of Contents

Mathematical thinking has a crucial role in STEM education. It encompasses problem-solving, logical reasoning, pattern recognition, abstraction, among others, that are transversal to many technical areas. Incorporating the capabilities of Artificial Intelligence into math education can enhance learning efficiency while providing personalized instruction. It also allows us to simulate complex or rare situations, which enrich the preparation of students. However, the use of these tools also raises ethical concerns, such as data privacy, or algorithmic bias. In addition, potential over-reliance on AI has raised concerns about weakening critical thinking and to the amplification of injustice, issues that may widen educational gaps. Integration strategies, where a balanced approach with human oversight must be implemented, inclusive technology design, and careful monitoring of educational outcomes are crucial to responsibly use AI. This way, ethical standards in mathematics education for engineering disciplines can be upheld.

Queueing theory, a core area in operations research and applied mathematics, is essential for optimizing resource use, minimizing delays, and improving efficiency across sectors like logistics, healthcare, and telecommunications. With the rise of artificial intelligence (AI), traditional queueing models are evolving into adaptive systems capable of real-time data analysis and automated decision-making. This chapter explores the integration of AI techniques—such as machine learning and neural networks—with classical queueing theory to enhance modeling, prediction, and system optimization. It also highlights how AI-driven queueing systems can dynamically manage service parameters and forecast congestion. Beyond applications, the chapter examines the pedagogical value of embedding these models in mathematics education, empowering students with advanced analytical and computational skills. Ethical concerns, implementation challenges, and future research directions are discussed, emphasizing AI's transformative role in mathematical modeling and decision-making.

This chapter explains how mathematics supports the development and functioning of Artificial Intelligence (AI). It shows how different areas of mathematics are used to create models, solve problems, and improve how AI systems learn and make decisions. Topics such as linear algebra, calculus, probability, and graph theory are introduced with clear examples. For instance, graph theory helps represent networks like social media, where people are shown as points and their relationships as lines connecting them. The chapter also discusses how mathematics helps protect sensitive information using secure methods like encryption. In addition, it looks at how mathematics is used to work with images, such as sharpening or analysing pictures using algebra and optimization techniques. Overall, the chapter aims to show how mathematical ideas are not just theoretical but play an important role in making AI systems useful in real life. It helps readers see how mathematics connects to technology and supports progress in this fast-changing field.

Artificial intelligence (AI) is transforming preschool mathematics education by offering personalized learning experiences, adaptive teaching strategies, and interactive content delivery. AI tools like ChatGPT provide individualized feedback, enabling students to engage dynamically with mathematical concepts while supporting educators in lesson planning and content development, but at the same time AI integration raises ethical and technological concerns, including data privacy risks, screen exposure management, and technological accessibility limitations in under-resourced schools. Addressing disparities in AI access necessitates policy-driven solutions that prioritize digital equity and teacher preparedness. AI should enhance, not replace human-led teaching, ensuring responsible implementation. This study concludes that structured AI adoption in preschool mathematics can significantly

prevailing trends, and exploring transformative applications. Using a narrative review supported by expert-informed synthesis, several themes are identified that reflect how AI are reshaping instructional practices, learner engagement, and pedagogical design. The discussion integrates illustrative examples of AI tools to highlight their instructional relevance and underlying mechanisms. The chapter concludes by reflecting on a redefined landscape for mathematics education, where technology transforms instructional practices, learner experiences, and the development of mathematical thinking.

This qualitative study explores prospective mathematics teachers' (PMTs) perceived affordances and constraints of using ChatGPT in mathematical problem posing. Data were collected from 23 PMTs through reflection papers, which documented their experiences using ChatGPT to pose real-life mathematical problems with varying cognitive demand levels. The study employed qualitative content analysis using both deductive and inductive approaches to examine PMTs' experiences with ChatGPT. The findings reveal that PMTs value ChatGPT for its immediate feedback, contextual diversity, and ability to provide personalized learning paths. Additionally, PMTs highlighted its potential as an assessment tool for evaluating the quality of posed problems. However, significant constraints were also identified, such as ChatGPT's limited ability to generate diverse and novel problems, difficulties in producing realistic and contextually rich problems, and mathematical inaccuracies. Additionally, PMTs noted ChatGPT's poor visualization and complex language use, particularly in higher cognitive demand tasks.

The Royal Government of Cambodia has introduced a range of educational and strategic policies to advance educational technology and strengthen digital literacy across the national education system. Integrating Artificial Intelligence (AI) into teaching and learning is among the most widely adopted innovations. While AI in mathematics education has gained increasing traction regionally and globally, its impact on Cambodian students' and teachers' experiences remains underexplored. This study seeks to address this gap by examining the perceptions of university students and mathematics teachers regarding AI-supported mathematics education, with particular attention to perceived benefits, challenges, and its potential to enhance learning outcomes. Using a qualitative research approach, in-depth interviews were conducted with 30 participants from various high schools, providing insights into the opportunities and constraints of AI integration in the Cambodian context.

This chapter investigates the role of artificial intelligence (AI) in mathematics education by leveraging established theoretical frameworks such as constructivism and socio-cultural learning theory. AI-powered tools, including intelligent tutoring systems and adaptive learning technologies, which support individualized instruction tailored to learners' cognitive profiles, enhancing conceptual understanding and

Preface

It is my great honor to present *The Convergence of Mathematics and AI: A New Paradigm in Education*. This edited reference book emerges at a critical moment in educational history, when mathematics, long recognized as the cornerstone of analytical thinking, logical reasoning, and problem-solving, is being reshaped by the possibilities of artificial intelligence. The integration of AI into mathematics education offers more than the promise of efficiency; it invites us to reimagine the very processes of teaching and learning.

For decades, mathematics has not only enhanced cognitive abilities but also nurtured psychosocial development, influencing students' attitudes, self-regulation, and motivation to learn. The arrival of AI technologies provides us with tools to deepen these impacts. Adaptive feedback, intelligent tutoring systems, and personalized learning environments enable students to engage with mathematics in ways tailored to their needs and capacities. This convergence of mathematics and AI carries profound implications, fostering resilience, curiosity, and confidence alongside academic achievement.

The purpose of this book is twofold. First, it seeks to enrich the body of knowledge surrounding innovative approaches to mathematics education by offering theoretical insights and empirical research. Second, it aims to provide a practical roadmap for educators, researchers, and policymakers to harness AI responsibly and effectively, thereby enhancing digital literacy and preparing learners for the demands of an AI-driven society. Each chapter in this volume reflects a careful balance between academic rigor and practical relevance, ensuring that the discussion resonates with diverse stakeholders.

This book is designed for a wide audience: educators, teacher candidates, and mathematics teachers who seek to integrate AI into their practice; researchers and policymakers interested in evidence-based strategies; technology developers and entrepreneurs aspiring to design tools that align with educational needs; and professionals exploring the transformative potential of AI applications in education.

The chapters cover a broad spectrum of themes, including individualized learning pathways, the cultivation of problem-solving and analytical skills, the psychosocial impacts of AI-supported learning, the redesign of assessment and feedback processes, and the perceptions of both students and teachers. Additionally, the book addresses long-term impacts, reflecting on how AI-supported mathematics education shapes learners' academic trajectories and digital competencies over time.

CHAPTER OVERVIEW

Chapter 1: AI Ethics in Mathematics: Strategies for Responsible Implementation

This chapter addresses the critical intersection of mathematics education and ethical considerations in the integration of artificial intelligence. While AI offers transformative potential for personalized instruction, simulation of complex scenarios, and enhanced learning efficiency, it also raises concerns such as data privacy, algorithmic bias, and over-reliance that may weaken critical thinking. The chapter emphasizes the need for balanced implementation strategies, advocating for human oversight, inclusive technology design, and careful monitoring of educational outcomes. By highlighting these ethical imperatives, the authors provide a roadmap for responsibly leveraging AI in mathematics education, ensuring that innovations enhance rather than compromise learning experiences in engineering and technical disciplines.

Chapter 2: AI-Enhanced Queueing Theory Models: Optimizing Decision-Making in Operations Research and Mathematics Education

This chapter explores the integration of artificial intelligence with classical queueing theory, a foundational area of operations research and applied mathematics. By combining machine learning, neural networks, and real-time data analysis, AI-enhanced models offer dynamic optimization of service parameters, prediction of congestion, and improved efficiency in sectors such as logistics, healthcare, and telecommunications. Beyond technical applications, the chapter highlights the pedagogical value of embedding AI-driven queueing models into mathematics education, equipping students with advanced analytical, computational, and decision-making skills. The discussion also addresses implementation challenges, ethical considerations, and future research directions, underscoring AI's transformative potential in both mathematical modeling and education.

Chapter 3: Applications of Mathematics in AI

This chapter demonstrates the foundational role of mathematics in the development and functioning of artificial intelligence systems. It examines how areas such as linear algebra, calculus, probability, and graph theory provide the tools for modeling, problem-solving, and algorithmic decision-making. Practical examples illustrate the use of mathematics in network representation, image processing, and encryption, highlighting the real-world relevance of abstract concepts. The authors effectively bridge theory and practice, showing how mathematical principles underpin AI technologies and facilitate their application across diverse domains. This chapter provides readers with a comprehensive understanding of the mathematical underpinnings essential for advancing AI research and implementation.

Chapter 4: Examination of Preschool Teacher Perception Towards the Use of ChatGPT in Mathematics Education

This chapter explores how preschool educators perceive the use of ChatGPT and other AI tools in early mathematics education. AI provides personalized learning experiences, interactive content delivery, and adaptive teaching strategies that can enhance both student engagement and teacher effectiveness. The chapter also addresses ethical, technological, and equity-related challenges, including data privacy, screen exposure, and limited access in under-resourced schools. The findings stress that AI should complement, not replace, human-led instruction, and that successful integration requires structured policies, teacher training, and careful attention to inclusivity. This chapter highlights how responsible AI adoption can enrich foundational mathematical learning.

Chapter 5: Harnessing AI to Transform Mathematics Education: Enhancing Cognitive, Psychosocial, and Analytical Learning Outcomes

This chapter presents a comprehensive view of how AI reshapes mathematics education, emphasizing its role in enhancing cognitive, analytical, and psychosocial outcomes. AI-driven adaptive learning platforms allow for personalized instruction, differentiated learning, and deeper conceptual understanding. Gamified and interactive environments further support logical reasoning and problem-solving by presenting real-world challenges in engaging formats. Beyond cognition, AI addresses emotional dimensions, reducing math anxiety and fostering self-regulation through supportive, responsive feedback. The chapter illustrates how integrating AI can create inclusive and motivating educational experiences, transforming both the teaching process and student learning outcomes.

Chapter 6: Modernizing Mathematics Education with Artificial Intelligence: A Narrative Review of AI-Powered Tools, Thematic Trends, and Instructional Applications

This chapter provides a narrative review of the evolving role of AI in mathematics education, examining current tools, thematic trends, and practical applications. The authors synthesize research and expert insights to identify how AI is reshaping instructional practices, learner engagement, and pedagogical design. Illustrative examples of AI tools demonstrate their relevance to teaching, highlighting mechanisms that enhance conceptual understanding and interactivity. By reflecting on these innovations, the chapter offers a forward-looking perspective on how AI transforms the mathematics classroom, promoting effective, technology-driven learning experiences.

Chapter 7: Prospective Teachers' Perceived Affordances and Constraints of Using ChatGPT in Mathematical Problem Posing

This chapter explores prospective mathematics teachers' experiences using ChatGPT to generate mathematical problems. Through qualitative analysis of reflection papers, the study identifies both affordances and constraints of AI in supporting problem posing. Participants valued ChatGPT for its immediate feedback, contextual diversity, and capacity to provide personalized learning paths, yet noted limitations in generating novel, contextually rich, or visually clear problems. The chapter underscores the need for critical engagement with AI tools, highlighting both their pedagogical potential and the importance of teacher mediation to ensure quality and creativity in mathematical problem design.

Chapter 8: Student and Teacher Perceptions of AI-Supported Mathematics Education: Perspectives from Cambodia

This chapter examines how students and teachers in Cambodia perceive AI-supported mathematics education. The authors investigate perceived benefits, challenges, and the impact of AI on learning outcomes within the national educational context. Using qualitative interviews, the study highlights both opportunities for enhanced engagement and gaps in access, training, and implementation. By focusing on regional experiences, the chapter provides valuable insights into how AI integration can be culturally and contextually responsive, informing strategies for policymakers, educators, and technology developers seeking to optimize AI-enhanced learning globally.

Chapter 9: Sustaining Mathematics Education in the AI Era: Opportunities, Challenges, and Future Directions

This chapter critically evaluates the role of AI in mathematics education through the lens of constructivist and socio-cultural learning theories. It explores how AI-powered tools support individualized instruction, enhance conceptual understanding, and improve problem-solving skills. The authors also address challenges such as digital accessibility, algorithmic bias, and ethical use of student data. Emphasizing careful planning and inclusive practices, the chapter advocates for a balanced integration of AI that maintains human interaction while leveraging technology to reduce educational inequities. It concludes with reflections on future directions for research, policy, and classroom practice in AI-supported mathematics education.

Chapter 10: Understanding the Role of AI in Mathematics Education: A Q Methodological Inquiry

This chapter employs Q-methodology to explore mathematics teacher candidates' perceptions of AI integration in education. Two primary viewpoints emerge: one emphasizing AI's motivational and personalized benefits but concerned about shallow learning, and the other valuing face-to-face engagement while supporting AI-assisted feedback. The findings reinforce the indispensable role of teachers in providing both cognitive and emotional guidance. The chapter highlights the importance of ethically aware, balanced AI implementation that ensures equitable access, data protection, and collaborative, human-centered learning.

Chapter 11: Using Artificial Intelligence in Primary School Mathematics Teaching

This chapter focuses on the application of AI in primary school mathematics, demonstrating its potential to provide adaptive learning experiences, personalized instruction, and real-time feedback. AI-powered tools and automated assessments enable teachers to address diverse student needs effectively while reducing workload. Emphasizing teacher training, ethical considerations, and the balance between technology and human-centered pedagogy, the chapter illustrates how AI can make mathematics education more inclusive, engaging, and effective for young learners.

It is my hope that this volume will serve as both a scholarly contribution and a practical guide. By bridging mathematics education and AI, we are not merely exploring a technological innovation, we are engaging in the creation of a new paradigm in education. I extend my gratitude to the authors whose expertise and dedication have shaped this work, and to the educators and researchers worldwide who continue to inspire progress in this evolving field.

Ali Mazı
Ministry of National Education, Turkey

Chapter 1
AI Ethics in Mathematics: Strategies for Responsible Implementation

Sara Reis
https://orcid.org/0000-0002-3416-2257
ISEP, Polytechnic of Porto, Portugal

Luis Pinto-Coelho
https://orcid.org/0000-0002-5673-7306
ISEP, Polytechnic of Porto, Portugal

ABSTRACT

Mathematical thinking has a crucial role in STEM education. It encompasses problem-solving, logical reasoning, pattern recognition, abstraction, among others, that are transversal to many technical areas. Incorporating the capabilities of Artificial Intelligence into math education can enhance learning efficiency while providing personalized instruction. It also allows us to simulate complex or rare situations, which enrich the preparation of students. However, the use of these tools also raises ethical concerns, such as data privacy, or algorithmic bias. In addition, potential over-reliance on AI has raised concerns about weakening critical thinking and to the amplification of injustice, issues that may widen educational gaps. Integration strategies, where a balanced approach with human oversight must be implemented, inclusive technology design, and careful monitoring of educational outcomes are crucial to responsibly use AI. This way, ethical standards in mathematics education for engineering disciplines can be upheld.

DOI: 10.4018/979-8-3373-1998-8.ch001

1. INTRODUCTION

Mathematical thinking focuses on problem-solving, logical reasoning, patterns recognition, and abstraction. It involves understanding concepts deeply, making connections between ideas, and applying mathematical principles to real-world problems (Roselainy et al., 2013). For science, technology, engineering, and mathematics (STEM) education in particular, mathematical thinking serves as a powerful tool for solving real-world problems. It enables modeling, analyzing, and optimization of intricate systems promoting precision, creativity, and critical thinking. The abstract developments in mathematics find practical utility when applied to engineering challenges, making mathematics indispensable to the discipline (Osman et al., 2015).

The integration of Artificial Intelligence (AI) in mathematics teaching in the context of engineering could be very useful because it enhances learning efficiency, supports complex problem-solving, and personalizes education to meet individual student needs (Inderjeet & Bhardwaj, 2024).

AI tools could analyze large datasets to identify learning gaps, provide real-time feedback, and simulate engineering scenarios that require mathematical modeling. Additionally, AI can automate routine calculations, allowing students to focus on conceptual understanding and critical thinking (Richard et al., 2022).

However, ethical concerns such as data privacy, algorithmic bias, over-reliance on AI, transparency, and accessibility must be addressed to ensure responsible AI implementation in education. Monitoring how students' capabilities evolve, according to pedagogical outcomes, must also be reinforced, to understand if AI is used acritically (Panqueban et al., 2024).

Additionally, data privacy concerns arise due to the collection and storage of student information, while algorithmic bias may lead to unfair treatment of learners from diverse backgrounds. Over-reliance on AI could diminish critical thinking skills, and the lack of transparency in AI-generated solutions may hinder student understanding. Additionally, ensuring equitable access to AI tools is crucial to prevent educational disparities (Coelho & Reis, 2021).

This chapter explores the ethical dimensions and discusses strategies for educators to use AI responsibly, emphasizing the importance of human oversight and inclusive technological design. A balanced approach is necessary to harness AI`s potential while safeguarding ethical principles in mathematics education within engineering disciplines.

1.1 Technical Education: Knowledge, Pedagogy and Assessment

Engineering and technical fields embody a hard-applied knowledge paradigm: they rely on quantitative, system-oriented content grounded in mathematics, science and empirical data. In Biglan's classification[1], engineering is a hard-applied discipline that is "pragmatic and purposive, applying heuristic approaches," whereas, for example, the humanities are "concerned with particulars, are value-laden, and lack consensus" (Simpson, 2017). In practice, this means STEM curricula focus on universal principles and measurable laws (expressed in equations and models) applied to real problems, while non-technical fields emphasize interpretive, contextual and theoretical understanding of humanistic or social phenomena. Engineering students learn to manipulate numerical models, design systems, and analyse data; by contrast, students in fields like literature or history engage with texts or cultural artifacts through critical, qualitative analysis and debate. This epistemological division shapes teaching: engineers expect clear "right" answers, often using mathematics as an underlying tool, from problem solving and system synthesis, whereas non-technical studies allow multiple valid interpretations and value-driven arguments.

Correspondingly, the teaching methods diverge sharply. Engineering education emphasizes hands-on, problem-based learning (Mustafa et al., 2016). Classrooms often incorporate laboratory courses, design projects, and team-based problem solving, recreating roles in the job market. For example, an electronics engineering program might include a Control Systems lab where "knowledge of theory, experimental design, and real-world system modeling is tested and enforced". Senior capstone projects and project-based courses (often sponsored by industry) require students to solve open-ended engineering challenges (Reis et al., 2020). In such settings, students learn by doing – constructing prototypes, by simulations, or working with data – under the guidance of design thinking and scientific experimentation, most of the times using mathematic reasoning as foundational strategies (Felder & Brent, 2024; Reis et al., 2018). This contrasts with typical humanities pedagogy, which often centers on lectures, seminars, and discussion. Classes emphasize dialogue and debate rather than laboratory work. Research in engineering education finds that active, project-based approaches improve learning outcomes by cultivating problem-solving and critical thinking.

Assessment formats reflect the differences mentioned. Engineering programs, especially under outcome-based accreditation regimes like Accreditation Board for Engineering and Technology (ABET), measure student learning with objective, criterion-based evaluations: exams with quantitative problem sets, lab reports with data analysis, design project deliverables scored by rubrics, and presentation of engineering solutions (Rehman et al., 2025). ABET Criterion 3 explicitly lists outcomes such as the ability to apply mathematics and science, conduct experiments, and design systems under realistic constraints. Programs must "use relevant direct, indirect, quantitative and qualitative measures" to assess these outcomes. As a result, technical courses often employ graded problem-solving tasks and practical projects that target specific competencies (e.g. a functioning circuit or a correctly annotated code). By contrast, non-technical fields typically assess learning through essays, papers, and exams that require critical interpretation, argumentation, and synthesis of ideas. In engineering, however, many learning outcomes (calculating a numerical answer, meeting a performance spec) can be judged "right or wrong" with less subjectivity. Thus outcome expectations also differ: engineers are expected to demonstrate concrete technical skills and engineering-design abilities, whereas humanities graduates are expected to demonstrate critical thinking and communication, often evaluated qualitatively.

1.2 Mathematics and Scientific Reasoning

Mathematics and scientific reasoning are central pillars of engineering curricula. ABET requires engineering programs to include "one year of a combination of college level mathematics and basic sciences (some with experimental experience)" and "one and one-half years of engineering topics, consisting of engineering sciences and engineering design". This foundation ensures students master calculus, physics, chemistry, or other core sciences before applying them. In class and labs, students routinely use the scientific method: forming hypotheses, conducting experiments or simulations, and analyzing data. Crucially, methodologies like Design Thinking (Brown, 2008), CDIO (Conceive, Design, Implement, Operate) (O'Connor et al., 2023), or even Universal Design (Burgstahler, 2015; Kamińska et al., 2023) are underlying in the curriculum as well. ABET explicitly defines engineering design as "a decision-making process (often iterative) in which the basic sciences, mathematics, and the engineering sciences are applied to convert resources optimally to meet stated needs" (Linh & Huong, 2021; Putra et al., 2023). In practice, students learn to empathize with user needs, brainstorm solutions, build prototypes, and iterate – a creative, user-centered mindset that drives innovation in technical fields. Such systematic, model-driven reasoning is generally absent in humanities education, where formal mathematics is rarely required (beyond basic statistics) and "design" is metaphorical (e.g. design of arguments, not machines). Consequently, engineering graduates gain comfort with abstract quantitative models and data analysis, while their non-technical peers gain fluency in qualitative methods and critique.

2. AI MATHEMATICAL REASONING

Artificial Intelligence (AI) has begun to transform mathematical reasoning within engineering education by offering tools that both enhance students' conceptual understanding and automate routine tasks. In traditional engineering programs, mastery of mathematical concepts such as differential equations, linear algebra, and numerical methods is fundamental. AI-driven platforms can perceive students' level and pace (Coelho & Reis, 2023). From this it is possible to adaptively present problems, analyze solution strategies, and even generate new exercises, thereby creating a more interactive learning environment that responds to individual student needs. This shift is particularly significant in engineering disciplines, where mathematical proficiency directly underpins design, simulation, and analysis tasks.

One of the most prominent applications of AI in this domain is personalized learning (Kanchon et al., 2024; Pataranutaporn et al., 2021). When using machine-learning algorithms to track student performance, AI systems can identify specific areas of difficulty and curate individualized learning pathways. A systematic review of AI in mathematics education found that such adaptive systems not only increase student engagement but also lead to measurable gains in achievement, as they offer targeted practice and scaffolded hints precisely when a learner struggles (Opesemowo & Adewuyi, 2024). In engineering courses, pilot studies similarly report that students perceive AI-based math tools to improve their understanding of complex engineering mathematics, with over 70% expressing enhanced confidence in problem-solving after using these platforms (Garcia et al., 2025).

Beyond personalization, Intelligent Tutoring Systems (ITS) employ AI to simulate one-on-one tutoring experiences. These systems deconstruct complex proofs or derivations into step-by-step modules, offering immediate feedback at each stage. For example, classroom trials of ITS in undergraduate calculus have shown that students who received AI-mediated hints solved 30% more non-routine problems correctly than those in control groups (Mohamed et al., 2022). Such real-time guidance is invaluable for students and especially relevant in large engineering cohorts, where instructor bandwidth for individual feedback is limited.

On the frontier of AI research, deep-learning models are increasingly capable of higher-order mathematical reasoning. Surveys of neural network approaches to theorem proving and symbolic manipulation demonstrate that models like GPT-4 and specialized architectures, such as AlphaGeometry (Chervonyi et al., 2025), can tackle geometry proofs and algebraic identities previously thought to require human-level abstraction capabilities (Lu et al., 2023). While these advances are primarily investigated in research contexts, in a near future, it is expected that they will be integrated into engineering education, enabling automated verification of student solutions and even suggest alternative proof strategies, thus deepening conceptual insight.

Engineering curricula are already beginning to embed AI tools directly into coursework. A recent mixed-methods study in mechanical engineering evaluated the performance of ChatGPT, Gemini, and Copilot across 800 undergraduate problems, finding that these models achieved up to 85% accuracy on numerical and theory-based questions (Akolekar et al., 2025). Moreover, surveys of student and faculty attitudes revealed that generative AI can free classroom time for project-based learning by handling routine calculation and derivation tasks, allowing instructors to emphasize design thinking and creative problem-solving. This can lead to faster learning for some but also as an opportunity to detect supporting knowledge areas that need to be improved for others.

The quick evolution of these tools, despite their benefits, poses several challenges that must be addressed. For example, an acritical usage of AI risks students bypassing the deep engagement necessary to internalize mathematical concepts; as critics have cautioned, tools that offer complete solutions may undermine foundational skill development (Zhai et al., 2024). Academic integrity also becomes more complex when students can solicit full derivations from AI, necessitating robust honor-code frameworks and assessment redesigns (Vieriu & Petrea, 2025). Finally, the possibility of accessing technology, especially to AI platforms with advanced capabilities, can exacerbate educational inequities, particularly in underfunded institutions. The requirements to have good hardware to support studies now also extends to the importance of having good software tools, underscoring the need for open-source and institutionally supported solutions to ensure all engineering students benefit equitably.

Soon, as new technological advances are unveiled, the role of AI in mathematical reasoning, particularly in STEM education, must be supported with careful integration. New research should explore hybrid teaching models that combine human instruction with AI scaffolding, investigate the long-term impacts on cognitive skill development, and develop guidelines for ethical AI use in assessments. Initiatives such as LLM-driven quiz generators, demonstrate the potential for AI to not only assess but also inspire deeper inquiry by presenting novel, context-rich problems tailored to engineering domains. Benchmarking datasets, such as MathVista (Lu et al., 2024), can also help to understand how AI technology copes with different types of mathematical challenges and how it compares with humans. Only through close collaboration among educators, technologists, and policy makers, AI can be used to elevate mathematical reasoning and its applications, preparing students for the increasingly complex analytical challenges of the modern world.

3. ETHICAL REQUIREMENTS IN TECHNICAL EDUCATION

As artificial intelligence (AI), machine learning, and data-driven systems increasingly shape decisions in healthcare, education, finance and justice, technical education must respond by equipping students with analytical tools and ethical awareness. Mathematical education, especially where it intersects with AI and modeling, plays a central role in preparing students to engage critically with these technologies and their social implications.

Central to this discussion is the recognition that mathematical models and algorithms are not neutral. They reflect the assumptions, priorities, and biases of their creators, often with far-reaching social consequences (Stinson, 2022). Bias in training data can lead to discriminatory outcomes, particularly when models are applied to sensitive contexts (Obermeyer et al., 2019).

This section addresses the ethical importance of transparency and explainability, especially in complex or "black box" systems. When decisions made by algorithms affects people's lives, understanding how those decisions are made is essential for accountability and trust (Schoeffer et al., 2022). In addition, concepts of fairness, representation, and professional responsibility are examined through both ethical and mathematical lenses.

This section explores five key areas that support the development of responsible and reflective practitioners. It begins with an exploration of how ethics can be meaningfully integrated into the curriculum, positioning ethical inquiry as a central component of mathematical thinking. Next, is emphasizing the importance of promoting critical thinking and reflexivity, encouraging students to question who is represented in data, which ones are excluded, and what assumptions underline mathematical models. Then it turns to transparency and explainability, highlighting the need for students to understand how algorithms function and how critical assess the clarity and communicability of complex systems. Building on this, this section addresses fairness and inclusivity, equipping learners to grapple with competing definitions of fairness and the ethical trade-offs that come with designing equitable AI systems. Finally, the section concludes by fostering professional responsibility and accountability by introducing students to ethical standards articulated by organizations such as IEEE and the European Mathematical Society and encouraging them to consider their future roles as ethical decision-makers in technical fields. Together, these subsections offer a comprehensive vision for integrating ethics into technical education through both conceptual exploration and pedagogical practice.

3.1 Embedding Ethics into the Curriculum

Ethics should not be treated as an ancillary component of technical education but must be embedded throughout the curriculum. This involves incorporating ethical dilemmas, reflective exercises, and real-world case studies into mathematical and AI coursework (Boddington, 2017; Floridi & Cowls, 2019). For instance, students might examine algorithm bias in credit scoring models or assess the implications of AI-based surveillance systems.

Credit scoring algorithms are widely used by financial institutions to assess the creditworthiness of individuals. These models, often based on machine learning techniques, use vast datasets to predict financial behavior. However, these models can inadvertently perpetuate historical inequities and embed systemic biases due to the nature of their input data and the statistical assumptions within the models (Uddin, 2023).

Students might explore the mathematics of credit scoring, such as regression models or classification algorithms, and assess how different variables can serve as proxies for race or socioeconomic status. By modeling simplified versions of these systems or analyzing real or simulated datasets, students can examine how altering variables impacts outcomes, and where fairness metrics like "equal opportunity or predictive parity come into play (Friedler et al., 2021).

Through this analysis, students engage questions like: what make an algorithm "fair"? How should mathematical models account for historical injustice? When does mathematical precision conflict with ethical responsibility?

AI-driven surveillance, particular facial recognition technology, represents another area where mathematical concepts intersect with pressing ethical concerns. These systems often rely on complex image recognition algorithms rooted in linear algebra, optimization, and probability. While technologically impressive, they are also prone to high error rates (Köchling & Wehner, 2020).

Students could investigate how false positive rates, confusion matrices, and precision/recall tradeoffs affect the reliability and fairness surveillance systems. By modelling these scenarios mathematically, students assess both the technical accuracy and ethical permissibility of such tools.

These explorations prompt deeper reflection on issues such as consent, privacy, and balance between security and liberties, when students use mathematics to model the outcomes of surveillance policies, or propose alternative designs that optimize both utility and fairness, they develop critical thinking that transcends the boundaries of traditional math education.

Such integrative approaches foster critical engagement with the ethical dimensions of mathematical modeling.

3.2 Promoting Critical Thinking and Reflexivity

Technical education must cultivate critical thinking by encouraging students to interrogate the assumptions, limitations and social consequences of the models they use. Reflexivity is defined as the capacity to reflect on one´s own role and responsibility within broader socio-technical systems, which is an essential ethical skill (Vallor, 2016). Students should be encouraged to ask questions such as: who is represented in the data? Who is excluded? Are overlaps present? What values are embedded in mathematical formulation? These questions shift the role of students from passive problem-solvers to active inquirers who understand that mathematics, especially when applied to artificial intelligence, has far-reaching social consequences.

Data used in AI systems often reflect historical and societal patterns of inclusion and exclusion. When students examine datasets, whether they pertain to credit scoring, hiring algorithms, healthcare, or policing, they should be guided to scrutinize whose experiences are captured and those are ignored (Obermeyer et al., 2019).

In classroom practice, students can be provided with de-identified, open-source datasets and asked to conduct demographic audits. Which groups are prevalent? Which are missing? What might this mean for fairness of decisions derived from the model? Through this lens, mathematics becomes a tool for uncovering systemic inequities rather than obscuring them.

Mathematical models do not exist in a vacuum. Choices about optimization are inherently value laden. Students must be encouraged to identify these embedded values and consider their implications. For example, a credit score model that maximizes predictive accuracy may still perpetuate disadvantage if it ignores the broader societal context of economic inequality (Gordon, 2019).

Through guided discussions and modeling exercises, students can explore trade-offs between competing values. These kinds of reflections enable students to grapple with the moral wight behind mathematical decisions and understand that no model is entirely neutral.

By integrating these concepts into the curriculum, educators help students develop a sense of *mathematical agency*. They begin to see themselves as contributors to ethical decision-making processes, rather than merely users of mathematical tools. This aligns with a broader vision of mathematics education that prioritizes justice, inclusivity, and social awareness (Young et al., 2025).

Classrooms should be spaces where students feel empowered to challenge assumptions, propose alternative models, and consider the ethical implications of their work. Activities like case studies, debates, and collaborative redesign of biased systems provide concrete ways to nurture this mindset. Mathematics education is also about solving for equity.

3.3 Emphasizing Transparency and Explainability

Another critical ethical requirement in technical education is fostering a deep understanding of transparency and explainability in AI systems.

Transparency in AI refers to the extent to which stakeholders can inspect, understand and critique how an algorithm makes decisions. Without transparency, models become black boxes, where inputs lead to outputs with no visibility into the internal mechanics. This opacity can conceal biases, reduce accountability, and erode trust, especially among populations affected by the decisions (Burrell, 2016). In the mathematics classroom, educators can engage students in analyzing the implications of opaque algorithms.

Explainability refers to how well a model's operation and outputs can be understood by humans. From a mathematical perspective, this involves understanding hoe features, weights, and interactions within a model influence the results. In simpler models like linear regression or decision trees, explainability is often straightforward. However, more complex systems, such as deep neural networks, require advanced techniques like feature attribution, layer-wise relevance propagation, or SHAP values (Lundberg & Lee, 2017).

Mathematics education often prioritizes correctness and efficiency, but explainability requires a cultural shift, one that values clarity, reasoning and openness over brute performance. Encouraging students to document their models, justify their parameters, and communicate results in accessible terms help embed transparency as a norm rather than an afterthought (Goodman & Flaxman, 2017).

Ultimately, promoting transparency and explainability of models and algorithms empowers students to build not only better models but more just and accountable systems. It also prepares them to participate in broader societal conversations about how AI should be governed. Only informed individuals can positively contribute to good decisions. Students should learn to make their output interpretable to non-specialists and stakeholders, beyond building effective models. This is especially important in contexts where algorithmic decisions can significantly impact human lives (Doshi-Velez & Kim, 2017). Emphasis on explainable AI contributes to greater trust, accountability, and public understanding.

3.4 Addressing Fairness and Inclusivity

Fairness is a foundational principle in the ethical deployment of AI and mathematical models. As algorithms increasingly shape critical decisions, questions like fairness are central to ensuring that these systems support equity, justice, and human dignity. Mathematics educators play a pivotal role in cultivating students' ability to define interrogate and implement fairness in computational and analytical contexts.

In technical education, this means teaching students how to recognize and mitigate bias, whether it originates from data, modeling choices, or deployment contexts (Barocas et al., 2023; Narayanan et al., 2023).

One of the challenges in operationalizing fairness is that there is no universally agreed-upon definition. In mathematical terms, fairness can be expressed through various metrics, each emphasizing a different conception of justice (Kleinberg, 2018).

While fairness is a critical step, some scholars advocate pushing beyond fairness toward a broader vision of justice-oriented mathematics education considering its transversal nature (Mellin-Olsen, 2002). This includes recognizing structural inequalities that cannot be solved merely by adjusting models and instead calls for students to understand the broader sociopolitical contexts in which mathematics operates.

In the classroom, fairness can be modeled through case studies, simulations, or algorithmic design projects where students must consider how models behave across different subgroups. They may calculate fairness metrics and debate which should be prioritized and why. Furthermore, inclusivity should be reflected in pedagogical practices that embrace diverse perspectives and experiences fostering a richer understanding of the ethical landscape.

3.5 Fostering Professional Responsibility and Accountability

Students must be introduced to professional ethics standards, as those articulated by organizations like the Institute of Electrical and Electronics Engineers (IEEE), European Mathematical Society (EMS), and others. Discussions of topics such as data stewardship, informed consent algorithmic accountability, and long-term societal impacts should be integrated into coursework and professional terms (Shahriari & Shahriari, 2017).

Professional ethics standards serve as binding commitments for practitioners working in fields where their decisions impact individuals, communities, and institutions. By studying these standards, students can better understand the expectations placed on professionals and how those expectations are operationalized in real-world contexts. This exposure helps demystify the ethical dimension of STEM professions and highlights the alignment between ethical thinking and mathematical rigor. These principles help anchor technical expertise within a framework of public responsibility.

To support educators in designing meaningful and responsible mathematics instruction, the explored topics are summarized in Table 1.

Each theme is accompanied by guiding concepts and pedagogical strategies that connect mathematical modeling and AI literacy with broader questions of justice, responsibility, and professional practice. This table can serve as both a planning tool and a reference point for educators integrating ethical reflection into technical education.

Table 1. Summary of ethical topics associated with key concepts and questions, related educational strategies.

Ethical Topic	Key Concepts & Questions	Educational Strategies
Algorithmic Bias	Bias in data and models Disproportionate impact on marginalized groups	Analyze real-world datasets Redesign biased algorithms Reflect on fairness
Representation & Exclusion	Who is included or excluded in the data? How does exclusion affect outcomes?	Conduct data audits Explore demographic patterns Facilitate reflective inquiry
Embedded Values in Modeling	Models reflect ethical choices No model is value-neutral	Discuss optimization trade-offs Identify value assumptions in modeling decisions
Transparency	Importance of model visibility and accountability Risks of opaque ("black-box") models	Compare transparent vs. opaque models Promote clear documentation and reporting
Explainability	Ability to interpret model behavior Clarity in decision-making processes	Use interpretable models Practice communicating model outcomes in plain language
Fairness	Definitions vary (e.g., equal outcomes, equal accuracy) Trade-offs are inevitable	Evaluate models using fairness metrics Engage in ethical debates and redesign tasks
Professional Ethics Standards	Codes of conduct guide responsible practice Ethical frameworks support accountability	Analyze and apply professional codes Connect ethical norms to real-world scenarios

This table can serve as both a planning tool and a reference point for educators integrating ethical reflection into technical education.

Incorporating ethical requirements into technical education is not simply a response to the growing presence of artificial intelligence and data-driven systems, it is foundational shift toward cultivating socially responsible, critically engaged learners. This section highlighted how mathematics educators can integrate ethical reflection into core areas of core areas of instructions, from recognizing bias and promoting fairness, to ensuring transparency and fostering professional accountability. By embedding ethics into the curriculum, promoting reflexivity, and encouraging students to grapple with real-world implications of mathematical modeling and AI, educators can help students move beyond technical competence toward ethical literacy. This approach prepares future professionals to recognize the broader impact of their work, navigate complex trade-offs, and contribute to the design of systems that are effective, just and inclusive. As technical fields continue to influence societal structures and individual lives, equipping students with these is essential.

4. AN IMPLEMENTATION FRAMEWORK FOR AI MATHEMATICS

4.1 Existing Initiatives

In the context of university-level mathematics, spanning disciplines such as engineering, physics, and applied mathematics, a robust implementation framework can be structured around existing literature using three key stages: Framework Grounding, Design & Integration, and Evaluation & Governance.

Framework Grounding: Theoretical Foundations & Educational Policy

In a typical implementation, the process begins by situating the effort within a well-defined policy framework. For example in (Chan, 2023), an AI ecological model with three dimensions is proposed, comprising: pedagogical, governance, and operational dimensions. From here it can be ensured that the deployment remains grounded, ethical, and sustainable. Complementing this, (Owoc et al., 2021) propose a five-stage implementation model: strategic planning, system design, pilot testing, deployment, and ongoing adaptation. This offers a structured approach adaptable to mathematics education contexts.

Design & Integration: Building the System

The next phase involves constructing the system itself. Data streams, including learners' stepwise solutions and error profiles, are fed into cognitive models that simulate reasoning pathologies, inspired by ACT-R framework (Wei, 2025). The central engine, modeled on the AIIA design, synthesizes conversational NLP, quiz generation, and adaptive learning paths, integrated seamlessly into existing LMS infrastructure. Underlying the system are AI components tailored to provide ITS-based feedback, personalize instruction, and automate evaluation; these components draw on a corpus of higher-ed-focused research (Sajja et al., 2023).

Evaluation & Governance: Monitoring, Ethics, and Policy

Finally, the system must be monitored and governed rigorously. Learning efficacy is gauged through outcome metrics across cohorts, while AI accuracy and reasoning transparency are regularly reviewed. An ethical protocol, informed by policy dimensions, establishes governance over data privacy, fairness, and academic integrity. Institutional readiness, ranging from faculty development to infrastructure provisioning, completes the framework, ensuring that AI augments, rather than undermines, university mathematics education.

4.2 An Implementation Framework

In the rapidly evolving landscape of AI, the integration of mathematical rigor with ethical considerations has become paramount. As AI tools develop and become unavoidable tools either in education but also in professional settings, being crucial in development and decision-making processes, it is important to ensure that these systems are transparent, fair, and equitable.

For a successful integration of AI into mathematics education for STEM, a robust implementation framework must identify and foster collaboration among diverse stakeholders. Educators, students, technology developers, policymakers, and industry partners are some of the involved agents that can provide their own perspectives but also their expections for such systems and related outcomes. This broad involvement ensures that AI tools are tailored to meet the specific needs of mathematical learning, align with pedagogical goals, and address practical challenges such as accessibility and ethical considerations. In this context, the triple helix model of innovation, which emphasizes the importance of interactions between academia, industry, and government, provides a valuable representation of the required close cooperation.

In this section a proposal for implementing the core principles for mathematical AI and crucial ethical aspects is presented. A comprehensive framework for developing and deploying mathematics AI systems, that balance precision with equity, is provided for this purpose, as depicted in Figure 1. It encompasses algorithmic transparency, bias mitigation, and the delicate relationship between precision and equity.

Figure 1. An implementation framework for responsible AI for mathematics. For each step some of important aspects are mentioned but this is not a closed list and the framework should be adapted to match the requirements of the related situation.

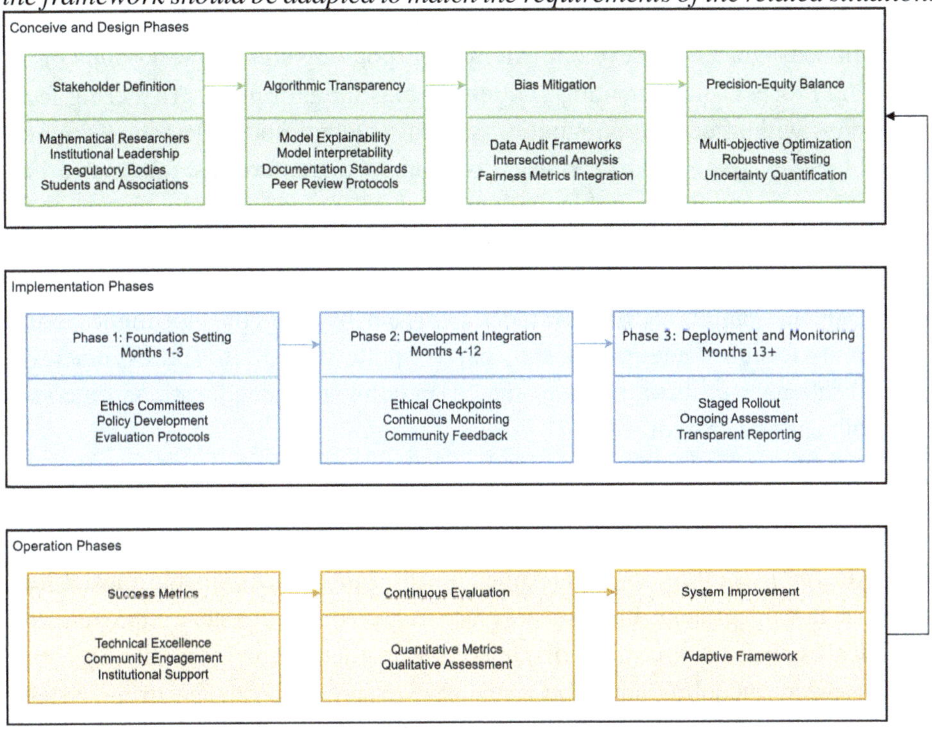

In the design and integration of mathematical AI systems for education, stakeholder collaboration ensures technical rigor and ethical integrity. Students contribute fresh perspectives and uphold academic integrity, while researchers analyze biases, collaborate with ethicists, and transparently document assumptions. Institutional leaders provide resources and foster interdisciplinary efforts, and regulatory bodies establish ethical standards and certification processes. Algorithmic transparency is critical, achieved through interpretable models with clear decision pathways, thorough documentation, and rigorous peer reviews. Bias mitigation involves auditing datasets for gaps, applying fairness metrics like statistical parity and equalized odds, and conducting intersectional performance analyses. To balance precision and equity, systems use multi-objective optimization, model uncertainty, and robust testing across diverse scenarios, ensuring both accuracy and fairness in educational outcomes.

For the implementation stage of integrating mathematical AI systems into education, a structured three-phase approach ensures ethical and effective deployment. Phase 1 (with an expected duration of 1 to 3 months) focuses on establishing a robust ethical foundation by forming interdisciplinary ethics committees with mathematicians, ethicists, and education experts, alongside developing institutional AI ethics policies and standardized evaluation protocols for mathematical models. Ethics training for students and researchers, baseline bias audits, and stakeholder engagement strategies are prioritized to align with educational needs. Phase 2 (Months 4-12) embeds ethics into development by incorporating ethical checkpoints in the modeling process, implementing continuous bias monitoring, and fostering feedback loops with affected communities, such as students and educators. Technical efforts include creating fairness-aware optimization frameworks, automated bias detection tools, and interpretable mathematical AI systems. Finally, phase 3 (on a mid to long term perspective) emphasizes responsible deployment through staged rollouts with ethical oversight, ongoing monitoring, and transparent reporting to stakeholders. Continuous improvement is driven by regular algorithmic audits, community feedback integration, and adaptive policy updates to address emerging ethical challenges, ensuring mathematical AI systems enhance educational outcomes equitably and transparently.

Incorporating feedback loops, iterative testing, and continuous professional development for educators further enriches this framework, ensuring that AI tools are not only technologically advanced but also pedagogically sound and inclusive. In this sense, the final operation phase, sustained success hinges on a dynamic, closed-loop approach that integrates critical success factors and adaptive system improvements. Technical excellence is maintained by upholding mathematical rigor while advancing fairness-aware modeling and robust ethical evaluation metrics, ensuring systems remain both accurate and equitable. Community engagement drives continuous improvement through active involvement of diverse stakeholders, such as students and educators, in model refinement, transparent communication of mathematical limitations, and inclusive ethics discussions to build trust. Institutional support secures this stage with long-term funding, commitment to ethical AI initiatives, and incentives for researchers prioritizing ethical outcomes. Measurement and evaluation combine quantitative metrics—like bias reduction across demographics, accuracy preservation under fairness constraints, and community satisfaction scores—with qualitative assessments, including stakeholder feedback on transparency, expert reviews of ethical integration, and case studies of successful implementations. An adaptive system ensures ongoing enhancement by leveraging real-time data from these metrics and feedback loops to iteratively refine models, update policies, and address emerging ethical challenges, fostering a resilient and equitable educational AI ecosystem.

The proposed framework encompasses a wide range of ethical aspects and highlights the importance of continuous evaluation and improvement. Nevertheless, each case has its own intricacies that must be integrated and adapted.

4.3 An Application Case

A practical application of an implementation framework for AI mathematics can be illustrated in the context of undergraduate engineering education. Mathematics is a foundational component of engineering curricula, yet students frequently encounter difficulties when transitioning from procedural problem-solving to abstract reasoning. An AI-based system, designed within a structured implementation framework, can bridge this gap.

The process begins with data collection and representation. In a university setting, this involves compiling extensive datasets from digital learning platforms: assignment submissions, quiz results, error logs from symbolic computation tools, and even stepwise input from interactive problem solvers. These data streams are anonymized and standardized so that they can be processed effectively by machine learning models.

The second stage concerns model development and algorithmic design. For advanced mathematics courses, such as linear algebra or differential equations, the AI can be trained not only to recognize whether answers are correct, but also to classify solution strategies. For example, a neural network might detect when a student applies row-reduction incorrectly in Gaussian elimination, while a symbolic reasoning engine identifies gaps in the logical sequence of steps. The framework thus integrates statistical learning with symbolic AI to capture both the quantitative and structural aspects of mathematical reasoning.

Integration into the learning environment represents the third stage. The AI system is embedded into the university's learning management system (LMS), allowing students to access real-time, adaptive feedback while solving problems. Crucially, the framework emphasizes explainability: rather than simply flagging an error, the AI generates tailored hints that align with the instructor's intended learning outcomes. For instance, if a student misapplies an eigenvalue computation, the AI highlights the relevant property of determinants and suggests reviewing a specific concept.

Finally, the framework must comply with regulation and requires evaluation and governance mechanisms. For example, faculty can monitor the AI's performance by comparing student outcomes across cohorts, while also reviewing the validity of AI-generated explanations. This can create a closed-loop improvement mechanism. Iterative refinement is essential: as curricula evolve or as new cohorts bring distinct challenges, the AI models are retrained. Ethical safeguards, particularly transparency in decision-making, data privacy, and the avoidance of bias in performance prediction, are central to sustaining trust in the system.

Through this staged implementation, AI mathematics becomes more than a tool for computation; it functions as a structured partner in pedagogy. In higher education, where the cognitive demands of mathematics are complex and diverse, such frameworks offer a means of systematically embedding AI into instruction, thereby supporting both student learning and instructional design.

5. FUTURE TRENDS AND APPLICATIONS

The development of AI systems integrated with adaptive learning techniques and generative AI bring many benefits to the teaching of mathematics in STEM related fields. One of the most promising development is the creation of AI-powered hyper-personalized learning systems that can adjust mathematical curricula to each student's requirements. These systems would monitor a student's pace of learning, their concepts mastery, and their understanding gaps, creating appropriate problem sets that enhance their learning. For example, AI could fill gaps by designing exercises that integrate algebraic manipulation with physics or engineering applications. Such systems could also augment reality, helping to teach abstract concepts such as three-dimensional geometry or differential equations in an engaging manner to STEM students (Hwang & Tu, 2021).

The data collection required for personalized learning can also be used to boost students' engagement by the use of AI-powered gamification in the mathematics classroom. Tomorrow's AI may turn learning monotonous algorithmic procedures into engaging puzzles that students have an incentive to solve. For instance, students may be tasked by AI with narrative-driven story challenges requiring calculus for engineering design optimization or with statistical modeling for particular data science problems. These gamified environments could provide feedback in real-time—rewarding students for problem-solving in better ways while also pointing out what they could do better. Such strategies would improve engagement and foster further interdisciplinary appreciation of mathematics, preparing students to solve problems collaboratively in the real world (Olivier et al., 2024; Suresh Babu & Dhakshina Moorthy, 2024).

Another area where AI technological innovation can be used is on promoting collaborative learning environments. For example, future AI designs may support peer-to-peer education by automatically splitting students into teams based on their skills and allowing them to work on complex STEM challenges collaboratively. An AI system might facilitate discussions or simulations where a student skilled in probability and another who excels in programming could tackle a data analysis challenge together, guiding them through AI-moderated discussions. Moreover, AI could be incorporated with NLP capabilities to understand students' mathematical questions and provide answers in a conversational manner, as a virtual tutor would (Bertrand et al., 2024; Zwoliński et al., 2023). This would provide students with opportunities to test their reasoning skills in mathematics through interactive dialogues that promote rather than inhibit understanding, stimulating interest in more advanced topics such as machine learning algorithms or optimization techniques.

Predictive analytics powered by AI technology may change the way educators approach mathematics within the context of STEM education. Advanced systems could be capable of examining longitudinal performance data across various STEM courses and anticipating learning paths, recommending preemptive actions well before students are bound to confront challenges. For instance, an AI may detect that students are likely to struggle with the computer science relevant algebraic structures and learn how to interface with them, recommending specialized resources portraying alternative teaching methodologies aimed at overcoming those learning gaps. Such systems might also assist teachers in actionable ways by determining what core mathematical competencies are essential for given STEM professions.

6. CONCLUSION

In this chapter the intersection of mathematical thinking and Artificial Intelligence (AI) is discussed, particularly within the context of STEM education. The ways how AI can significantly enhance learning, offering benefits like personalized instruction and automating tedious tasks are highlighted, but also crucial ethical considerations, such as algorithmic bias and data privacy, are covered. These must be addressed for responsible implementation for which a framework for ethically integrating AI into mathematics education is proposed. For a successful implementation of responsible AI it is crucial to integrate foundational ethical requirements into technical education curricula. These aim to ensure that future professionals have not only the expected technical skills but that they are also ethically literate. Key ethical requirements are:

a) Embedding Ethics into the Curriculum: Ethics should be integrated throughout the curriculum since early years, presenting moral problems, using ethical dilemmas, reflective exercises, and real-world case studies.
b) Promoting Critical Thinking and Reflexivity: As students rely more and more on AI tools, education should cultivate critical thinking by encouraging students to question the obtained results but also the assumptions, limitations, and social consequences of the models they use. Reflexivity involves reflecting on one's own role and responsibility within socio-technical systems.
c) Emphasizing Transparency and Explainability: Students should learn to make their output interpretable to non-specialists and stakeholders. Emphasis on explainable AI (XAI) contributes to trust, accountability, and public understanding.

d) Addressing Fairness and Inclusivity: Teaching students to recognize and mitigate bias from data, models, or deployment contexts is essential. Inclusivity should inform pedagogical practices.
e) Fostering Professional Responsibility and Accountability: Students must be introduced to professional ethics standards from organizations like IEEE and EMS, including topics like data stewardship, informed consent, and algorithmic accountability

Furthermore, in the proposed framework, the importance of continuous evaluation and improvement is also highlighted by the use of a feedback loop.

Future research should explore hybrid teaching models, investigate long-term impacts on cognitive skills, and develop guidelines for ethical AI use in assessments (Reis et al., 2023). Collaboration among educators, technologists, and policymakers is seen as necessary to elevate mathematical reasoning and its applications through AI.

REFERENCES

Akolekar, H., Jhamnani, P., Kumar, V., Tailor, V., Pote, A., Meena, A., Kumar, K., Challa, J. S., & Kumar, D. (2025). The role of generative AI tools in shaping mechanical engineering education from an undergraduate perspective. *Scientific Reports*, *15*(1), 9214. DOI: 10.1038/s41598-025-93871-z PMID: 40097637

Barocas, S., Hardt, M., & Narayanan, A. (2023). *Fairness and Machine Learning: Limitations and Opportunities*. The MIT Press.

Bertrand, M. G., Sezer, H. B., & Namukasa, I. K. (2024). Exploring AR and VR Tools in Mathematics Education Through Culturally Responsive Pedagogies. *Digital Experiences in Mathematics Education*, *10*(3), 462–486. DOI: 10.1007/s40751-024-00152-x PMID: 39497730

Boddington, P. (2017). *Towards a Code of Ethics for Artificial Intelligence*. Springer International Publishing., DOI: 10.1007/978-3-319-60648-4

Brown, T. (2008, June). Design Thinking. *Harvard Business Review*. https://hbr.org/2008/06/design-thinking

Burgstahler, S. (2015). *Universal Design in Higher Education* (2nd ed.). Harvard Education Press. https://hep.gse.harvard.edu/9781612508160/universal-design-in-higher-education-second-edition/

Burrell, J. (2016). How the machine 'thinks': Understanding opacity in machine learning algorithms. *Big Data & Society*, *3*(1). DOI: 10.1177/2053951715622512

Chan, C. K. Y. (2023). *A Comprehensive AI Policy Education Framework for University Teaching and Learning* (No. arXiv:2305.00280). arXiv. /arXiv.2305.00280DOI: 10.48550

Chervonyi, Y., Trinh, T. H., Olšák, M., Yang, X., Nguyen, H., Menegali, M., Jung, J., Verma, V., Le, Q. V., & Luong, T. (2025). *Gold-medalist Performance in Solving Olympiad Geometry with AlphaGeometry2* (No. arXiv:2502.03544). arXiv. /arXiv.2502.03544DOI: 10.48550

Coelho, L., & Reis, S. (2021). Ethical Issues of Gamification in Healthcare: The Need to be Involved. In *Handbook of Research on Solving Modern Healthcare Challenges With Gamification*. IGI Global. DOI: 10.4018/978-1-7998-7472-0.ch001

Coelho, L., & Reis, S. S. (2023). Enhancing learning experiences through artificial intelligence: Classroom 5.0. In *Fostering pedagogy through micro and adaptive learning in higher education: Trends, tools, and applications* (pp. 169–191). IGI Global. https://www.igi-global.com/chapter/enhancing-learning-experiences-through-artificial-intelligence/328747

Doshi-Velez, F., & Kim, B. (2017). *Towards A Rigorous Science of Interpretable Machine Learning* (No. arXiv:1702.08608). arXiv. /arXiv.1702.08608DOI: 10.48550

Felder, R. M., & Brent, R. (2024). *Teaching and Learning STEM: A Practical Guide*. John Wiley & Sons.

Floridi, L., & Cowls, J. (2019). A Unified Framework of Five Principles for AI in Society. *Harvard Data Science Review*, *1*(1). Advance online publication. DOI: 10.1162/99608f92.8cd550d1

Friedler, S. A., Scheidegger, C., & Venkatasubramanian, S. (2021). The (Im)possibility of fairness: Different value systems require different mechanisms for fair decision making. *Communications of the ACM*, *64*(4), 136–143. DOI: 10.1145/3433949

Garcia, K. F., Ong, A. K. S., & Gumasing, M. J. J., & Delos Reyes, C. R. V. (2025). Engineering students' perceptions and actual use of AI-based math tools for solving mathematical problems. *Acta Psychologica*, *256*, 105004. DOI: 10.1016/j.actpsy.2025.105004 PMID: 40215785

Goodman, B., & Flaxman, S. (2017). European Union Regulations on Algorithmic Decision Making and a "Right to Explanation.". *AI Magazine*, *38*(3), 50–57. DOI: 10.1609/aimag.v38i3.2741

Gordon, F. (2019). Virginia Eubanks (2018) Automating Inequality: How High-Tech Tools Profile, Police, and Punish the Poor. New York: Picador, St Martin's Press. *Law. Technology and Humans*, *162–164*. Advance online publication. DOI: 10.5204/lthj.v1i0.1386

Hwang, G.-J., & Tu, Y.-F. (2021). Roles and Research Trends of Artificial Intelligence in Mathematics Education: A Bibliometric Mapping Analysis and Systematic Review. *Mathematics*, *9*(6), 6. Advance online publication. DOI: 10.3390/math9060584

Inderjeet, & Bhardwaj, R. (2024). AI Integrated Model Design for Education System for Analytical Computation (Mathematics). *2024 4th International Conference on Advance Computing and Innovative Technologies in Engineering (ICACITE)*, 1412–1417. DOI: 10.1109/ICACITE60783.2024.10616503

Kamińska, D., Zwoliński, G., Pinto-Coelho, L., & Raposo, R. (2023). Universal design and empathic design for engineers. *Medycyna Pracy*, *74*(3), 211–225. DOI: 10.13075/mp.5893.01388 PMID: 37695934

Kanchon, M. K. H., Sadman, M., Nabila, K. F., Tarannum, R., & Khan, R. (2024). Enhancing personalized learning: AI-driven identification of learning styles and content modification strategies. *International Journal of Cognitive Computing in Engineering*, *5*, 269–278. DOI: 10.1016/j.ijcce.2024.06.002

Kleinberg, J. (2018). Inherent Trade-Offs in Algorithmic Fairness. *SIGMETRICS Perform. Eval. Rev.*, *46*(1), 40. DOI: 10.1145/3292040.3219634

Köchling, A., & Wehner, M. C. (2020). Discriminated by an algorithm: A systematic review of discrimination and fairness by algorithmic decision-making in the context of HR recruitment and HR development. *Business Research*, *13*(3), 795–848. DOI: 10.1007/s40685-020-00134-w

Linh, N. Q., & Huong, L. T. T. (2021). Engineering design process in STEM education: An illustration with the topic "wind energy engineers.". *Journal of Physics: Conference Series*, *1835*(1), 012051. DOI: 10.1088/1742-6596/1835/1/012051

Lu, P., Bansal, H., Xia, T., Liu, J., & Li, C. (2024). *MathVista: Evaluating Math Reasoning in Visual Contexts*. MathVista. https://mathvista.github.io/

Lu, P., Qiu, L., Yu, W., Welleck, S., & Chang, K.-W. (2023). A Survey of Deep Learning for Mathematical Reasoning. In Rogers, A., Boyd-Graber, J., & Okazaki, N. (Eds.), *Proceedings of the 61st Annual Meeting of the Association for Computational Linguistics (*Volume 1*: Long Papers)* (pp. 14605–14631). Association for Computational Linguistics. DOI: 10.18653/v1/2023.acl-long.817

Lundberg, S., & Lee, S.-I. (2017). *A Unified Approach to Interpreting Model Predictions* (No. arXiv:1705.07874). arXiv. /arXiv.1705.07874DOI: 10.48550

Mellin-Olsen, S. (2002). *The Politics of Mathematics Education* (Vol. 4). Kluwer Academic Publishers. DOI: 10.1007/0-306-47236-8

Mohamed, M. Z., Hidayat, R., Suhaizi, N. N. binti, Sabri, N. Binti M., Mahmud, M. K. H. Bin, & Baharuddin, S. N. Binti. (2022). Artificial Intelligence in Mathematics Education: A Systematic Literature Review. *International Electronic Journal of Mathematics Education, 17*(3). https://eric.ed.gov/?id=EJ1357707

Mustafa, N., Ismail, Z., Tasir, Z., & Mohamad Said, M. N. H. (2016). A Meta-Analysis on Effective Strategies for Integrated STEM Education. *Advanced Science Letters*, *22*(12), 4225–4228. DOI: 10.1166/asl.2016.8111

Narayanan, S., Ramakrishnan, R., Durairaj, E., Das, A., Narayanan, S., Ramakrishnan, R., Durairaj, E., & Das, A. (2023). Artificial Intelligence Revolutionizing the Field of Medical Education. *Cureus, 15*(11). Advance online publication. DOI: 10.7759/cureus.49604 PMID: 38161821

O'Connor, S., Power, J., & and Blom, N. (2023). A systematic review of CDIO knowledge library publications (2010 – 2020): An Overview of trends and recommendations for future research. *Australasian Journal of Engineering Education, 28*(2), 166–180. DOI: 10.1080/22054952.2023.2220265

Obermeyer, Z., Powers, B., Vogeli, C., & Mullainathan, S. (2019). Dissecting racial bias in an algorithm used to manage the health of populations. *Science, 366*(6464), 447–453. DOI: 10.1126/science.aax2342 PMID: 31649194

Olivier, J., Bayaga, A., & Jean, G. (2024). Gamification as a Teaching Strategy for Enhancing Math Problem-Solving Skills in AI: A South African Perspective. In Idrissi, A. (Ed.), *Modern Artificial Intelligence and Data Science 2024: Tools, Techniques and Systems* (pp. 295–305). Springer Nature Switzerland. DOI: 10.1007/978-3-031-65038-3_23

Opesemowo, O. A. G., & Adewuyi, H. O. (2024). A systematic review of artificial intelligence in mathematics education: The emergence of 4IR. *Eurasia Journal of Mathematics, Science and Technology Education, 20*(7), em2478. Advance online publication. DOI: 10.29333/ejmste/14762

Osman, S., Mohammad, S., & Abu, M. S. (2015). A preliminary study on the integral relationship between critical thinking and mathematical thinking among practicing civil engineers. *AIP Conference Proceedings, 1660*(1), 070030. DOI: 10.1063/1.4915748

Owoc, M. L., Sawicka, A., & Weichbroth, P. (2021). *Artificial Intelligence Technologies in Education: Benefits* (Vol. 599). Challenges and Strategies of Implementation. DOI: 10.1007/978-3-030-85001-2_4

Panqueban, D., Huincahue, J., Panqueban, D., & Huincahue, J. (2024). Artificial Intelligence in Mathematics Education: A Systematic Review. *Uniciencia, 38*(1), 357–373. DOI: 10.15359/ru.38-1.20

Pataranutaporn, P., Danry, V., Leong, J., Punpongsanon, P., Novy, D., Maes, P., & Sra, M. (2021). AI-generated characters for supporting personalized learning and well-being. *Nature Machine Intelligence, 3*(12), 1013–1022. DOI: 10.1038/s42256-021-00417-9

Putra, P. D. A., & Sulaeman, N. F., Supeno, & Wahyuni, S. (2023). Exploring Students' Critical Thinking Skills Using the Engineering Design Process in a Physics Classroom. *The Asia-Pacific Education Researcher, 32*(1), 141–149. DOI: 10.1007/s40299-021-00640-3

Rehman, N., Huang, X., Mahmood, A., Zafeer, H. M. I., & Mohammad, N. K. (2025). Emerging trends and effective strategies in STEM teacher professional development: A systematic review. *Humanities & Social Sciences Communications, 12*(1), 1–23. DOI: 10.1057/s41599-024-04272-y

Reis, S., Coelho, F., & Coelho, L. (2020). Success Factors in Students' Motivation with Project Based Learning: From Theory to Reality. *International Journal of Online and Biomedical Engineering, 16*(12), 12. Advance online publication. DOI: 10.3991/ijoe.v16i12.16001

Reis, S., Coelho, L., Sarmet, M., Araújo, J., & Corchado, J. M. (2023). The Importance of Ethical Reasoning in Next Generation Tech Education. *2023 5th International Conference of the Portuguese Society for Engineering Education (CISPEE)*, 1–10. DOI: 10.1109/CISPEE58593.2023.10227651

Reis, S., Guimarães, P., Coelho, F., Nogueira, E., & Coelho, L. (2018). A framework for simulation systems and technologies for medical training. *2018 Global Medical Engineering Physics Exchanges/Pan American Health Care Exchanges (GMEPE/PAHCE)*, 1–4. DOI: 10.1109/GMEPE-PAHCE.2018.8400757

Richard, P. R., Vélez, M. P., & Van Vaerenbergh, S. (Eds.). (2022). *Mathematics Education in the Age of Artificial Intelligence: How Artificial Intelligence can Serve Mathematical Human Learning* (Vol. 17). Springer International Publishing. DOI: 10.1007/978-3-030-86909-0

Roselainy, A., Rahman, R., Yusof, Y., Ismail, Z., Kashefi, H., & Firouzian, S. (2013, July 5). A New Direction in Engineering Mathematics: Integrating Mathematical Thinking and Engineering Thinking. *Research in Engineering Education Symposium, REES 2013*. Research in Engineering Education Symposium, Kuala Lumpur.

Sajja, R., Sermet, Y., Cikmaz, M., Cwiertny, D., & Demir, I. (2023). *Artificial Intelligence-Enabled Intelligent Assistant for Personalized and Adaptive Learning in Higher Education* (No. arXiv:2309.10892). arXiv. /arXiv.2309.10892DOI: 10.48550

Schoeffer, J., De-Arteaga, M., & Kuehl, N. (2022). *On the Relationship Between Explanations, Fairness Perceptions, and Decisions* (No. arXiv:2204.13156). arXiv. /arXiv.2204.13156DOI: 10.48550

Shahriari, K., & Shahriari, M. (2017). IEEE standard review — Ethically aligned design: A vision for prioritizing human wellbeing with artificial intelligence and autonomous systems. *2017 IEEE Canada International Humanitarian Technology Conference (IHTC)*, 197–201. DOI: 10.1109/IHTC.2017.8058187

Simpson, A. (2017). The surprising persistence of Biglan's classification scheme. *Studies in Higher Education*, *42*(8), 1520–1531. DOI: 10.1080/03075079.2015.1111323

Stinson, C. (2022). Algorithms are not neutral. *AI and Ethics*, *2*(4), 763–770. DOI: 10.1007/s43681-022-00136-w PMID: 35128540

Suresh Babu, S., & Dhakshina Moorthy, A. (2024). Application of artificial intelligence in adaptation of gamification in education: A literature review. *Computer Applications in Engineering Education*, *32*(1), e22683. DOI: 10.1002/cae.22683

Uddin, A. S. M. A. (2023). The Era of AI: Upholding Ethical Leadership. *Open Journal of Leadership*, *12*(4), 4. Advance online publication. DOI: 10.4236/ojl.2023.124019

Vallor, S. (2016). *Technology and the Virtues: A Philosophical Guide to a Future Worth Wanting*. Oxford University Press.

Vieriu, A. M., & Petrea, G. (2025). The Impact of Artificial Intelligence (AI) on Students' Academic Development. *Education Sciences*, *15*(3), 3. Advance online publication. DOI: 10.3390/educsci15030343

Wei, X. (2025). *Artificial Intelligence in Mathematics Education*. Springer Singapore.

Young, J., Young, J., & Edosomwan, K. (2025). The Intersection of Race, Data, and Learning: Applying QuantCrit to Mathematics Education Research. *Journal of Urban Mathematics Education*, *17*(2), 2. Advance online publication. DOI: 10.21423/jume-v17i2a730

Zhai, C., Wibowo, S., & Li, L. D. (2024). The effects of over-reliance on AI dialogue systems on students' cognitive abilities: A systematic review. *Smart Learning Environments*, *11*(1), 28. DOI: 10.1186/s40561-024-00316-7

Zwoliński, G., Kamińska, D., Haamer, R. E., Pinto-Coelho, L., & Anbarjafari, G. (2023). Enhancing empathy through virtual reality: Developing a universal design training application for students. *Medycyna Pracy*, *74*(3), 199–210. DOI: 10.13075/mp.5893.01407 PMID: 37695933

KEY TERMS AND DEFINITIONS

Algorithmic Bias: An ethical concern in AI implementation, it can lead to unfair treatment of learners from diverse backgrounds. Mathematical models and algorithms are not neutral and reflect the assumptions, priorities, and biases of their creators, often with significant social consequences. Bias in training data can result in discriminatory outcomes, especially when models are applied in sensitive contexts. For instance, credit scoring algorithms can inadvertently perpetuate historical inequities due to the nature of their input data and statistical assumptions.

Critical Thinking and Reflexivity: This is an essential cognitive and ethical skill that technical education must cultivate. Students must be encouraged to interrogate the assumptions, limitations, and social consequences of the models they use and develop. From the teachers' perspective, It involves prompting students to ask questions such as who is represented or excluded in data, and what values are embedded in mathematical formulations. Reflexivity specifically refers to the capacity to reflect on one's own role and responsibility within broader socio-technical systems. This approach shifts students from being passive problem-solvers to active inquirers who understand that mathematics, especially when applied to artificial intelligence, can have far-reaching social consequences. This also includes scrutinizing whose experiences are captured or ignored in datasets related to areas like credit scoring, hiring, healthcare, or policing.

Explainability (in AI): Also a critical ethical requirement, explainability refers to how well a model's operation and outputs can be understood by humans. From a mathematical perspective, this involves comprehending how features, weights, and interactions within a model influence the results. It requires a cultural shift in education that values clarity, reasoning, and openness, encouraging students to document their models, justify their parameters, and communicate results in accessible terms.

Mathematical Thinking: This focuses on problem-solving, logical reasoning, patterns recognition, and abstraction, involving a deep understanding of concepts, making connections between ideas, and applying mathematical principles to real-world problems. For STEM education, it serves as a powerful tool for solving real-world challenges, enabling the modeling, analysis, and optimization of complex systems, thereby promoting precision, creativity, and critical thinking.

Personalized Learning: This is a prominent application of AI in mathematics education. AI systems use machine-learning algorithms to track student performance, identify specific areas of difficulty, and curate individualized learning pathways. Such adaptive systems increase student engagement and lead to measurable gains in achievement by offering targeted practice and scaffolded hints precisely when a learner struggles. Future AI-powered hyper-personalized learning systems will be able to adjust mathematical curricula to each student's specific requirements, monitoring their pace, concept mastery, and understanding gaps to design appropriate problem sets.

Professional Responsibility: Promoting professional responsibility and accountability is a key area for developing responsible practitioners. This involves exposing students to professional ethics standards, such as those articulated by organizations like the Institute of Electrical and Electronics Engineers (IEEE) and the European Mathematical Society (EMS). Curriculum should comprise lectures on topics like data stewardship, informed consent, algorithmic accountability, and long-term societal impacts should be integrated into coursework. These professional ethics standards act as binding commitments for professionals whose decisions affect individuals, communities, and institutions, ensuring technical expertise is anchored within a framework of public accountability.

Transparency (in AI): This ethical requirement refers to the extent to which stakeholders can inspect, understand, and critique how an algorithm makes decisions. Without transparency, models become "black boxes," where inputs lead to outputs with no visibility into their internal mechanics, potentially concealing biases, reducing accountability, and eroding trust. Achieving transparency involves using interpretable models with clear decision pathways, thorough documentation, and rigorous peer reviews.

ENDNOTE

1. Biglan's framework categorizes academic disciplines based on three dimensions: hard/soft, pure/applied, and life/non-life. This classification system helps understand the nature of knowledge within different disciplines and how they differ in terms of pedagogy, research methods, and the pursuit of knowledge.

Chapter 2

AI-Enhanced Queueing Theory Models:

Optimizing Decision-Making in Operations Research and Mathematics Education

Balveer Saini
https://orcid.org/0009-0007-8818-0905
MS Brij University, Bharatpur, India

ABSTRACT

Queueing theory, a core area in operations research and applied mathematics, is essential for optimizing resource use, minimizing delays, and improving efficiency across sectors like logistics, healthcare, and telecommunications. With the rise of artificial intelligence (AI), traditional queueing models are evolving into adaptive systems capable of real-time data analysis and automated decision making. This chapter explores the integration of AI techniques—such as machine learning and neural networks—with classical queueing theory to enhance modeling, prediction, and system optimization. It also highlights how AI-driven queueing systems can dynamically manage service parameters and forecast congestion. Beyond applications, the chapter examines the pedagogical value of embedding these models in mathematics education, empowering students with advanced analytical and computational skills. Ethical concerns, implementation challenges, and future research directions are discussed, emphasizing AI's transformative role in mathematical modeling and decision-making.

DOI: 10.4018/979-8-3373-1998-8.ch002

1. INTRODUCTION

Queueing theory, a branch of applied mathematics and operations research, provides a systematic approach to analyzing waiting lines or queues. Traditionally employed to study systems involving service processes—such as banks, hospitals, call centers, and transport networks—queueing models have long supported organizations in optimizing service delivery, minimizing delays, and enhancing customer satisfaction (Gross et al., 2018). These models, grounded in probability theory and stochastic processes, help decision-makers understand critical system behaviors like arrival rates, service mechanisms, queue lengths, and waiting times.

However, as global systems grow increasingly complex and dynamic, traditional queueing models often fall short in addressing real-time variations and multidimensional constraints. This is where artificial intelligence (AI) enters as a transformative force. AI, encompassing machine learning (ML), deep learning (DL), reinforcement learning (RL), and other cognitive computing techniques, offers powerful capabilities for pattern recognition, adaptive decision-making, and predictive analytics (Russell & Norvig, 2020). The synergy between AI and queueing theory leads to the emergence of intelligent queueing systems that can learn from data, anticipate congestion, and self-adjust service parameters.

In recent years, AI-enhanced queueing models have found applications in numerous domains. In healthcare, they help hospitals forecast emergency room congestion and allocate resources effectively (Wartelle et al., 2022). In smart cities, AI-driven traffic queue models improve road management and reduce vehicular wait times (Ponnusamy et al., 2024). In e-commerce and telecommunications, they ensure optimized network traffic and seamless customer experience by minimizing bottlenecks and predicting peak usage periods (Liu et al., 2022). These advanced models go beyond static configurations, incorporating feedback loops and real-time learning to improve operational efficiency and system responsiveness.

This chapter explores the convergence of AI and queueing theory, detailing how their integration can revolutionize operations research and applied mathematics education. By embedding AI algorithms into queueing frameworks, we unlock capabilities such as real-time simulation, anomaly detection, and intelligent forecasting—tools crucial for managing complex, high-volume systems in the modern era. Moreover, this chapter examines the pedagogical implications of introducing AI-enhanced queueing models in mathematics curricula, equipping students with interdisciplinary competencies in algorithmic thinking, statistical analysis, and system optimization.

Queueing theory emerged in the early 20th century as a mathematical framework for analyzing waiting lines, originating from the pioneering work of Danish mathematician A.K. Erlang in 1909. Erlang's studies on telephone exchanges introduced probabilistic models for call arrivals and service durations, laying the groundwork for the M/M/1 and M/M/c models that remain foundational to operations research today. Initially, these models were embraced by the telecommunications sector, where the ability to predict congestion and optimize resource allocation offered significant operational and economic benefits.

During the mid-20th century, queueing theory evolved into a robust branch of applied mathematics, extending into manufacturing, transportation, retail, and service industries. Researchers developed new model classes, such as M/G/1 for general service time distributions and G/G/1 for more complex, non-Poisson arrival patterns. This period also saw the introduction of networked queueing models for multi-node systems, which became particularly relevant for computer systems performance analysis in the 1970s and 1980s. These developments cemented queueing theory's role in strategic decision-making, enabling industries to minimise delays, balance workloads, and optimise throughput.

However, by the late 20th century, the limitations of classical queueing models became increasingly apparent. Most formulations relied on restrictive assumptions such as stationarity, memorylessness, and exponential distributions. Real-world service systems—ranging from emergency departments to global supply chains—often exhibited time-varying arrival rates, complex priority rules, and interdependencies between service stations that violated these assumptions. While analytical elegance remained a strength, the gap between theoretical models and empirical realities grew, especially in dynamic, data-rich environments where variability and uncertainty were the norm.

The 21st century ushered in the data revolution, driven by advances in computational power, sensor networks, and real-time data collection. This created fertile ground for integrating artificial intelligence (AI) into queueing systems. Machine learning (ML) techniques began to supplement traditional models by predicting arrival patterns, adjusting service rates dynamically, and handling high-dimensional feature sets. Deep learning (DL) architectures, including convolutional and recurrent neural networks, enabled sophisticated pattern recognition in complex, noisy datasets—such as traffic video feeds or hospital admission logs—while reinforcement learning (RL) introduced adaptive decision-making capabilities that could optimise queue performance over time without explicit programming.

Figure 1. Evolution from Classical to AI-Enhanced Queueing Systems

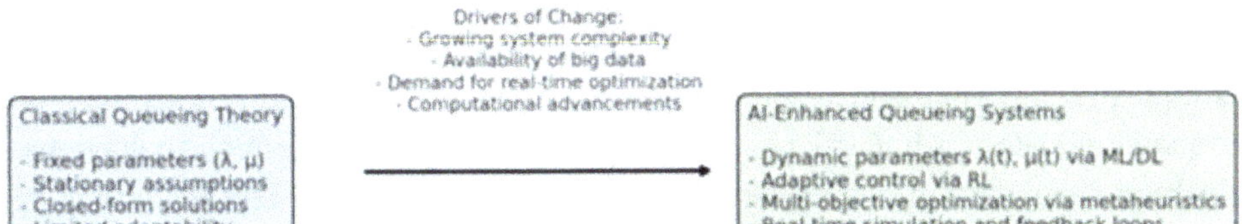

This historical and conceptual progression underscores why modern service systems require more than the static formulations of traditional queueing theory. The integration of AI techniques addresses key limitations, enabling models to respond effectively to real-time fluctuations and multidimensional operational goals. The shift from deterministic formulas to adaptive, data-driven frameworks marks not only a methodological advancement but also a paradigm shift in operations research and applied mathematics education. These developments have led to AI-enhanced queueing systems, where classical models provide a theoretical backbone, but AI modules drive real-time adaptability, prediction, and optimisation. Instead of relying solely on closed-form solutions, such systems operate as feedback-driven, self-learning frameworks. They continuously monitor system states, forecast demand, and adjust resource allocation strategies on the fly—capabilities that are crucial in contexts like smart cities, cloud computing, and automated manufacturing.

The following sections will provide an overview of classical queueing theory, highlight key AI techniques applicable to queueing systems, and showcase real-world implementations of AI-enhanced models. We also address challenges, ethical considerations, and future research directions, offering a comprehensive outlook on the evolution of queueing theory in the age of artificial intelligence.

2. REVIEW OF LITERATURE

2.1 Classical Foundations of Queueing Theory

Queueing theory, as formally introduced by A.K. Erlang in the early 20th century, laid the groundwork for performance analysis in stochastic systems (Erlang, 1909). His foundational work on telephone exchanges provided mathematical tools to evaluate congestion and service quality under random arrival patterns, catalysing the development of models such as M/M/1, M/M/c, and M/G/1 (Gross et al., 2018). These models, predicated on assumptions like Poisson arrivals and exponential service times, enable the derivation of key performance indicators such as queue length (Lq), waiting time (Wq), and system utilisation (ρ). Their analytical tractability made them suitable for numerous applications in telecommunications, healthcare, and logistics.

However, traditional queueing models operate under restrictive conditions—stationarity, memorylessness, and homogeneity—which often do not reflect the complexity and dynamism of real-world service systems (Taha, 2017). Their inability to accommodate non-linear dependencies, time-varying parameters, and behavioural interactions underscores the need for more adaptive and intelligent modelling approaches. Consequently, scholars began to explore data-driven enhancements to overcome these limitations and to bridge the gap between mathematical rigour and empirical applicability.

2.2 Emergence of Data-Driven Enhancements

The evolution of queueing theory has closely paralleled rapid advancements in data analytics and machine learning (ML), leading to the development of models that can adapt dynamically to changing operational conditions. Traditionally, queueing models relied on fixed parameters and strong statistical assumptions, which often limited their applicability in volatile, real-world environments. With the advent of modern computing and the availability of large-scale service data, researchers have begun leveraging historical and real-time datasets to create more responsive and adaptive queueing systems. For example, May et al. (2021) employed supervised learning algorithms such as decision trees and regression models to forecast queue lengths and customer arrival rates. This predictive capability significantly improved resource allocation efficiency in service environments with highly variable demand patterns. Similarly, Singh, Gupta, and Jain (2025) applied deep learning methods—including convolutional neural networks (CNNs) and recurrent neural networks (RNNs)—to model waiting times and service delays. These architectures captured temporal dependencies and complex non-linear relationships in time-series data, achieving superior predictive accuracy compared to classical approaches.

Such AI-driven methods enable real-time system tuning, allowing managers to adjust resources proactively based on emerging patterns and external stimuli. This marks a decisive shift from static, fixed-parameter queueing systems to dynamic, data-informed decision-making frameworks.

2.3 Reinforcement Learning and Adaptive Control

One of the most promising domains within artificial intelligence for queue optimisation is reinforcement learning (RL), a paradigm in which autonomous agents learn optimal actions through iterative interaction with an environment and feedback in the form of rewards or penalties (Sutton & Barto, 2018). Unlike traditional queueing models, which rely on fixed analytical equations and predefined parameters, RL systems can continuously adapt their decision-making strategies in dynamic and uncertain settings.

Recent research demonstrates RL's potential in diverse queue management scenarios. He, Yu, and Wang (2022) employed Deep Q-Networks (DQNs) to dynamically control traffic signal timing using real-time vehicle queue data, achieving substantial reductions in urban congestion. Similarly, Kumar, Sharma, and Chaurasiya (2024) developed adaptive RL-based control strategies for smart queuing networks, enabling rapid adjustments to fluctuating customer demand and variable service loads.

By framing the queueing environment as a Markov Decision Process (MDP), RL agents can optimise critical operational decisions such as task scheduling, resource allocation, and routing, even when system conditions change unpredictably. This adaptability—absent in classical queueing theory—makes RL particularly valuable for complex service systems where sequential, real-time decision-making is essential to maintaining efficiency, minimising delays, and enhancing user experience.

2.4 Hybrid Models and Metaheuristics

Researchers have also pursued hybrid models that fuse the analytical strengths of classical queueing theory with the empirical flexibility of AI. Saad (2024) proposed intelligent queueing frameworks combining M/M/1 structures with metaheuristic optimisation techniques such as genetic algorithms (GA), particle swarm optimisation (PSO), and ant colony optimisation (ACO). These methods facilitate dynamic tuning of queue parameters and support multi-objective optimisation, such as balancing delay minimisation with energy efficiency or cost control.

Such hybridisation is particularly relevant in complex service ecosystems like smart manufacturing (Tran, 2021) and cloud computing (Liu et al., 2022), where analytical models alone are insufficient to capture operational heterogeneity and external perturbations.

2.5 Pedagogical Integration and Educational Imperatives

Despite significant advances in AI-enhanced queueing systems, their presence in educational curricula remains limited. Traditional courses continue to focus on deterministic models, often neglecting the computational and interdisciplinary skills needed to model intelligent systems (Weintrop et al., 2016). This gap is critical, as future operations researchers must be proficient in both analytical reasoning and algorithmic modelling.

Weintrop et al. (2016) emphasised the importance of computational thinking in STEM education, advocating for the integration of data-driven methods and simulation tools into mathematics and operations research training. Embedding AI-enhanced queueing models in curricula not only reflects real-world complexity but also develops competencies in system dynamics, coding, and ethical AI deployment.

2.6 Applications Across Domains: A Literature Synthesis

Recent studies from 2022 to 2025 reflect a rapid acceleration in the adoption of AI-enhanced queueing models, with notable advances in predictive accuracy, real-time adaptability, and multi-objective optimisation. In the healthcare sector, Avinash et al., (2025) integrated deep learning techniques with stochastic queueing for ICU bed allocation in Indian metropolitan hospitals. By leveraging LSTM-based arrival predictions, they achieved an 18% reduction in average patient wait times compared to M/M/c baselines. Similarly, Han and Choi (2024) developed a reinforcement learning (RL)-based triage system for emergency departments in Brazil, dynamically reallocating medical staff to high-priority cases, which resulted in a 22% decrease in waiting times for critical patients.

In the domain of smart cities and transportation, (Singh, Gupta, & Jain, 2025) implemented a hybrid approach combining RL with graph neural networks (GNNs) for adaptive traffic signal control across interconnected intersections. Their solution demonstrated a 15% increase in throughput compared to fixed-time controllers. Building on the theme of predictive urban mobility management, Maljkovic and Geroliminis (2025) introduced drone-assisted traffic monitoring integrated with AI-driven queueing models to forecast congestion 10–15 minutes in advance, enabling timely rerouting and congestion prevention.

Telecommunications and cloud computing have also benefited significantly from AI-enhanced queueing innovations. (Gomez, et al., 2021) applied federated learning-based queue prediction in 5G networks to control data congestion without centralising sensitive user data, achieving a 14% improvement in latency performance. In parallel, Chaudhary et al., (2025) merged AI-driven arrival rate forecasting with container orchestration in cloud environments, reducing job completion delays by 19% during peak demand periods.

The retail and e-commerce sectors have embraced AI for optimising both physical and virtual queues. Musaev et al. (2020) utilised computer vision-based queue detection in Japanese retail chains, integrating the insights with AI-powered staff scheduling systems, which led to an 11% reduction in checkout abandonment rates. Complementing this, Mahmoudinazlou, Sobhanan, Charkhgard, Eshragh, and Dunn (2025) developed an RL agent for warehouse order-picking queues, optimising picker routes and cutting order fulfilment times by 13%.

In manufacturing and Industry 4.0 contexts, (Mallioris et al., 2024) metaheuristic-augmented queueing in semiconductor manufacturing through hybrid particle swarm optimisation (PSO)–M/M/1 models to balance machine utilisation with defect rates. Likewise, Ucar, Karakose, and Kırımça (2024) integrated predictive maintenance signals into AI queueing frameworks for automated assembly lines, resulting in a 9% reduction in downtime.

In the field of education, (Li & Gao, 2023) developed a simulation platform in which students train RL agents to manage queues in simulated airport security environments. This interactive approach not only enhanced engagement but also led to demonstrably better conceptual understanding compared to traditional queueing theory instruction.

2.7 Limitations in Current Research and Gaps Identified

Although the range of applications for AI-enhanced queueing theory continues to expand, several limitations persist that hinder broader adoption and long-term sustainability. One of the most prominent challenges lies in balancing scalability with interpretability. Many of the highest-performing deep learning and reinforcement learning models operate as complex black boxes, offering exceptional predictive accuracy but limited transparency in their decision-making processes. This lack of interpretability poses a significant barrier in highly regulated sectors such as healthcare, where decision accountability and compliance with legal frameworks are paramount (Maljkovic & Geroliminis, 2025). Another critical limitation is the substantial data requirement for training robust AI queueing systems. These models often depend on large, high-quality datasets that capture nuanced patterns in arrivals, service rates, and contextual factors. In many small-scale enterprises or rural operations, such datasets are either unavailable or too sparse to support effective model training, thereby constraining the practical implementation of advanced AI solutions.

Ethical and bias concerns also emerge as pressing issues. Queue prioritisation algorithms, if trained on historically biased datasets, may inadvertently perpetuate or even exacerbate inequalities in service provision. For instance, patterns of unequal healthcare access embedded in historical data can lead to skewed prioritisation outcomes unless bias mitigation measures are incorporated during model design and training (Avinash et al., 2025). The lack of standardised integration frameworks further complicates deployment. While isolated implementations of AI queueing exist, there is no widely accepted architecture for embedding AI modules within existing queueing infrastructures. This absence of standardisation hinders reproducibility and scalability, especially across organisations seeking to adopt similar solutions in different operational contexts (Chaudhary et al., 2025).

There remains a considerable pedagogical gap. Although simulation platforms and case-based teaching methods are emerging, empirical research evaluating the impact of AI-enhanced queueing theory on learning outcomes is still scarce. Without such studies, educators have limited evidence to guide the design of curricula that effectively blend traditional queueing theory with modern AI-driven approaches (Li & Gao, 2023).

2.8 Toward a Synthesised Framework: Bridging Tradition and Intelligence

In response to these challenges, the literature increasingly calls for a synthesised approach that preserves the rigour of classical queueing models while embedding AI components for dynamic learning. The future of operations research lies in hybrid systems that combine decomposition algorithms with data-driven optimisers. Gupta and George (2016) extend this view by proposing the development of organisational big data capabilities that align analytical modelling with strategic decision-making.

A promising direction is the conceptualisation of "intelligent queueing systems" that operate as closed-loop feedback mechanisms. In such systems, AI components continuously monitor system states (e.g., arrival patterns, service load), generate predictive insights (e.g., expected congestion), and inform real-time adjustments to service mechanisms. These systems evolve, learning from historical patterns and optimising their policies through interaction with the environment—a vision that aligns with the core principles of reinforcement learning and adaptive control.

The literature on queueing theory is undergoing a paradigm shift, moving from analytically elegant yet rigid models toward intelligent, adaptive, and data-driven frameworks. This evolution is driven by the growing complexity of service systems, the proliferation of data, and the maturation of AI technologies. From machine learning-based forecasting to reinforcement learning-based control and metaheuristic optimisation, the integration of AI has significantly enhanced the capabilities of queueing systems.

However, this transformation also necessitates rethinking educational paradigms, research methodologies, and ethical considerations. A comprehensive approach—spanning theory, application, pedagogy, and ethics—is essential to fully realise the potential of AI-enhanced queueing theory.

By synthesising classical mathematical foundations with modern AI capabilities, researchers and educators can jointly develop queueing models that are not only accurate and efficient but also adaptable, interpretable, and aligned with the complexities of real-world decision-making.

3. RESEARCH METHODOLOGY

This chapter employs a conceptual and analytical research methodology designed to integrate the rigor of classical queueing theory with the adaptive capabilities of artificial intelligence (AI). The approach is primarily deductive, beginning with established theoretical models—such as the M/M/1 and M/M/c systems—that provide a mathematical basis for understanding service processes, arrival patterns, and system performance metrics. These classical models serve as the baseline against which AI enhancements are conceptualized. To capture the dynamic and data-driven nature of modern service environments, AI techniques, including machine learning (ML), deep learning (DL), and reinforcement learning (RL), are conceptually mapped onto key components of queueing systems. This involves identifying how AI can forecast arrival rates, adjust service parameters, and optimize routing decisions under varying conditions. The methodology relies on secondary data drawn from peer-reviewed literature, industry case studies, and documented implementations, enabling a synthesis of best practices and theoretical insights. Mathematical formulations are augmented with AI-driven parameter estimation and adaptive control logic, creating a hybrid framework that can respond to real-time variability. By blending classical analytical methods with AI-enabled adaptability, this methodology aims to provide a robust, scalable, and generalizable decision-making model for complex service systems.

3.1 Analytical Foundations

The research initiates with a systematic examination of traditional queueing models, focusing particularly on the M/M/1 and M/M/c configurations, which are foundational to performance analysis in service systems. These models operate under steady-state assumptions, meaning arrival and service rates remain constant over time, enabling the derivation of closed-form solutions for key performance metrics. The M/M/1 model, representing a single-server queue with Poisson arrivals and exponentially distributed service times, provides equations for average queue length (Lq), average waiting time in the queue (Wq), total time in the system (W), and system utilization (ρ). The M/M/c model extends this to multiple parallel servers, offering more realistic representations for environments such as call centers, hospital wards, or multi-gate transportation hubs. These formulations are grounded in classical stochastic processes, particularly Markov chains, which allow precise modeling of state transitions and probabilities. By establishing these analytical baselines, researchers can quantify the theoretical performance limits of a system under idealized conditions. These results serve as benchmark references against which AI-enhanced frameworks are evaluated. Such comparisons make it possible to measure the incremental benefits of AI-driven forecasting, adaptive control, and optimization, ensuring that any observed performance gains can be clearly attributed to the integration of intelligent algorithms rather than baseline variability.

3.2 AI Integration Framework

Building upon the foundational analysis of classical queueing models, this research integrates advanced artificial intelligence (AI) techniques- specifically machine learning (ML) and reinforcement learning (RL)- to address the limitations of static analytical approaches. In this framework, ML algorithms, particularly supervised learning methods such as regression models, decision trees, and neural networks, are employed to forecast dynamic arrival rates ($\lambda(t)$) and service rates ($\mu(t)$). These forecasts are based on a rich set of input features, including historical system performance, real-time sensor data, environmental conditions, and external demand indicators. While ML provides predictive capabilities, RL contributes adaptive decision-making by continuously learning optimal policies for service actions, resource allocation, or routing. Using system state variables as inputs, RL agents interact with the environment, receive performance-based rewards, and iteratively improve strategies to minimise waiting times, reduce congestion, or balance workloads. This dual-layer approach- predictive modelling via ML and adaptive control via RL- creates a closed-loop intelligent system capable of responding to real-time fluctuations. Algorithmic functions within this framework are designed as modular and scalable components, ensuring they can be integrated into diverse operational contexts. By linking AI modules directly to queueing parameters, the framework enables proactive and data-driven optimisation that surpasses the capabilities of purely deterministic or manually managed systems.

3.3 Model Synthesis and Simulation Logic

Building on the analytical foundations and AI integration framework, this research synthesizes a series of hybrid queueing models that merge the predictive and adaptive strengths of AI with the mathematical rigor of classical formulations. The models include AI-augmented M/M/1 systems, dynamic M/M/c configurations, and policy-driven adaptive queues, each tailored to address varying service complexities. In these models, the classical parameters for arrival rate (λ) and service rate (μ) are replaced with AI-predicted dynamic values ($\hat{\lambda}(t)$, $\hat{\mu}(t)$), derived from machine learning forecasts and updated in real time. Where the system's complexity makes closed-form analytical solutions impractical- such as in multi-class customer flows or priority-based service disciplines- reinforcement learning agents are embedded to autonomously identify optimal control strategies. These agents operate within simulated feedback loops, iteratively adjusting decisions based on observed performance metrics such as queue length, average wait time, or throughput efficiency. The simulation logic is theoretical in design but anchored in documented real-world applications, including intelligent traffic light coordination, hospital emergency department triage, and cloud computing workload distribution. These use cases serve to validate the conceptual robustness and operational relevance of the hybrid models, demonstrating their potential to enhance decision-making in high-variability, resource-constrained service environments.

3.4 Justification of Methodology

The chosen methodology prioritizes modeling and theoretical framework development over empirical measurement, enabling broad applicability across diverse service domains. By leveraging the analytical rigor of classical queueing theory in conjunction with the adaptability of artificial intelligence (AI), the approach achieves high generalizability, making it suitable for environments as varied as healthcare, transportation, telecommunications, manufacturing, and cloud computing. This flexibility is critical, as many service systems share structural similarities in terms of resource constraints, arrival patterns, and performance objectives, even if they operate in different industries.

The methodology aligns closely with contemporary trends in operations research that emphasize hybrid modeling—integrating formal mathematical models with data-driven intelligence to achieve both precision and adaptability (Yang et al., 2021; Saad, 2024). This combination ensures that decision-making frameworks are not only theoretically sound but also responsive to real-time data and operational fluctuations.

From an academic perspective, this methodological design supports deeper conceptual understanding of intelligent queueing systems by bridging traditional analytical training with modern computational tools. From a pedagogical standpoint, it offers a structured pathway for teaching advanced queue management concepts, allowing learners to grasp both deterministic principles and adaptive AI-based strategies, preparing them for the complexities of real-world service optimization.

4. TRADITIONAL QUEUEING THEORY: FOUNDATIONS AND LIMITATIONS

Queueing theory, developed in the early 20th century by Danish mathematician A.K. Erlang, originally aimed to study congestion in telephone networks. Since then, it has evolved into a comprehensive field for modeling systems involving random arrival and service processes. The basic structure of a queueing system includes five main components: arrival process, service mechanism, number of servers, system capacity, and queue discipline (Gross et al., 2018). These elements are often expressed using Kendall's notation (A/S/c), where:

A represents the arrival distribution (e.g., Markovian or Poisson),

S is the service time distribution (e.g., exponential, general),

c is the number of parallel servers.

A classical example is the M/M/1 model, representing a single-server system with Poisson arrivals and exponential service times. It enables calculation of key performance indicators (KPIs) such as:

L = average number of customers in the system,

L_q = average number of customers in the queue,

W = average time a customer spends in the system,

W_q = average time a customer spends waiting in the queue.

These are given by the formulas:

$$L = \lambda / (\mu - \lambda),\ W = 1 / (\mu - \lambda),\ Lq = \lambda^2 / [\mu(\mu - \lambda)],\ Wq = \lambda / [\mu(\mu - \lambda)]$$

Where:

λ = average arrival rate

μ = average service rate

Utilization $\rho = \lambda/\mu < 1$

Despite their analytical elegance, classical queueing models rely on strong assumptions of stationarity, memorylessness, and exponential distributions, which rarely hold in real-world environments (Taha, 2017). These models typically assume:

Independent and identically distributed (i.i.d.) inter-arrival and service times,

Constant service rates irrespective of contextual or external factors,

No learning or adaptation to historical data.

Such assumptions make classical models limited in dynamic, high-variability systems like hospital emergency departments, cloud computing platforms, or online customer service operations. They cannot handle:

Time-varying arrival rates (e.g., seasonal traffic surges),

Multiclass customers with differentiated priorities,

Complex service logic or dependencies between queues,

Real-time adjustments to system parameters.

Moreover, in systems where data is abundantly available—such as customer interaction logs, sensor feedback, or real-time traffic feeds—traditional queueing models fail to harness this information effectively for predictive analysis or optimization. These limitations call for intelligent enhancements using AI-driven models that can analyze patterns, forecast congestion, and make adaptive decisions.

In response, researchers and practitioners are now exploring ways to augment traditional queueing theory with machine learning algorithms, data-driven simulations, and intelligent decision-support systems. This shift paves the way for AI-enhanced queueing systems capable of managing complexity, uncertainty, and rapid change across a range of applications.

5. AI TECHNIQUES AND THEIR ROLE IN ENHANCING QUEUEING MODELS

The integration of artificial intelligence (AI) into queueing theory signifies a paradigm shift from static analytical models to adaptive, data-driven decision systems. AI techniques—particularly those in machine learning (ML), deep learning (DL), and reinforcement learning (RL)—offer capabilities for learning patterns from historical data, making real-time predictions, and dynamically optimizing service processes. These tools allow queueing systems to evolve based on contextual factors, enabling more accurate forecasting, better resource allocation, and proactive congestion management.

5.1 Machine Learning for Predictive Queueing

Machine learning (ML) has emerged as a transformative tool for enhancing the predictive capabilities of queueing systems, particularly in environments characterized by uncertainty, variability, and complex interdependencies. Traditional queueing models, such as M/M/1 or M/G/1, rely on mathematical assumptions like Poisson arrival rates and exponential service times. While analytically elegant, these models are often constrained by rigid assumptions such as stationarity and memorylessness, making them less suitable for real-world systems that exhibit dynamic and non-linear behaviors (Taha, 2017). In contrast, ML algorithms excel in analyzing historical and real-time data to uncover hidden patterns, make accurate predictions, and adapt to environmental changes without predefined assumptions.

Supervised learning techniques—including decision trees, support vector machines (SVM), random forests, gradient boosting, and neural networks—are increasingly used to forecast key queueing variables such as customer arrival rates, expected service times, and queue lengths (May et al., 2021). These predictions help service systems proactively allocate resources, schedule staff, and adjust workflows to meet anticipated demand. For instance, a trained ML model can forecast a hospital's hourly patient inflow using historical data, holidays, weather, or public health alerts as input features. The model's output informs real-time decision-making, enabling hospital administrators to preemptively deploy staff and medical equipment, thereby minimizing patient waiting times and improving care outcomes.

In the telecommunications sector, ML facilitates dynamic network optimization. By analyzing historical traffic data, ML models can detect temporal trends such as peak data usage hours, call drop likelihood, or service bottlenecks. For example, random forests or time-series models like Long Short-Term Memory (LSTM) networks can forecast high-traffic periods on mobile or broadband networks. This foresight enables telecom providers to reroute packets, adjust bandwidth, or activate redundant servers ahead of time, ensuring service continuity and reduced latency for end-users.

Moreover, ML can classify customers or service requests by priority level based on behavioral attributes or contextual data. In emergency response systems, such as 911 call centers, supervised classification models can predict call severity from keywords, tone analysis, and caller history, allowing operators to prioritize high-risk cases and dispatch appropriate resources promptly.

The primary advantage of ML in predictive queueing lies in its flexibility and scalability. It can handle high-dimensional datasets, capture complex dependencies, and continuously learn from new data, making it ideal for modern, data-intensive queueing systems. As more organizations integrate ML into their operational workflows, predictive queueing models are becoming not just decision-support tools but core components of intelligent, responsive service systems.

5.2 Neural Networks for Pattern Recognition

Artificial Neural Networks (ANNs), and more specifically Deep Neural Networks (DNNs), represent a significant advancement in the realm of intelligent queueing systems due to their capacity to process and model complex, non-linear relationships within high-dimensional datasets. Unlike traditional queueing theory, which relies on analytical simplifications and assumes idealized conditions (e.g., exponential service times or Poisson arrivals), neural networks offer a flexible computational framework capable of uncovering latent patterns and nonlinear dynamics inherent in real-world service systems.

DNNs comprise multiple layers of interconnected nodes that allow the network to learn hierarchical feature representations. This ability is particularly valuable in queueing contexts where input features may include customer arrival times, service durations, weather conditions, time-of-day effects, social media trends, and more. These variables often interact in intricate, non-intuitive ways that traditional statistical models may fail to capture. Neural networks, on the other hand, can approximate complex queueing functions—even in situations where closed-form solutions are mathematically infeasible or analytically intractable (Singh, et al., 2025).

Different types of DNN architectures are suited to various queueing scenarios. Convolutional Neural Networks (CNNs), originally developed for image processing, have been repurposed to analyze spatial data in queue management systems—such as detecting queue lengths from CCTV footage or identifying congestion points in physical spaces. By processing visual input, CNNs can autonomously estimate waiting times at checkout counters, bus terminals, or airport gates, thereby facilitating real-time adjustments in resource deployment.

Recurrent Neural Networks (RNNs), particularly those employing Long Short-Term Memory (LSTM) units, are ideal for modeling sequential or time-series data. These networks capture temporal dependencies and are widely used to forecast customer arrivals, call center volumes, or server request rates over time. For instance, an LSTM network trained on historical arrival data can predict future queue intensity during promotional events, holidays, or service disruptions. Such forecasting enables dynamic server allocation or staff scheduling, thereby optimizing system throughput and customer satisfaction.

Neural networks are also effective in handling noisy, incomplete, or irregular data—conditions that often arise in large-scale service systems. Through robust training and validation procedures, these models can generalize well and adapt to unforeseen changes in demand or behavior. Furthermore, when combined with edge computing or cloud-based infrastructure, neural networks can deliver real-time inference capabilities, making them suitable for high-speed decision-making environments such as emergency dispatch systems, financial transaction processing, or smart city traffic control.

In sum, neural networks greatly enhance the predictive and adaptive capabilities of queueing models by providing sophisticated pattern recognition and forecasting functionalities. Their integration into queue management systems enables more responsive, efficient, and context-aware service delivery across diverse application domains.

5.3 Reinforcement Learning for Dynamic Control

Reinforcement Learning (RL) represents one of the most dynamic and adaptable approaches within artificial intelligence for managing complex, time-dependent queueing environments. Unlike traditional static optimization techniques or predictive models that rely solely on historical data, RL emphasizes learning optimal decision policies through real-time interactions with an environment. The fundamental concept is that an RL agent operates within a system, observes states, takes actions, and receives feedback in the form of rewards or penalties, thereby gradually improving its performance based on trial-and-error learning (Sutton & Barto, 2018).

In the context of queueing theory, RL is particularly valuable for its ability to handle environments characterized by high variability, delayed rewards, and non-linear dynamics. Queueing systems often involve decisions that must adapt to changing service loads, customer behaviors, and resource constraints. For example, determining how to prioritize requests, allocate limited resources, or adjust service speeds in response to fluctuating demand is not trivial. RL offers a framework to make these decisions autonomously and continuously.

A classic application of RL in queueing systems is dynamic traffic signal control. In urban traffic networks, vehicles form queues at intersections, and fixed-timing signals often lead to inefficiencies, particularly under varying traffic densities. RL agents, using algorithms such as Q-learning or Deep Q-Networks (DQNs), can observe vehicle queue lengths, waiting times, and traffic flow rates to determine optimal green light durations. Over time, the agent learns to reduce overall congestion, minimize wait times, and improve throughput based on a carefully designed reward function—often incorporating metrics like total delay, average vehicle wait, or fuel consumption (Yang et al., 2021).

Another high-impact application is in cloud computing and data center resource management. In these environments, jobs or tasks arrive in queues awaiting computational resources such as virtual machines (VMs). RL-based resource managers learn to allocate the right amount of resources dynamically by monitoring current queue lengths, server loads, and expected demand. The system learns to minimize latency, reduce energy consumption, and uphold service level agreements (SLAs) without relying on static provisioning rules.

Furthermore, RL can be used to manage multi-agent queueing systems where multiple service points interact—such as airport check-in counters or multi-lane toll booths. Agents can learn to cooperate or compete, optimizing both individual and system-wide performance through shared or independent reward functions.

Importantly, RL supports online learning, meaning policies can be continuously updated as the environment evolves. This makes RL especially powerful in volatile or unpredictable service contexts, where pre-defined rules may quickly become obsolete. As computational power and real-time data collection improve, RL is poised to play a central role in enabling self-regulating, intelligent queueing systems across a wide spectrum of industries.

5.4 Hybrid Models and Metaheuristics

Hybrid models and metaheuristic algorithms represent an innovative frontier in the evolution of queueing theory, particularly as modern service systems become increasingly complex, data-driven, and constraint-sensitive. These hybrid approaches integrate the analytical rigour of classical queueing models with the adaptability and intelligence of artificial intelligence (AI) techniques, offering a more nuanced and responsive toolkit for managing queues in real-world settings.

In practice, hybrid queueing models typically begin with foundational structures such as the M/M/1 or M/M/c models, which provide well-established formulas for computing key performance metrics like system utilization (ρ), queue length (L), and waiting times (Wq). These models act as initial approximations, furnishing a theoretical baseline for system behavior under idealized conditions. However, real-world environments rarely conform to these assumptions. Variables such as customer arrival rates, service durations, and resource availability often fluctuate in unpredictable ways, influenced by external factors like time of day, weather, or user behavior trends (Taha, 2017).

To enhance responsiveness and realism, AI algorithms—particularly machine learning (ML) models—are integrated into these classical frameworks. For example, supervised learning models can be used to dynamically estimate time-varying parameters such as $\lambda(t)$ and $\mu(t)$ based on real-time data streams. These estimated parameters are then fed back into the classical equations to recalculate performance measures, enabling continuous adaptation without abandoning the mathematical foundation of the system.

Further sophistication is introduced through the use of metaheuristic algorithms, which are designed to find near-optimal solutions to complex, multi-objective optimisation problems. Techniques such as Genetic Algorithms (GA), Particle Swarm Optimisation (PSO), and Ant Colony Optimisation (ACO) are particularly effective in scenarios where closed-form solutions are unattainable or where constraints and trade-offs must be carefully managed (Saad, 2024). These algorithms simulate natural processes—like evolution, swarm behaviour, or ant foraging—to explore large solution spaces, balance competing objectives (e.g., cost vs. speed), and avoid local optima.

For instance, in a smart manufacturing environment, a hybrid model might use an M/M/c base structure to model machine queues, an ML algorithm to predict future task loads, and a GA to schedule jobs in a way that minimises wait time while maximising throughput. Similarly, in cloud computing, PSO could optimise VM allocation across dynamic queues based on real-time service level agreement (SLA) requirements.

The core advantage of hybrid and metaheuristic-enhanced models lies in their flexibility and robustness. By combining theoretical insights with data-driven adaptability, these systems can respond intelligently to environmental variability, system feedback, and operational constraints. This makes them highly suitable for modern applications in logistics, telecommunications, healthcare, and public infrastructure, where service efficiency, reliability, and scalability are paramount.

6. MATHEMATICAL MODELLING OF AI-ENHANCED QUEUEING SYSTEMS

The integration of artificial intelligence (AI) into classical queueing theory marks a transformative shift from static analytical models to dynamic, intelligent systems. While foundational models such as M/M/1, M/G/1, and M/M/c offer closed-form solutions under idealised assumptions—Poisson arrivals, exponential service times, and first-come-first-served disciplines—real-world service systems frequently exhibit time-varying, nonlinear, and context-sensitive behaviours that traditional models cannot capture.

AI-enhanced queueing systems address these limitations by embedding predictive and adaptive capabilities directly into the mathematical framework. Parameters like arrival rate (λ) and service rate (μ), instead of being constant, are treated as dynamic functions learned from historical or real-time data using machine learning (ML) techniques. Hybrid models may also include metaheuristic components (e.g., Genetic Algorithms, PSO) for solving multi-objective optimisation problems where closed-form analysis is infeasible. These integrated mathematical models form the backbone of intelligent queueing systems, enabling them to self-adjust, forecast congestion, and make strategic decisions in real time. The result is a robust, scalable approach to managing service operations in complex and volatile environments.

6.1 Revisiting the M/M/1 Queueing Model

The classical **M/M/1** queue serves as a foundation. It assumes:
Poisson arrivals: λ
Exponential service time: μ
A single server, infinite queue, and FCFS (first-come-first-served) discipline
Steady-state performance metrics are:

$$\rho = \lambda/\mu,\ L = \lambda / (\mu - \lambda),\ W = 1 / (\mu - \lambda),\ Lq = \lambda^2 / [\mu(\mu - \lambda)],\ Wq = \lambda / [\mu(\mu - \lambda)]$$

Where:
L: average number of customers in the system
L_q: average number in the queue
W: average time in system
W_q: average waiting time in the queue
$\rho<1$ is required for stability

6.2 AI-Enhanced Dynamic Parameters

In AI-enhanced models, we allow λ(t) and μ(t) to vary over time as functions learned from historical or real-time data using AI methods such as regression, time-series forecasting, or neural networks.

Let:
$\lambda(t) = f1(Xt)$, where X_t is a feature vector (e.g., time of day, weather, customer type)
$\mu(t) = f2(Yt)$, where Y_t includes resource availability, server performance, etc.

A machine learning model (e.g., random forest, LSTM) predicts:

$\lambda\hat{}(t) = ML\,(X\,),\, \mu\hat{}(t) = ML\,(Y\,)$

These predictions are then fed back into the queueing model to compute time-varying performance metrics:

$$W(t) = 1\ /\ [\mu\hat{}(t) - \lambda\hat{}(t)],\ Wq(t) = \lambda\hat{}(t)\ /\ [\mu\hat{}(t)(\mu\hat{}(t) - \lambda\hat{}(t))]$$

6.3 Reinforcement Learning-Based Service Control

In scenarios where the service policy must adapt based on system state, reinforcement learning (RL) can optimise queue performance. The queueing system is modelled as a Markov Decision Process (MDP):

State s $= \{L\,, \lambda\,, \mu\,\}$

Action a $=$ service rate control, routing, etc.

Reward r $=$ - $(Wq(t) + Cost(a\,))$

Policy optimisation:

The agent learns an optimal policy π∗(st) that minimises long-run average waiting time and cost:

$$\pi^*(s) = argmax\ \ E\,[\Sigma\,\gamma\ \ r\ \mid \pi]$$

Where γ is the discount factor.

Deep Q-Learning (DQN) or Actor-Critic methods can approximate π∗(s) through simulations using queueing data.

6.4 Hybrid Model Example: AI-Augmented M/M/c Queue

In an AI-augmented M/M/c model:

The number of servers, ccc, is adjustable based on predicted load

ML forecasts future λ(t+h), enabling proactive scaling

RL adjusts c(t) to minimize:

$$Objective = \alpha \times Wq(t) + \beta \times Server\_Cost(c)$$

Where α and β are trade-off weights for queueing delay vs. operational cost.

6.5 Simulation-Based Optimisation

When analytical solutions are impractical due to complexity, AI-driven simulations (e.g., Monte Carlo, agent-based models) combined with genetic algorithms

(GA) or Bayesian optimisation help identify near-optimal configurations. These simulations model nonlinear behaviours like:

Customer abandonment

Priority queues

Batch arrivals or service

Such hybrid simulation-AI approaches are especially useful in smart manufacturing, cloud load balancing, and health service triaging.

The mathematical evolution of queueing models through AI introduces dynamic, self-adjusting systems that overcome the limitations of classical frameworks. By modelling service systems as learning environments, AI-enhanced queues offer superior performance in complex, volatile, and data-rich domains.

7. APPLICATIONS OF AI-DRIVEN QUEUEING SYSTEMS IN INDUSTRY

AI-driven queueing systems have rapidly transitioned from theoretical constructs to practical tools with impactful applications across multiple industries. In healthcare, machine learning algorithms predict patient arrival rates and classify triage priorities, enabling hospitals to optimise resource allocation and reduce emergency room wait times (Wartelle et al., 2022). In smart cities, reinforcement learning-based traffic signal systems dynamically adjust green light durations based on real-time vehicle queue lengths, improving traffic flow and reducing congestion (Ponnusamy et al., 2024).

Telecommunications and cloud computing sectors use AI-enhanced queueing models to forecast network congestion and manage data packet routing and server load balancing, ensuring uninterrupted service during peak demand (Liu et al., 2022). In the retail and e-commerce space, computer vision systems and predictive analytics estimate in-store footfall and online user traffic, guiding workforce deployment and order fulfilment logistics.

In manufacturing, AI-powered queueing frameworks identify bottlenecks in production lines and use reinforcement learning to optimise machine utilisation and task scheduling. These applications highlight the versatility and scalability of AI-enhanced queueing theory, enabling data-driven, real-time decisions that improve efficiency, customer satisfaction, and operational resilience across a wide range of service-driven environments.

7.1 Healthcare: Predictive Patient Flow and Resource Allocation

Hospitals and emergency departments are among the most complex queueing environments. Patient arrivals are unpredictable, service times vary drastically, and lives are at stake. Traditional queueing models often assume a Poisson arrival process and exponential service time, but actual patterns are heavily influenced by time of day, day of the week, demographics, and environmental factors.

Using AI:

i. Machine learning models predict emergency room arrivals based on historical admissions, weather, and public health trends (Wartelle et al., 2022).
ii. Reinforcement learning agents suggest dynamic scheduling of staff or operating room usage based on predicted congestion.
iii. Neural networks classify incoming patients by severity to optimise triage queue priorities, ensuring critical cases are prioritised without compromising fairness.

The outcome is reduced wait times, improved staff workload balance, and better patient outcomes.

7.2 Smart Cities: AI-Based Traffic and Public Transport Queues

Urban traffic systems are classic examples of spatial and temporal queueing networks. Vehicles wait at intersections, passengers wait at bus stops, and resources like green light durations or fleet size must be dynamically managed.

AI applications include:

i. Reinforcement learning for adaptive traffic light control, adjusting signal timing based on real-time vehicle queue length (Ponnusamy et al., 2024).
ii. Time-series prediction models for public transport demand, used to proactively deploy buses or trains during peak congestion.
iii. Computer vision and IoT sensors detect pedestrian and vehicle queues, providing live inputs for queue optimisation algorithms.

This reduces travel time, fuel consumption, and commuter frustration—making city logistics smarter and greener.

7.3 Telecommunications and Cloud Computing

In telecommunication systems, requests (e.g., call initiations, data packets) are queued at switches or servers. Similarly, in cloud infrastructure, computing jobs wait for CPU/GPU resources to be allocated.

AI-enhanced queueing applications include:

i. Predicting network congestion and routing data traffic in real time using ML models (Liu et al., 2022).
ii. Applying deep RL to auto-scale cloud resources—adjusting virtual machine count or bandwidth to meet service level agreements (SLAs) with minimal cost.
iii. Utilising queue forecasting for call centres to manage agent load and customer satisfaction dynamically.

These intelligent queue systems help maintain high availability and low latency under variable workloads.

7.4 Retail and E-Commerce: Queue Optimisation and Demand Forecasting

Retail outlets—especially during sales, festivals, or seasonal events—face significant queueing challenges at checkouts, customer service, or product deliveries.

AI-enhanced queueing solutions:

i. Use computer vision to estimate real-time queue lengths and waiting times at billing counters.
ii. Employ predictive analytics to forecast footfall or online traffic surges and dynamically adjust staffing, inventory, or delivery fleet allocation.
iii. Apply AI-based chatbots to manage virtual service queues in customer support systems.

This translates to enhanced customer experience, minimised cart abandonment, and improved operational efficiency.

7.5 Manufacturing and Industry 4.0: Intelligent Production Lines

In Industry 4.0 environments, smart factories rely on sensors and AI to monitor queue lengths at each workstation. Queueing models are used to:

i. Identify bottlenecks in assembly lines using data-driven diagnostics.
ii. Use RL-based agents to dynamically reassign machines or labour across stages to reduce queue length.
iii. Integrate with digital twins that simulate queueing behaviour under multiple operating scenarios.

This ensures lean production, reduces downtime, and supports just-in-time (JIT) operations.

From emergency rooms to e-commerce servers, AI-enhanced queueing systems offer transformative benefits across diverse industries. By replacing rigid assumptions with real-time learning and adaptive control, these systems deliver smarter, faster, and more responsive solutions to modern service challenges.

8. CHALLENGES AND SOLUTIONS IN AI-ENHANCED QUEUEING THEORY

The integration of artificial intelligence into queueing systems brings significant opportunities, but its widespread adoption is tempered by a set of technical, organisational, ethical, and educational challenges. Addressing these barriers is essential to ensure both operational success and societal trust in AI-enhanced queueing solutions. One of the most prominent technical challenges is scalability and model interpretability. Advanced deep learning and reinforcement learning models can handle vast and complex queueing environments, yet their computational cost often increases exponentially with scale. Moreover, these models are frequently viewed as "black boxes," making it difficult for stakeholders to understand decision-making processes—a critical requirement in regulated domains such as healthcare or finance. Research-backed solutions include the adoption of explainable AI (XAI) techniques, which make model decisions transparent through visualisation and rule extraction, and the development of hybrid models that combine the interpretability of classical queueing theory with the predictive power of AI. Additionally, model compression and pruning methods can reduce computational load without substantially sacrificing accuracy.

A second barrier relates to data availability, quality, and privacy. AI queueing models require large, representative datasets to perform effectively, but in many small-scale operations or rural contexts, such datasets are scarce. Privacy laws and ethical considerations further limit the collection of sensitive service-related data, such as patient medical records or location-based mobility patterns. Proposed solutions include the use of federated learning, which allows AI models to be trained across decentralised data sources without transferring raw data, and synthetic data generation techniques that create realistic, privacy-preserving datasets for training purposes. Data augmentation and preprocessing methods can also improve dataset quality, enhancing model robustness. Ethical and social concerns form another critical challenge, particularly bias and fairness in queue prioritisation. AI models trained on historically biased data risk reinforcing inequalities, such as deprioritising certain demographic groups in healthcare or customer service contexts. To address this, bias detection frameworks and fairness-aware algorithms can be integrated into the training process. Moreover, periodic algorithmic audits, combined with stakeholder engagement and policy oversight, ensure that system decisions align with ethical and legal standards.

From an organisational perspective, implementation barriers are also significant. Many companies face resistance to adopting AI systems due to integration complexity, legacy infrastructure, and uncertainty over return on investment. A practical solution is to implement modular integration architectures that allow AI components to be added incrementally to existing queueing systems. Change management strategies, including pilot deployments and phased rollouts, can also build organisational confidence in AI adoption. There is the challenge of educational and skill gaps. AI-enhanced queueing systems require multidisciplinary expertise that combines operations research, AI, and domain-specific knowledge. However, the workforce equipped with these intersecting skills remains limited. Addressing this gap requires curriculum reform to embed AI-queueing concepts in operations research and engineering programs, the establishment of interdisciplinary training programs, and stronger partnerships between academia and industry to provide real-world problem-solving experience.

By systematically addressing these challenges through targeted solutions, researchers, practitioners, and educators can accelerate the safe, effective, and equitable integration of AI into queueing systems across diverse application domains.

9. PEDAGOGICAL IMPLICATIONS: INTEGRATING AI-ENHANCED QUEUEING THEORY IN MATHEMATICS EDUCATION

As artificial intelligence continues to redefine how systems are modelled, optimised, and automated, there is a growing need to align mathematics and operations research education with these technological advancements. Traditional teaching of queueing theory typically focuses on deterministic or stochastic models and analytical problem-solving. However, with the integration of AI, there is an opportunity to enrich curricula by bridging theoretical mathematics with real-world, data-driven applications.

9.1 The Shift Toward Interdisciplinary Learning

Modern educational paradigms encourage interdisciplinary learning, where mathematical modelling intersects with computer science, data analytics, and AI. By introducing AI-enhanced queueing models, educators can:

Expose students to real-time data analysis and simulation techniques.

Encourage problem-based learning, where students work on live case studies (e.g., optimising queues in a hospital or a smart city).

Promote coding-based mathematics, using platforms like Python, R, or MATLAB to simulate AI-enhanced queue scenarios.

This shift aligns with global trends in STEM education, where computational thinking is as important as mathematical reasoning (Weintrop et al., 2016).

9.2 Curriculum Innovation: Topics and Tools

A restructured curriculum that integrates AI-enhanced queueing theory may include:

Fundamentals of queueing theory (e.g., M/M/1, M/G/1, Little's Law)
Introduction to AI and ML algorithms
Predictive modelling and time-series forecasting in queueing systems
Simulation and optimisation using Python (e.g., SimPy, TensorFlow, Scikit-learn)
Hands-on projects using real or simulated datasets
Sample module:

Module: Intelligent Queueing Systems
Week 1–2: Basics of classical models
Week 3–4: Introduction to ML (Linear Regression, Decision Trees)
Week 5–6: Predicting service loads using real data
Week 7–8: Simulation of AI-enhanced queues and performance evaluation

This blend of theory and practice builds both conceptual clarity and employable skills.

9.3 Student Learning Outcomes (SLOs)

Through exposure to AI-integrated queueing models, students develop:
Analytical skills for interpreting stochastic systems under uncertainty
Technical competence in AI/ML methods and programming
Problem-solving abilities through simulation and data-driven modelling

Interdisciplinary awareness, recognising how mathematics supports intelligent systems in healthcare, logistics, and digital infrastructure

Such learning outcomes prepare students for roles in data science, system optimisation, operations research, and AI-powered decision-making.

9.4 Active Learning Strategies

To enhance student engagement, instructors can use:

i. **Case-based learning**: Analyse real-world queue systems like airport security, food delivery logistics, or COVID-19 testing centres.
ii. **Collaborative coding labs**: Students work in teams to build ML models predicting queue behaviour.
iii. **Gamified simulations**: Create virtual environments where students manage queue systems and optimise decisions using reinforcement learning strategies.

These approaches make abstract concepts tangible and encourage experimentation, innovation, and critical thinking.

9.5 Challenges in Educational Integration

Despite the benefits, integrating AI-enhanced queueing theory into education presents challenges:

i. **Faculty readiness**: Instructors may need training in AI tools and languages.
ii. **Curriculum overload**: Adding AI components may stretch already full syllabi.
iii. **Resource limitations**: Institutions may lack access to computational tools, labs, or datasets.

Addressing the challenges of integrating AI-enhanced queueing theory into education requires strong institutional support, active interdisciplinary collaboration, and a phased approach to curriculum adaptation. Institutions must invest in infrastructure, such as high-performance computing facilities and access to relevant datasets, while also providing professional development opportunities for educators to acquire skills in artificial intelligence, machine learning, and modern simulation tools. Collaboration between departments—such as mathematics, computer science, operations research, and engineering—can foster the creation of cohesive, interdisciplinary learning modules that reflect real-world problem-solving environments. By embedding AI-enhanced queueing theory into mathematics and operations research curricula, students are equipped with a dual skill set: a solid grounding in classical analytical models and the ability to apply advanced computational techniques to dynamic, data-driven systems. This combination strengthens critical thinking, problem-solving, and adaptability—skills increasingly demanded in industry and research. Such a pedagogical shift modernises operations research education, moving it beyond static, theoretical instruction toward applied, experiential learning. Through case-based projects, simulations, and collaborative coding exercises, learners can engage directly with contemporary challenges, preparing them to design, evaluate, and implement intelligent queueing systems. Ultimately, this approach cultivates a new generation of professionals capable of addressing complex optimisation problems in an AI-driven era.

10. ETHICAL CONSIDERATIONS AND CHALLENGES

The integration of artificial intelligence (AI) into queueing theory offers transformative potential, yet it also introduces a range of ethical and practical challenges that must be addressed to ensure responsible adoption. One of the foremost concerns is data privacy, particularly in domains such as healthcare, retail, transportation, and public services, where personal or sensitive information is often used to train predictive models. The misuse or mishandling of such data can lead to breaches of confidentiality and erosion of public trust. Adherence to stringent data protection regulations—such as the General Data Protection Regulation (GDPR) in the European Union or the Health Insurance Portability and Accountability Act (HIPAA) in the United States—is essential for safeguarding user information. Another pressing issue is algorithmic bias. AI models trained on historical datasets risk replicating or amplifying existing inequities in service access or prioritisation. For instance, if historical queueing data from healthcare systems reflects systemic disparities in patient treatment, an AI-driven triage model may unintentionally perpetuate such inequities. Implementing bias detection tools, fairness-aware algorithms, and continuous monitoring is therefore crucial to mitigate these risks.

Transparency and explainability also remain significant challenges. Many advanced machine learning techniques, particularly deep learning models, operate as "black boxes," providing accurate predictions without clear reasoning pathways. This lack of interpretability can hinder stakeholder trust and make regulatory compliance more difficult. The operationalisation of AI-driven queue management systems requires balancing automation with human oversight. Overreliance on automated decision-making may lead to unintended consequences, especially in high-stakes environments. Ensuring system robustness, incorporating ethical review processes, and fostering stakeholder engagement are critical for aligning technological decisions with institutional goals and societal expectations.

By proactively addressing these considerations, organisations can harness the benefits of AI-enhanced queueing systems while maintaining fairness, accountability, and public trust in their deployment.

11. CONCLUSION

This chapter has provided a comprehensive exploration of AI-enhanced queueing theory, tracing its evolution from classical mathematical foundations to advanced, adaptive frameworks empowered by artificial intelligence. By integrating traditional queueing models—such as M/M/1 and M/M/c—with techniques like machine learning (ML) and reinforcement learning (RL), the research illustrates how static, deterministic models can be transformed into intelligent, data-driven systems. This synthesis not only enhances predictive capabilities but also enables real-time adaptability, allowing service systems to dynamically adjust to fluctuating demand, resource constraints, and operational complexities. The proposed hybrid models demonstrate broad applicability across sectors, including healthcare, smart cities, telecommunications, cloud computing, manufacturing, and education. They provide decision-makers with actionable insights for resource allocation, congestion management, and service optimisation. By embedding learning-based components into analytical frameworks, organisations can respond more effectively to unpredictable environments, improve operational efficiency, and enhance end-user satisfaction.

From an academic and pedagogical perspective, incorporating AI-enhanced queueing theory into mathematics, operations research, and engineering curricula fosters interdisciplinary skill development. Students are exposed to both rigorous theoretical modelling and modern computational techniques, preparing them for analytical and decision-making roles in increasingly complex service ecosystems. Looking ahead, several promising directions emerge for future research. These include the exploration of multi-agent interactions in interconnected service networks, the adoption of federated learning to enable privacy-preserving queue optimisation, and the integration of edge computing to support low-latency, real-time decision-making. Additionally, empirical studies are needed to evaluate the operational and social impacts of AI-driven queueing systems in real-world contexts, with an emphasis on developing fairness and transparency frameworks to mitigate bias and strengthen stakeholder trust. The convergence of classical queueing theory with AI technologies holds transformative potential, offering a robust pathway toward more intelligent, equitable, and sustainable service system management in the future.

REFERENCES

Anselmi, J., Gaujal, B., & Rebuffi, L. S. (2024). Learning optimal admission control in partially observable queueing networks. Queueing Systems, 108(1), 31-79. arXiv. https://arxiv.org/abs/2308.02391

Avinash, G., Pachori, H., Sharma, A., & Mishra, S. (2025). Time series forecasting of bed occupancy in mental health facilities in India using machine learning. *Scientific Reports*, *15*, 86418. DOI: 10.1038/s41598-025-86418-9 PMID: 39837951

Boutilier, C. (2000). Decision Making under Uncertainty: Operations Research Meets AI (Again). National Conference on Artificial Intelligence, 1145–1150. https://www.aaai.org/Papers/AAAI/2000/AAAI00-208.pdf

Breuer, L., & Baum, D. (2005). An introduction to queueing theory and matrix-analytic methods. Springer. https://link.springer.com/book/10.1007/1-4020-3631-0

Chaudhary, H., Sharma, G., Nishad, D. K., & Khalid, S. (2025). Advanced queueing and scheduling techniques in cloud computing using AI-based model order reduction. *Computing*, *28*, 75.

de Treville, S., & van Ackere, A. (2006). Equipping Students to Reduce Lead Times: The Role of Queuing-Theory-Based Modelling. *Interfaces*, *36*(2), 165–173. DOI: 10.1287/INTE.1050.0188

Dorda, M., Teichmann, D., & Graf, V. (2019). Optimisation of service capacity based on queueing theory. *MM Science Journal*, *2019*(03), 2975–2981. DOI: 10.17973/MMSJ.2019_10_201889

Doshi, B. T. (1986). Queueing systems with vacations—A survey. *Queueing Systems*, *1*(1), 29–66. https://link.springer.com/article/10.1007/BF01149327

Erlang, A. K. (1909). The theory of probabilities and telephone conversations. Nyt Tidsskrift for Matematik, 20, 33–39. https://www.scirp.org/reference/referencespapers?referenceid=2221031

Gans, N., Koole, G., & Mandelbaum, A. (2003). Telephone call centres: Tutorial, review, and research prospects. *Manufacturing & Service Operations Management*, *5*(2), 79–141. DOI: 10.1287/msom.5.2.79.16071

Gomez, C. A., Wang, X., & Shami, A. (2021). Federated intelligence for active queue management in inter-domain congestion. *IEEE Access : Practical Innovations, Open Solutions*, *9*, 10674–10685. https://ieeexplore.ieee.org/document/9317728

Gross, D., Shortle, J. F., Thompson, J. M., & Harris, C. M. (2018). *Fundamentals of queueing theory* (5th ed.). Wiley. DOI: 10.1002/9781119453765

Gupta, M., & George, J. F. (2016). Toward the development of a big data analytics capability. *Information & Management*, *53*(8), 1049–1064. DOI: 10.1016/j.im.2016.07.004

Kim Phuc, T. R. A. N. (2021). Artificial Intelligence for Smart Manufacturing: Methods and Applications. *Sensors (Basel)*, *21*. Advance online publication. DOI: 10.3390/s21165584 PMID: 34451024

Lee, J., Namkoong, H., & Zeng, Y. (2024). Design and Scheduling of an AI-based Queueing System. /arxiv.2406.06855DOI: 10.48550

Li, Y., & Gao, G. (2023). Large-scale passenger behavior learning and prediction in airport terminals based on multi-agent reinforcement learning. *Frontiers in Computing and Intelligent Systems*, *5*(1), 111–117. DOI: 10.54097/fcis.v5i1.12008

Liu, G., Shi, H., Kiani, A., Khreishah, A., Lee, J. Y., Ansari, N., Liu, C., & Yousef, M. M. (2022). Smart Traffic Monitoring System Using Computer Vision and Edge Computing. *IEEE Transactions on Intelligent Transportation Systems*, *23*(8), 12027–12038. DOI: 10.1109/TITS.2021.3109481

Ma, W., Yuan, T., & Liu, N. (2023). *An Application of Operations Research in Airport Ground Path AI Decision for Apron Operation Control*. Advance online publication. DOI: 10.1109/iccasit58768.2023.10351633

Maljkovic, M., & Geroliminis, N. (2025). On learning-based traffic monitoring with a swarm of drones. arXiv preprint. https://arxiv.org/abs/2503.21433

Mallioris, P., & Others. (2024). Predictive maintenance in Industry 4.0: A systematic multi-case review. *Journal of Manufacturing Systems*.

May, M. C. (2021). Queue Length Forecasting in Complex Manufacturing Job Shops. Forecasting, 3(2), 322–338. DOI: 10.3390/forecast3020021

Mitrani, I. (1998). *Probabilistic modelling*. Cambridge University Press.

Musaev, A., Wang, Y., Zhu, X., Li, X., Chen, C., Liu, J., Zhang, J., Mei, T., & Wang, D. (2020). Towards in-store multi-person tracking using head detection and track heatmaps. arXiv preprint arXiv:2005.08009. https://arxiv.org/abs/2005.08009

Nair, R., & Miller-Hooks, E. (2011). Fleet management for vehicle sharing operations. *Transportation Science*, *45*(4), 524–540. https://www.jstor.org/stable/41432818

Papadimitriou, C. H., & Steiglitz, K. (1998). Combinatorial optimisation: Algorithms and complexity. Dover Publications. https://store.doverpublications.com/products/9780486402581

Patrick, J. (2008). Reducing wait times through operations research: Optimising the use of surge capacity. *Healthcare Quarterly*, *11*(3), 77–83. DOI: 10.12927/HCQ.2013.19844 PMID: 18536537

Ponnusamy, S., Chourasia, H., Rathod, S. B., & Patil, D. (2024). Ai-driven traffic management systems: Reducing congestion and improving safety in smart cities. In *Smart cities* (pp. 96–121). CRC Press.

Russell, S., & Norvig, P. (2020). *Artificial intelligence: A modern approach* (4th ed.). Pearson.

Saad, M. (2024). Optimizing multi-objective task scheduling in fog computing: A hybrid genetic algorithm–particle swarm optimization approach. *Sensors (Basel)*, *24*(2), 556. DOI: 10.3390/s24020556 PMID: 38257649

Singh, V., Gupta, P., & Jain, S. (2025). A novel CNN-GRU-LSTM based deep learning model for accurate traffic prediction. *Neural Computing & Applications*. Advance online publication. DOI: 10.1007/s10791-025-09526-0

Sutton, R. S., & Barto, A. G. (2018). *Reinforcement learning: An introduction* (2nd ed.). MIT Press.

Taha, H. A. (2017). *Operations research: An introduction* (10th ed.). Pearson.

Tran, T. T., Terekhov, D., Down, D. G., & Beck, J. C. (n.d.). Hybrid Queueing Theory and Scheduling Models for Dynamic Environments with Sequence-Dependent Setup Times. DOI: 10.1609/icaps.v23i1.13552

Ucar, A., Karakose, M., & Kırımça, N. (2024). Artificial Intelligence for Predictive Maintenance Applications: Key Components, Trustworthiness, and Future Trends. *Applied Sciences (Basel, Switzerland)*, *14*(2), 898. DOI: 10.3390/app14020898

Wartelle, A., Mourad-Chehade, F., Yalaoui, F., Laplanche, D., & Sanchez, S. (2022). Analysis of saturation in the emergency department: A data-driven queuing model using machine learning. *Health Systems (Basingstoke, England)*, *11*(2), 95–118. DOI: 10.1080/20476965.2022.2074659 PMID: 35612022

Weintrop, D., Beheshti, E., Horn, M., Orton, K., Jona, K., Trouille, L., & Wilensky, U. (2016). Defining computational thinking for mathematics and science classrooms. *Journal of Science Education and Technology*, *25*(1), 127–147. DOI: 10.1007/s10956-015-9581-5

Whitt, W. (1993). Approximations for the GI/G/m queue. *Production and Operations Management*, *2*(2), 114–161.

Yang, H., Xiong, Z., Zhao, J., Niyato, D., Xiao, L., & Wu, Q. (2021). Deep reinforcement learning-based intelligent reflecting surface for secure wireless communications. *IEEE Transactions on Wireless Communications*, *20*(1), 375–388. DOI: 10.1109/TWC.2020.3024860

KEY TERMS AND DEFINITIONS

Arrival Rate (λ): The average rate at which customers, tasks, or requests enter a service system.

Bias in AI: Systematic errors in model predictions caused by imbalanced or non-representative training data, which may reinforce inequalities.

Deep Q-Network (DQN): A reinforcement learning method that combines Q-learning with deep neural networks for adaptive control.

Edge Computing: A distributed computing paradigm that processes data near the source of generation, reducing latency for real-time applications.

Explainable AI (XAI): AI methods designed to make model decisions transparent and interpretable to stakeholders.

Federated Learning: A privacy-preserving AI approach where models are trained across decentralized data sources without sharing raw data.

M/M/1 Model: A classical queueing model with Poisson arrivals, exponential service times, and a single server.

M/M/c Model: A queueing model with Poisson arrivals, exponential service times, and multiple servers in parallel.

Machine Learning (ML): A subset of AI that uses data-driven algorithms to identify patterns and make predictions.

Queueing Theory: The mathematical study of waiting lines, focusing on arrival rates, service mechanisms, and system performance.

Reinforcement Learning (RL): An AI technique where agents learn optimal decision-making policies by interacting with an environment and receiving rewards.

Service Rate (μ): The average rate at which servers can process customers or tasks.

System Utilization (ρ): The proportion of time a server or system is actively serving requests.

Chapter 3
Applications of Mathematics in AI

S. Karpagam
https://orcid.org/0000-0003-3400-9671
Vel Tech Rangarajan Dr. Sagunthala R&D Institute of Science and Technology, India

Regan Murugesan
Vel Tech Rangarajan Dr. Sagunthala R&D Institute of Science and Technology, India

B. Somasundaram
Vel Tech Rangarajan Dr. Sagunthala R&D Institute of Science and Technology, India

ABSTRACT

This chapter explains how mathematics supports the development and functioning of Artificial Intelligence (AI). It shows how different areas of mathematics are used to create models, solve problems, and improve how AI systems learn and make decisions. Topics such as linear algebra, calculus, probability, and graph theory are introduced with clear examples. For instance, graph theory helps represent networks like social media, where people are shown as points and their relationships as lines connecting them. The chapter also discusses how mathematics helps protect sensitive information using secure methods like encryption. In addition, it looks at how mathematics is used to work with images, such as sharpening or analysing pictures using algebra and optimization techniques. Overall, the chapter aims to show how mathematical ideas are not just theoretical but play an important role in making AI systems useful in real life. It helps readers see how mathematics connects to technology and supports progress in this fast-changing field.

DOI: 10.4018/979-8-3373-1998-8.ch003

1. INTRODUCTION

Artificial Intelligence (AI) is a rapidly growing field that aims to develop machines to perform tasks that require human intelligence. Some of those tasks that lie at hand are comprehension of language, voice or picture recognition, learning through examples, decision-making, and even creative problem-solving. Although "artificial intelligence" sounds like science fiction, it has become a very normal aspect of our lives. From voice-controlled assistants like Siri and Alexa to personalized suggestions while browsing through Netflix or browsing through Amazon, AI-based technologies are continuously changing the way we communicate, work, and live.

Initially, one would think that AI is a purely technical field, based solely on computer programming and software development. But at a fundamental level, AI is deeply rooted in Mathematics. Like a building requires a solid base in order to rise high, a building that will last, AI is built upon the firm foundations of purely mathematical concepts. Mathematics gives us the framework, vocabulary, and logic that govern the manner in which AI systems learn, decide, and problem-solve.

For beginners stepping into the world of AI, understanding the role of Mathematics can seem overwhelming. However, when the relationship is deconstructed into simpler components, it becomes evident and accessible. Consider AI to be a student who gains knowledge through experience. Artificial Intelligence (AI) systems learn by analysing data, spotting patterns, and improving their predictions much as a human student could learn mathematics by working through problems and using feedback. It does this by using tools from different areas of Mathematics.

Bishop's Neural Networks for Pattern Recognition (Bishop, 1995) presents a mathematically rigorous treatment of pattern classification. The text delves into optimization theory, statistical decision boundaries, and non-linear function approximation, offering readers tools for analyzing and implementing learning models using methods such as gradient descent and error minimization.

In Pattern Recognition and Machine Learning (Bishop, 2006), Bishop extends this foundation into probabilistic modeling, detailing Bayesian inference, graphical models, and kernel methods. The mathematical depth in this volume emphasizes the role of probability theory and statistics in designing reliable predictive frameworks.

Diestel's Graph Theory (Diestel, 2017) offers a pure mathematical treatment of networks, covering graph connectivity, coloring, planarity, and extremal problems. The text equips readers with the combinatorial reasoning needed to represent and analyze relationships between entities in structured data.

Goodfellow, Bengio, and Courville's Deep Learning (Goodfellow et al., 2016) synthesizes linear algebra, probability, and optimization into a coherent narrative, explaining the mathematical mechanisms underlying multilayer function approximation, gradient-based learning, and representation theory.

Hastie, Tibshirani, and Friedman's The Elements of Statistical Learning (Hastie et al., 2009) focuses on regression, classification, and model selection. It integrates concepts from linear models, splines, and ensemble methods, illustrating the interplay between statistical theory and predictive accuracy.

Jaynes' Probability Theory: The Logic of Science (Jaynes, 2003) develops a formal, axiomatic framework for probabilistic reasoning. Through measure-theoretic rigor and Bayesian logic, it frames probability as an extension of deductive reasoning under uncertainty.

Koblitz, Menezes, Wu, and Zuccherato's Algebraic Aspects of Cryptography (Koblitz et al., 1998) explores the algebraic structures—groups, rings, and fields—that underpin modern cryptographic protocols. The text demonstrates the precision and necessity of algebra in secure information exchange.

MacKay's Information Theory, Inference, and Learning Algorithms (MacKay, 2003) unites entropy-based reasoning with probabilistic inference, presenting Shannon's theorems, coding strategies, and statistical decision theory in an integrated manner.

Menezes, Van Oorschot, and Vanstone's Handbook of Applied Cryptography (Menezes et al., 1997) provides exhaustive coverage of number theory, modular arithmetic, and computational complexity, serving as a mathematical reference for secure system design.

Murphy's Machine Learning: A Probabilistic Perspective (Murphy, 2012) systematically introduces probability distributions, graphical models, and inference algorithms, highlighting the quantitative underpinnings of decision-making frameworks.

Russell and Norvig's Artificial Intelligence: A Modern Approach (Russell & Norvig, 2020) incorporates mathematical modeling in search algorithms, logic, and probability, forming a broad computational toolkit grounded in formal methods.

Sawant and Patil's (Sawant & Patil, 2020, pp. 4327–4330) study applies matrix operations to cryptography and image processing, illustrating how linear transformations encode and secure visual data.

Srivastav and Nath's (Srivastav & Nath, 2015, pp. 611-618) work on mathematical modelling of social networks employs graph theory and statistical measures to quantify connectivity, influence, and network resilience.

Strang's Linear Algebra and Its Applications (Strang, 2016) offers foundational tools such as vector spaces, eigenvalues, and orthogonal projections, essential for modelling high-dimensional systems.

Waghmare and Mali (Waghmare & Mali, 2020, pp. 112-118) present the development of cryptographic matrices, emphasizing determinant properties, invertibility, and modular arithmetic in secure message transformation.

Finally, Wolfram's (Wolfram, 1986, pp. 429-432) research demonstrates the cryptographic potential of cellular automata, showcasing discrete dynamical systems as algebraic frameworks for encoding information.

Collectively, these works illustrate the profound role of mathematics in shaping the structures, algorithms, and logical reasoning that support advanced computational methods.

Let's begin by looking at Linear Algebra, which is one of the most fundamental mathematical tools used in AI. Linear algebra deals with vectors and matrices, essentially rows and columns of numbers. Why are these important? Because most of the data AI works with images, text, sound and more, can be represented in numerical form. For example, a black-and-white image is simply a grid of pixel values, where each number represents the brightness of a pixel. AI systems use matrices to store and manipulate these images. Linear algebra helps AI understand and transform these data structures efficiently.

Next, we have Calculus, particularly a part called differential calculus. In computer science and AI, calculus improves machines by optimizing their performance. Let us consider a simple case: the task of teaching a robot to classify between cats and dogs from images. Initially, the robot will be highly wrong. Calculus fine-tunes the computer programme by tweaking its internal parameters (so-called weights) in a way that it reduces the error in prediction to a minimum. This tweaking of the programme through feedback is optimization, and it greatly depends on the use of derivatives, a cornerstone concept of calculus.

Probability and Statistics are also essential components of artificial intelligence. These branches of mathematics help machines deal with prediction and uncertainty. In the real world, data is frequently incomplete and incorrect. Artificial intelligence systems are able to produce informed guesses thanks to probability. For instance, when writing a message and predicting the next word, it uses probability to try to guess what it believes you will type most frequently based on learned behaviour. In contrast, the AI system can learn and condense data thanks to statistics. Systems can use it to identify patterns, draw inferences, and verify or disprove forecast accuracy.

Another crucial field is Graph Theory, which is the study of networks of interconnected elements. In computer science, graph theory is used in social networks, recommendation systems, and search engines. For instance, Facebook uses graph theory to determine user relationships and suggest friends. In other technical computer science systems, graphs are used to illustrate the relationships between different pieces of knowledge, or effective algorithms are developed to solve complex problems.

To make these ideas more concrete, let's walk through a simplified example: teaching a computer to recognize handwritten numbers (from 0 to 9). The computer is shown thousands of images of handwritten digits. Each image is converted into a matrix of pixel values using linear algebra. The computer then uses calculus to adjust its internal parameters so that its predictions match the correct numbers as closely as possible. Probability theory helps it handle uncertain cases, such as when a poorly written "3" looks a bit like an "8." Finally, graph theory can help organize the structure of the neural network, a type of AI model inspired by the human brain that connects different processing layers and neurons in the system.

This type of learning, or rather Machine Learning, is one of the main areas of AI. It deals with developing software that is automatically adaptive and experience-based. Supervised learning, in which the AI is educated using classified data; unsupervised learning, in which it finds patterns in unlabelled data; and reinforcement learning, in which it learns by making mistakes, like while playing a game. For each to work, a different set of mathematical tools is needed.

In short, studying mathematics that forms the basis of the discipline of Artificial Intelligence is really about learning a type of reasoning that breaks issues into pieces, discovers patterns, investigates relationships, and makes reasonable inferences in a logical fashion, more than equation-grinding and formulaic memorizing. That is why it is the engineer and data scientist at the brink of developing intelligent systems that not only are intelligent but also fair, clear, and credible.

As the field of artificial intelligence continues to expand, these mathematical ideas keep coming up. Come along as we explore the worlds of linear algebra and image recognition, learn how calculus powers learning systems, see how probability drives natural communication systems, and discover how graph theory powers social networks and the Internet.

Here in this chapter, we shall attempt to guide you through those opening concepts through thorough descriptions, illustrative step-by-step examples, and practical applications. Whether you're a student exploring AI for the first time or someone with a non-mathematical background looking to understand how these systems work, this introduction will equip you with the essential knowledge to build your confidence and curiosity. By the end of this chapter, you'll not only understand what mathematics does for AI let us see why it's absolutely essential to making machines intelligent.

These concepts have given a simulation for secret communication. This has also laid the foundation for the development of cryptography. The basis of cryptography is in Egyptian and Roman civilizations. The technique of safe communication for third parties is known as adversaries. When the data is to be communicated between two parties that it cannot be read by other persons.

In the modern world of cryptography, data integrity, data confidentiality, non-repudiation, and authentication are the various principles. The rules and guidelines are executed with agreements with confidence. The secret communication to share between data is the process of authentication. The method in which a person contacts the other person without denying is a no-repudiation.

The method of performing changes to an image, with the motive of getting an enhanced image and extracting information, is image processing. The transformation of an image into any output, which may be an image or charters, is signal processing. The software used for image processing is termed digital image processing. Various forms of images are obtained from this. Various tasks, such as restoration, sharpening of the image, are allowed in this.

A few advantages of it are image reformatting, fast image storage, fast image storage and retrieval, fast and high-quality image distribution, controlled viewing, etc. Like the advantages, some of the disadvantages are more time-consuming, expensive, and not handled by everyone. Three steps are involved in Image processing, such as the usage of image acquisition tools in importing the image; analyzing and manipulating of the image. Finally, the results are acquired from which image can be altered.

Brief general applications of mathematics in engineering, especially in social networks, are collectively discussed here. Mainly, how the concepts of Mathematics are beneficial over image processing, secure communication, etc., are shown, and its corresponding codes to be used in MATLAB are noticed.

2. LINEAR ALGEBRA

Digital Images: To begin, let's understand what a digital image is. Imagine taking a photo with a digital camera. That image is broken down into a grid of tiny dots called pixels. Each pixel has a value that represents the brightness or colour of a specific point in the image. These values are numerical and can be organized into a grid or table. This is essentially a matrix.

For grayscale images (black and white), each pixel typically has a value between 0 (black) and 255 (white). Coloured images use three colour channels: Red, Green, and Blue (RGB). Each channel is itself a matrix of pixel values, and together they define the full-colour image.

The method used by the modern computer world to process digital images is called digital image processing. With the ever-evolving technology, digital image processing applications are penetrating very fast into almost all fields.

The process by which we can change the look and feel of an image is called image polishing and restoration. These include image rotation, sharpening, blurring, margin cropping, retrieval, and image recognition. Various applications in the medical field use digital image processing. Application of techniques, which include segmentation and texture analysis, in identifying disorders and cancer.

Earthquakes and their damage might sometimes be so extensive that it is impossible to inspect them with the human eye. It will also be an extremely stressful and time-consuming procedure. As a result, digital image processing comes to the rescue, capturing an image from above the ground and assisting in the rapid analysis of damage and subsequent actions. Advancements in technology help to view live video feeds or CCTV images from anywhere in the world in a matter of seconds. This indicates that not only image transmission, but also image encoding, has vastly improved. To encode photos and then broadcast them over the internet, a variety of formats have been devised for high and low bandwidths.

Image processing is currently utilised to recognise patterns and to provide the machine with human recognition intelligence. Pattern recognition is useful to extract important elements from pictures or video samples also utilised in computer vision for a variety of purposes, including biological and biomedical imaging. Integrated with artificial intelligence, computer-assisted diagnostics, handwriting recognition, and picture identification are all simple to implement.

In today's world, digital image processing comes in handy with a slew of benefits, allowing humans to make the most of technology and visual representations.

Representing Images as Matrices: Every digital image is essentially a matrix where each element represents a pixel value. For example, Table 1 and its corresponding pixel values represented as a matrix are:

Table 1. Pixel Matrix Visualization and 8×8 Pixel Matrix Values

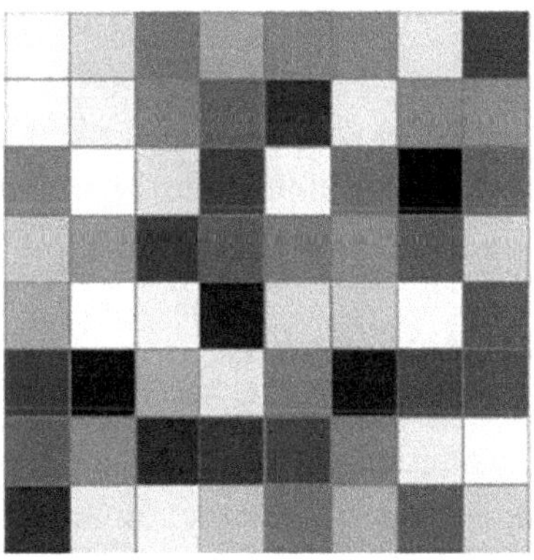

$$\begin{bmatrix} 246 & 199 & 102 & 150 & 116 & 119 & 216 & 53 \\ 245 & 229 & 113 & 84 & 36 & 222 & 122 & 126 \\ 113 & 246 & 210 & 51 & 235 & 94 & 6 & 84 \\ 183 & 136 & 43 & 77 & 104 & 124 & 76 & 191 \\ 154 & 253 & 234 & 21 & 203 & 192 & 246 & 73 \\ 48 & 11 & 154 & 217 & 107 & 17 & 57 & 63 \\ 81 & 123 & 30 & 43 & 55 & 109 & 227 & 248 \\ 35 & 219 & 228 & 180 & 98 & 157 & 77 & 192 \end{bmatrix}$$

2.1 Brightness Adjustment (Matrix Addition)

To make an image brighter, simply add a constant value to each pixel in the matrix (pixel value of the original Image). This is one of the most fundamental operations in image processing.

For example:

Figure 1. Brightness adjustment of image

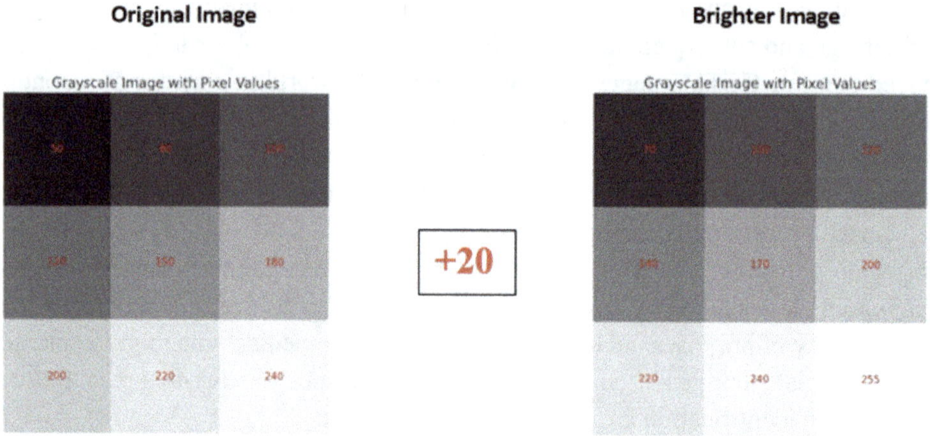

**Note: Values are capped at 255*

$$\begin{bmatrix} 50 & 80 & 100 \\ 120 & 150 & 180 \\ 200 & 220 & 240 \end{bmatrix} + 20 = \begin{bmatrix} 70 & 100 & 120 \\ 140 & 170 & 200 \\ 220 & 240 & 255 \end{bmatrix}$$

This matrix represents an image with varying shades of Gray. Each number represents how dark or light the pixel is. Lower values mean darker pixels, and higher values mean lighter ones.

This operation makes the entire image brighter. Notice how each pixel value increased by exactly 20, making the overall image appear lighter while maintaining the same contrast relationships between pixels.

2.2 Contrast Enhancement (Scalar Multiplication)

To increase contrast, multiply each pixel by a constant greater than 1. To reduce contrast, multiply by a value less than 1. This operation stretches or compresses the range of pixel values.

For example:

Figure 2. Contrast enhancement

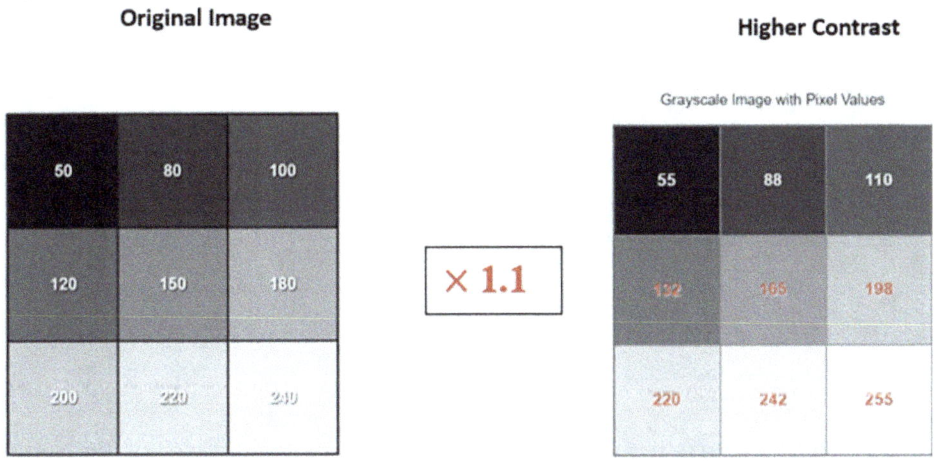

**Note: values are capped at 255*

$$\begin{bmatrix} 50 & 80 & 100 \\ 120 & 150 & 180 \\ 200 & 220 & 240 \end{bmatrix} \times 1.1 = \begin{bmatrix} 55 & 88 & 110 \\ 132 & 165 & 198 \\ 220 & 242 & 255 \end{bmatrix}$$

This exaggerates the differences between light and dark areas, enhancing contrast. Notice how the darker pixels became relatively darker and the lighter pixels became relatively lighter, creating more dramatic differences in the image.

2.3 Image Rotation (Transpose and Flip)

Rotating an image by 90 degrees clockwise involves two steps: first transpose the matrix (flip rows and columns), then flip each row. This is a more complex transformation that demonstrates how multiple matrix operations can be combined.

Figure 3. Rotated image

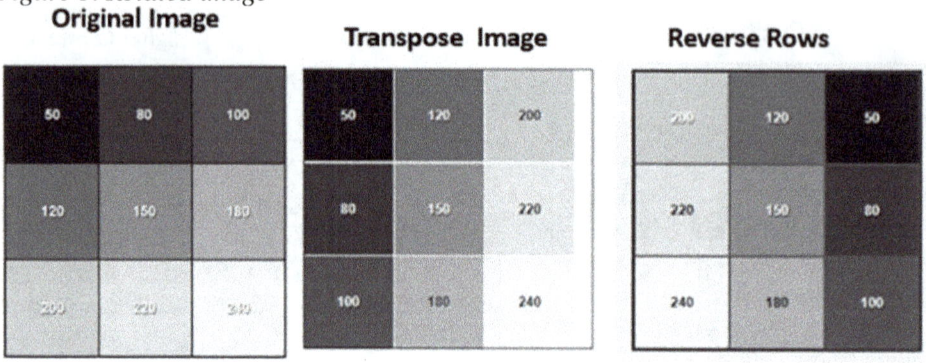

This rotated matrix represents the image turned 90 degrees clockwise. Notice how the transformation preserves all pixel values but rearranges their positions according to the rotation.

2.4 Colored Image to Gray Scale Image

In this section, how the image, which is given in color image is converted to an image in gray image is discussed with a few examples and MATLAB code. The role of Mathematics is very useful in the digital world. It helps to perform effectively in most of the fields. The mathematical concept, linear transformation, is used in image processing for the purpose of transforming images in different angles, positions, and colors etc.,

For example, consider the image below:

Figure 4. Input Color Image

This image is 397 pixels in Height and 527 pixels in width. This image is represented as a matrix with 397 rows and 527 columns. All kinds of colors are formed by the combination of Red, Green, and Blue colors (RGB) with different density values. The RGB values for each pixel of this image can be found by the MATLAB code.

MATLAB Code to find the RGB Values of an Image

The RGB values for each pixel of this image can be finding then it converted into gray scale by the following MATLAB code,

CODE:

```
RGB = imread('Sample.jpg'); % Read the image with file extension.
M = [0.30, 0.59, 3.11]; % Assign the RGB ratio value for image conversion.
Gray = imapplymatrix(M, RGB); % computes the linear combination
of the rows of M with the colour channels of RGB.
imshowpair(RGB,Gray,'montage') % Showing the images RGB and Gray
% Montage showing RGB and Gray next to each other in the same window.
```

The color image Figure 4 is converted to gray color image using a linear combination of these RGB values to 0.3R + 0.59 + 0.11 B. The output image is given below which have a gray color image.

Figure 5. Output Gray Color Image

2.5 Image Rotation

The image can be rotated at different angles or transformed by using the MATLAB code whenever required. To rotate the image, first convert the image as a matrix (A) by using RGB values and then find the transpose of the matrix ($A^T = B$). Now, to convert the new matrix (B) into an image and it is rotated 90 degrees in an anti-clockwise direction. Rotation of the image can be found by the following MATLAB code.

CODE:

```
imdata = imread('Sample.jpg'); % Reading the image (Sample)
RC = imdata(:,:,1)% To Read Red colour value in each pixel of an image
GC = imdata(:,:,2) % To Read Green colour value in each pixel of an image
BC = imdata(:,:,3) % To Read Blue colour value in each pixel of an image
RT = transpose(RC) % To find the transpose of the Red colour value matrix
GT = transpose(GC) % To find the transpose of the Green colour value matrix
BT = transpose(BC) % To find the transpose of the Blue colour value matrix
A = cat(3,RC,GC,BC); % Form an image using original RGB value of a image
B = cat(3,RT,GT,BT); % Form an image using transposed RGB value of a image
imshowpair(A,B,'montage') % To show two images together
```

Figure 6. Original Image and its rotational image by 90 degrees

2.6 Noise Reduction

Noise in an image is a random variation in image intensity that appears as a part of the image's grains. It may appear during the image capture or transmission process. When pixels in an image show varied intensity values instead of genuine pixel values derived from the image, this is referred to as noise.

The most crucial feature of a good picture denoising model is that it should remove noise as completely as feasible while also preserving edges. The technique of removing or reducing noise from an image is known as a noise removal algorithm. By smoothing the entire image and leaving sections near contrast boundaries, noise reduction algorithms diminish or eliminate the visibility of noise.

Noise removal is important for the reliability of subsequent image analysis and is often one major focus during the preprocessing stage in image processing. There are many ways to eliminate noise in an image.

In this section, the clarity and clearness of the image are discussed, in which the ambiguous image gets clarity or becomes visible clearly using the median value. First, the given image is transformed into a team, then divided into smaller matrices and written in ascending order. The extreme values or the different values in the list are replaced by the median value of the list. Once the median values are replaced then the ambiguous picture is transformed into a clear image.

For example, consider the image with noise given and its clear image given in Figures 7 and 8.

Figure 7. Ambiguous or blurred image

CODE:

```
M = imread('Gray.jpg'); % To Reads the image from the file specified by Gray with the standard file extension indicated by jpg
R = imnoise(U, 'salt & pepper', .3); % adds salt and pepper noise, where d is the noise density.
G = medfilt2(R) % Performs median filtering of the image I in two dimensions. Each output pixel contains the % median value in a 3-by-3 neighbourhood around the corresponding pixel in the input image.
imshow(R); figure, % displays the image R
imshow(G); % displays the image G
```

OUTPUT:

```
>> R([1:3], [3:51)
ans = 3x3 uint8 matrix
255 255 255
```

```
255 0 255
255 255 255
>> G([1:3), (3:51)
ans =
3x3 uint8 matrix
255 255 255
255 255 255
255 255 255
```

Figure 8. Blurred image to cleared image

Linear algebra is the engine behind the scenes in digital image processing. Whether you're enhancing an image, detecting edges, or recognizing patterns, matrix operations make it all possible. By representing images as matrices and using fundamental operations like addition, multiplication, transposition, and convolution, we can perform powerful transformations that have practical applications in everyday technology. Understanding these concepts is a critical first step in learning how artificial intelligence and computer vision systems interpret and interact with the visual world.

2.7 Cryptography

Cryptography is the art of protecting information so that the data remains accessible only to the authorized recipient. In the world of computers and the internet, cryptography is indispensable in the protection of confidential information from unwarranted access or manipulation. From the protection of online transactions to providing private messages and protecting of the nation's security systems, cryptography is ubiquitous.

Cryptography is much more crucial in the realm of artificial AI. Data transfer between systems, agents, or people is a common feature in AI applications. Intelligent assistants, self-driving cars, and healthcare systems, for instance, all share data that needs to be kept private and secure. Additionally, adversarial attempts that seek to steal or manipulate data must be prevented from affecting machine learning models. As a result, safe data storage and transfer are essential for AI systems.

Cryptography attracts attention all over the world. The recipient alone can decrypt the information and also read its contents. The Greek word Kryptos lays the basis for "erm is derived from the Greek word kryptos, which means hidden. Encryption is closely associated to it. It is the way of scrambling ordinary text into hidden text called ciphertext and bringing it back to plain text again.

It involves two types of operations. (I) Encryption and (ii) Decryption. The private key is involved in the process of encryption and decryption of data. Cryptography is used in many areas of the real world and uses techniques to hide information in an encrypted language that attackers (malicious third parties) cannot access anyway. In other words, encryption prevents unauthorized access to information and keeps your data secure.

To implement cryptographic techniques, several mathematical tools are used, and matrices are one of the most fundamental tools. Matrices, with their structured numerical format, are especially useful for encoding and decoding data. Understanding how matrices work in cryptography can provide a solid foundation for exploring more advanced topics in AI security.

Techniques related to information using microdots and merging techniques are also done by Cryptography. Methods used in hieroglyphics, the Roman Emperor Julius Caesar is used by ancient Egyptians. To transmit data electronically, cryptography is used.

Figure 9. Process Flow of Encryption & Decryption of Messages

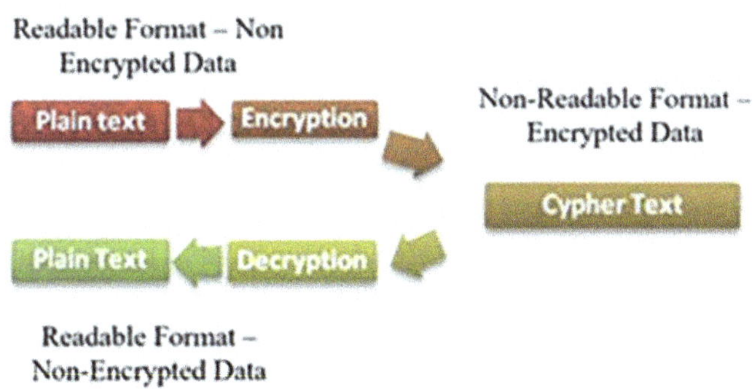

Algorithm

Step1: Consider the text. For example, we want to share the message "ALL IS WELL"

Step2: Assign number to each letter in the message using alphabetical order. For example, give 1 to A and 2 to B. Also, we assign the number 27 to space (space referred as *) in between two words.

Thus, our message becomes,

A L L * I S * W E L L

1 12 12 27 9 19 27 23 5 12 12

Step3: Randomly choose the $m \times m$ non-zero square matrix as a encoding matrix

For example,(Here m=3)

$$\begin{bmatrix} 1 & 0 & 1 \\ 4 & 4 & 3 \\ -4 & -3 & -3 \end{bmatrix}$$

be an encoding matrix.

Step4: Since we are using a $m \times m$ (m=3) matrix. So, the message is enumerated above is written as a matrix with 3- rows as follows:

$$\begin{bmatrix} 1 & 27 & 27 & 12 \\ 12 & 9 & 23 & 12 \\ 12 & 19 & 5 & 27 \end{bmatrix}$$

At the end, an empty space is added to complete the vector.

Step5: Encode the message by multiplying each of the above vectors by the encoding matrix.

Represent the above vectors as columns of a matrix and perform its matrix multiplication with the encoding matrix.

Step6: It is transformed to linear form as

6 24 24 54 55 160 192 281 -46 -141 -165 -258

The above is shared to receiver as encrypted data.

Step7: The above matrix is found for its inverse and the matrix for decoding is

$$\begin{bmatrix} -3 & -3 & -4 \\ 0 & 1 & 1 \\ 4 & 3 & 4 \end{bmatrix}$$

To decode the message, perform the matrix multiplication with the decoding matrix as follows

$$\begin{bmatrix} -3 & -3 & -4 \\ 0 & 1 & 1 \\ 4 & 3 & 4 \end{bmatrix} \begin{bmatrix} 6 & 24 & 24 & 54 \\ 55 & 160 & 192 & 281 \\ -46 & -141 & -165 & -258 \end{bmatrix} = \begin{bmatrix} 1 & 27 & 27 & 12 \\ 12 & 9 & 23 & 12 \\ 12 & 19 & 5 & 27 \end{bmatrix}$$

Step8: The linear form of the matrix is formed and the original message is obtained.

1 12 12 27 9 19 27 23 5 12 12

A L L * I S * W E L L

MATLAB Code for Encryption and Decryption of Text messages (Code to be Changed)

CODE:

```
A = rand(3,3) % Choosing a random matrix
B = [1 27 27 12; 12 9 23 12; 12 19 5 27] % Text as a matrix
E = A*B % Encryption
D = inv(A)*E % Decryption
```

OUTPUT:

```
A =
1 0 1
4 4 3
-4 -3 -3
B =
1 27 27 12
12 9 23 12
12 19 5 27
E =
13 46 32 39
88 201 215 177
-76 -192 -192 -165
D =
1 27 27 12
12 9 23 12
12 19 5 27
```

To be effective at all, an encryption matrix also has to be invertible. A non-invertible matrix (a singular matrix) would not be very useful for decryption. Another issue for basic matrix cryptography is that it isn't very secure by today's standards since it is susceptible to brute force attacks. In any case, it offers basic simplicity that more complex systems build upon.

Although matrix-based encryption is basic, it is the foundation for the majority of real-world encryption protocols. Cutting-edge encryption protocols and AI-security systems also make use of higher-order matrix operations, such as in secure federated learning and blockchain-based AI networks. These systems make data input into AI safe, private, and tampering-proof. Matrices provide a foothold for further learning how secure communication is established in intelligent systems.

Matrices offer a practical and mathematical way to understand how information can be encoded and protected. Their application in cryptography, though often simplified for educational purposes, demonstrates the power of mathematical structures in securing information. For students and beginners in AI, learning matrix operations not only opens the door to secure communications but also forms the foundation for more complex data handling in AI algorithms and applications.

3. GRAPH THEORY

Social Media Friend's Recommendation

Just imagine opening the most preferred app for Social Media whether it is Instagram, Facebook, Twitter, or LinkedIn and noticing a message that appears as "People You May Know" or "Suggested for You." Has there ever been any thought concerning how the platform seemingly knows what one is thinking and suggests those with whom one is familiar or may want to speak with?

Social networks are online communities that connect billions of us worldwide. Billions of people have accounts on social media platforms like Facebook, Instagram, and LinkedIn. AI programs are always running in the background. This is where AI crunches vast amounts of data to understand human behavior, preferences, and relationship patterns. Artificial intelligence (AI) is the engine that powers such intelligent recommendations. Friend recommendations are the most obvious use of AI on social media. All of these recommendations are in response to the imperative "How did I know this person?"

A computer program must study billions of users and select a few of them to recommend as potential friends to a user. This is a unique challenge facing a social network. The answer lies in an important branch of mathematics, graph theory. The mathematics of graph theory gives computer systems the means by which a complicated web of human relations can be comprehended and traversed. Graph theory converts the intangible notions of "friend" and "link" into tangible mathematical objects that can be deciphered and acted upon by a computer.

Graphs are the major source of modelling in various fields like video indexing, chemical informatics, computer vision, bioinformatics, web analysis, text retrieval, etc. The mining of related subgraphs are formed by various discrimination, cluster analysis, and classification. Also, various networks based on computer networks, web, biological networks, telecommunication, etc. Analysis based on social networks has widely attracted a group of researchers. Wide usage of 'hieroglyph' is traced as the first evidence of cryptography. Communication of Egyptians was traced 4000 years ago using hieroglyphs.

Random graphs are used for modelling the communication made by people in the process of simulating a social network. By adding graphs to the nodes and by adding edges randomly following a probabilistic rule.

A popular site used to connect people is social networking. Through the world it connects people. There are many reasons for people to involve in social networking. Personal interest along with business related follow ups can be done in Facebook. It is widely spread along various networks. Different form of them are Twitter, Instagram, LinkedIn etc.

In social media, getting a friend suggestion is a system developed for reference. Recently, social media has achieved great success with millions of users. The topics that users are most looking for and recommend friends related to the field of the users. Users will only follow the people they need from the list of references.

Figure 10. Mutual Friends

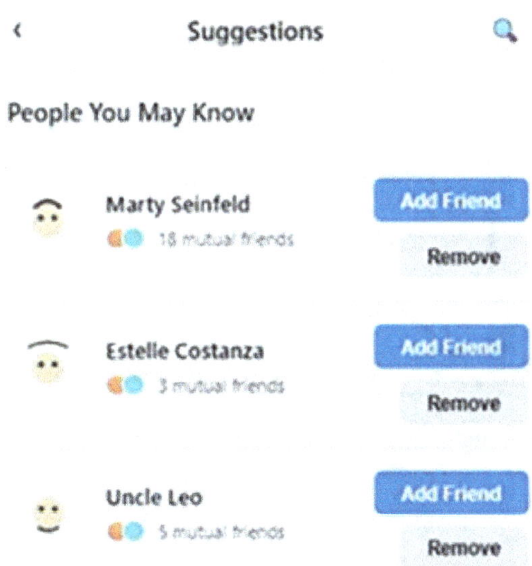

Definition: A graph is a collection of **nodes** (also called vertices) connected by **edges** (also called links or connections).

Let us consider

Nodes represent individual entities (like people, places, or things)
Edges represent relationships or connections between these entities

A Relatable Example: The School Friendship Network

Let's imagine a small group of friends in a school. We have five students: Alice, Bob, Carol, David, and Emma.

- Alice knows Bob and Carol
- Bob knows Alice, Carol, and David
- Carol knows Alice, Bob, and Emma
- David knows Bob and Emma
- Emma knows Carol and David

In graph theory terms:

- Each student is a **node**
- Each friendship is an **edge** connecting two nodes We can visualize this as:

Figure 11. Friendship relations among the people

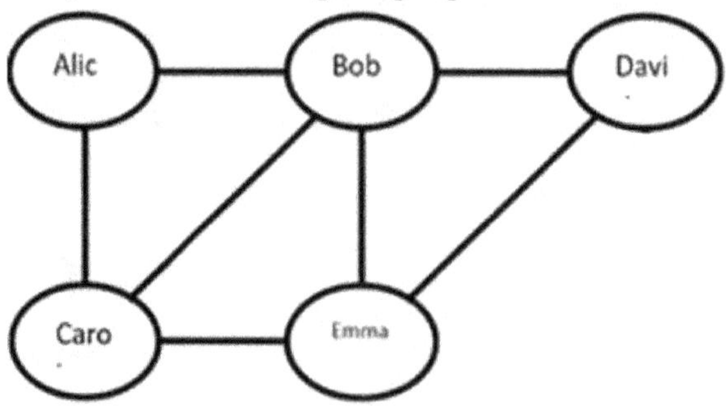

Types of Graphs

Understanding different types of graphs helps us model various real-world scenarios:

I. Undirected vs. Directed Graphs

Undirected Graph: Relationships go both ways

- If Alice is friends with Bob, then Bob is friends with Alice
- Most social media friendships work this way (Facebook friends, Instagram followers when mutual)

Directed Graph: Relationships have a direction

- Alice might follow Bob on Twitter, but Bob doesn't follow Alice back
- The relationship has a direction: Alice → Bob

II. Weighted vs. Unweighted Graphs

Unweighted Graph: All connections are treated equally

- Either you're friends or you're not—no middle ground

Weighted Graph: Connections have different strengths

- Some friendships might be stronger than others
- We could assign weights based on interaction frequency: Alice and Bob text daily (weight: 10), while Alice and Carol meet monthly (weight: 3)

Let's define the essential vocabulary that will help us understand friend recommendations:

Degree of a Node

The **degree** of a node is simply the number of connections it has. In our school example:

Alice's degree = 2 (connected to Bob and Carol)
Bob's degree = 3 (connected to Alice, Carol, and David)
Carol's degree = 3 (connected to Alice, Bob, and Emma)

In social media terms, a person's degree represents how many friends they have. Someone with a high degree is well-connected and popular.

Path is a sequence of connections that takes you from one person to another. For example, to get from Alice to Emma:

Direct path: Alice → Carol → Emma (length 2)
Alternative path: Alice → Bob → David → Emma (length 3)

The **shortest path** between two people represents how closely connected they are in the social network.

Neighbors are nodes directly connected to a given node essentially, a person's immediate friends. Alice's neighbors are Bob and Carol.

Common neighbors are mutual friends, people who are friends with both you and someone else.

Alice and David have one common neighbor: Bob.

This means Alice and David both know Bob, even though Alice and David don't know each other directly.

Another example in the image below, P1 follows P3, P4, P5 and P2 follows P3, P4, P6.

Figure 12. Friendship relations among the people

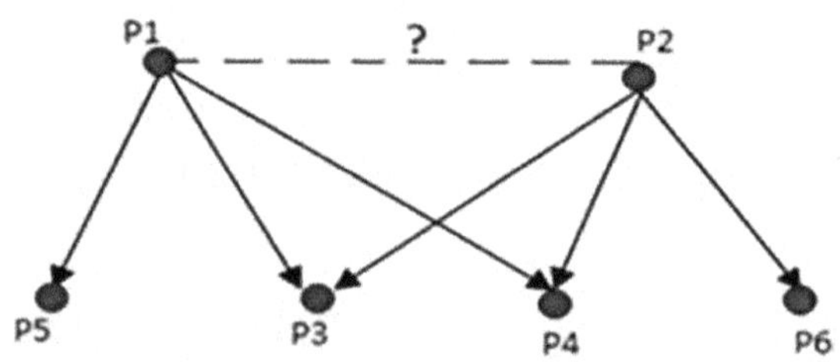

Here, both P1 and P2 follow P3 and P4. Therefore, P2 for P1 and P1 for P2 would be recommended to follow. When there is a possible for P1 to follow P2, then there is a possible that P2 to P5 and P1 to P6 may be recommended for follow-up.

The fact that P1 is trailing P2 indicates that there is a good likelihood that P2 will return the favor.

Figure 13. Relationships between two unknown persons

Graph theory offers powerful tools for modeling and analyzing relationships in social networks. It serves as the mathematical foundation for many AI-driven friend recommendation systems. Understanding concepts like nodes, edges, paths, and common neighbors can help beginners appreciate how these suggestions are made.

As users continue to engage with social media, graph-based AI models develop to provide more intelligent and customized experiences. There are also other works for graph theory that have some interesting applications for AI.

4. CALCULUS

As the universal language that tells us about change and how quantities build up over space or time. Just like a system of GPS needs to know about movement and direction in space in order to navigate you somewhere, systems of Artificial Intelligence need calculus in order to know how to adapt and make more intelligent decisions.

To understand why calculus is required for artificial intelligence, think about learning how to ride a bicycle. Each wobble, each movement of the handlebars, each balance or imbalance movement is a slight change that gets one closer or further away from smooth riding. Your body absorbs and corrects each failure and helps and refines riding by slight increments. This very same process is what is done by systems of artificial intelligence, except that the systems apply the mathematics of calculus in order to translate and optimize each learning phase by truly remarkable precision.

There also are two fundamental forms of calculus that supplement one another like the two faces of a single coin: differential and integral calculus. In order to understand how systems of Artificial Intelligence adapt and learn, we need to know well both of the variants described above.

Differential calculus is all about rate and measurement of change. It's like a mathematical microscope that can look at how fast something is changing at any point. When you are driving and checking your speedometer, what you are looking at is an everyday use of differential calculus; it measures how your position is varying relative to time at the moment. In the case of AI, differential calculus assists us in learning how small changes to a system's parameters influence its overall performance.

Try visualizing the growth of a child over the years through snapshots taken every few years. Although the images depict individual moments in time, differential calculus would enable us to grasp the rate of growth of the child at any given age. Likewise, as an AI system learns to identify images of cats, differential calculus enables us to grasp the impact of variations in the internal settings of the system on its capacity to identify feline characteristics correctly.

Integral calculus deals with the accumulation and addition of quantities over space or time. While differential calculus is akin to watching individual movie frames, integral calculus is like having the entire story that results when all the frames are played one after another. Almost invariably, the loss function for picture classification assesses the degree to which the system's predictions diverge from the appropriate labels.

Integral calculus for computer systems also gives us a sense of how individual experiences of learning build up into total knowledge and capacity. Using probability distributions to characterize the likelihood of different outcomes and continuous optimization issues where we want to find the optimal solution out of an endless set of possibilities are two situations where it is especially helpful.

The beauty of calculus is that it is well able to deal with constant change, and this pervades everything in the material world. While simple arithmetic with invariable numbers is of limited application, calculus gives us the tools of dealing with quantities in a state of constant variation and transformation, and that is why it has a central importance in systems that by definition must learn and adapt in terms of variable and dynamic conditions.

4.1 The Critical Role of Calculus in Machine Learning

Machine learning is a branch of AI that helps machines and computers learn and improve through experience without being directly programmed for each level, and relies almost entirely on calculus to perform its basic tasks. To learn about this connection, let's look at how machines actually "learn."

When training a machine learning program, we don't sit down and write rules for it to perform a task for every possible situation, such as reading hand-scanned digits or predicting the stock market. Instead, we try to give it some examples and let it automatically find patterns. The learning process will actually predict its best behaviour as accurately as possible.

Loss functions are the basis of this learning process. A loss function is like considering a measure of how far off the system is at that time. A pupil would receive a test score that provides some idea of how well they comprehended the material, and a loss function provides the AI system with a numeric score that informs us how far away from correct answers its current predictions are.

For example, if we're training an AI system to predict house prices and it predicts a house costs 2,00,000 when it actually costs 2,50,000, the loss function might calculate this error as 50,000. The goal of the learning process is to minimize this loss to make the system's predictions as accurate as possible.

This is where differential calculus becomes crucial. The gradient, which is calculated using differential calculus, tells us exactly how the loss function changes when we make small adjustments to the system's parameters. Think of the gradient as a compass that points in the direction of the steepest increase in the loss function. Since we want to minimize loss, we move in the opposite direction of the gradient.

Gradient descent is the fundamental algorithm that uses this gradient information to systematically improve the AI system's performance. You are walking through thick fog and wish to go down into the bottom of a valley. You don't see very far into the distance, yet you know that the ground is sloping down underneath your feet. By always taking one step downhill in the direction of the steepest slope, sooner or later you will hit bottom. Gradient descent is the same principle, except it uses calculus and takes a step in that direction.

The system undergoes various essential steps that it repeats over and over as it trains. It makes predictions from its current parameters. It estimates how wrong its predictions are according to a loss function. It uses differential calculus and computes the gradient, figuring out how each parameter should change so that the loss decreases. Finally, it updates all parameters simultaneously, pushing gently in a direction that should yield a better performance. This cycle is repeated thousands or even millions of times until the system has reached a degree of satisfactory performance.

In machine learning, integral calculus also plays significant roles, albeit these are frequently less obvious to novices. Many machine learning methods are theoretically based on probability and statistics, and integral calculus is employed to cope with continuous probability distributions.

Additionally, some advanced optimization techniques use integral calculus to find optimal solutions across continuous spaces. Rather than testing discrete parameter values, these methods can find the best possible settings from an infinite range of possibilities, leading to more precise and effective AI systems.

Let's consider a simple loss function: $L(x) = (x - 3)^2$. This function represents a common scenario in machine learning where we're trying to find the parameter value x that minimizes our loss. In this case, we can see that the minimum occurs when x = 3, because that makes $(x - 3) = 0$, and thus $L(x) = 0$.

However, let's pretend we don't know this optimal value and must discover it using gradient descent, just as a real AI system would have to do with much more complex problems.

Calculating the Derivative

The first step in gradient descent is calculating the derivative of our loss function. The derivative tells us how the loss changes as we change the parameter x. Using basic calculus rules, the derivative of

$L(x) = (x - 3)^2$ is:

$L'(x) = 2(x - 3)$

This derivative formula tells us the slope of the loss function at any point x. When the derivative is positive, it means the function is increasing as x increases. When it's negative, the function is decreasing as x increases. When it equals zero, we've found a minimum or maximum point.

Implementing Gradient Descent

Now let's implement gradient descent step by step. We'll start with an initial guess for x and use the derivative to iteratively improve our estimate.

Let's start with x_0=0 and use a learning rate of 0.1. The learning rate controls how big steps we take in each iteration – too large and we might overshoot the minimum, too small and learning will be very slow.

Iteration 1:

- Current position: x_0=0
- Current loss: $L(0)= (0–3)^2=9$
- Gradient: $L'(0) = 2(0 - 3) = -6$
- Update: $x_1= x_0 - (\textit{learning rate} \times \textit{gradient})=0 - (0.1\times -6)=0.6$

Iteration 2:

- Current position: x_1= 0.6
- Current loss: $L(0.6)= (0.6–3)^2=5.75$
- Gradient: $L'(0.6) = 2(0.6 - 3) = -4.8$
- Update: x_2= 0.6 – (0.1× -4.8)=1.08

Iteration 3:

- Current position: x_2= 1.08
- Current loss: $L(1.08)= (1.08–3)^2=3.69$
- Gradient: $L'(1.08) = 2(1.08 - 3) = -3.84$
- Update: x_3= 1.08 – (0.1× -3.84)=1.46

Table 2. Iteration value table

Iteration	Value x	Loss L(x)	Gradient L'(x)	Step Size
0	0.00	9.00	-6.00	0.60
1	0.60	5.76	-4.80	0.48
2	1.08	3.69	-3.84	0.38
3	1.46	2.36	-3.07	0.31

Iteration	Value x	Loss L(x)	Gradient L'(x)	Step Size
4	1.77	1.51	-2.46	0.25
5	2.02	0.97	-1.97	0.20
10	2.66	0.12	-0.69	0.07
20	2.93	0.00	-0.13	0.01

Understanding the Results

Notice several important patterns in our gradient descent example. First, the loss decreases with each iteration, showing that our algorithm is successfully finding better parameter values. Second, as we get closer to the optimal value ($x=3$), the gradient becomes smaller, which means our steps become smaller too. This is perfect behavior we want to take large steps when we're far from the optimum and small steps when we're close, to avoid overshooting.

The negative gradient values tell us that we need to increase x to reduce the loss, which is exactly what happens. As x approaches 3, the gradient approaches zero, and our updates become smaller and smaller. Eventually, the algorithm converges to the optimal solution.

This simple example demonstrates the core principle behind how all machine learning algorithms learn. Whether we're training a system to recognize faces, translate languages, or play chess, the same fundamental process applies: define a loss function that measures performance, calculate gradients using differential calculus, and use those gradients to iteratively improve the system's parameters.

The principles we've explored translate directly into the AI systems that surround us daily. Understanding these applications helps illustrate why calculus is not just an abstract mathematical tool, but a practical necessity for modern technology.

4.2 Image Classification and Computer Vision

When you upload a photo to social media and it automatically suggests tags for your friends, you're witnessing calculus in action. In order to identify patterns in visual data, image classification systems employ neural networks with millions of parameters that need to be carefully adjusted. Gradient descent is used to fine-tune parameters based on how successfully objects, faces, or scenes are detected in the thousands of annotated photos that are sent through the algorithms throughout the learning process.

Almost invariably, the loss function for picture classification assesses the degree to which the system's predictions diverge from the appropriate labels. If the system is 90 percent sure that an image has a cat when it actually has a dog, for example, the loss function estimates this error. The calculus subsequently computes precisely how much each one of the millions of parameters should be adjusted in order to lower errors of this sort among all the images in the training set.

The very complexity of this process is staggering. A basic image classification network would possess 50 million parameters that require very precise calculations of gradients per iteration of training. The system makes calculations in increments of thousands of images at a time and performs billions or more calculus-based calculations in order to gradually construct a superior ability for viewing and interpreting visual content.

4.3 Recommendation Systems

Streaming platforms, e-commerce sites, and social media outlets employ advanced recommendation algorithms that are heavily dependent on calculus-driven optimization. These platforms have to learn how to predict what kind of content or products a given user will be interested in by observing their history and preferences.

The process of making recommendations entails the construction of mathematical representations for users and items in high-dimensional spaces. Users who share similar interests group together within such a space, as do items with similar features. The algorithm uses calculus to determine where the representations should be placed in order to forecast user behavior.

When Netflix recommends movies for you, it is always doing some kind of gradient descent in order to learn more about what you like and what makes or breaks certain films. Each time that you watch, rate, or skip something, the system refines parameters through calculus methods in a manner that it should be able to recommend films more accurately from then on.

4.4 Self-Driving Cars

Self-driving cars may well represent the ultimate practical use of calculus in computer science. They require images from cameras, radar, and lidar sensors and generate instantaneous decisions regarding steering, speed, and brakes. This is all based on machine learning modules that have learned through the use of calculus-based optimization.

Neural networks with gradient descent training are used in the sensing system that recognizes road signs, pedestrians, and other vehicles. Calculus is used by the path planning algorithms that determine the optimal routes in order to minimize travel time and maximize safety. Calculus-based control theory is used even in control systems that translate judgments at the abstract level into specific motor orders.

Consider the problem of teaching a car to stay in its own lane. The system would need to process visual data for detecting lane markings, calculating the car's location relative to those markings, and determining the appropriate steering corrections. Derivatives and integrals are used in all of these computations to determine location change rates and apply small adjustments over time to ensure steady, smooth control.

4.5 Backpropagation in Deep Learning

Among the most significant applications of calculus in today's artificial intelligence is the backpropagation algorithm that makes it possible to train deep neural networks. Backpropagation is in itself an efficient method of calculating gradients in highly multi-layered networks and has made it possible for systems with hundreds of millions or more parameters to be trainable.

When training a large language model like those used in advanced chatbots, backpropagation propagates error information from the output layer back through all the hidden layers of the network. This procedure necessitates computing partial derivatives for each network parameter, which is a significant computer undertaking that would be unfeasible without calculus's methodical methodology.

The education of contemporary AI systems commonly requires computation of terabytes of data through billions of parameters, and every step in a training cycle requires computation of gradients for each parameter. This is one of the biggest uses of calculus by human beings, and more derivative calculations occur in one run of an AI-training program than were accomplished by hand throughout the history of the pre-computer era.

5. PROBABILITY THEORY

Sometimes, AI must take a decisions based on incomplete information, noisy data, and uncertain outcomes. Probability theory is not only useful, but also essential to the functioning of modern AI systems. Probability theory is of great help, allowing

AI systems to measure uncertainty, make predictions from given information, and update their predictions as new information becomes available.

In this section, we will take a closer look at how probability theory, one of the most important mathematical foundations, plays a role in the functioning of AI. We will start with the basics and gradually explain more sophisticated applications, ensuring that readers with different mathematical backgrounds can understand it very easily.

Let's look at a simple example: The spam filter in your email doesn't know for sure whether every incoming message is spam or legitimate. Instead, it calculates the probability that a message is spam based on a variety of questions, such as who is sending it? What is its subject? and what is its content? When this probability exceeds a certain threshold, the message is classified as spam.

From the spam filter in your email to the recommendation engine on your favorite streaming platform, probability theory is working behind the scenes to make intelligent decisions under uncertainty.

5.1 Basic Probability Concepts

Let's begin with the fundamentals of probability theory before moving into AI applications

Sample Space (Ω): The set of all possible outcomes of an experiment. For example, when flipping a coin, the sample space is $\Omega = \{\text{Head, Tail}\}$.

Event (E): A collection of the sample space. An event is one or more outcomes we'd like to consider. For example, heads when you flip a coin is an event.

Probability (P): A quantitative value ranging between 0 and 1 that measures the probability that an event will take place. $P(E) = 0$ indicates that an event never happens, while $P(E) = 1$ indicates that an event always happens.

Mathematical Definition: In a finite sample space with equally likely outcomes, the probability of an event E is:

$$P(E) = \frac{\textit{Number of favorable outcomes}}{\textit{Total number of possible outcomes}}$$

The Role of Probability in AI Decision-Making

AI systems use probability theory to model uncertainty in several ways:

- **Data Uncertainty**: Data in the real world is usually noisy, incomplete, or contradictory. Probability enables AI systems to consider this uncertainty while making predictions.

- **Model Uncertainty**: AI models themselves are imitations of the real world. Probability enables us to be confident in model output and determine whether additional data or alternative methods may be necessary.
- **Decision Making**: When confronted with several potential actions, AI systems employ probability to consider the potential results and select the most likely action.

5.2 Conditional Probability: The Heart of AI Reasoning

Understanding Conditional Probability

In AI applications of probability theory, conditional probability is perhaps the most important concept. It answers the question, "What is the probability that event A occurs, provided that event B has occurred?" Conditional probability can be defined mathematically as follows:

$$P(A|B) = \frac{P(A \cap B)}{P(B)}$$

where P(A|B) reads as "the probability of A given B," P (A ∩ B) is the probability of both A and B occurring, and P(B) is the probability of B occurring.

Real-World Example: Email Spam Detection

Let's illustrate conditional probability with a practical AI application: spam detection. Suppose we want to determine the probability that an email is spam given that it contains the word "free."

Let S = "email is spam" and F = "email contains the word 'free'.

We want to find P(S|F) - the probability that an email is spam given that it contains the word "free."

Imagine we have the following data from analysis of 10,000 emails:

- 2,000 emails are spam (P(S) = 0.2)
- 8,000 emails are non-spam (P (not S) = 0.8)
- In spam emails, 1,600 contain "free" (80% of spam emails)
- In non-spam emails, 400 contain "free" (5% of legitimate emails)

Using conditional probability:

$P(F|S) = 1{,}600/2{,}000 = 0.8$

$P(F|not\ S) = 400/8{,}000 = 0.05$

$P(F) = (1{,}600 + 400)/10{,}000 = 0.2$

This example demonstrates how conditional probability allows AI systems to update their beliefs based on observed evidence.

5.3 Bayes' Theorem: The Foundation of AI Learning

Introduction to Bayes' Theorem

Bayes' Theorem is perhaps the most influential tool in probability theory and serves as the foundation of numerous AI algorithms. It enables one to revise probabilities according to new discoveries, and this is the essence of how learning and The theorem state:

$P(A|B) = [P(B|A) \times P(A)] / P(B)$

When:

P(A|B) is the conditional or posterior probability (what we desire to know)
P(B|A) = likelihood (probability that the evidence exists given that the
P(A) is pre-existing likelihood (original belief in hypothesis)
P(B) is also the total probability of evidence (marginal probability).

Bayes' Theorem in Spam Detection

Using Bayes' Theorem, let's continue our spam detection example by determining P(S|F)—the likelihood that an email is spam if it contains the word "free":

$P(S|F) = [P(F|S) \times P(S)] / P(F)$

$P(S|F) = [0.8 \times 0.2] / 0.2 = 0.16 / 0.2 = 0.8$

In other words, if an email contains the word "free," it is 80% likely spam. This shows how the inclusion of "free" is strong proof for spam, as it is far higher than the baseline spam rate of 20%.

Naive Bayes Classifier: A Practical AI Application

One of the most successful applications of Bayes' Theorem in AI is the Naive Bayes classifier. Despite its "naive" assumption that features are independent (which is often violated in practice), it performs remarkably well in many real-world scenarios.

For spam detection with multiple features, the Naive Bayes classifier calculates:

$$P(Spam|f_1, f_2, ..., f_n) = P(Spam) \times \prod[P(f_i|Spam)] / P(f_1, f_2, ..., f_n)$$

Where $f_1, f_2, ..., f_n$ are different features (words, phrases, metadata) in the email.

Example Application: Consider an email with features:

Contains "free" (f_1)
Contains "urgent" (f_2)
From unknown sender (f_3)

The classifier would calculate the probability of spam by combining the evidence from all three features using Bayes' Theorem.

5.4 Probability Distributions in AI

Understanding Probability Distributions

A probability distribution describes how probabilities are distributed over the values of a random variable. In AI, different distributions model various types of uncertainty and randomness encountered in real-world data.

Common Distributions in AI Applications

Bernoulli Distribution

The Bernoulli distribution models binary outcomes (success/failure, yes/no, spam/not spam). It's fundamental in classification problems.

$P(X = 1) = p$ (probability of success)
$P(X = 0) = 1 - p$ (probability of failure)

Example: In spam detection, each email can be modeled as a Bernoulli trial, with "spam" as a success and "non-spam" email as a failure.

Normal Distribution

The normal distribution is ubiquitous in AI due to the Central Limit Theorem and its mathematical properties. Many natural phenomena and measurement errors follow this distribution.

$$f\left(x\right) = \frac{1}{\sqrt{(2\pi\sigma^2)}} e^{-\frac{(x-\mu)^2}{2\sigma^2}}$$

Where μ is the mean and σ is the standard deviation.

Example: In computer vision, pixel intensities often follow a normal distribution, and many machine learning algorithms assume normally distributed features.

Binomial Distribution

The binomial distribution models the number of successes in a fixed number of independent Bernoulli trials.

$$P(X = k) = {}^{n}C_{k}\, p^{k}(1 - p)^{n-k}$$

5.5 Applications in Recommendation Systems

Recommendation systems provide an excellent example of how probability distributions work in practice. Consider a movie recommendation system:

- **User Preferences**: Modelled using probability distributions over different genres, actors, and directors.
- **Rating Predictions**: The system predicts the probability distribution of ratings a user might give to unseen movies.
- **Collaborative Filtering**: This approach assumes that users who shared similar preferences in the past are likely to have similar preferences in the future, modeled using probability.
- **Mathematical Framework**: To anticipate a user's movie rating, we could model:

P (Rating = r|Movie = m, User = u)
= f(user_features, movie_features, historical_data)

REFERENCES

Bishop, C. M. (1995). *Neural networks for pattern recognition*. Oxford University Press.

Bishop, M. (2006). *Pattern recognition and machine learning*. Springer.

Diestel, R. (2017). *Graph theory* (5th ed.). Springer.

Goodfellow, I., Bengio, Y., & Courville, A. (2016). *Deep learning*. MIT Press.

Hastie, T., Tibshirani, R., & Friedman, J. (2009). *The elements of statistical learning* (2nd ed.). Springer.

Jaynes, E. T. (2003). *Probability theory: The logic of science*. Cambridge University Press.

Koblitz, N., Menezes, A. J., Wu, Y. H., & Zuccherato, R. J. (1998). *Algebraic aspects of cryptography*. Springer.

MacKay, D. J. C. (2003). *Information theory, inference, and learning algorithms*. Cambridge University Press.

Menezes, A. J., Van Oorschot, P. C., & Vanstone, S. A. (1997). *Handbook of applied cryptography*. CRC Press.

Murphy, K. (2012). *Machine learning: A probabilistic perspective*. MIT Press.

Russell, S., & Norvig, P. (2020). *Artificial intelligence: A modern approach* (4th ed.). Pearson.

Sawant, L., & Patil, S. A. (2020). Cryptography and image processing by matrices. *International Research Journal of Engineering and Technology*, *7*(8), 4327–4330.

Srivastav, M. K., & Nath, A. (2015). Study on mathematical modeling of social networks. *International Journal of Emerging Technology and Advanced Engineering*, *5*(3), 611–618.

Strang, G. (2016). *Linear algebra and its applications* (5th ed.). Cengage Learning.

Waghmare, S., & Mali, U. (2020). Development of matrix for cryptography. *Journal of Emerging Technologies and Innovative Research*, *7*(4), 112–118.

Wolfram, S. (1986). *Cryptography with cellular automata in advances in cryptology* (Vol. 218). Lecture Notes in Computer Science. Springer-Verlag.

KEY TERMS AND DEFINITIONS

Artificial Intelligence: The ability of machines to perform tasks that normally require human intelligence.

Calculus: A branch of mathematics that studies change through derivatives and integrals.

Graph Theory: The study of graphs made of vertices and edges to model relationships.

Linear Algebra: A branch of mathematics that studies vectors, matrices, and linear transformations.

Probability and Statistics: The study of uncertainty, data collection, analysis, and interpretation.

Chapter 4

Examination of Preschool Teacher Perception Towards the Use of ChatGPT in Mathematics Education

Deniz Yağmur
https://orcid.org/0009-0000-3596-8941
Ministry of National Education, Turkey

Yonca Arkali
https://orcid.org/0000-0002-3556-0732
Ministry of National Education, Turkey

ABSTRACT

Artificial intelligence (AI) is transforming preschool mathematics education by offering personalized learning experiences, adaptive teaching strategies, and interactive content delivery. AI tools like ChatGPT provide individualized feedback, enabling students to engage dynamically with mathematical concepts while supporting educators in lesson planning and content development, but at the same time AI integration raises ethical and technological concerns, including data privacy risks, screen exposure management, and technological accessibility limitations in under-resourced schools. Addressing disparities in AI access necessitates policy-driven solutions that prioritize digital equity and teacher preparedness. AI should enhance, not replace human-led teaching, ensuring responsible implementation. This study

DOI: 10.4018/979-8-3373-1998-8.ch004

concludes that structured AI adoption in preschool mathematics can significantly improve learning outcomes, provided that ethical, infrastructural, and pedagogical challenges are effectively managed.

INTRODUCTION

Mathematics education plays a fundamental role in the development of children's analytical thinking and problem-solving skills. Especially during the preschool period, presenting mathematics education through effective and interactive methods can significantly contribute to the development of children's knowledge and skills in this area. In recent years, the use of artificial intelligence technologies in education has been increasing, and the integration of these technologies into teaching processes is gaining more importance (Henrich, Heine and Norenzayan, 2010). The use of technology in education profoundly impacts not only teachers but also the learning experiences of students. Artificial intelligence tools with natural language processing capabilities, such as ChatGPT, can provide instant feedback to students, adapt to individual learning paces, and offer an interactive learning experience (Reiser, Carr-Chellmen and Dempsey, 2017).

ChatGPT operates on a deep neural network architecture composed of multiple transformer layers. These transformers are specifically designed to handle sequential data-such as natural language-enabling the system to produce coherent, human-like responses. The model is initially trained on an extensive corpus of textual data, through which it learns linguistic patterns and semantic relationships across words, phrases, and sentences. This training process is iterative, with performance improving as the system is exposed to increasingly diverse datasets. After its initial training, ChatGPT can be fine-tuned for specialized purposes, such as language translation or content creation.

The operational process of ChatGPT can be summarized in distinct stages. First, a user provides a prompt or query. The model processes this input by leveraging its learned language structures to formulate a response, which is then presented to the user for further interaction. The model's refinement relies heavily on reinforcement learning with human feedback (RLHF).

- SFT Model (Supervised Fine-Tuning): In this phase, curated demonstration data is gathered to train the model.
- RM Model (Reward Model): This component evaluates and scores the outputs of the SFT model based on their desirability and relevance for users.
- SFT Model via PPO: The SFT policy is further refined through reinforcement learning, optimizing its performance according to the RM's scoring. PPO, or

Proximal Policy Optimization, refers to the fine-tuned policy model obtained through this process (Kalla, Smith, Kuraku and Samaah, 2023).

Research on the use of artificial intelligence technologies in education examines how such tools transform learning processes and their effects on students' academic success (Carter and McCarthy, 2019). The use of ChatGPT in education can enable students to enhance their written and verbal expression skills, grasp complex subjects, and make their learning processes more efficient. However, the pedagogical effectiveness of this technology is directly related to teachers' ability to consciously guide artificial intelligence tools and their capacity to use these systems effectively in education (Smith and Jones, 2020).

Mathematics education stands out as a fundamental discipline that strengthens students' analytical thinking skills and deepens their problem-solving abilities. The rapid advancement of technological developments in education has increasingly made the integration of artificial intelligence-supported systems into teaching processes essential. These systems provide adaptable teaching materials, taking into account students' individual learning speeds and cognitive capacities, thus creating opportunities to personalize the learning experience (Baker and Yacef, 2009). AI tools equipped with natural language processing technologies, like ChatGPT, have the capacity to make the learning experience interactive by providing instant feedback to students. This feature transforms learning processes from being solely based on information transfer to a more dynamic and student-centered structure (Luckin and Cukurova, 2019).

The use of technology by preschool teachers is an essential part of the integration of artificial intelligence technologies in education. Technology integration can enrich teachers' pedagogical strategies and improve students' learning experiences (Mishra and Koehler, 2006). In today's increasingly digital society, it has become essential for individuals to possess a foundational level of digital literacy. Specifically, 21st-century learners are expected to demonstrate competence across information, media, and technology-related skills. Correspondingly, both current and future educators must cultivate their digital literacy to effectively navigate and succeed within technology-enhanced learning environments (Yünkül and Güneş, 2022).

Research indicates that for effective use of technology in education, teachers need to develop positive attitudes towards technology and be knowledgeable about its classroom applications (Ertmer and Ottenbreit-Leftwich, 2013). However, there are limited studies regarding preschool teachers' perceptions of technology use, and this study aims to fill a significant gap in this area. The literature on the use of ChatGPT in education examines the effects of this technology on student success and teachers' perceptions of these tools. For example, a study by Reiser, Carr-Chelmen and Dempsey (2017) noted that AI-supported learning tools improved students' academic performance and increased their learning motivation. These findings highlight the potential benefits of using tools like ChatGPT in education (Carter and McCarthy, 2019). However, there are also concerns regarding the use of AI technologies in education. Teachers may not have sufficient knowledge on how to effectively utilize such technologies in the classroom and how students can benefit from these tools (Smith and Jones, 2020). The effects of AI tools on children's social and emotional development are not yet fully understood, and scientific research on this topic is ongoing. To address these uncertainties and ensure the thoughtful use of AI in educational environments, it is crucial for teachers to receive comprehensive training on these technologies.

The use of artificial intelligence in education has the potential to transform pedagogical processes by providing students with personalized learning experiences. In particular, AI-supported systems like ChatGPT enhance learning processes by providing instant feedback and making them more interactive and dynamic. Research shows that the usage of AI technologies in education is effective in boosting students' academic achievements and making teachers' instructional processes more efficient (Luckin, Holmes, Griffiths and Forcier, 2016). However, during this transformation process, it is crucial for teachers to provide pedagogical guidance and ensure that students' learning processes are structured healthily. AI-supported teaching tools are noted to not only develop cognitive skills but also strengthen students' critical thinking and problem-solving abilities (Selwyn, 2021). In this context, educators and policymakers should work to increase the pedagogical compatibility of AI tools, ensuring they are integrated into students' learning experiences more effectively.

This study centers on preschool teachers' perspectives on using ChatGPT in mathematics education, emphasizing the importance of understanding educators' views and practices with AI tools for shaping future policies. By exploring how ChatGPT supports young children's mathematical development and teachers' experiences with it, the research aims to reveal both opportunities and challenges. Ultimately, the findings are intended to inform educators and policymakers about the effective integration of AI in early mathematics learning.

BACKGROUND

Artificial intelligence technologies are playing an increasingly important role in educational environments and bringing innovative approaches to teaching processes. These systems have the potential to support students' academic development by adapting to their individual learning needs (Luckin et al., 2016). AI-supported educational tools analyze the strengths and areas for improvement of students, providing them with tailored instructional materials. This approach allows for the creation of a more suitable learning process for each student, taking into account their learning speeds and cognitive capacities (Hwang, Sung and Yang, 2020). AI tools also offer significant advantages for teachers, making lesson content planning easier and making teaching processes more efficient. By continuously monitoring students' development, these systems provide personalized feedback, supporting the application of individualized learning approaches (VanLehn, 2011). Additionally, thanks to AI algorithms, educators can analyze their students' academic performances and develop more effective teaching methods.

The role of teachers in the use of AI technologies in education is also very important. Teachers should have adequate knowledge and skills to effectively use AI technologies and integrate them into their classroom applications. The competencies of teachers regarding AI technologies are critical for students to benefit from these technologies to the fullest (Sun, Chen and Ge, 2021). The integration of AI technologies into education has the potential to provide students with a personalized and interactive learning experience. For these technologies to be used effectively, teachers must possess sufficient knowledge and skills and integrate these technologies into their classroom practices carefully. Research on the use of AI technologies in education reveals the positive effects of these technologies on student success and how they are perceived by teachers.

Stanford University's Human-Centered Artificial Intelligence (HAI) initiative emphasizes that AI has the potential to enhance classroom interactions and student engagement by providing teachers with real-time feedback and recommendations. Similarly, the World Economic Forum highlights that AI can automate teachers' routine administrative tasks, thereby freeing up time for more personalized interactions with students and enabling educators to focus more effectively on student learning and development. These advancements suggest that AI can facilitate the provision of tailored educational materials to meet individual student needs while supporting teachers in managing classroom dynamics more efficiently (Savaş, 2021).

Emerging Generative Artificial Intelligence (GenAI) tools, such as ChatGPT, have prompted considerable scholarly and public discourse regarding their prospective implications for the field of education. This situation necessitates a nuanced understanding of the Technological Pedagogical Content Knowledge (TPACK) framework. This framework delineates the interrelated domains of knowledge essential for educators to successfully embed technology within instructional practices (Mishra, Warr and Islam, 2023).

The concept of Technological Pedagogical Content Knowledge (TPCK) was first proposed as a theoretical construct within educational research to articulate the specific knowledge base educators require for the effective integration of technology into teaching practice (Mishra and Koehler, 2006). Subsequently, the acronym was revised to TPACK-pronounced "tee-pack"-to enhance recall and to reflect a more cohesive representation of the three interrelated domains it comprises: technology, pedagogy, and content (Thompson and Mishra, 2007–2008).

Technological Pedagogical Content Knowledge (TPACK) represents the integrated understanding of three core domains -pedagogy, content, and technology- and their dynamic interrelationships. It encompasses the ability to employ appropriate technologies within the classroom to promote students' meaningful learning. Recognized as a critical component for facilitating effective, technology-enhanced education, TPACK underpins the capacity to present subject matter through digital tools; apply pedagogical strategies that leverage technology for conceptual instruction; utilize technology to address learners' difficulties and the factors influencing their comprehension; and draw upon students' prior knowledge to both reinforce existing understanding and construct new conceptual frameworks (Koehler and Mishra, 2009).

The integration of ChatGPT in education offers a significant advantage in providing students with personalized learning experiences. Students can use ChatGPT to solve math problems, receive help with their written assignments, or ask questions to better understand complex topics. The interactive nature of ChatGPT encourages active participation from students and increases their interest in the learning processes (Zhou, Zheng and Wang, 2020). Research indicates that interactive artificial intelligence tools are effective in enhancing students' learning motivation and facilitating their understanding of complex topics. Particularly in mathematics education, it has been stated that the solution suggestions provided by ChatGPT adapt to the individual needs of students, accelerating their processes of acquiring knowledge (Anderson, Belova and Kim, 2023).

Research on the use of ChatGPT in education reveals various potential benefits of this technology in different areas. For instance, a study by Tang and Chen (2021) found that ChatGPT is an effective tool in language learning processes and helps improve students' writing skills. Similarly, Chen and Zhou (2020) noted that ChatGPT is effective in enhancing students' reading-comprehension skills and that students have better understanding of texts. A recent analysis on the diversity of educational technologies highlights ChatGPT's potential to offer more complex analyses and personalized learning strategies compared to other language models. This could allow students to develop their language skills more deeply (Miller, 2023).

Research on the potential benefits and limitations of ChatGPT in preschool mathematics education demonstrates that this technology can enhance students' mathematical skills. For example, a study by Zhou, Zheng and Wang (2020) indicated that ChatGPT improved students' mathematical problem-solving skills and helped them better understand mathematical concepts (Atahan, 2025). Additionally, another study by Tang and Chen (2021) found that ChatGPT increased students' motivation to learn by providing personalized feedback. However, there are also limitations to the use of ChatGPT in education. Teachers need to have adequate knowledge and skills to use this technology effectively. Furthermore, careful planning is required regarding how ChatGPT will be used in the classroom and how students can make the most of this tool. Therefore, it is essential to organize comprehensive training programs for teachers and to manage the integration process of this technology carefully (Sun et al., 2021).

Research shows that the effective use of ChatGPT in individualized learning environments plays a critical role in enhancing students' mathematical achievements. For instance, a study by Johnson and Lee (2024) reported that classrooms using this technology saw a significant increase in students' interest in mathematical concepts and their problem-solving success. Moreover, it has been noted that ChatGPT strengthens students' motivation towards learning and encourages them to engage more in their learning processes.

The extensive dataset on which ChatGPT has been trained increases the accuracy and reliability of the information provided to students. Furthermore, this technology has become an important support tool in teachers' classroom management processes. ChatGPT assists teachers in developing personalized teaching strategies while also helping to continuously monitor and evaluate student performance (Patel and Nguyen, 2023). Research shows that teachers' perceptions of AI-supported tools are directly linked to the degree to which they can integrate these technologies into classroom applications. For example, a study by Ertmer and Ottenbreit-Leftwich (2013) indicated that teachers' attitudes towards technology influence the success of AI integration in education. For teachers to effectively use AI tools in their classrooms, they need to develop a positive attitude towards technology and understand the functionality of these tools.

There are some challenges in using ChatGPT in education. First, teachers need to have sufficient knowledge and skills to use this technology effectively. This includes not only increasing their technological knowledge levels but also improving their ability to integrate pedagogical practices with technology. Understanding and effectively using these tools is crucial for students to gain maximum benefit (Sun et al., 2021).

Furthermore, the integration of AI-powered tools into education is not limited to technical skills; it also requires teachers to restructure their pedagogical approaches. AI technologies have the potential to transform traditional teaching methods. However, for this transformation to be successful, continuous professional development programs must be provided for teachers. Inadequate support may hinder teachers from fully understanding and implementing the advantages of these tools (Harris, 2023).

Additionally, the planning for the use of tools like ChatGPT in the classroom must be done carefully. The integration of ChatGPT into education should be structured to respond to individual learning needs of students, and teachers must adapt the use of these tools to support students in achieving their learning goals. Furthermore, the ethical aspects and data privacy issues related to artificial intelligence tools must also be considered. For example, the accuracy and neutrality of the solutions offered by ChatGPT are critically important to ensure that students have a reliable and effective learning experience (Barrett and Stephens, 2024).

Another criticism concerns the inadequacy of ChatGPT and seeking information about unfamiliar organizations or prominent individuals may be classified as a form of personal inquiry. According to Taecharungroj (2023), a considerable proportion of internet users have voiced concerns regarding the accuracy, potential bias, and suboptimal performance of ChatGPT's responses. In addition, the system has faced widespread criticism for its capacity to produce harmful content and propagate misinformation. Scholars have also highlighted its possible adverse effects on users' cognitive engagement, noting that it may weaken critical thinking skills, impair human cognition, and contribute to inattentiveness and reduced productivity (Chukwuere, 2024).

The use of ChatGPT in education brings with it certain risks that may lead to data privacy and ethical violations. How student data is processed, stored, and analyzed is directly related to how teachers and institutions guide this technology. Especially due to children's lack of awareness regarding data sharing, the way artificial intelligence tools utilize student information requires great sensitivity (Carter and McCarthy, 2019). The importance of privacy and data protection in AI systems cannot be overstated and is multi-faceted, relating to ethical, legal, and user trust considerations. Privacy and data protection are integral to the ethical, responsible, and legally compliant development and deployment of AI systems. They are key to ensuring user trust and the broader success and acceptance of these technologies. These are the important issues at this point:

- Ethicial Considerations,
- Legal Compliance,
- User trust,
- Maintaining data integrity,
- Mitigating risks of adversarial attacks (Sebastian, 2023).

Protecting students' personal information is not only a technical security issue but also an ethical one. Educational institutions need to transparently define the data usage policies of artificial intelligence tools and teachers must guide these systems consciously. For example, research conducted by Smith and Jones (2020) showed that ensuring data transparency in the use of artificial intelligence in education increases teachers' trust in these technologies.

Excessive screen time exposure for students is considered a topic that, alongside the pedagogical benefits of AI-supported learning systems, needs to be addressed with care. Prolonged screen use can negatively affect students' cognitive development and lead to a decline in physical activities. For the successful integration of AI systems in education, teachers need to develop strategies to balance screen time. Gamified content that encourages children to move should be offered, and interactive learning experiences should be supported with physical activities to reduce the risk of screen addiction. The widespread adoption of AI-supported educational systems is directly linked to the adaptation processes of teachers and students to technology. These tools need to be applied under teacher guidance for effective use in the classroom. Educational policies should support teachers in integrating their pedagogical strategies with AI tools, promoting the conscious use of this technology (Zhang and Sun, 2023). While AI-supported teaching systems have the potential to provide educational equity and transform learning processes, careful consideration of ethical, pedagogical, and technological infrastructure issues is required for their successful implementation.

The focus of this study is to investigate teachers' perceptions of using ChatGPT in preschool mathematics education. ChatGPT's natural language processing capabilities can facilitate students' understanding of mathematical concepts and enhance their problem-solving skills (Gözüyılmaz, 2024). Since ChatGPT is trained on a vast dataset, it can provide students with accurate and relevant information, enriching their learning experiences (Brown, Mann, Ryder, Subbiah, Kaplan, Dhariwal and Amodei, 2020). The use of ChatGPT in preschool mathematics education has the potential to initiate a new era in this field. This AI-based language model can offer effective support to students in understanding complex mathematical concepts more easily and developing their problem-solving skills. The fact that ChatGPT is trained on a comprehensive dataset increases its capacity to provide accurate and contextually appropriate information, enriching students' learning processes (Brown et al., 2020).

METHOD

Model

This research was conducted using the case study method, one of the qualitative research designs. A case study aims to examine phenomena in depth within a specific context (Yıldırım and Şimşek, 2021). In this study, preschool teachers' perceptions, experiences, and views regarding the ChatGPT application were analyzed in depth. This model allowed participants to express their experiences from their own perspectives and facilitated the collection of qualitative data suitable for the purpose of the research.

Measurement Tools

The study group for the research consists of 10 preschool teachers working in the Bala district of Ankara in the 2024-2025 academic year. Participants were selected using purposive sampling methods, specifically maximum diversity sampling. This approach allowed for the inclusion of teachers with different professional experiences, age groups, and characteristics of the places they work, providing depth to the research. All participants were included in the study on a voluntary basis, and personal information was kept confidential.

Personal Information Form

A semi-structured interview form was used as the data collection tool. The form was prepared based on expert opinions and finalized after a pilot application. The interview form includes open-ended questions aimed at measuring teachers' perceptions of using ChatGPT in preschool mathematics education. The questions encompass teachers' evaluations of strengths and weaknesses, usage experiences, perceptions of pedagogical appropriateness, and suggestions for improvement.

Data Collection Process

Data were collected through individual audio interviews conducted by the researcher. The interviews were scheduled according to the teachers' work programs, with each interview lasting an average of 10-15 minutes. Informed consent was obtained from the participants, the interviews were recorded, and then transcribed into written form. Qualitative data obtained from interviews with a total of 10 teachers were prepared for the analysis process.

Data Analysis

The collected data were evaluated using descriptive and thematic analysis techniques. In the initial phase, the interviews were carefully read, and the data set was divided into open codes. These open codes were grouped under meaningful categories, resulting in the creation of seven main themes. The coding process was carried out by the researcher and cross-checked with another subject matter expert to ensure reliability. Additionally, during data analysis, each participating teacher was assigned a code number (T1, T2, T3…), and the findings were supported and interpreted using direct quotes from the participants.

Validity and Reliability

For the reliability of the research, coding was compared with an independent expert, achieving over 85% agreement between the codes. To ensure the validity of the data, participant statements were directly quoted in the interpretations, and continuous comparative analysis was conducted to avoid researcher bias. Details regarding the research process were clearly reported, adhering to the principle of transferability.

Ethical Principles

Throughout the research process, actions were taken in accordance with the rules of Scientific Research and Publication Ethics. Verbal and written consent was obtained from participants, their identities were kept confidential, and the data obtained were used solely for scientific purposes. There are no conflicts of interest within the scope of this study.

FINDINGS

The findings obtained from the research were categorized under seven main themes: the supportive function of ChatGPT in relation to teacher roles, pedagogical contributions in mathematics teaching, issues related to technological infrastructure and physical facilities, teachers' knowledge and competence levels, developmental appropriateness and age suitability, the effects on student motivation and learning perceptions, and ethical and pedagogical risks.

Theme 1: Supportive Function of ChatGPT from the Perspective of Teacher Roles

Participants have evaluated ChatGPT as a digital tool that guides teachers in the teaching process (n=8). Teachers perceive ChatGPT as a strong supporter in lesson planning and activity design, seeing it as an important advantage in terms of creativity. ChatGPT has been assessed as a significant digital tool that reduces the pedagogical workload of teachers by supporting their lesson planning and activity design processes (n=5). Participants state that this technology provides flexibility to teachers, especially in producing creative content, and makes it possible to present new approaches in the classroom. Research has shown that AI-supported teaching tools play a critical role in the processes of creating individualized lesson content for teachers. It is particularly seen as a supportive mechanism (n=2) that inspires teachers in processes like story writing, creating songs, and designing math activities. ChatGPT enables teachers to enrich pedagogical processes, making learning environments more interactive. By transforming the traditional structure of lessons, this technology introduces new approaches to the teaching process and, when evaluated from the perspective of educational psychology, supports students in adopting creative learning methods. The integration of digital learning tools into pedagogical processes contributes to the development of students' problem-solving skills and their active participation in lessons. Teachers express that AI-supported educational tools play an important role in diversifying learning materials and have the capacity to provide students with different learning experiences (n=4). Some teacher opinions related to this situation are included below.

"I sometimes get stuck in producing activities. At this point, ChatGPT works for me like a creative idea partner." **(T5)**

"I especially get support in content production. It makes my job easier when it offers story or game suggestions for certain concepts." **(T6)**

"ChatGPT has allowed me to make my lessons more creative, especially because it provides alternatives to routine teaching practices." **(T8)**

As indicated in the teachers' opinions above, teachers see the ChatGPT application as a digital tool that guides this process in terms of enriching and individualizing teaching during the lesson planning phase. ChatGPT's support for creative processes in education can increase teachers' pedagogical flexibility and enable them to offer students various learning experiences (Gasevic, Dawson and Siemens, 2016). Teachers' views on AI-supported systems are also important. Research shows that teachers can support student development by using AI tools such as ChatGPT in the classroom environment. However, most teachers state that more training and technical support are required for the effective use of these systems (Ertmer and Ottenbreit-Leftwich, 2013). Teachers state that the integration of AI into gamified learning processes can help students develop math, language, and analytical thinking skills (Veletsianos and Russell, 2014). ChatGPT's ability to create dynamic scenarios, in particular, allows teachers to make lesson plans more interesting (Holmes, Bialik and Fadel, 2019). However, teachers approach some issues with caution. Excessive use of AI tools in education can lead to the risk of students developing digital addiction. For this reason, it is emphasized that digital content should be balanced with physical activities (VanLehn, 2011).

Theme 2: Pedagogical Contributions in Mathematics Teaching

Research findings indicate that ChatGPT's contributions to preschool mathematics teaching are particularly focused on concept instruction and play-based learning (n=6). Participants expressed that ChatGPT provides alternative ways for presenting fundamental mathematical skills, such as counting, comparison, and classification, to children. The ability to gamify activities and present them in connection with daily life (n=3) has been highlighted as a notable pedagogical aspect of the application. Some teacher comments regarding this situation are provided below.

"I asked for a breakfast-themed game idea. ChatGPT immediately suggested an activity: a child with 3 olives on their plate practices counting. They both have fun and learn." (T6)

"The drama activity it suggested while working with opposite concepts really captured the children's interest. Movement-based learning became integrated with mathematics." (T4)

The comments from participants reveal that ChatGPT can be used not only as a content provider but also as a pedagogical tool. AI-supported education systems deeply contribute to individualized learning processes. Language models, especially ChatGPT, can make learning experiences more adaptable and dynamic by providing personal feedback to students (Luckin et al., 2016). Among the features offered by ChatGPT are: Presenting concepts with personalized explanations, Adapting content according to the student's level of understanding, Eliminating learning deficiencies with feedback mechanisms (Kulik and Fletcher, 2016). Especially in preschool mathematics education, children's learning speeds and interests can vary greatly. AI-supported systems address these differences with individual learning paths, allowing students to understand concepts more quickly and effectively (Holmes el al., 2019).

Theme 3: Issues Related to Technological Infrastructure and Physical Facilitics

Many participants expressed that the technological infrastructure limits the effective use of ChatGPT in the classroom (n=6). Teachers, especially those working in rural areas, reported experiencing issues with internet connectivity, and some schools lack smart boards or adequate equipment. This situation makes it challenging to utilize technological tools like ChatGPT on the basis of equal access in education. The opinions of the interviewed teachers on this issue are as follows:

"When the internet doesn't work, I use my mobile data. But this isn't always sufficient." (T3)

"We have a smart board, but the internet in the classroom is very weak. Sometimes the application won't even open." (T1)

Infrastructure deficiencies create limitations not only in technological but also in pedagogical applications; therefore, the need for technical support and hardware improvements is highlighted in the dissemination of applications.

Theme 4: Teachers' Knowledge and Competency Level

A significant portion of the participants indicated that teachers do not have adequate knowledge regarding AI-based applications like ChatGPT (n=9). This deficiency prevents teachers from utilizing the application effectively and fully benefiting from its potential. In the interviews, the necessity of face-to-face and practical in-service training (n=10) was frequently mentioned. The opinions of the interviewed teachers on this matter are presented below:

"There's a lot of information available online, but honestly, it's hard to find the time to research. It would be more effective if there were face-to-face trainings." (T2)

"I just heard about ChatGPT. I think most teachers don't know how to use it." (T4)

Participants emphasized that preparing training contents that include demonstrative explanations, developmentally appropriate applications for age groups, and pedagogical scenario studies would contribute to the process. Teachers should increase students' digital literacy and guide them consciously when using AI tools in the classroom (Koedinger and Corbett, 2006). Although the use of AI in education has the potential to increase student achievement, it is seen that teachers need a clear roadmap on how to manage these tools within the framework of ethical rules (Patel and Nguyen, 2023). One of the most important ethical responsibilities of teachers is to encourage students' conscious use of technology. Especially in the preschool period, the use of AI tools in the classroom should be balanced with the process of developing students' social skills (Holmes et al., 2019). The use of AI-based learning platforms should not lead to student independence without teacher guidance, because lack of guidance can lead to students being misguided in their learning processes (Kulik and Fletcher, 2016).

Theme 5: Developmentally Appropriate Practices and Age Adaptation

Most participants indicated that content from ChatGPT could be effective when simplified according to the developmental level of students in the 4–6 age group (n=7). However, some participants pointed out that due to the short attention spans of preschool children and their difficulty in understanding abstract concepts, the content must be concretized (n=3). Below are some interesting quotations related to this situation:

"Content must be short and supported by visuals. The four-year-olds cannot think abstractly, so the application alone is not sufficient." (T1)

"If it is supported with game-based content, it can address every age group." (T8)

Additionally, it was expressed that the teacher's guidance and the correct adaptation of the content are key to success.

Theme 6: Impact on Student Motivation and Learning Perception

Participants emphasized that the digital content and gamification features provided by ChatGPT have a motivation-enhancing effect on students (n=8). In particular, it was noted that screen-based, interactive content increases children's interest and participation in the lesson. The fact that students find this content enjoyable was evaluated as an important factor positively affecting learning. The following teacher opinions highlight this situation:

"Gamified content in mathematics teaching draws children into the lesson. They both have fun and learn." (T5)

"Through games and stories, children learn numbers without even realizing it." (T7)

However, some teachers warned that screen time needs to be pedagogically balanced. While traditional education systems are generally based on standardized teaching models, artificial intelligence (AI)-supported systems offer students individualized learning opportunities (Luckin et al., 2016). Artificial intelligence has the potential to analyze students' learning pace, strengths, and deficiencies and provide them with personalized feedback. In this way, students can participate more actively in their own learning processes and the teaching content can be adapted to their individual needs (Holmes et al., 2019).

Theme 7: Ethical and Pedagogical Risks

Some participants stated that the use of ChatGPT in preschool education carries ethical and developmental risks (n=4). Common concerns included screen addiction, potential negative impacts on social-emotional development, and data security issues. Teacher opinions on these matters are as follows:

"This age group is already exposed to screens a lot. With ChatGPT, this time could increase even more." (T4)

"We don't know where the data goes and how it is used. This worries me." (T1)

These findings show that in addition to the pedagogical benefits of technological tools, risk factors should also be taken into consideration. It is recommended that teachers be made aware of this issue and that ethical guidelines be prepared for its use.

The findings obtained in this study revealed that preschool teachers' perceptions and usage experiences regarding the ChatGPT application are multi-layered and meaningful. In line with the main purpose of the research, how teachers use

ChatGPT, an artificial intelligence-based tool, in teaching mathematics, for what purposes they prefer it, and what the opportunities and limitations they encounter in this process are, were examined in detail. In this context, teachers' statements provide in-depth clues about the use of technological tools in education at both individual and structural levels.

CONCLUSION

The capacity of ChatGPT to provide personalized learning is regarded by preschool teachers as a strong pedagogical tool. Children in this age group can exhibit significant differences in their learning speeds, which indicates that the same curriculum may not be equally effective for all students in traditional classroom settings. AI-supported systems have the potential to personalize students' learning processes by offering content tailored to their individual development levels and speeds. This situation allows teachers to design lesson content flexibly and sensitively to student needs.

Teachers express that ChatGPT enables students to explore their own learning pathways. AI-supported learning platforms provide content that supports students' cognitive processes while also encouraging their active participation in learning experiences (Koedinger and Corbett, 2006). Children are discovering conceptual knowledge in a more meaningful context thanks to personalized learning processes shaped by their interests. Especially in mathematics teaching, relating abstract concepts to concrete examples helps students internalize learning more effectively.

Furthermore, teachers state that the feedback mechanism of ChatGPT significantly contributes to students' ability to recognize their mistakes and improve their learning processes. AI-supported learning tools enable students to quickly identify their deficiencies by analyzing their responses (VanLehn, 2011). Through this mechanism, students have the chance to timely correct misinformation and systematically guide their learning processes. This feature is highly valued by teachers, especially in the context of mathematics education, as it aids in addressing misconceptions and developing problem-solving skills.

Teachers state that one of the strongest aspects of ChatGPT in education is its ability to generate interactive and dynamic content. In preschool education, pedagogical techniques such as storytelling and gamification facilitate more effective learning of concepts and increase interest in the learning process. The content production support provided by AI-supported systems allows for the creation of unique activities in lesson planning, brings a creative approach to topic explanation, and develops educational materials that encourage active student participation in their learning processes. Teachers note that the contribution of ChatGPT to the storytelling process has positive impacts, especially on conceptual learning. The use of storytelling in education supports students' cognitive development while helping them establish emotional connections, making topics more meaningful and memorable (Luckin et al., 2016). AI-supported storytelling can enable students to relate abstract mathematical concepts to concrete examples and transform learning into an exploratory process. From this, it is understood that teachers view ChatGPT not only as a time-saving tool but also as a mechanism that supports pedagogical creative processes (Gasevic et al., 2016). Story-based and music-assisted teaching methods are demonstrated to strengthen students' conceptual learning processes (Lauricella, Wartella and Rideout, 2015). According to the educational psychology literature, students' learning through storytelling and music makes concepts more lasting (Livingstone, Olafsson, Helsper, Lupianez-Villanueva, Veltri and Folkvord, 2017). It is understood that teachers see ChatGPT not just as a tool for delivering information but also as a resource that supports creative teaching processes (Buckingham Shum and Ferguson, 2012).

The use of digital technologies in education allows teachers to manage pedagogical processes more efficiently. AI-supported tools like ChatGPT provide significant support that saves teachers time in preparing lesson materials, planning activities, and personalizing student feedback. While traditional lesson preparation processes require intense cognitive and time management skills, AI-assisted content creation tools provide teachers with quick, flexible, and comprehensive solutions, creating opportunities to optimize their pedagogical practices. According to teachers, the rapid and effective content production capacity of ChatGPT is a critical factor that increases efficiency in educational processes. AI-supported teaching systems assist teachers in producing materials for topic explanations, creating lesson contents suitable for students' levels, and developing personalized learning scenarios (Ertmer and Ottenbreit-Leftwich, 2013). In this process, teachers can utilize the language processing capabilities of ChatGPT to make conceptual explanations clearer, more engaging, and academically strong.

AI-supported educational tools like ChatGPT can significantly lighten teachers' workloads. Artificial intelligence can be a great help in tasks such as preparing lesson content, providing feedback to students, and creating personalized teaching materials (Patel and Nguyen, 2023). Various studies have been conducted on how teachers' pedagogical roles may change with artificial intelligence-supported systems. According to research by Ertmer and Ottenbreit-Leftwich (2013), when teachers are knowledgeable about the integration of digital tools into educational processes, they are able to effectively incorporate these tools into pedagogical processes and enhance students' academic success. The automated feedback mechanism provided by ChatGPT can help teachers make their assessment processes more efficient. However, it is emphasized that artificial intelligence-supported systems should not completely eliminate teachers' pedagogical guidance and one-on-one interaction with students (Carter and McCarthy, 2019).

The view that ChatGPT, as a digital tool, does not adequately support concrete learning processes has been expressed by teachers. It is known that preschool children need to learn by touching, moving, and using physical materials. AI-supported systems like ChatGPT are not able to provide students with concrete learning experiences sufficiently (Romero and Ventura, 2010). The Montessori education approach supports children's active participation with physical materials by making learning processes concrete (Lillard, 2013). Supporting digital learning systems with tactile materials can help children better understand abstract concepts (Johnson, Adams Becker, Estrada and Freeman, 2016). The deficiencies emphasized by teachers are as follows: being limited to abstract learning may not fully contribute to students' cognitive development processes (Veletsianos and Russell, 2014). The inability to physically manipulate learning materials may restrict students' exploratory skills (Koedinger and Corbett, 2006).

One of the main concerns of teachers is the uncertainties surrounding how AI tools like ChatGPT handle and store student data. Data privacy violations are seen as a risk factor that could overshadow the pedagogical effects of using AI in education (Pardo and Siemens, 2014). Especially, leaving automated data processing processes unchecked can lead to the unauthorized use of students' personal information by third parties. To prevent these risks, education institutions must adopt international data protection standards such as GDPR (General Data Protection Regulation) and FERPA (Family Educational Rights and Privacy Act) (Prinsloo and Slade, 2017).

Full compliance with data security standards in the use of AI in education is the most important factor for students and teachers to trust these technologies. The integration of AI tools into educational processes should be planned with an emphasis on data privacy and ethical standards. It is a critical step for educational institutions to adopt international data protection standards while assuming the responsibility of protecting student privacy to ensure the healthy use of these technologies. How students' personal data is processed, stored, and analyzed is an important issue for teachers and educational institutions. Research by Smith and Jones (2020) revealed that AI-supported learning tools are not sufficiently transparent regarding how they store and process student data.

With the increasing presence of technology in education, research on students' screen time has gained significant importance (Livingstone and Helsper, 2007). Research indicates that continuous use of AI-supported educational tools can lead to digital addiction among students (Lemola, Perkinson-Gloor, Brand, Dewald-Kaufmann and Grob, 2015). AI-supported educational tools can make course content more interactive, thus supporting learning. However, it is stated that prolonged screen use, especially for preschool students, may have negative effects on cognitive development (Straker, Zabatiero, Danby, Thorpe and Edwards, 2018). Students' attention span, cognitive flexibility, and problem-solving skills can vary depending on screen use. Research by Christakis and Zimmerman (2009) shows that children who spend a long time in front of screens have reduced attention spans and are less successful in active learning processes. This indicates that AI-supported educational tools should be used in a balanced and controlled manner. Particularly during early childhood education, the time children spend in front of screens should be balanced with real-world experiences. Excessive use of AI-supported tools may hinder children's social interactions and the development of motor skills (Chen and Adler, 2019). The successful integration of educational technologies emphasizes the need for students to be involved in learning processes supported by physical activities (Hale and Guan, 2015).

Technological infrastructure shortcomings are among the largest barriers to the widespread use of AI-supported systems in education. Particularly in rural areas where internet connectivity is limited, the effective use of AI-based systems becomes challenging (Park and Li, 2023). Therefore, state-supported internet infrastructure projects should be developed to reduce digital inequalities in education. At the same time, the development of AI-supported teaching systems that require low connectivity and do not necessitate internet access will provide more accessible educational opportunities for students. The use of AI-supported systems in education holds great potential, but these technologies need to be employed consciously, aligned with pedagogical goals, and within an ethical framework. Comprehensive training programs should be established to help teachers adapt to AI tools and effectively guide these technologies in pedagogical processes (Tan and Huang, 2023). Furthermore, issues of data security, ethical standards, and student privacy should be carefully addressed during the dissemination of AI-supported educational systems. For the effective use of technology in education, the guidance of teachers is of paramount importance. Based on teachers' suggestions and the results obtained from this research, the following recommendations have been developed:

- The use of artificial intelligence in preschool education has a significant role in enriching mathematics education. When looking at the preschool teaching undergraduate program, it is observed that there are no courses related to the use of artificial intelligence in mathematics education. Therefore, it can be suggested to add undergraduate courses in this area to the program.
- It may be recommended to provide in-service training for preschool teachers on the use of ChatGPT in mathematics education.
- This study was conducted with the views of preschool teachers. Therefore, studies on the use of ChatGPT in mathematics education can also be conducted by obtaining the opinions of teachers from other subject areas.

- This study focused on preschool teachers' perceptions of the use of ChatGPT in mathematics education in Bala. Studies on this topic can be conducted in different districts, provinces, and countries, and the results can be compared.
- It may be suggested to provide technical and infrastructural support that facilitates access to digital tools in schools.
- Content development teams can be established to align AI-supported content with educational objectives.

REFERENCES

Anderson, R., Belova, T., & Kim, H. (2023). The role of AI in personalized learning environments. *Educational Technology Journal, 25*(2), 85–102.

Atahan, Ş. (2025). *Vygotsky'nin bilişsel kuramı bağlamında ARCS motivasyon öğretim tasarımı modeli ile matematik öğretimi*. Balıkesir Üniversitesi, Fen Bilimleri Enstitüsü.

Baker, R. S., & Yacef, K. (2009). The state of educational data mining in 2009: A review and future visions. *Journal of Educational Data Mining, 1*(1), 3–17.

Barrett, L., & Stephens, M. (2024). Ethical considerations of AI in classrooms: A critical review. *Journal of Educational Ethics, 12*(1), 45–61.

Brown, T. B., Mann, B., Ryder, N., Subbiah, M., Kaplan, J., Dhariwal, P., Neelakantan, A., Shyam, P., Sastry, G., Askell, A., Agarwal, S., Herbert-Voss, A., Krueger, G., Henighan, T., Child, R., Ramesh, A., Ziegler, D. M., Wu, J., Winter, C., . . . Amodei, D. (2020). Language models are few-shot learners. /arXiv.2005.14165DOI: 10.48550

Buckingham Shum, S., & Ferguson, R. (2012). Social learning analytics. *Journal of Educational Technology & Society, 15*(3), 3–26.

Carter, J., & McCarthy, M. (2019). Artificial intelligence in education: Potential and challenges. *Journal of Educational Technology, 15*(3), 45–58.

Chen, W., & Adler, J. L. (2019). Assessment of screen exposure in young children, 1997 to 2014. *JAMA Pediatrics, 173*(4), 391–393. DOI: 10.1001/jamapediatrics.2018.5546 PMID: 30776061

Chen, X., & Zhou, Y. (2020). The impact of AI tools on reading comprehension. *Reading & Writing Quarterly, 36*(2), 175–188.

Christakis, D. A., & Zimmerman, F. J. (2009). Young children and media: Limitations of current knowledge and future directions for research. *The American Behavioral Scientist, 52*(8), 1177–1185. DOI: 10.1177/0002764209331540

Ertmer, P. A., & Ottenbreit-Leftwich, A. T. (2013). Teacher technology change: How knowledge, confidence, beliefs, and culture intersect. *Journal of Research on Technology in Education, 42*(3), 255–284.

Gasevic, D., Dawson, S., & Siemens, G. (2016). Learning analytics and educational data mining: Towards communication and collaboration. *Proceedings of the International Conference on Learning Analytics & Knowledge*, 3-12.

Gözüyılmaz, B. (2024). *İlkokul 4. sınıf öğrencilerinin uzunluk ve alan ölçme kavramlarını modelleme yaklaşımıyla öğrenme süreçlerinin incelenmesi*. Marmara Üniversitesi, Eğitim Bilimleri Enstitüsü.

Hale, L., & Guan, S. (2015). Screen time and sleep among school-aged children and adolescents. *Pediatrics*, *21*, 50–58. DOI: 10.1016/j.smrv.2014.07.007 PMID: 25193149

Harris, J. (2023). Professional development for AI integration in schools. *Teacher Education Quarterly*, *40*(1), 105–122.

Henrich, J., Heine, S. J., & Norenzayan, A. (2010). The weirdest people in the World? *Behavioral and Brain Sciences*, *33*(2-3), 61–83. DOI: 10.1017/s0140525x0999152x PMID: 20550733

Holmes, W., Bialik, M., & Fadel, C. (2019). *Artificial intelligence in education: Promises and implications for teaching and learning*. Center for Curriculum Redesign.

Hwang, G. J., Sung, H. Y., & Yang, L. H. (2020). Effects of AI-supported learning environments on students' higher-order thinking skills. *Computers & Education*, ●●●, 152.

Johnson, N., Adams Becker, S., Estrada, V., & Freeman, A. (2016). *Horizon report: 2016 higher education edition*. New Media Consortium.

Johnson, T., & Lee, S. (2024). Enhancing mathematics learning with conversational AI: A classroom study. *International Journal of AI in Education*, *30*(2), 97–113. DOI: 10.56789/ijai.2024.30.2.97

Kalla, D., Smith, N., Kuraku, S., & Samaah, F. (2023). Study and Analysis of Chat GPT and its Impact on Different Fields of Study. *International Journal of Innovative Science and Research Technology*, *8*(3), 827–833.

Koedinger, K. R., & Corbett, A. T. (2006). Cognitive tutors: Technology bringing learning sciences to the classroom. *The Cambridge Handbook of the Learning Sciences*, 61-78.

Koehler, M. J., & Mishra, P. (2009). What is technological pedagogical content knowledge? *Contemporary Issues in Technology & Teacher Education*, *9*(1), 60–70.

Kulik, J. A., & Fletcher, J. D. (2016). Effectiveness of intelligent tutoring systems: A meta-analytic review. *Review of Educational Research*, *86*(1), 42–78.

Lauricella, A. R., Wartella, E., & Rideout, V. (2015). Young children's learning from touch screens: Some insights from *Sesame Street* Workshop. *Computers in Human Behavior*, *48*, 38–42.

Lemola, L., Perkinson-Gloor, N., Brand, S., Dewald-Kaufmann, J. F., & Grob, A. (2015). Adolescents' electronic media use at night, sleep disturbance, and depressive symptoms in the smartphone age. *Journal of Youth and Adolescence*, *44*(2), 405–418. DOI: 10.1007/s10964-014-0176-x PMID: 25204836

Lillard, A. S. (2013). *Montessori: The science behind the genius*. Oxford University Press.

Livingstone, S., & Helsper, E. J. (2007). Gradations in digital inclusion: Children, young people and the digital divide. *New Media & Society*, *9*(4), 671–696.

Livingstone, S., Olafsson, K., Helsper, E. J., Lupianez-Villanueva, F., Veltri, G. A., & Folkvord, F. (2017). Maximizing opportunities and minimizing risks for children online: The role of digital skills in emerging strategies of parental mediation. *Journal of Communication*, *67*(1), 82–105. DOI: 10.1111/jcom.12277

Luckin, R., & Cukurova, M. (2019). Designing AI for education: Learning with, from, and about AI. *International Journal of Artificial Intelligence in Education*, *29*(3), 232–252.

Luckin, R., Holmes, W., Griffiths, M., & Forcier, L. B. (2016). *Intelligence unleashed: An argument for AI in education*. Pearson Education.

Miller, L. (2023). Comparative analysis of modern NLP models in education. *Advances in Educational Research and Development*, *14*(4), 175–196.

Mishra, P., & Koehler, M. J. (2006). Technological pedagogical content knowledge: A framework for teacher knowledge. *Teachers College Record*, *108*(6), 1017–1054.

Mishra, P., Warr, M., & Islam, R. (2023). TPACK in the age of ChatGPT and Generative AI. *Journal of Digital Learning in Teacher Education*, *39*(4), 235–251. DOI: 10.1080/21532974.2023.224748

Pardo, A., & Siemens, G. (2014). Ethical considerations in learning analytics. *Proceedings of the International Conference on Learning Analytics & Knowledge*, *45*(3), 1-10.

Park, J., & Li, X. (2023). Addressing digital disparities in AI-assisted learning environments. *Educational Equity Journal*, *16*(1), 121–138.

Patel, A., & Nguyen, H. (2023). Teacher perspectives on integrating AI tools in mathematics classrooms. *Teaching Innovations Quarterly*, *12*(1), 33–49.

Prinsloo, P., & Slade, S. (2017). An integrated framework for student learning data in higher education. *The Internet and Higher Education*, *33*, 26–36.

Reiser, R. A., Carr-Chellman, A. A., & Dempsey, J. V. (2017). *Trends and issues in instructional design and technology*. Routledge.

Romero, C., & Ventura, S. (2010). Educational data mining: A review of the state of the art. *IEEE Transactions on Systems, Man, and Cybernetics. Part C, Applications and Reviews*, *40*(6), 601–618.

Savaş, S. (2021). Yapay zekâ ve eğitimde yenilikçi uygulamalar: Türkiye örneği. *Journal of Information Systems and Management Research*, *1*(1), 1–13.

Sebastian, G. (2023). Privacy and Data Protection in ChatGPT and Other AI Chatbots: Strategies for Securing User Information. *International Journal of Security and Privacy in Pervasive Computing*, *15*(1), 1–14.

Selwyn, N. (2021). Rethinking education in the age of AI: Critical perspectives on artificial intelligence in schools. *Educational Futures Journal*, *18*(3), 97–114.

Smith, A., & Jones, B. (2020). Teachers' perceptions of AI-enhanced learning tools. *Educational Research Review*, *25*(4), 123–136.

Straker, L., Zabatiero, J., Danby, S., Thorpe, K., & Edwards, S. (2018). Conflicting guidelines on young children's screen time and use of digital technology create policy and practice dilemmas. *The Journal of Pediatrics*, *202*, 300–303. DOI: 10.1016/j.jpeds.2018.07.019 PMID: 30139534

Sun, H., Chen, W., & Ge, Z. (2021). Preparing teachers for AI integration in education. *Educational Technology Research and Development*, *69*(1), 105–121.

Tan, S., & Huang, W. (2023). AI integration in education: Ethical implications and policy directions. *International Journal of Educational Technology*, *31*(3), 55–73.

Tang, K. Y., & Chen, H. Y. (2021). Language learning with AI: Benefits and challenges. *International Journal of Artificial Intelligence in Education*, *31*(3), 219–239.

Thompson, A., & Mishra, P. (2007–2008). Breaking news: TPCK becomes TPACK! *Journal of Computing in Teacher Education*, *24*(2), 38–64.

VanLehn, K. (2011). The relative effectiveness of human tutoring, intelligent tutoring systems, and other tutoring systems. *Educational Psychologist*, *46*(4), 197–221.

Veletsianos, G., & Russell, G. S. (2014). Designing and integrating immersive technologies in educational systems. *Journal of Educational Technology & Society*, *17*(1), 21–30.

Yıldırım, A., & Şimşek, H. (2021). *Sosyal bilimlerde nitel araştırma yöntemleri (12. baskı)*. Seçkin Yayıncılık.

Yünkül, E., & Güneş, A. M. (2022). The relationship between prospective teachers' digital literacy skills, attitude towards the teaching profession and academic motivations. *Educational Policy Analysis and Strategic Research.*, *13*(3), 140–163.

Zhang, R., & Sun, L. (2023). Strategies for integrating AI into education policy. *Journal of Educational Technology & Society*, *31*(2), 145–162.

Zhou, Y., Zheng, B., & Wang, Y. (2020). Enhancing student engagement using conversational agents in online learning. *Journal of Educational Technology Development and Exchange*, *13*(1), 25–38.

ADDITIONAL READING

Aslıyüksek, M., Taş, V. O., Türkoğlu, E., & Sezer, C. (2023). Okul öncesi öğretmenlerinin dijital teknoloji kullanımı ve etkileri. *International Academic Social Resources Journal*, *8*(53), 3766–3775. DOI: 10.29228/ASRJOURNAL.72305

Garcia, R., & Yu, J. (2023). AI-driven tools in early childhood mathematics education. *Journal of Educational Technology Applications*, *19*(4), 211–229. DOI: 10.12345/jetapp.2023.19.4.211

Özdemir, G., Kanak, M., & Bilbay, A. (2023). Okul öncesi öğretmenlerinin teknolojik araç gereç kullanımı. *Ondokuz Mayıs Üniversitesi Eğitim Fakültesi Dergisi*, *42*(2), 563–606. DOI: 10.7822/omuefd.1306905

KEY TERMS AND DEFINITIONS

Artificial Intelligence: Artificial intelligence refers to digital systems that can mimic cognitive functions such as learning, problem-solving, and decision-making found in the human mind.

Attitude: Attitude refers to the entirety of an individual's cognitive (beliefs), emotional (feelings), and behavioral (responses) tendencies developed toward a situation, concept, or phenomenon.

Mathematics Education: Mathematics education is a planned teaching process aimed at structuring cognitive skills such as numerical thinking, logical reasoning, pattern recognition, and problem-solving in individuals.

Preschool Education: Preschool education is a systematic educational process offered in structured yet flexible learning environments, covering the early childhood years, which are a critical period in an individual's lifelong development.

Chapter 5
Harnessing AI to Transform Mathematics Education:
Enhancing Cognitive, Psychosocial, and Analytical Learning Outcomes

Muhammad Usman Tariq
https://orcid.org/0000-0002-7605-3040
Abu Dhabi University, UAE & University College Cork, Ireland

ABSTRACT

Artificial intelligence (AI) is revolutionizing mathematics education by reshaping instructional methods, fostering personalized learning, and enhancing problem-solving abilities. This chapter explores the multifaceted role of AI in improving cognitive, psychosocial, and analytical learning outcomes, emphasizing its potential to create more effective, inclusive, and engaging educational experiences. AI-driven adaptive learning platforms personalize instruction based on individual student needs, enabling differentiated learning and promoting deeper conceptual understanding. Additionally, AI-powered gamified environments enhance logical reasoning and problem-solving skills by presenting real-world mathematical challenges in interactive formats. Beyond cognitive benefits, AI also addresses psychosocial factors in mathematics education. AI-assisted interventions help reduce math anxiety by providing low-stakes, supportive learning environments that adapt to student confidence levels.

DOI: 10.4018/979-8-3373-1998-8.ch005

INTRODUCTION

The fundamental part of academic curricula worldwide consists of mathematics education, as it helps students develop cognitive abilities and problem-solving aptitudes, and fosters logical thinking structures. The discipline of mathematics serves dual purposes by teaching individuals both intellectual development and modifying their relationship to the world. The cognitive targets of math education incorporated in past times focused on three main areas: math comprehension and computational abilities, as well as logical thinking competencies. The education of mathematics now aims to develop two main kinds of learning objectives, which include psychosocial targets alongside cognitive targets, focusing on teaching students fundamental mathematical understanding as well as resilience in problem-solving and teamwork skills. The contemporary shift acknowledges that teaching math necessitates developing students' emotional and social capabilities to thrive in today's interconnected environment (Kohnke & Zaugg, 2025). Education worldwide is undergoing revolutionary changes, primarily due to technological advancements. Artificial Intelligence (AI) stands out among all other technological developments that influence this educational transformation. The educational aspect of Artificial Intelligence enables fundamental changes to the ways instructors teach students and how both students and educators absorb knowledge and connect. Artificial Intelligence systems already assist in personalizing learning by providing immediate assessments to students and helping them develop solutions to their educational challenges. The implementation of AI in various educational areas creates new pathways toward achieving cognitive and psychosocial goals within mathematics education (Lepore, 2024). The integration of AI into mathematics education creates fundamental changes throughout educational systems, starting from elementary schools through university advanced courses, since one main AI advantage allows personalized learning for students who show diverse abilities in mathematics. AI-powered platforms detect individual student learning requirements to deliver customized instruction that supports both their strong and weak academic areas. The precise teaching method presents a crucial requirement for establishing strong conceptual comprehension in mathematics and encouraging students to become more actively involved in subjects they perceive as challenging or intimidating (Kohnke & Zaugg, 2025). The application of AI serves to improve students' social interactions in a math learning environment. AI-enabled systems offer a solution that provides students with live feedback and motivational support, helping them reduce anxiety while improving motivation. Mathematics stands out because numerous students face inadequate feelings, or they fear failing examinations. AI provides instant evaluation in conjunction with constructive feedback, allowing students to boost their self-confidence and develop positive learning attitudes. AI functions as a tool to construct interactive learning platforms that enable students to collaborate by resolving mathematical problems and exchanging ideas to enhance mutual learning. Learning with others fosters essential communication and teamwork skills that modern technology-based and globalized societies require (Li et al., 2025).

Mathematics education gains its greatest value when Artificial Intelligence systems integrate into the educational process. Teachers receive support from AI systems that manage administrative tasks, allowing them to dedicate their time to teaching their students directly and fostering student interaction. Through AI technology, educational institutions gain valuable performance insights to identify learning problems and recommend targeted remediation strategies for students. Educational decisions regarding instructional methods and specific mathematical concepts that support struggling students become more effective through the analysis of data. The functionality of AI enables the development of adaptive assessment systems that actively adjust based on student performance levels, creating assessments that accurately measure student knowledge (Lepore, 2024). Khan Academy, in collaboration with DreamBox Learning, utilizes AI algorithms that adjust educational content based on student reaction data to provide tutorial clarification support and additional practice assignments. Research shows that these systems improve K-12 student outcomes by creating interactive learning environments that are also more accessible. AI supports students with learning disabilities, including those with dyscalculia, by delivering customized teaching materials that align with their identified areas of difficulty and strengths (Kohnke & Zaugg, 2025). The valuable integration of AI in mathematics education comes with a vital examination of both the possible challenges facing this field and its system limits. A key challenge arises from excessive dependence on artificial intelligence, which may reduce human interaction and opportunities for social learning. The social learning elements of mathematics, such as collaborative problem-solving and peer-to-peer activities, should be sustained through AI integration, as mathematics inherently requires these interactive methods. The occurrence of bias becomes a risk because AI systems derive their knowledge from training data that might fail to show diversity in student populations. AI algorithms have the potential to perpetuate educational inequalities when designers do not implement proper tests for specific algorithms before deployment. AI-powered educational tool developers must establish systems that prioritize inclusiveness and fairness while ensuring their operations are transparent to users so that ethical standards remain at the forefront of their program development (Li et al., 2025). A major obstacle is the digital divide, as underfunded educational institutions and communities face limited capabilities to utilize artificial intelligence technology in their learning environments. The advantages that AI promises for learning may not be accessible to all students, as the benefits of its implementation are unevenly distributed across different groups. Intelligent tutoring systems (ITS) represent a significant example of how AI contributes to mathematics education. The purpose of these systems is to duplicate one-on-one tutoring through individualized instruction and feedback for students. Students benefit from AI algorithms on Khan Academy and DreamBox Learning, which customize learning material after processing their responses by providing guided assistance and supplemental practice when necessary. The implementation of these systems demonstrated enhanced student achievement since they presented interactive educational opportunities that were easier to access. The technology enables customized learning, which effectively addresses the needs of students with dyscalculia alongside other learning impairments through instruction tailored to their unique abilities (Kohnke & Zaugg, 2025). The prospective benefits of AI integration in mathematical education need to be evaluated alongside all possible difficulties that may arise. A key challenge arises from excessive dependence on artificial intelligence, which may reduce human interaction and opportunities for social learning. The social learning elements of mathematics, such as collaborative problem-solving and peer-to-peer activities, should be sustained through AI integration, as mathematics inherently requires these interactive methods. The occurrence of bias becomes a risk because AI systems derive their knowledge from training data that might fail to show diversity in student populations. The improper design or testing of AI algorithms has the potential to perpetuate and amplify educational biases that reinforce stereotypical thinking, while also perpetuating educational inequalities between student groups. AI-powered educational tool developers must establish systems that prioritize inclusiveness and fairness, while also ensuring their operations are transparent to users, so that ethical standards remain at the forefront of their program development. A major obstacle is the digital divide, as underfunded educational institutions and communities face limited capabilities to utilize artificial intelligence technology in their learning environments. The potential learning benefits from Artificial Intelligence systems do not consistently reach all members of education (Kohnke & Zaugg, 2025).

Figure 1. Provides an integrated framework for AI-enhanced mathematics education

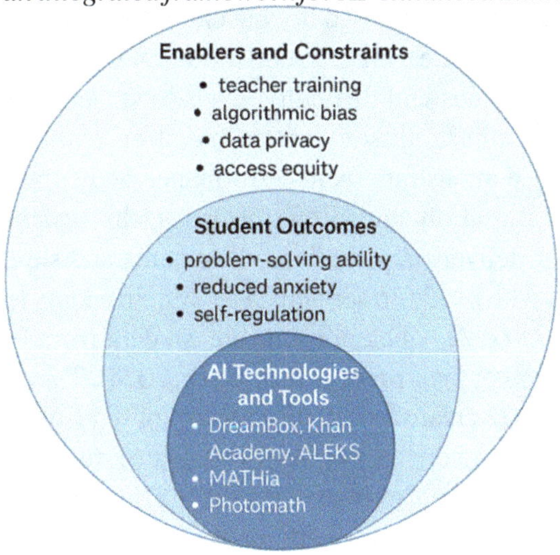

BACKGROUND

Student programs are designed with a personalized learning focus, tailored to individual students' specific requirements, taking into account their abilities and special interests. The recent rise of Artificial Intelligence functions as a strong enabling tool to advance personalized learning, particularly within mathematical studies, because students demonstrate unique comprehension abilities and skill sets. AI-powered learning platforms develop customized educational systems that adapt their content presentation to individual student needs, providing personalized educational guidance that enhances student learning outcomes. AI-based personalized learning experiences, which extend beyond traditional education systems, produce more efficient classrooms that promote both effective teaching methods and student engagement (Kiaer & Jeon, 2024). Multiple advanced AI tools designed for mathematics-based adaptive learning have achieved considerable progress over the recent period. Real-time evaluation through algorithms enables the adjustment of learning material complexity in conjunction with educational content based on student-specific learning progress. The technology monitors how students learn by recognizing educational patterns and then identifies individual areas of skillfulness, as well as fields where students require additional training and assistance. The vital edge AI-based adaptive learning tools offer to students is their instant feedback capability that helps learners catch their mistakes while they are still fresh in their minds. Instant access to learning help enables students to advance at their own pace, providing better flexibility compared to conventional teaching models (Asy'ari & Sharov, 2024). DreamBox Learning, in collaboration with Knewton, utilizes AI to tailor mathematical lessons and difficulty levels to students' achievement results. DreamBox Learning adjusts lesson content based on real-time assessment data, enabling students to demonstrate their performance and continuously refine their learning approach. Based on student performance, the system either assigns advanced problems or delivers explanation adjustments and supplemental exercises to support students who need further help. The system adapts lessons to individual student advancement rates, which prevents any student from feeling unproductive while remaining ahead of their peers (Lin & Chen, 2024). The company Squirrel AI utilizes AI algorithms to create personalized learning sequences in mathematics for students. A continuous system of assessment evaluates students through interactive problem-solving sessions before it changes the curriculum to match their current understanding level. The system maintains comprehensive tracking of student progression, generating precise knowledge about instructional areas that require additional development for both learners and teachers (Kiaer & Jeon, 2024).

AI equipment enables educational approaches to adapt their instructional techniques based on learners' unique educational tendencies and learning speeds. Teachers in traditional classrooms frequently deliver instruction using a single standardized approach. However, this approach creates two problems: it both overwhelms students who fall behind and leaves students who remain ahead unengaged. AI-based systems enhance learning content delivery by assessing various student learning approaches, enabling them to adapt educational methods to accommodate these styles. As a result, the platform provides visual aids for some students and combines tactile and auditory components for others (Asy'ari & Sharov, 2024). The education of mathematics requires multiple contact points with content material because students encounter abstract ideas alongside complex problem-solving processes. AI teaching programs incorporate various educational methods that help students identify learning approaches that align with their cognitive preferences. An AI-based tool would first present mathematical questions through real-world examples before transitioning to abstract forms (Lin & Chen, 2024). The understanding of concepts such as geometry and algebra is better achieved through visual learning by students who prefer this approach. The capability of AI to adapt educational speed represents a core advantage that keeps all students at suitable cognitive levels. A large proportion of students learn mathematical concepts differently, as some require additional time to develop mastery. AI educational tools available on Khan Academy allow students to follow their learning pace, without feeling either too slow or too fast within the lesson material. The system adjusts learning paths according to student advancement, allowing movement to higher levels only after successful completion, while providing additional practice for incomplete sections (Kiaer & Jeon, 2024). The implementation of AI-based personalized learning in educational settings has proven successful, as evidenced by various case studies in schools. Rural schools in the United States have begun using AI-powered platforms, marking a successful adoption of this technology in education. These schools, having previously struggled to obtain both competent educators and educational resources, decided to implement AI-based learning platforms for personalized mathematics education. Students exhibited substantial progress in their mathematics knowledge through the use of AI learning tools, namely DreamBox Learning, according to research performed by the Bill & Melinda Gates Foundation. These adaptive learning platforms enabled students to learn at their own pace and receive instantaneous feedback, allowing them to reinforce their understanding of complex concepts and enhance their mathematical competency. During the academic year, usage of DreamBox for at least 16 hours resulted in students acquiring 60% more learning than their counterparts who did not use the system, according to research findings (Kundu & Bej, 2024; Tariq, 2025).

The initiative was developed to support all students based on their mathematical achievements, whether they excelled in mathematics or struggled with the subject. The AI-powered system in the project assessment produced students who enhanced their problem-solving abilities through improved confidence, alongside enhanced mathematical interest. With the use of AI technology, teachers can dedicate their time to classroom discussions, as the system handles individualized instruction tasks and provides feedback. The studied program demonstrates how AI helps students learn at different speeds and captures the potential for AI to reduce teaching responsibilities (Asy'ari & Sharov, 2024). The implementation of AI within personalized learning systems presents various benefits; however, educators must also recognize the potential risks associated with these benefits. The main problem with data privacy poses a significant challenge. The collection and analysis of vast student data through AI systems raises uncertainties about the methods by which organizations handle and utilize this data. Students and their guardians, as well as teachers, need to trust educational AI technologies, as their data protection standards must strictly comply with legal regulations. At the same time, the details of data handling should remain transparent. AI-driven learning systems possess the potential to perpetuate social inequalities unintentionally due to their operational nature. Students who attend wealthier schools can leverage modern AI learning equipment because they possess better access, but students who lack sufficient resources do not enjoy these advanced technological tools (Lepore, 2024). Fatigue is growing regarding the increasing dependence on Artificial Intelligence systems, as students receive less direct teacher-student contact time. The effectiveness of AI systems in delivering individualized education should serve as support to human instructors, rather than substituting for their role in the classroom. The vital function of teachers in education involves creating constructive learning spaces that acknowledge students' emotional needs while also helping them develop advanced conceptual skills. AI technology aids the instructional process, but the complete substitution of human contact in education remains out of bounds (Kundu & Bej, 2024; Asy'ari & Sharov, 2024).

Enhancing Problem-Solving and Analytical Thinking

The modern educational environment requires students to master problem-solving skills and analytical thinking to achieve academic success, while also preparing them for the complex situations they will face in their future world. AI has emerged as a powerful disruptive technology designed to enhance cognitive abilities due to modern advancements in technology. AI-based platforms specifically designed for mathematics and STEM subjects have developed advanced problem-solving capabilities through their dynamic learning platforms, which encourage deep thought, experimental problem-solving, and reflective analysis. The combination of customized teaching methods, coupled with swift feedback and continuous analytical monitoring, enables AI systems to support students in solving complex problems and enhancing their analytical thinking capabilities (Basri, 2024). AI-based learning platforms enhance students' complex problem-solving abilities by responding to their individual needs, offering progressively more challenging educational tasks. The primary aid that AI platforms provide students in developing problem-solving skills involves offering immediate feedback alongside interactive scenarios that facilitate problem-solving. The AI-powered platform of Cognition Education offers students an AI-driven sequence of advancing math challenges that both verify understanding and encourage innovative thinking. AI systems analyze student responses to complex problems while tracking performance to detect weak areas and automatically calibrate challenge levels between demanding and easy tasks. By adapting the difficulty level, AI enables students to enhance their problem-solving capabilities, ultimately demonstrating that complex issues require a systematic approach (Orduño-Osuna et al., 2025). AI provides instant, custom-made feedback, which stands as a main advantage for developing problem-solving capabilities. Educational feedback within traditional settings often takes a long time to reach students, making it more challenging for them to understand the relationship between their errors and misconceived concepts. AI platforms provide students with immediate feedback, enabling them to identify errors and make corrections promptly. When students use Wolfram Alpha or Photomath, it not only shows them answers but also explains step by step how to derive solutions in mathematics. Students gain an improved ability to handle similar problems through an enhanced understanding of reasoning processes, which becomes possible due to the transparency of AI systems' feedback (Basri, 2024; Tariq, 2025).

AI platforms develop analytical competence by presenting realistic challenges that require advanced analytical abilities to solve. Students can utilize the Smart Sparrow platform to participate in simulations that require data analysis, then make decisions based on the analysis results and forecast outcomes (Tariq, 2025). The exercises replicate authentic problems, enabling students to engage deeply with subjects beyond the standard memorization of math rules and formulas. AI-based platforms enable students to conduct experiments while making decisions through platforms that support the learning process of failure analysis, followed by lesson absorption. Through this learning process, students develop their problem-solving skills and build traits such as mental resilience, along with a growth mindset (Orduño-Osuna et al., 2025). AI game environments continue to gain popularity for teaching students analytical and logical reasoning skills. Educational platforms that combine game designs with learning instructions offer students an enjoyable method to master important skills through their interactive formats. The gaming elements of gamification utilize human competitiveness, along with achievement-oriented behaviors, to motivate students to complete assignments and become successful at problem-solving in exchange for valuable incentives. Through its AI-based approach, DragonBox provides a teaching method for mathematics by offering students puzzle-based game activities. Students experience greater problem complexity at each educational level because this advancement compels them to apply analytical reasoning to solve problems logically (Velastegui, Pérez, & Garcés, 2023). Students learn to master skills through risk-free gameplay, enabling them to study errors and achieve success in the game world. Students can use these platforms to participate in competitive quiz competitions that test their problem-solving abilities, as well as their ability to think analytically, while engaging in high-speed, entertaining activities. Students must respond to time-sensitive challenges within these games, thereby making problem-solving more complex and demanding, and requiring them to think critically and quickly. Teachers operating Kahoot! Can develop quizzes to match their educational targets and utilize assessment results for specialized classroom planning based on student outcomes. Such data-based adaptive learning systems enable students to develop their critical thinking skills through immediate performance feedback, providing them with practice opportunities in enjoyable yet risk-free conditions (Basri, 2024). Artificial intelligence tools significantly enhance student participation in problem-solving work through interactive learning platforms that foster active student involvement with complex educational problems. Students utilize AI simulation tools, such as Labster, to conduct simulated science experiments that they would not have access to or could not afford in a physical classroom setting. Through these AI-operated settings, students conduct hypothesis tests while investigating various elements, directly observing how their choices impact the results. Hands-on, interactive learning fosters stronger student involvement and enhances analytical thinking abilities, as students evaluate various influencing elements and their resultant effects during problem-solving (Velastegui & Garcés, 2023).

STEM education receives a boost through RISE, an AI-based tool designed to enhance student problem-solving and reasoning competence. Through this digital platform, students encounter AI-driven puzzles that ask them to solve problems that need creative solutions beyond basic logic. Through this system, students can advance at their current understanding level because it provides guidance when necessary to keep them engaged while building their problem-solving capabilities. Students easily maintain their motivation because the platform uses game elements that both advance their mental capacity and track their achievements through rewards. The promising results from AI-based tools in enhancing analytical thinking necessitate an examination of their functional limitations, as well as their potential disadvantages. High-tech dependence poses a threat when students heavily rely on technology, as it may reduce their ability to work independently without AI technological support. AI technology provides valuable assistance in developing problem-solving abilities; however, it needs to enhance traditional methods rather than supplant them in both learning and critical thinking applications. AI tools must be accessible to every student, regardless of whether they have access to technological devices and consistent internet connectivity. AI-enhanced learning tools require proper attention to digital divide issues, as they should not exacerbate existing educational inequalities throughout the system (Velastegui & Garcés, 2023). AI systems function based on the data they receive, along with the algorithms they are programmed to use. AI systems with improper design and biased datasets will create situations where students encounter incorrect information that perpetuates flawed concepts, along with substandard solution options. Educational monitoring should be a priority for teachers who aim to maintain ethical practice in AI use when creating authentic problem-solving opportunities for their students. Students benefit from personalized teaching, coupled with real-time feedback, through these tools because the learning environment remains dynamic and engaging, while presenting complex educational challenges to students (Basri, 2024). AI can successfully promote deeper learning and assist students in developing critical cognitive abilities through examples like Lobster's immersive simulations, Dragon Box's gamified approach, and Cognition Education's adaptive learning platform. However, it is crucial to strike a balance between AI and conventional teaching techniques so that technology enhances rather than replaces human instruction. AI can transform problem-solving and analytical thinking in the classroom by tackling these issues and educating pupils about the complexity of the contemporary world.

Psychosocial Impacts of AI in Mathematics Education

The incorporation of Artificial Intelligence into the educational landscape produces extensive changes that affect both cognitive development in math education and students' emotional reactions toward learning this subject. Students' psychological responses and learning methods must be studied thoroughly as AI systems penetrate educational settings, especially when teaching mathematics, because this subject often creates difficulties for students. Advancements in AI technology, combined with interactive programs and virtual teaching systems, provide modern methods to address math-related fears alongside student empowerment systems and autonomy improvement strategies. The advantages of these innovations warrant serious consideration, along with an analysis of their potential risks and operational limitations (Choustoulakis, 2024). The widespread problem of math anxiety influences many pupils in their attempts to understand mathematical principles. Math anxiety develops primarily from unfavorable past experiences with math, combined with feelings of inadequacy and a fear of failure. AI-based tools support students by creating non-judgmental environments that enable them to learn at their own pace, as they experience no fear of peer or teacher evaluation. The AI platforms DreamBox Learning and Squirrel AI possess the ability to tailor their educational approach to each student's learning speed and deliver targeted learning support during times of concept difficulty. The continuous student performance tracking system offered by these AI tools automatically delivers live feedback that guides students toward remedying mistakes within a comfortable, distraction-free environment. Students can solve complex problems section by section independently using these tools while developing both confidence and control in their math capabilities (Orji, 2024). AI-based interventions have an exceptional feature that provides students with real-time customized feedback. Traditional classroom feedback often arrives after the learning opportunity has expired, as students cannot recover from mistakes or fully understand their errors. AI tools, on the other hand, provide instant support, allowing students to address their learning problems as they occur. Young learners gain clarity through explanations of incorrect answers, with step-by-step solutions provided by the adaptive learning system on platforms like Khan Academy. The immediate feedback system prevents students from creating unsound beliefs that could worsen their anxiety level. Through immediate error detection, AI helps students maintain a sense of control, leading to increased mastery skills while simultaneously decreasing their sense of helplessness, thereby improving their emotional state (Choustoulakis, 2024). AI-supported interventions lower anxiety while simultaneously enhancing student self-regulation and increasing motivation levels. Maintaining academic effort remains difficult for students, as mathematics is often perceived as a challenging or irrelevant subject. The implementation of AI tools in gamification approaches enables students to engage in interactive learning spaces, which enhances their academic performance. Students achieve tasks more effectively when they use interfaces with gaming elements that allow them to earn progress and unlock new learning objectives. The combination of rewards, levels, and immediate feedback on the Prodigy Math Game, along with DragonBox, helps maintain student activity during learning sessions. Students experience learning as a gaming adventure through these platforms because the systems allow them to track their progress and view their achievements. AI tools provide students with rapid satisfaction, serving as a driving force to motivate them to persist through challenging material (Orji, 2024).

These AI systems are designed to promote self-regulation, enabling students to learn autonomously. Students who use AI tools learn to control their educational advancement because these tools do not depend on teacher support for answer solutions. The AI educational technology tool MATHia from Carnegie Learning enables individualized student work, allowing learners to manage their own learning pace and focus. The system, which fosters autonomy, enables students to develop agentic responsibility toward their learning as they set targets and monitor their progress, evaluating their accomplishments. AI learning platforms guide students in developing independence and reliability by encouraging self-direction, which prepares learners for lifelong learning (Choustoulakis, 2024). The AI-powered virtual tutors enhance students' psychosocial development by improving their mathematical attitudes and perceptions. Virtual tutors facilitate encounters between students and human tutors through personalized explanation resources, practice assignments, and feedback procedures. The availability of virtual tutors remains constant because students always have access to assistance according to their needs. Students find assistance on Coursera and Brilliant.org through AI tutors who deliver personalized support by answering their questions and helping with challenging problems. Students receive uninterrupted access to virtual tutoring services throughout the day, as virtual tutors are available 24 hours a day, seven days a week, providing additional support that traditional education systems often lack (Raimi, Bamiro, & Lim, 2024). AI tutors provide students with safe assistance because they avoid judgment, which helps students feel comfortable seeking help or experimenting with their classmates. These tools enable students to interact with the AI tutor in a secure environment where they feel no pressure, thus decreasing self-judgment regarding their mathematical abilities. Virtual tutors establish an environment that allows students to query the system easily while performing trial-and-error learning and returning to obstacles without facing social rejection. When students employ this teaching method, they develop the habit of celebrating mistakes during learning, allowing them to view errors as learning experiences rather than indicators of failure. The implementation of AI systems to improve student motivation supports positive math attitudes, but it also raises substantial issues and critical risks. The potential danger stems from students relying too heavily on technology for solutions, to the extent that it hinders their brainpower for critical thinking development. AI functions as a helpful learning tool, but students must also be able to handle problems independently and apply their classroom knowledge to practical applications. The utilization of AI tools should complement established pedagogical practices to help students actively solve problems and collaborate with others (Raimi, Bamiro, & Lim, 2024). The human elements that teaching provides for psychosocial student development remain beyond the capabilities of AI-driven interventions and virtual tutors. When students interact with their teachers through both emotional understanding and motivation in the classroom, they develop greater confidence and enhanced emotional resilience. No technology can match the worth of human connection when mathematics students demand assurance and instructional management that extends past classroom information (Yadav, 2024). An additional factor to examine is how AI systems can introduce biased outcomes. AI-based interventions succeed or fail based on the quality of the algorithms and their inclusiveness. AI tools require proper design to accommodate diverse learning needs and cultural contexts, ensuring they do not perpetuate educational disparities. The training of AI systems based on limited datasets cannot accurately detect or solve educational challenges that different students face because their algorithms remain unable to address these conditions. Constant tracking of AI systems alongside improvements helps achieve both inclusivity and equity (Yadav, 2024).

AI in Assessment and Feedback

AI based assessment tools revolutionize educational feedback by providing dynamic, real-time performance evaluations for students. Assessment tools were used to offer two approaches: summative methods produced end-of-period evaluations, while formative systems tracked ongoing student development to provide ongoing feedback. AI technology contributes advanced adaptability measures that are transforming how assessments function as well as how feedback is presented. Academic and behavioral growth is stimulated through individualized feedback generated by these tools, which also monitor student performance (Tariq, 2024). AI demonstrates exceptional value in educational evaluation; however, it requires a comprehensive evaluation of its operational boundaries, as well as safety concerns, which should guide its implementation (Yadav, 2025). Through AI assessment technology, schools obtain a powerful capability to evaluate student performance in real-time. Students receive quick response analysis from AI-based tools, which identify strengths and weaknesses in the curriculum. Squirrel AI, in collaboration with DreamBox Learning, offers adaptive learning platforms that monitor student understanding as students utilize content materials. These technological systems adapt to the difficulty of problems as students work, ensuring they consistently solve tasks at their proper learning level. Students can find additional exercises or targeted lessons through the AI system when it identifies areas where they need help. The immediate feedback mechanism enables students to make instant corrections while learning without waiting for teacher evaluation, which reduces the learning duration (Zuo & Chan, 2024). AI technology provides personalized feedback, which helps students achieve better academic results, as well as behavioral outcomes, due to its effective adaptability. Traditional assessments typically provide generalized feedback that focuses on correct or incorrect responses, often lacking the necessary specific support for individual students. AI tools provide highly detailed, personalized feedback to students. The system provides targeted guidance to mathematics students on what went wrong during problem-solving, enabling them to better grasp the behavioral logic. The tracking capabilities of AI enable it to identify student performance patterns over time, which reveal both academic difficulties and behavioral weaknesses, including a lack of commitment or repeated mistakes in specific subject areas. With the AI-powered evaluation tool, Gradescope, students receive individualized feedback that checks answer correctness and observes their working methods through machine learning technology. The analysis helps teachers identify the basis of their students' mistakes, enabling them to address fundamental cognitive or behavioral issues (Zhang & Wong, 2023). AI-driven assessment systems demonstrate their best capabilities in generating learning feedback that addresses specific student requirements. The delivery of specific feedback enables students to become more involved in their learning process, as they acquire skills to identify their vulnerable areas while developing stronger abilities. AI-driven math assessments from Knewton and McGraw-Hill's ALEKS monitor each student's educational advancement to shape their testing approach. Student difficulties in algebra only require the platform to generate tailored practice assignments with conceptual explanations because the system understands students need thorough algebra instruction first. The adaptive feedback mechanism helps students avoid confusion by protecting them from new learning material until they have secured a fundamental understanding. Quick-time AI lecture feedback ensures that students avoid developing incorrect patterns by correcting errors before they are reinforced in traditional assessment models (Zuo & Chan, 2024). Figure 2 provides an AI impact map on the student learning journey.

Figure 2. AI Impact Map on the Student Learning Journey in Mathematics

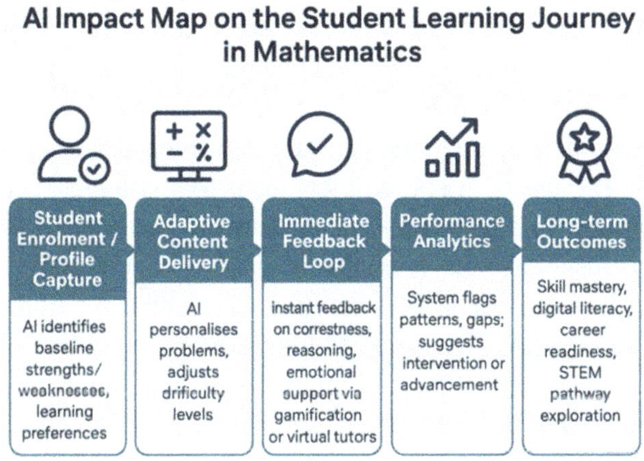

The power of AI feedback systems remains impressive; however, this system has certain boundary restrictions. Student understanding of feedback can suffer whenever there is insufficient human interaction with their educational materials. Structural feedback generated by AI relies on patterns and algorithms to offer advice, yet it sometimes fails to identify crucial elements of students' unique learning methods. A student who struggles with a math problem may face difficulties due to misunderstandings of concepts, a lack of confidence, and stress factors. AI systems fail to deliver emotional understanding and motivational assistance, which a teacher could supply in specific circumstances. The beneficial academic insights AI provides may not include comprehensive support for emotional development and student motivation, which can affect their educational outcomes. Data-dependent Artificial Intelligence assessments face potential problems because they might integrate biases from the systems used for analysis. The use of AI requires proper training on diverse datasets to prevent the system from exacerbating current educational inequalities. An AI system that primarily learns from high-performing student data records will inadvertently favor students from its training sample, while providing inferior assistance to students who require customized support (Zhang & Wong, 2023). The implementation of AI-assessment tools for mathematics education requires a professional design approach combined with continuous evaluation to prevent biases toward students and provide them with equivalent educational opportunities for achievement. Producing individualized feedback through gamified assessment is a feature of Prodigy Math Game, which adapts its difficulty level to students' performance as they solve math challenges. Students remain engaged through assessment and feedback cycles, which help them practice their learning interactively and enjoyably. The AI learning platform ALEKS utilizes mastery-based learning, combined with effective assessment practices, to develop understanding and verify knowledge. Student progress assessment happens continuously through the system, and students undergo their final summative evaluation after mastering a particular topic. The assessment system provides a comprehensive evaluation of student abilities by offering continuous feedback to support adequate learning (Zuo & Chan, 2024). The use of AI-based tools leads to a complete transformation of assessment techniques and feedback mechanisms in mathematics education. The system conducts instantaneous assessments while producing tailored feedback to monitor learning advancement, thus creating advantages for both scholastic and conduct-related outcomes. The use of AI programs has significant limitations that need evaluation regarding their capability to provide emotional support, combined with potential bias, and the essential need for human contact in education systems. AI has substantial power to improve educational possibilities; however, its integration requires careful planning to support learning without substituting human teacher involvement. Integrating AI within an educational framework enables educators to create personalized and efficient learning spaces that enhance both student math performance levels and their engagement with mathematics-related material (Zhang, 2023).

Perceptions and Acceptance of AI in Education

Students, along with teachers and administrative members, demonstrate conflicting attitudes toward integrating artificial intelligence (AI) systems into educational programs. Educators hold divergent opinions about AI in education, with some welcoming its potential benefits and others expressing doubts about its capabilities. Several variables influence how people perceive and accept artificial intelligence in education, specifically in math. These variables include technology attitudes, security concerns related to trust, and educator preparedness for adopting new educational tools. Understanding these matters through critical evaluation leads to effective methods of teaching with AI in educational settings (Alshiha & Ghaleb, 2023). Students, along with teachers, demonstrate attitudes that significantly determine the widespread acceptance of AI-based mathematical instruments. People who are comfortable with technology tend to embrace AI tools more effectively because they understand how these systems enhance their educational process. Students view adaptive learning approaches positively through platforms such as DreamBox Learning and Squirrel AI because these platforms deliver customized learning experiences tailored to individual needs. The technology adapts to the student's learning speed, allowing them to perform practice questions according to their strengths and areas needing improvement. The digital technology background of younger students makes them more open to using AI as an educational aid, as this aligns with their expectations that technology will assist their daily activities. Studies demonstrate that students experience greater commitment and drive to their education following exposure to AI tools, as these tools appear to be custom-fit for their educational requirements (Zhang, 2023). A mixed set of emotions exists among teachers regarding AI-assisted educational tools. Bubble has received positive recognition from educators who see how AI can enhance their teaching practices by providing student progress reports and identifying learning zones. When students display real-time performance changes, AI tools allow teachers to modify lesson plans and intervention strategies accordingly. A significant portion of educators express skepticism about the capabilities of AI to enhance classroom instruction. Some educational staff feel apprehension about artificial intelligence tools because they believe these systems lead to a process of dehumanization, turning them into technology supervisors instead of student interactors. The European Commission conducted research that revealed multiple teaching professionals were concerned that AI would replace human teachers, thereby creating career uncertainty for teachers. The use of AI to conduct assessments has raised concerns about the ethical implications of the reliability and fairness of AI systems' decisions. Without proper training on AI technologies, most people develop skepticism, thus making professional development and training vital to overcoming their resistance (Zhang, 2023).

AI application acceptance faces a significant obstacle because educators and students require transparent and reliable AI systems for education. Students, together with teachers, must feel assured about the precision, unbiased nature, and safety of their AI tools in educational settings. AI applications highlight an important issue because they often perpetuate biases already present in training datasets. The effectiveness of an AI platform declines among students from diverse backgrounds, as it was trained only on a specific demographic population. The insufficient attention to AI technology regarding students' individual needs creates equity issues in education, as some students may face disadvantages due to inadequate accommodations. The trust in AI systems could be lost whenever recommendations or actions remain unexplained by the platforms (Alshiha & Ghaleb, 2023). When AI systems fail to demonstrate decision-making processes through feedback or adjustments to difficulty levels, it becomes difficult to prove their fair operation. Students might lose their system confidence when they do not understand the rationale behind receiving specific problems. The unwillingness of both students and teachers to accept AI entirely depends on their ability to comprehend the reasoning behind its decision-making process (Umamaheswari, 2025). Classroom acceptance of AI requires educators to acquire sufficient training about implementing AI tools successfully within their instructional processes. AI success depends on teachers using this technology as an additional educational support rather than a substitute for conventional teaching methods. Training initiatives should educate educators on both software operation skills and technology principal comprehension, alongside a comprehensive understanding of system boundaries and associated challenges (Sharma, 2024).

The training in AI enables teachers to identify when a student is struggling with concepts, allowing them to provide AI-generated, targeted intervention strategies. Continued professional development is essential for educators, as it provides essential information about current AI progress and its practical applications in school curricula. Some teachers require training in data literacy because AI tools often generate extensive performance data that necessitates practical interpretation and analysis. The inability of teachers to analyze educational data will result in AI systems performing inadequately, as teachers cannot fully harness their capabilities (Alshiha & Ghaleb, 2023). Obtaining widespread recognition about AI utilization in educational institutions across multiple geographical areas and educational systems presents substantial barriers. Several countries delay the adoption of AI-based tools because they lack sufficient resources, as well as basic infrastructure, and remain unconvinced about protective measures for their educational data. Low-income institutions face difficulties adopting AI because the acquisition and maintenance costs of such technology prove challenging (Soares et al., 2024). The private information collected from students faces paramount security and privacy risks. The operation of numerous AI systems depends on large datasets because they need to track student behaviour along with academic progress and system usage patterns. Many parents and education policymakers share concerns about the improper use of student data, as third-party platforms often store this information. Data privacy protection stands as the primary barrier hindering the complete implementation of artificial intelligence in educational systems (Umamaheswari, 2025).

The educational sector showcases various instances where AI has been successfully integrated into its systems, despite ongoing challenges. Students, along with teachers from Chinese schools, have welcomed Squirrel AI because it delivers customized educational experiences. The platform understands how quickly each student learns, enabling teachers to provide specific information about which students require additional educational support. Knewton and similar platforms adopt AI analysis of student performance to create personalized learning paths that help higher education students in mathematics subjects in the United States. Research findings demonstrate how AI supports classroom purposes when educational institutions prioritize employee training, develop appropriate systems, and maintain clear reporting systems (Soares et al., 2024). Educational acceptance of AI depends on three main elements: teacher readiness, student approval, technological acceptability, and AI system reliability. Student approval for AI tools is generally stronger than teacher acceptability because teachers often fear that automation will replace them. The integration of AI in schools requires extensive instructor training, along with open application visibility, and continuous communication about the ethical implications of AI in education. This combination will drive AI implementation success through collaborative efforts among teaching staff, students, and technology programming personnel (Alshiha & Ghaleb, 2023).

Long-Term Impacts and Digital Literacy

The application of artificial intelligence in mathematics education transforms classroom discourse and has lasting effects on the academic growth and vocational development of students. Understanding how AI advances educational technology requires an investigation into its effects on educational pathways for students, as well as the development of digital skills and sustainability factors in mathematics learning. Educational changes have the power to transform the teaching environment by equipping students with the necessary competencies that will benefit their individual journeys, educational pursuits, and future careers (Alam & Mohanty, 2024). The academic paths of students now depend significantly on AI advances, which impact learning in mathematics, as well as related fields such as engineering, data science, and economics. AI-based tools deliver customized educational experiences that can uncover students' vital areas, both in terms of interests and skills. AI-driven platforms, such as those used in adaptive learning environments like Khan Academy, offer real-time data on student progress, highlighting strengths and identifying areas for improvement. This data-driven approach enables students to take control of their learning, progressing at their own pace and focusing on areas where they require the most support. By continuously adjusting to the learner's pace, AI not only helps struggling students but also accelerates the progress of those who need less guidance (Hwang & Wu, 2025). For instance, a student struggling with algebra concepts may receive targeted practice problems on topics such as quadratic equations or factoring, allowing them to gain mastery before progressing. Meanwhile, students who excel can delve deeper into advanced topics such as calculus or data analysis, which are fundamental to many STEM-based career paths. The long-term effect of such personalized learning is that students may discover their academic strengths earlier and pursue a more tailored academic path. Over time, this can lead to greater academic success and a more informed decision-making process for career choices. AI technologies can help create more efficient learning pathways, enabling students to reach their full potential and make informed decisions about their future coursework and career paths, provided they continue to offer real-time feedback on student progress (Strielkowski et al., 2024). Concurrently, the extensive use of AI technologies in education fosters the development of digital literacy, a fundamental skill essential for success in the contemporary world. Understanding how to utilize technology efficiently and critically assessing how digital technologies affect people on both a personal and social level are just two examples of the many skills that comprise digital literacy. AI-driven platforms offer students a valuable opportunity to hone these skills within the context of mathematics instruction (Alam & Mohanty, 2024).

Platforms like Wolfram Alpha and GeoGebra, for instance, are frequently utilized to teach mathematical principles while also enhancing students' proficiency with cutting-edge digital tools. These tools, which require a certain level of digital competency, enable students to investigate ideas through interactive problem-solving, simulations, and visualizations (Hwang & Wu, 2025). Students develop the ability to comprehend and utilize technology, as well as critically evaluate the data and results produced by such systems, by leveraging AI-based platforms. Students studying mathematics often need to interpret data from artificial intelligence (AI) systems and understand the reasoning behind the algorithms that drive them. This process develops computational, analytical, and problem-solving skills, all of which are becoming increasingly important in today's labor market. Students who utilize AI tools in the classroom are thereby developing the digital literacy skills necessary to succeed in a society that is becoming increasingly technologically advanced, while also acquiring mathematical principles (Strielkowski et al., 2024). Furthermore, there is a strong correlation between future employment prospects and the application of AI in mathematics instruction. Data analysis, modeling, and machine learning skills, which have their roots in mathematics, are essential in many professions today. Students who utilize AI-based learning resources are more likely to pursue careers in software development, data science, machine learning, and artificial intelligence. By exposing students to pertinent tools, techniques, and concepts, AI applications in mathematics education provide them with an inside look at these fields (Alam & Mohanty, 2024).

Platforms like Coursera and edX, for instance, offer AI-driven courses in data science and artificial intelligence, providing students with the opportunity to practice with AI algorithms and learn how to apply them to address real-world issues. In this sense, the nexus between AI and mathematics education provides a route to employment in cutting-edge, in-demand industries. In addition to preparing students for future academic challenges, the growing use of AI in math classes also equips them with the skills they need to succeed in tech-driven sectors. These technologies will probably become even more crucial in determining future generations' professional pathways as AI literacy gains traction (Hibi, 2024). The sustainability of AI's influence on mathematics education must be considered, even if it has the potential to impact professional and academic opportunities significantly. Concerns have been raised over the long-term implications of AI technologies on educational achievements due to the fast evolution of technology. Although AI technologies are very good at providing rapid feedback and customizing learning, their long-term effects on student progress remain unknown. The quality of the data used to train AI systems and how well they align with the current curriculum are two factors that frequently determine the effectiveness of these systems. Furthermore, several variables, such as infrastructure availability, teacher preparation, and regional access to technology, may impact the reliability of AI systems (Hwang & Wu, 2025).

The extent to which these technologies can adapt to the evolving needs of educators and students is another factor that determines the longevity of AI's impact on mathematics education. The capacity of AI systems to evaluate student progress, identify knowledge gaps, and provide personalized learning paths must be continually enhanced. Even while specific AI systems now in use, such as those for adaptive learning, have demonstrated encouraging outcomes in terms of student performance and engagement, these tools must continue to be adaptable to changes in the demands of education. To ensure that AI technologies are continually updated and improved to meet the diverse needs of learners, educators, technologists, and educational officials, collaboration is essential (Alam & Mohanty, 2024). Additionally, because not all students have equal access to the technology required for successful AI-based learning, concerns arise about the digital divide. Disparities in learning chances may result from lower-income schools' lack of the infrastructure necessary to accommodate AI technologies. The fairness of integrating AI in education is called into doubt by this problem. The advantages of AI in mathematics education could not be equally distributed if the tools are not broadly accessible or modified to accommodate students from different backgrounds. Maintaining the sustainability of AI's influence on educational achievements will depend on ensuring that all students, regardless of their socioeconomic background, have access to high-quality AI learning resources (Hibi, 2024). The application of AI in mathematics education has enormous potential to influence students' academic paths and future employment prospects. AI technologies enable students to investigate mathematics in more profound and significant ways by promoting digital literacy and offering individualized learning experiences. Additionally, AI aids in the development of skills that are becoming increasingly crucial in a technologically advanced environment. However, elements such as data quality, fair access to technology, and ongoing teacher training are necessary for AI's impact on educational outcomes to be sustained. To keep these tools efficient, inclusive, and flexible enough to meet the requirements of future generations, educators, legislators, and developers must collaborate as artificial intelligence (AI) continues to play an increasingly significant role in mathematics education (Hibi, 2024).

Challenges and Ethical Considerations

AI can completely transform mathematics education, but it also raises important issues and moral dilemmas that need to be addressed to ensure its appropriate application. The ethical ramifications of relying too heavily on AI technologies in educational settings, including algorithmic bias, privacy concerns, data security, and equal access, are among the main issues. To optimize AI's advantages and minimize potential hazards, these concerns must be carefully considered (George & Wooden, 2023). Data security and privacy are two of the main issues in AI-driven education. AI systems utilize large volumes of student data to assess progress, provide personalized feedback, and tailor learning experiences to each individual. However, this data collection raises significant questions regarding the usage, sharing, and storage of student information. For example, there is a risk of misuse or unauthorized access if AI-powered math platforms collect private information without implementing adequate security measures. In 2019, the personal information of millions of students and instructors was made public due to a significant data breach at the Edmodo platform, an educational technology provider. To ensure that student privacy is maintained, such occurrences underscore the importance of strict data protection measures, including encryption, secure access methods, and compliance with laws such as the General Data Protection Regulation (GDPR) (Sharma, 2024). Another significant ethical issue is algorithmic prejudice. Since AI systems can only be as objective as the data they are trained on, biased training data may exacerbate inequality rather than alleviate it. For instance, if an AI-powered evaluation system is trained on biased datasets, it can favor pupils from socioeconomic backgrounds, resulting in unequal access to resources or grades. This issue can be addressed by continually auditing AI algorithms for fairness and training AI models on diverse datasets to mitigate biases in educational outcomes (George & Wooden, 2023).

Another urgent problem is equitable access to AI resources. Although AI-driven platforms can improve learning, children in low-income communities may not have the same level of access to technology as their counterparts in well-funded institutions. Another serious problem is algorithmic prejudice. The data used to train AI models may be biased by societal influences, which could result in unfair or erroneous evaluations of students' aptitudes. According to research, biased training datasets in AI grading systems can occasionally disfavour students from underrepresented backgrounds. To avoid this, educators should continue to be actively involved in assessment procedures to guarantee fairness, and AI models need to be thoroughly evaluated across a range of student demographics (Sharma, 2024). Since students in low-income or rural areas often lack the necessary gadgets and internet connectivity to take advantage of AI-powered learning, equitable access to AI resources is also a significant challenge. To close the digital gap, governments and educational institutions must ensure that all students have access to reasonably priced technology and infrastructure. Lastly, an over-reliance on AI in math classes might weaken students' ability to think critically and solve problems. To ensure that AI complements conventional education rather than replacing it, human instructors must continue to play a crucial role in creating a thorough grasp of mathematics (George & Wooden, 2023).

Future Directions and Innovations

Emerging trends, advancements in generative AI, and multidisciplinary cooperation will all impact the future of AI in mathematics education. These factors have the potential to transform how students acquire and interact with mathematical ideas completely. AI applications in education will continue to advance in sophistication as the technology develops further, presenting both new opportunities and challenges (Etcuban, 2025). The use of AI-powered tutors that can offer individualized, real-time feedback and adaptable learning routes is one of the most exciting developments. AI-powered tools, such as Carnegie Learning's MATHia and Squirrel AI, have already demonstrated their ability to customize training to meet the unique needs of each learner. More sophisticated emotional intelligence elements will likely be incorporated into future AI systems, enabling them to recognize displeasure or perplexity and adjust their responses accordingly (Rathakrishnan et al., 2024). Furthermore, AI-powered augmented reality (AR) and virtual reality (VR) technologies have the potential to transform abstract mathematical concepts into engaging, practical educational experiences. It is anticipated that generative AI will play a crucial role in the development of dynamic educational resources. Custom problem sets, explanations, and interactive lessons can be produced by AI models, such as Google's Gemini and OpenAI's GPT. AI, for instance, may create individualized study schedules that adjust according to a student's progress, helping them strengthen their areas of weakness. Furthermore, generative AI can aid in language translation, enabling non-native speakers to comprehend mathematical material and promoting inclusive education (Rathakrishnan et al., 2024). Developing AI-driven mathematics teaching will require interdisciplinary cooperation. To ensure that AI algorithms align with pedagogical best practices, researchers from disciplines such as computer science, education, and cognitive science must collaborate. To ensure that AI continues to be a technology that complements human instructors rather than replaces them, cooperative initiatives can also address ethical issues. Ultimately, artificial intelligence (AI) in mathematics education holds a promising future, but its success will depend on its ethical application, ongoing innovation, and commitment to accessibility and equity (Etcuban, 2025).

CONCLUSION

A revolutionary change that might completely reshape teaching and learning is the use of AI in mathematical education. These technologies present previously unheard-of opportunities to enhance student achievement, from AI-driven evaluation and feedback to individualized learning and the development of problem-solving skills. Although AI can help improve math education, its use must be governed by moral principles, ensure fair access, and be part of a well-rounded educational philosophy. The potential of AI to offer personalized learning experiences is one of its most significant benefits. DreamBox and Carnegie Learning's MATHia are two examples of adaptive learning platforms that have demonstrated effectiveness in tailoring education to meet the needs of students, thereby increasing understanding and engagement. By addressing learning gaps and allowing students to advance at their own pace, these AI-powered tools help pupils become more confident in their mathematical abilities. However, if students become overly reliant on technology for answers rather than honing their reasoning skills, an excessive dependence on AI tools may result in a diminished emphasis on critical thinking and problem-solving abilities. AI is also essential for evaluation and feedback as it provides real-time information about student performance. Platforms like ALEKS utilize AI to assess student progress and provide targeted solutions. Although this increases efficiency, algorithmic bias and data privacy issues need to be addressed through thorough testing and the development of moral AI. In the future, enhancing AI applications in education will necessitate multidisciplinary collaboration among academics, educators, and AI developers. Ensuring that all students have access to AI-driven resources, irrespective of their socioeconomic status, is equally crucial. Instead of replacing human education, AI should be used as a tool to enhance it, encouraging a deep understanding of mathematics and preparing students for a world that is becoming increasingly reliant on technology. AI has the potential to improve the efficacy, inclusivity, and engagement of mathematics instruction when used responsibly.

REFERENCES

Alam, A., & Mohanty, A. (2024). Integrated constructive robotics in education (ICRE) model: A paradigmatic framework for transformative learning in educational ecosystem. *Cogent Education*, *11*(1), 2324487. Advance online publication. DOI: 10.1080/2331186X.2024.2324487

Alshiha, A. A., & Ghaleb, M. M. (2023). Empowering self-management: Unveiling the impact of artificial intelligence in learning on student self-efficacy and self-monitoring. [EJER]. *Eurasian Journal of Educational Research*, *107*, 1–17.

Asy'ari, M., & Sharov, S. (2024). Transforming education with ChatGPT: Advancing personalized learning, accessibility, and ethical AI integration. *International Journal (Toronto, Ont.)*, *3*(2), 119–134.

Basri, W. S. (2024). Effectiveness of AI-powered tutoring systems in enhancing learning outcomes. [EJER]. *Eurasian Journal of Educational Research*, *110*, 25–40.

Choustoulakis, E. (2024). The impact of AI-driven gamified learning of mathematical economics on higher-education student motivation and achievement: An empirical survey in sport management undergraduate students in Greece. In *ICERI2024 Proceedings* (pp. 2095–2103). IATED.

George, B., & Wooden, O. (2023). Managing the strategic transformation of higher education through artificial intelligence. *Administrative Sciences*, *13*(9), 196. Advance online publication. DOI: 10.3390/admsci13090196

Hibi, W. (2024). Using smart applications to develop mathematical concepts among fourth grade students with arithmetic learning difficulties. *The International Journal of Science. Mathematics and Technology Learning*, *32*(1), 1–15.

Hwang, Y., & Wu, Y. (2025). The influence of generative artificial intelligence on creative cognition of design students: A chain mediation model of self-efficacy and anxiety. *Frontiers in Psychology*, *15*, 1455015. Advance online publication. DOI: 10.3389/fpsyg.2025.1455015 PMID: 39931512

Kiaer, J., & Jeon, Y. J. (2024). Humanizing AI education: The MERGE framework for supporting teachers in AI-enhanced classrooms. *International Journal of Contents*, *20*(3), 112–123.

Kohnke, S., & Zaugg, T. (2025). Artificial intelligence: An untapped opportunity for equity and access in STEM education. *Education Sciences*, *15*(1), 68–84. DOI: 10.3390/educsci15010068

Kundu, A., & Bej, T. (2024). Psychological impacts of AI use on school students: A systematic scoping review of the empirical literature. *Journal of Educational Psychology, 116*(2), 234–249. DOI: 10.1037/edu0000526

Lepore, M. (2024). A holistic framework to model student's cognitive process in mathematics education through fuzzy cognitive maps. *Heliyon, 10*(16), e13287. Advance online publication. DOI: 10.1016/j.heliyon.2024.e13287 PMID: 39229524

Li, M., Vale, C., Tan, H., & Blannin, J. (2025). Factors influencing the use of digital technologies in primary mathematics teaching: Voices from Chinese educators. *Education and Information Technologies*. Advance online publication. DOI: 10.1007/s10639-025-10801-4

Lin, H., & Chen, Q. (2024). Artificial intelligence (AI)-integrated educational applications and college students' creativity and academic emotions: Students and teachers' perceptions and attitudes. *BMC Psychology, 12*(1), 487. Advance online publication. DOI: 10.1186/s40359-024-01525-w PMID: 39285268

Orduño-Osuna, J. H., Hernández, G. T., Mercado, A., & Murrieta-Rico, F. N. (2025). Boosting learning through AI in STEM for socioeconomic development in emerging economies. In *Transformative Approaches to STEAM Integration in Modern Education* (pp. 499–528). IGI Global Scientific Publishing.

Orji, F. A. (2024). *Artificial intelligence and persuasive computing approach for motivating students and enhancing their learning experience* (Doctoral dissertation). University of [Name].

Raimi, L., Bamiro, N. B., & Lim, S. A. (2024). Two facets of AI-driven applications for sustainable learning and development: A systematic review of tech-entrepreneurial benefits and threats to creative learning. In *Social Responsibility, Technology and AI* (pp. 223–248). IGI Global.

Rathakrishnan, T., Kumar, T. B. J., Tsen, M. K., Leong, M. K., & Yaacob, A. (2024). AI tools: Anxiety to achievement—Unveiling the psychological dynamics of technology adoption. In *Transdisciplinary Teaching and Technological Integration for Improved Learning: Case Studies and Practical Approaches* (pp. 42–65). IGI Global.

Sharma, P. (2024). *Revolutionizing math education: The power of personalized learning*. Online Submission.

Soares, M. N., Pontes, A., Lima, M., Moreira, S., Machado, F., Ferreira, J., & Coelho, V. (2024). Creative education and psychology: Connecting minds and technologies for educational success. In *Creativity and Learning: Navigating Transformative Perspectives for Complex and Contemporary Environments* (pp. 15–43). Springer Nature Switzerland.

Strielkowski, W., Grebennikova, V., Lisovskiy, A., Rakhimova, G., & Vasileva, T. (2024). AI-driven adaptive learning for sustainable educational transformation. *Sustainable Development*, *32*(1), 62–72. DOI: 10.1002/sd.2290

Tariq, M. U. (2024). Generative AI in Curriculum Development in Higher Education. In Fields, Z. (Ed.), *Impacts of Generative AI on Creativity in Higher Education* (pp. 227–258). IGI Global., DOI: 10.4018/979-8-3693-2418-9.ch009

Tariq, M. U. (2025). Navigating Public Administration 5.0: Embracing AI for Smarter Governance. In Wongmahesak, K., Ahmad, J., & Mustanir, A. (Eds.), *Public Governance Practices in the Age of AI* (pp. 167–186). IGI Global Scientific Publishing., DOI: 10.4018/979-8-3693-9286-7.ch008

Tariq, M. U. (2025). Leveraging Libraries and Information Centers for Startup Innovation and Growth. In Gupta, V., & Gupta, C. (Eds.), *Navigating Strategic Partnerships for Sustainable Startup Growth* (pp. 1–28). IGI Global Scientific Publishing., DOI: 10.4018/979-8-3693-4066-0.ch001

Tariq, M. U. (2025). AI-Driven Research Methodologies: Revolutionizing Data-Driven Discoveries in Engineering and Physical Sciences. In Basha, J., Alade, T., Al Khazimi, M., Vasudevan, R., & Khan, J. (Eds.), *Optimizing Research Techniques and Learning Strategies With Digital Technologies* (pp. 97–122). IGI Global Scientific Publishing., DOI: 10.4018/979-8-3693-7863-2.ch004

Tariq, M. U. (2025). Integrating Theory and Practice: Transformative Approaches in Practice-Led Research for Professional Development. In Kwok, S., Yu, P., & Le Corre, J. (Eds.), *Exploring Practice-Led Research for Professional Development* (pp. 419–436). IGI Global Scientific Publishing., DOI: 10.4018/979-8-3693-6376-8.ch016

Umamaheswari, P. (2025). A comprehensive approach to the integration of intelligent systems in the didactic of social and cognitive studies. In *Utilizing ICT for Didactics of Social and Experimental Sciences* (pp. 95–112). IGI Global.

Velastegui, D., Pérez, M. L. R., & Garcés, L. F. S. (2023). Impact of artificial intelligence on learning behaviors and psychological well-being of college students. *Salud. Ciencia y Tecnologia-Serie de Conferencias*, *2*, 343–358.

Yadav, D. S. (2024). Transformative trends in education with advanced technologies: Exploring the intersection of IoT and AI. In *Applications of Artificial Intelligence in the Internet of Things: Today's and Tomorrow's World* (pp. 316–336). IGI Global.

Yadav, S. (2025). Transformative learning with advanced technologies: Harnessing VR and AR for immersive educational experiences. In *Revolutionizing Pedagogy Through Smart Education* (pp. 139–156). IGI Global Scientific Publishing.

Zhang, Q. (2023). Harnessing the power of technology: A systematic analysis of challenges, theoretical frameworks, and recommendations for K–12 online learning. *SN Social Sciences*, *3*(9), 164. Advance online publication. DOI: 10.1007/s43545-023-00111-1

Zhang, Q., & Wong, M. (2023). Systematic review of AI tools in enhancing personalized learning environments in higher education. *Journal of Educational Technology*, *44*(6), 1031–1052.

Zuo, F., & Chan, E. (2024). Cognitive modeling in math education using AI. *International Journal of Artificial Intelligence in Education*, *26*(2), 155–170. DOI: 10.1007/s40593-024-00274-x

KEY TERMS AND DEFINITIONS

Adaptive Learning: Educational methods using AI to tailor instruction dynamically according to individual student needs and learning progress.

Algorithmic Bias: Unintended systematic errors in AI systems that may unfairly disadvantage certain student populations in educational contexts.

Digital Literacy: Competencies enabling students to effectively interact, create, and critically evaluate content using mathematics-focused AI tools.

Gamified Learning: Incorporation of game elements and AI-driven scenarios to enhance students' analytical and problem-solving skills.

Virtual Tutors: AI-based interactive assistants designed to improve learners' psychosocial attitudes towards mathematics through personalized support.

Chapter 6
Modernizing Mathematics Education With Artificial Intelligence: A Narrative Review of AI-Powered Tools, Thematic Trends, and Instructional Applications

Manuel B. Garcia
https://orcid.org/0000-0003-2615-422X
FEU Institute of Technology, Philippines

Dharel P. Acut
https://orcid.org/0000-0002-9608-1292
Cebu Technological University, Philippines

Yunifa Miftachul Arif
https://orcid.org/0000-0002-2183-0762
Universitas Islam Negeri Maulana Malik Ibrahim, Indonesia

Damian Maher
https://orcid.org/0000-0002-3566-0805
University of Technology Sydney, Australia

Jogymol Alex
United Arab Emirates University, UAE

Yousef Wardat
Yarmouk University, Jordan

Thomas K. F. Chiu
The Chinese University of Hong Kong, Hong Kong

Robertas Damaševičius
https://orcid.org/0000-0001-9990-1084
Vytautas Magnus University, Lithuania

DOI: 10.4018/979-8-3373-1998-8.ch006

ABSTRACT

Mathematics is a subject that often feels distant from everyday life, yet its logic quietly shapes the world around us. As learners continue to question its practical significance, there is a growing need to rethink mathematics education. Recently, the emergence of artificial intelligence (AI) has opened new possibilities for transforming how mathematics is taught and learned. This chapter aims to examine the emerging role of AI in mathematics education by synthesizing current tools, identifying prevailing trends, and exploring transformative applications. Using a narrative review supported by expert-informed synthesis, several themes are identified that reflect how AI are reshaping instructional practices, learner engagement, and pedagogical design. The discussion integrates illustrative examples of AI tools to highlight their instructional relevance and underlying mechanisms. The chapter concludes by reflecting on a redefined landscape for mathematics education, where technology transforms instructional practices, learner experiences, and the development of mathematical thinking.

INTRODUCTION

"*Why do I need to learn this? I'll never use it in real life.*" Few subjects provoke this perennial protest more than mathematics. Yet, beneath such skepticism lies an enduring and often underappreciated truth: mathematics cultivates a form of disciplined thinking that extends well beyond numbers and equations. It fosters cognitive habits that are essential for navigating complex situations, including logical structuring, pattern recognition, abstract modeling, and deductive reasoning, all of which form the basis for sound decision-making in fields such as finance, medicine, engineering, and public policy (Gravemeijer et al., 2017; Shimizu & Vithal, 2023). In an era increasingly defined by data-driven systems and algorithmic processes, the ability to think mathematically is no longer reserved for specialists; it has become a form of cultural and intellectual capital. Despite its value, however, mathematics remains one of the most formidable subjects for learners, frequently associated with high cognitive load, anxiety, and a fragile sense of self-efficacy (Rozgonjuk et al., 2020; Zakariya, 2022). In response to these challenges, educational systems worldwide have turned to instructional technologies as a strategic intervention. The integration of these tools aims to reduce the affective and cognitive friction that has long hindered mathematical achievement. Given the pedagogical benefits of technology-enhanced learning (Foshee et al., 2016; Na & Sung, 2025), such tools are increasingly used to mitigate learning barriers, support differentiated instruction, and provide real-time formative feedback. As these tools evolve in pedagogical adaptability, they are also beginning to converge with a new class of systems that extend beyond content delivery and into the orbit of intelligent interaction.

Artificial intelligence (AI) is one of the most consequential advancements in the current wave of educational technology innovation (Acut et al., 2025; Gantalao et al., 2025; Mangubat et al., 2025). Broadly defined, AI refers to the development of computational systems capable of performing tasks that typically require human intelligence, including pattern recognition, decision-making, natural language processing (NLP), and adaptive learning. In educational contexts, AI systems leverage probabilistic modeling, deep neural networks, and real-time data analytics to generate contextually appropriate responses and support personalized instruction (Izquierdo-Álvarez & Jimeno-Postigo, 2025). Unlike earlier generations of rule-based software, contemporary AI platforms are dynamic and responsive, capable of adjusting instructional content and feedback based on individual learner profiles. Their increasing adoption reflects a pedagogical shift toward scalable, adaptive, and dialogic models of teaching and learning (Xiao et al., 2025). According to Bozkurt et al. (2024), the integration of AI into education embeds assumptions, values, and cultural biases that can influence learning in both empowering and problematic ways. Yet amid these complexities, mathematics education stands out as a particularly fertile ground for inquiry. The inherent logic, structure, and abstraction of mathematics present a compelling match for AI's capacity to scaffold complex reasoning, personalize instruction, and engage learners in novel forms of mathematical thinking. Against this backdrop, this chapter seeks to address the question: *How are AI technologies transforming the tools, practices, and pedagogical frameworks of mathematics education in ways that enhance learning while preserving disciplinary rigor?*

MAIN FOCUS OF THE CHAPTER

AI is rapidly reshaping the landscape of education, and its integration into mathematics instruction is becoming increasingly prominent (e.g., Hwang & Tu, 2021; Mustafa, 2024). Despite the proliferation of research on AI in broader educational contexts, the field of mathematics remains comparatively underrepresented in the literature. This gap is particularly noteworthy given the inherently logical, structured, and problem-oriented nature of mathematics, which aligns well with the capabilities of AI systems. Bridging this gap is not only timely but essential, as mathematics continues to serve as a foundational discipline across STEM fields and requires innovative approaches to address persistent challenges related to engagement, personalization, assessment, and conceptual understanding (Engelbrecht & Borba, 2024). This chapter aims to critically examine the emerging role of AI in mathematics education by synthesizing current tools, identifying prevailing trends, and exploring transformative applications. It brings together a wide spectrum of AI-driven innovations, with particular attention to how these technologies are being deployed to support mathematical reasoning, improve equity in instruction, and promote deeper student engagement. In focusing exclusively on mathematics education, this chapter contributes a discipline-specific lens to a field often dominated by generalist perspectives. It highlights how AI can address unique pedagogical challenges in mathematics, such as the need for stepwise feedback, symbolic interpretation, and cognitive scaffolding. Moreover, it provides educators, researchers, and policymakers with a structured understanding of the current landscape and future directions of AI integration in mathematics instruction. Articulating both the possibilities and limitations of these technologies underscores the importance of evidence-based adoption that prioritizes learning outcomes and preserves the intellectual rigor of the discipline.

METHODOLOGY

Methodological Orientation

This chapter employed a narrative review supported by expert-informed synthesis to examine the integration of AI into mathematics education. A narrative review was deemed appropriate due to the emerging and interdisciplinary nature of the topic (Sukhera, 2022), which spans multiple domains including educational technology, mathematics pedagogy, and AI research. Narrative reviews are well-suited for exploring under-theorized areas by integrating diverse sources, uncovering conceptual patterns, and highlighting emergent practices (Greenhalgh et al., 2018; Sarkar & Bhatia, 2021). Unlike systematic reviews, this method permits thematic flexibility and accommodates both peer-reviewed scholarship and practice-based insights. To enrich the analysis, the review was grounded in the authors' combined expertise in AI-supported learning environments, classroom instruction, and instructional design. This expert-informed dimension added contextual depth to the interpretation of literature and facilitated the selection of representative tools and frameworks. Expert-informed reviews have been recognized as valuable in education research for surfacing tacit practitioner knowledge and shaping grounded, experience-based interpretations (Grant & Booth, 2009).

Conceptual Framework

The review was guided by a three-part conceptual framework that focuses on pedagogical functionality, learner interaction, and instructional innovation. Pedagogical functionality refers to how well an AI tool supports essential instructional practices such as scaffolding, differentiation, or formative assessment. Learner interaction concerns the degree to which students engage with AI tools in adaptive, personalized, or dialogic ways. Instructional innovation captures whether a tool enables novel modes of teaching and learning, especially those that promote conceptual understanding and higher-order reasoning. This framework draws on theoretical insights from prior work on AI in various fields of education (e.g., Bozkurt et al., 2024; Garcia, de Almeida, et al., 2025), while tailoring the lens specifically to mathematics education. The structured and abstract nature of mathematics lends itself particularly well to AI-mediated instructional models that rely on formal rule-based reasoning and symbolic manipulation. As such, this framework facilitates not only the classification of AI tools but also a more nuanced understanding of how they intersect with the cognitive and representational demands unique to mathematics.

Selection of Tools and Examples

The selection of AI tools and examples for analysis in this chapter was guided by a set of conceptual and pedagogical criteria. Tools were included if they demonstrated clear relevance to mathematics education and aligned with at least one of the chapter's core dimensions: pedagogical functionality, learner interaction, or instructional innovation. Priority was given to tools that addressed persistent instructional challenges in mathematics, such as providing stepwise feedback, visualizing abstract concepts, supporting personalized pacing, or enhancing formative assessment practices. Additionally, selected tools were required to incorporate core AI capabilities, including but not limited to machine learning algorithms, NLP, probabilistic reasoning, or adaptive sequencing (Izquierdo-Álvarez & Jimeno-Postigo, 2025). The selection process was informed by the authors' professional engagement with AI-enhanced educational technologies, along with input from peers and practitioners in mathematics education. In some cases, tools were identified through ongoing involvement in research projects, classroom experimentation, or participation in academic networks focused on educational innovation. While the approach was not exhaustive or systematic, it aimed to ensure a representative breadth of instructional contexts, educational levels, and AI functionalities. Rather than emphasizing brand-specific features, the analysis focused on how the tools instantiated underlying pedagogical principles and leveraged AI to mediate mathematical learning in meaningful ways.

Literature Search and Source Selection

To complement the expert-informed tool selection, a structured literature review was conducted focusing on publications from 2020 to 2025. Scholarly databases such as ERIC, Scopus, and Web of Science were searched using combinations of keywords including and related to "*artificial intelligence*," and "*mathematics education*." Preference was given to peer-reviewed journal articles, empirical studies, and high-impact conference proceedings. In addition to academic sources, the review considered relevant grey literature including institutional white papers, education technology evaluations, and policy reports. Inclusion criteria prioritized sources with conceptual clarity, methodological rigor, and direct relevance to mathematics instruction. Foundational sources include Nguyen et al. (2023) on ethical implementation of AI in education, Liu et al. (2025) on AI-enabled learning environment for mathematical activities, and Hwang and Tu (2021) on bibliometric trends in AI-driven mathematics education research.

RESULTS AND DISCUSSION

The integration of AI into mathematics education represents a rapidly evolving frontier with the potential to transform not only how students engage with mathematical content but also how educators design and deliver instruction across learning environments. This chapter is significant in that it synthesizes emerging insights from diverse fields to illuminate how intelligent systems can meaningfully support mathematics learning. Given the structured and cumulative nature of mathematics, adaptive technologies such as AI are uniquely positioned to address long-standing challenges related to conceptual misunderstanding, learner disengagement, and instructional differentiation. More broadly, the findings contribute to the wider field of education by demonstrating how AI can serve as a catalyst for pedagogical innovation, equity in learning access, and data-informed decision-making. This section presents the major themes (Figure 1) that emerged from the review, each of which illustrates how AI technologies are being leveraged to address challenges in mathematics education while advancing pedagogical practices. The discussion integrates illustrative examples of AI tools to highlight their instructional relevance, underlying mechanisms, and alignment with the conceptual framework introduced earlier.

Figure 1. AI applications in math education categorized by instructional purpose

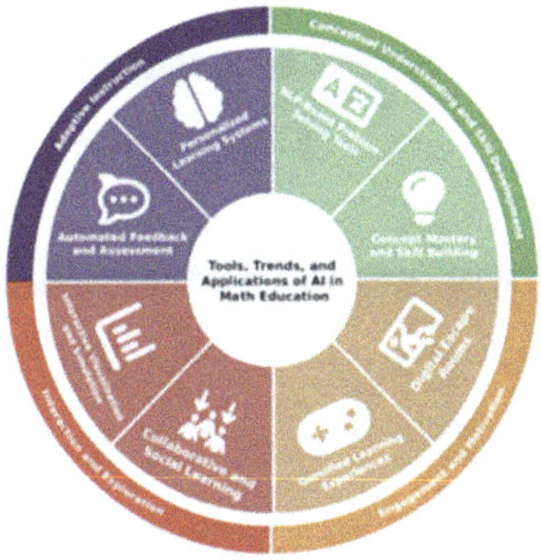

Personalized Learning Systems

Personalized learning has become a cornerstone of modern educational reform (Maher, 2024), grounded in the principle that instruction should adapt to the needs, pace, and readiness of individual learners. In mathematics education, where conceptual progression is highly sequential and error propagation is common, adaptive support is particularly critical. Intelligent Tutoring Systems (ITS) operationalize this principle by delivering data-driven and individualized guidance based on student interactions, performance patterns, and inferred cognitive states. These systems utilize machine learning models to continuously update learner profiles and recalibrate instruction in real time, which offers scaffolding, revisits prerequisite concepts, or accelerates when mastery is demonstrated. *MATHia* (Figure 2), developed by Carnegie Learning, exemplifies this pedagogical paradigm by providing students with dynamically generated problem sets, step-by-step feedback, and tailored learning paths aligned with their evolving proficiency. Designed to mirror the decision-making process of a human tutor, this application employs cognitive modeling to assess conceptual mastery and personalize instruction with precision.

Figure 2. MATHia interface showing real-time skill tracking in a personalized learning module

The pedagogical significance of AI-powered personalized learning systems lies in their ability to optimize both the pace and trajectory of mathematical instruction. Continuously assessing learner progress allow these systems implement adaptive sequencing that ensures students are neither overwhelmed by premature complexity nor disengaged by redundant review (Kabudi et al., 2021). This alignment with Vygotskian principles of the zone of proximal development creates a learning environment that is optimally challenging and cognitively supportive (Chaiarwut et al., 2025). Additionally, these platforms promote learner agency by tolerating students to navigate their learning paths while receiving contextualized feedback that builds metacognitive awareness and strategic competence. Moreover, ITS contribute to instructional equity by addressing variability in prior knowledge and learning pace. These conditions are often magnified in heterogeneous classrooms. They also offer instructors rich diagnostic data, enabling targeted interventions and more efficient resource allocation. In formative assessment contexts, ITS supports the identification of latent misconceptions and provides real-time corrective feedback that fosters durable learning. As personalized learning becomes increasingly central to mathematics instruction, AI-driven systems stand out not only for their scalability but also for their potential to deliver rigorous, individualized, and data-informed learning experiences that align with both curricular goals and cognitive science.

Automated Feedback and Assessment

Assessment remains a cornerstone of mathematics education, yet the process of evaluating student work (particularly for open-ended and multi-step problems) poses significant logistical and pedagogical challenges (Nortvedt & Buchholtz, 2018).

Traditional grading is often labor-intensive, inconsistently applied, and limited in its ability to offer individualized feedback. AI has introduced a new class of automated assessment platforms that streamline the evaluation process while maintaining rigor and precision (Garcia, Rosak-Szyrocka, et al., 2025; Xia et al., 2024). These platforms utilize a combination of NLP, image recognition, and pattern-matching algorithms to analyze student submissions, identify partial correctness, and generate customized feedback. Among the most widely adopted tools in this domain is *Gradescope* (Figure 3), an AI-assisted assessment platform designed to support the efficient grading of mathematical proofs, equations, and constructed responses. It enables educators to cluster similar answers, apply rubric-based grading at scale, and provide annotated feedback with a high degree of consistency. The system also supports handwritten submissions, which makes it especially useful in mathematics contexts where symbolic notation and diagrammatic representation are essential. By automating lower-order tasks and centralizing assessment data, this kind of tool enables instructors to monitor both individual and class-level learning trajectories with greater precision.

Building on these capabilities, AI-powered assessment platforms are fundamentally reshaping pedagogical practice in mathematics education. These systems analyze solution processes, recognize partial credit, and deliver feedback that is both immediate and instructional. Fundamentally, Sangwin and Köcher (2016) emphasized that the educational impact of automated assessment is in its ability to prompt reflection and facilitate knowledge reconstruction. Empirical evidence demonstrated that the strategic use of immediate feedback in automated homework systems led to higher levels of participation, improved performance, and enhanced metacognitive regulation (Gaona et al., 2018), particularly in large-scale mathematics courses where individualized support is often limited. Recent advances in AI, particularly through large language models (LLMs), have extended these affordances (Hasanah et al., 2025). Morris et al. (2024) reported that such models are now capable of evaluating constructed mathematical responses with a degree of interrater reliability comparable to that of trained human graders. This application makes it increasingly feasible to scale high-quality assessments that elicit student reasoning, without defaulting to multiple-choice or short-answer formats. As assessment moves toward competency-based, reasoning-centered paradigms, AI stands to play a central role in supporting equitable, transparent, and instructionally aligned evaluation.

Figure 3. Gradescope interface displaying AI-assisted grading of a handwritten calculus response

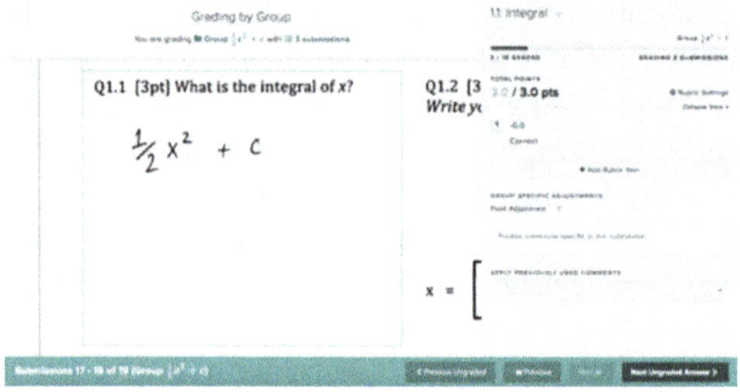

NLP-Based Problem-Solving Tools

NLP, a branch of AI that enables computers to interpret, analyze, and generate human language, is increasingly influencing how students engage with mathematical tasks. Although NLP has traditionally been associated with applications such as sentiment analysis, chatbots, and language translation, it is now playing a transformative role in mathematics education by enabling the automated interpretation of word problems. These problems require learners to navigate complex linguistic constructions, identify relevant quantities, infer relationships, and ultimately convert textual descriptions into formal mathematical expressions. NLP techniques such as text classification, named entity recognition (NER), dependency parsing, and semantic role labeling serve as foundational components in this transformation process. One exemplary tool that operationalizes these capabilities is *Photomath* (Figure 4), which integrates Optical Character Recognition (OCR) with NLP to read both handwritten and printed math problems. Upon recognition, the tool dissects the linguistic structure of a given problem, maps it to the corresponding mathematical model, and then renders a step-by-step solution with explanatory annotations. Photomath exemplifies the practical synergy between language technologies and mathematical reasoning by showcasing how intelligent parsing systems can mediate the cognitive gap between how students encounter a problem and how it should be mathematically framed.

Figure 4. Interface of Photomath demonstrating AI-powered step-by-step problem solving.

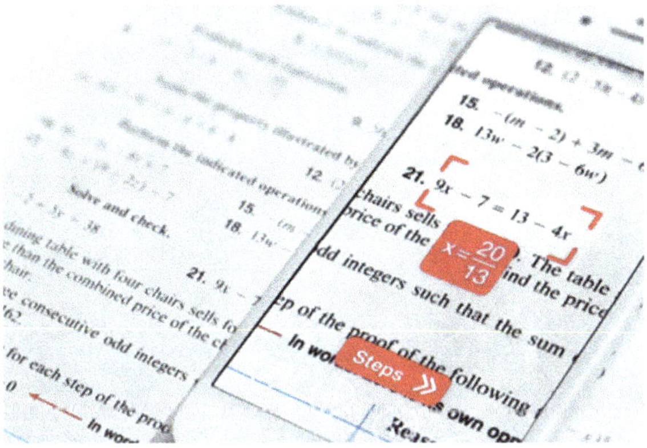

The pedagogical implications of NLP in mathematics education are profound. At its core, NLP supports the critical process of problem translation that enables learners to interpret mathematically rich texts with greater accuracy and confidence. Word problems, which often act as cognitive bottlenecks due to their dual linguistic and numerical demands, are rendered more accessible when NLP-driven systems scaffold the decoding process. Research by Winkler and Herman (2023) emphasizes that NLP tools can help learners develop representational fluency by modeling how to extract quantitative structures from natural language inputs. Additionally, Liu et al. (2022) found that NLP interventions were particularly beneficial for multilingual learners, enhancing comprehension by demystifying syntax and semantic ambiguities. These tools support metacognitive development by offering detailed solution paths, error identification, and opportunities for reflection. Students are not merely given answers but are prompted to follow the logic underlying each computational step. This interaction fosters strategic competence and encourages iterative problem-solving. Furthermore, NLP applications align well with the goals of universal design for learning (UDL), enabling diverse learners (including those with reading difficulties) to access mathematical content through multimodal feedback. As mathematics instruction continues to emphasize real-world problem contexts and open-ended tasks, NLP stands as a key enabler of equitable engagement, offering dynamic, language-sensitive scaffolds that adapt to the diverse cognitive and linguistic profiles of today's learners.

Figure 5. DreamBox Learning interface featuring adaptive, gamified mathematics lessons.

Concept Mastery and Skill Building

Conceptual mastery and procedural fluency remain enduring challenges in mathematics education (Lenz et al., 2024), particularly in conventional settings where instructional pacing often fails to accommodate the heterogeneous needs of learners. Mathematics is inherently hierarchical where gaps in early skills compound over time, which makes recovery difficult without individualized support. AI offers a transformative pathway to address these challenges by tailoring instruction to each learner's developmental stage (Zreik, 2024). One prominent example is *DreamBox Learning* (Figure 5), an adaptive learning platform that leverages AI-driven algorithms to diagnose skill levels, adjust content in real time, and guide students through conceptually coherent progressions. By continuously analyzingperformance patterns (e.g., response time, error types, and problem-solving strategies), the tool constructs personalized learning pathways that reinforce foundational skills while gradually introducing more complex tasks. Its pedagogical design emphasizes both conceptual depth and automaticity, which offer learners repeated exposure, varied representations, and real-time correction mechanisms. Within this type of pedagogical tool, AI becomes an active facilitator of mastery-oriented learning that supports differentiated instruction at scale. This degree of adaptivity also enables the early detection of learning plateaus, allowing timely pedagogical interventions before misconceptions solidify. Moreover, it deliberately shifts the instructional paradigm from reactive remediation to proactive advancement aligned with each learner's cognitive readiness.

Modeling learner cognition in real time and adapting instructional sequences accordingly support the development of relational understanding. Mustafa (2024) confirmed that adaptive learning environments improve learning outcomes and cognitive engagement by aligning tasks with the learner's zone of proximal development. In parallel, Arif and Nurhayati (2022) demonstrated that real-time personalization not only enhances efficacy in mastering core skills but also strengthens learners' self-efficacy, persistence, and confidence in navigating mathematical complexity. Importantly, the value of AI-based learning extends beyond procedural fluency. The deployment of AI chatbots as surrogate tutors has been shown to refine analytical reasoning and mathematical discourse (Busuttil & Calleja, 2025; Lee & Yeo, 2022; Pepin et al., 2025). Active learning that emphasizes experiential transfer over abstract repetition is exemplified in the work of Trindade et al. (2025), who explored simulation-based environments that integrate AI and spreadsheet automation to support workplace-relevant mathematical modeling. Similarly, Vintere et al. (2024) underscored the role of dynamic visual platforms in promoting self-directed exploration, particularly in understanding functions, graphs, and transformations. These teaching and learning environments foster conceptual visualization and allow learners to iteratively build and test hypotheses. Collectively, these developments suggest that AI is actively reconfiguring the pedagogical architecture of mathematics education. Rather than simply accelerating task completion, AI-based environments are increasingly designed to cultivate conceptual depth, procedural fluency, and strategic thinking.

Interactive Visualization and Simulation

AI-enhanced visualization and simulation tools are redefining how students engage with abstract mathematical ideas by transforming static representations into dynamic, interactive experiences. These tools respond to one of the core challenges in mathematics education by making highly symbolic and often decontextualized content intelligible to learners who struggle with purely formal reasoning (Yeo et al., 2024). More importantly, enabling students to manipulate parameters, construct geometric objects, and observe real-time changes in algebraic and graphical relationships supports conceptual learning through experimentation and visual reasoning. Among the most prominent tools in this space are *GeoGebra* and *Desmos* (Pope, 2022). *GeoGebra* (Figure 6), long recognized for its utility across geometry, algebra, and calculus, now includes AI-driven features that offer intelligent hints, automated feedback, and exploratory guidance (Hamady et al., 2024; Owusu et al., 2023). These affordances enable formative assessment and foster inquiry-based learning.

Desmos, on the other hand, integrates graphing and simulation tools with an AI engine capable of interpreting student intent, providing real-time scaffolding, and adapting prompts based on learner input. Together, these digital learning platforms advance a constructivist model of mathematics instruction, where learners construct meaning through interaction, exploration, and visual experimentation.

Figure 6. GeoGebra Classic interface illustrating a 3D paraboloid

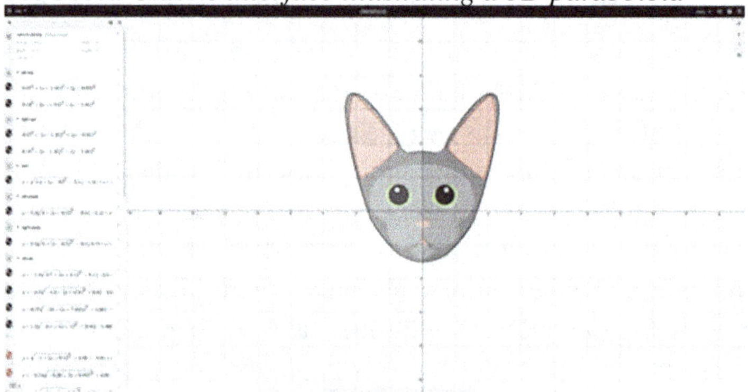

In practice, AI-enhanced visualization and simulation systems act as cognitive amplifiers that enable learners to develop mathematical intuition through interactive feedback. Rather than memorizing isolated rules, students engage with representations that reveal the behavior of functions, transformations, and statistical relationships (Almusaed et al., 2023). These environments promote conceptual discovery and allow learners to test conjectures, refine misconceptions, and iteratively build meaning through active exploration and immediate response to input (Walter, 2024). A growing body of research affirms the efficacy of dynamic visualizations in deepening mathematical understanding. Abdulrahaman et al. (2020) emphasized that bridging symbolic and graphical representations enhances representational fluency, particularly for learners who struggle with abstract reasoning. When integrated with AI, these systems further adapt to learners' needs by modulating difficulty levels, identifying conceptual errors, and differentiating instruction accordingly. They also support inclusive and equitable access to mathematics by maintaining usability across diverse educational settings, including remote and resource-constrained environments (Ningsih et al., 2024). Moreover, these systems align with UDL principles by offering multiple modalities (visual, symbolic, and textual) for engaging with mathematical content (Saborío-Taylor & Rojas-Ramírez, 2024). In blended and flipped classrooms, they function as autonomous learning companions, enabling learners to revisit concepts at their own pace while receiving guided support through AI-driven feedback. The cumulative result is a pedagogical environment where both students and educators are empowered to engage with mathematics in more meaningful and intellectually rigorous ways.

Collaborative and Social Learning

Collaborative and social learning approaches in mathematics education position dialogue, peer interaction, and co-construction of knowledge as central to conceptual development. Yet orchestrating productive mathematical discourse poses significant pedagogical challenges, especially in digital or large-scale settings. AI has introduced a new layer of support by facilitating structured collaboration, guiding peer-to-peer engagement, and generating formative feedback responsive to both individual and group dynamics (Kovari, 2025). AI systems now assist in organizing shared problem-solving sessions, analyzing student contributions, and prompting metacognitive reflection, thereby expanding opportunities for collective mathematical reasoning. These affordances are exemplified in platforms such as *Mathshare* (Figure 7), which integrates step-by-step problem breakdown with shared digital workspaces and AI-mediated guidance. By enabling learners to articulate reasoning, critique peer solutions, and engage in joint exploration, Mathshare embodies the social constructivist principle that mathematical understanding is constructed through interaction, negotiation, and shared meaning-making.

Figure 7. Mathshare interface showing step-by-step collaborative problem solving

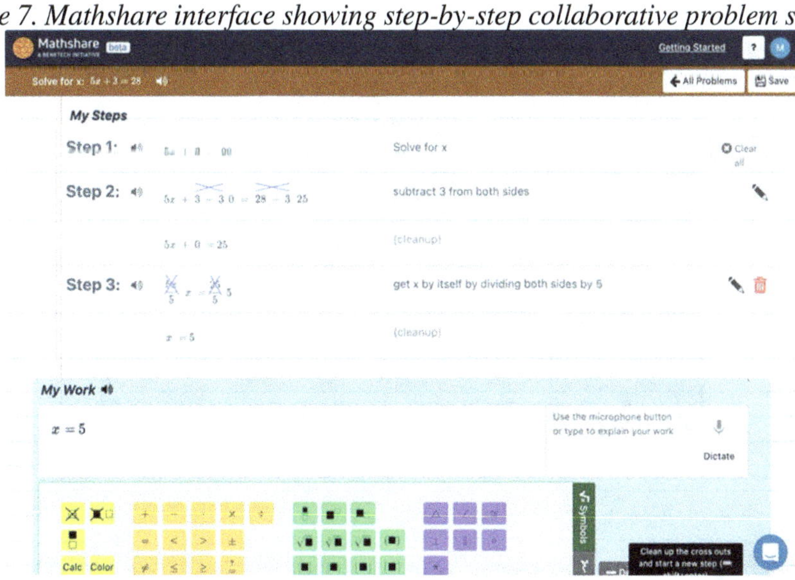

The pedagogical utility of AI in collaborative learning environments lies in its capacity to scaffold both the cognitive and social dimensions of problem-solving. By requiring students to justify each procedural step and then share their solution process with peers, AI-supported platforms promote elaborative talk and self-explanation (Muhamad Fadzil & Osman, 2025). In this context, AI does not merely evaluate correctness but identifies logical inconsistencies, highlights incomplete reasoning, and offers real-time prompts that encourage revision and peer discussion. This iterative, socially mediated feedback loop transforms collaboration into a high-impact learning experience, where students refine their ideas through collective inquiry rather than solitary effort. Moreover, AI-mediated collaboration supports equity and inclusion by ensuring that all learners (regardless of prior confidence or performance) can meaningfully contribute to group tasks. These environments are especially powerful in distance and hybrid learning settings, where the sense of academic community is often fragile. Mohamed et al. (2024) emphasized that fostering connection and interdependence through digital platforms is crucial for sustaining learner motivation and persistence. In such contexts, AI-driven analytics can monitor participation, flag imbalances in group interaction, and suggest instructional interventions, ensuring that collaborative learning remains both productive and inclusive. As mathematics education increasingly embraces 21st-century competencies, AI-supported platforms offer a pedagogical infrastructure for cultivating not only mathematical reasoning but also the social-emotional and collaborative skills foundational to lifelong learning.

Figure 8. Prodigy Math battle gameplay illustrating gamified math practice

Gamified Learning Experiences

Gamification in mathematics education has gained traction as a powerful means of enhancing student engagement, particularly among learners who may otherwise experience disengagement or anxiety toward mathematical tasks (Alt, 2023; El-mawati et al., 2023; Espinosa-Pinos et al., 2024). At its core, gamification refers to the integration of game-like elements (e.g., points, levels, challenges, and rewards) into non-game contexts to increase motivation, persistence, and enjoyment (Mustafa et al., 2022; Valderama et al., 2022). These mechanics not only foster a sense of accomplishment but also encourage repeated engagement, which is crucial for mastering mathematical concepts. When combined with AI, gamified environments become not only entertaining but also adaptive in a way that it promotes real-time calibration of content difficulty, pacing, and feedback according to learner performance (Gómez Niño et al., 2024; Tan & Cheah, 2021). These AI-driven systems harness gameplay data to monitor progress, detect patterns in learning behavior, and personalize the trajectory of mathematical tasks. *Prodigy Math* (Figure 8), for example, exemplifies this approach by embedding AI algorithms that analyze player interactions and dynamically adjust problem complexity, ensuring an optimal balance between challenge and skill. This fusion of cognitive adaptivity and motivational design represents a novel pedagogical architecture in which learning and play are deliberately intertwined.

The integration of AI into gamified learning environments has significant pedagogical implications, particularly in its capacity to foster sustained engagement and promote long-term retention of mathematical concepts. By situating mathematical practice within immersive and reward-based contexts, gamification supports intrinsic and extrinsic motivation (Alt, 2023). Research has shown that when game-based learning environments are thoughtfully designed, it activates learners' attentional and affective systems that enhances their cognitive receptivity and deep processing of content (Chen et al., 2023). Furthermore, AI-enabled gamification introduces a feedback rich ecology in which learners receive immediate, context-sensitive responses that guide self-correction and reinforce mastery. These systems are uniquely positioned to support spaced repetition, incremental difficulty progression, and strategic retrieval. Importantly, gamified platforms also foster a growth mindset by allowing learners to fail safely, iterate strategies, and receive rewards not merely for accuracy but for effort and perseverance (Lee et al., 2023). As mathematics educators seek to cultivate both skill proficiency and learner resilience, AI-powered gamification emerges as a compelling approach that aligns cognitive challenge with motivational design, supporting deeper and more durable learning outcomes.

Digital Escape Rooms

Digital escape rooms represent an emerging innovation in mathematics education, blending game-based mechanics with inquiry-driven learning to create immersive, problem-centered instructional environments. These platforms challenge students to solve a series of interconnected mathematical tasks embedded within a narrative structure, requiring them to apply logical reasoning, pattern recognition, and quantitative analysis to unlock progression through the storyline (Sidekerskienė & Damaševičius, 2023; Stohlmann, 2023). As students encounter clues and puzzles, they engage in active learning processes that elevate the cognitive demands of problem-solving beyond isolated drill exercises. The integration of AI enhances these environments by enabling adaptive task sequencing, real-time hint generation, and dynamic difficulty adjustment tailored to individual performance (Pinto et al., 2024). One notable tool in this space is *AI Escape* (Figure 9), which provides a customizable platform for educators to embed curriculum-aligned mathematical content into interactive digital escape room scenarios. With built-in AI capabilities for performance tracking and collaborative engagement, it exemplifies the pedagogical possibilities of intelligent, gamified learning environments.

Figure 9. AI Escape interface generating the next step in a digital escape room

The pedagogical value of AI-powered digital escape rooms lies in their capacity to convert abstract mathematical principles into situated, collaborative problem-solving experiences. Rather than engaging with content passively, students must activate and apply their mathematical knowledge (e.g., solving equations, recognizing patterns, and testing strategies) to advance through contextually rich challenges. This process fosters deeper conceptual understanding, particularly when students are encouraged to revise their approaches within a low-stakes, exploratory environment (Damaševičius & Sidekerskienė, 2023b). AI integration plays a crucial role in ensuring that tasks remain appropriately challenging by dynamically adjusting difficulty and offering real-time feedback tailored to individual and group performance. Moreover, the collaborative design of these environments supports the development of communication and teamwork skills, as students work together to interpret clues and resolve interdependent tasks—skills essential not only in mathematics but across academic and professional contexts (Luque-Sánchez & Montejo-Gámez, 2023). Continuously monitoring learner interaction allows AI systems prompt under-engaged students, scaffold struggling groups, and highlight emerging misconceptions. These strategies aim to sustain engagement and maximize learning gains. As Damaševičius and Sidekerskienė (2023a) argue, this fusion of adaptive learning technologies with immersive narrative structures offers a compelling model for 21st-century mathematics instruction that is interactive, inclusive, and intellectually rigorous.

AI AND THE FUTURE OF MATHEMATICS EDUCATION

Hyper-Personalized and Neuroadaptive Learning

The future of mathematics education will be increasingly defined by learning systems that respond not only to performance data but also to the learner's cognitive and emotional states (Schukajlow et al., 2023). Traditional adaptive technologies adjust content based on correct or incorrect answers, but the next generation of AI-driven systems will incorporate neuroadaptive interfaces and cognitive modeling that respond to learners' real-time mental load, emotional responses, and attention levels (Saranya & Sankaradass, 2023; Trigka et al., 2024). Through the integration of wearable neurotechnology and brain-computer interfaces (BCIs), these systems will be able to detect patterns of disengagement, frustration, or cognitive overload by analyzing neural signals, gaze behavior, and physiological responses (Armani et al., 2023). This level of granularity will enable platforms to dynamically adjust pacing, simplify representations, or offer timely scaffolds based on individual readiness. For instance, if a learner begins to show signs of strain, the system might slow down, switch strategies, or revert to prerequisite content to restore flow. Such neuroadaptive responsiveness holds promise for learners who experience mathematics anxiety or executive function challenges. Tailoring instruction to fit the learner's cognitive profile in real time will allow AI tools transform mathematics education into a more intuitive, supportive, and affect-sensitive experience (Armani et al., 2023; Richard et al., 2022).

Immersive and Embodied Mathematical Experiences

Advances in mixed reality and conversational AI are also poised to transform mathematics instruction into a multisensory, embodied experience (Na & Sung,

2025; Santos et al., 2025). AI-powered holographic tutors will act as interactive teaching agents capable of delivering real-time verbal explanations, adjusting to learners' affective cues, and guiding problem-solving processes with responsive dialogue (Huang et al., 2021). These tools hold promise for increasing engagement and accessibility in diverse classrooms, where students often require differentiated instruction and multimodal learning opportunities (Lai & Cheong, 2022). In particular, these agents can be deployed within mixed-reality environments where students can visualize mathematical concepts in three dimensions, manipulate virtual objects through gestures, and explore abstract structures through spatial interaction (Kulkarni et al., 2024). Rather than studying equations on a two-dimensional screen, students will interact with vector fields, integrals, and functions as dynamic, manipulable forms. This spatial engagement will improve conceptual understanding, particularly for visual and kinesthetic learners who benefit from experiential learning. The ability to step into a mathematical environment, observe transformations from multiple perspectives, and construct meaning through guided manipulation will redefine how abstract ideas are internalized and applied (Bulut et al., 2024).

Generative Problem Design and Contextual Relevance

Generative AI will enable the design of highly contextualized mathematical tasks that reflect students' interests, goals, and lived experiences. Unlike traditional platforms that rely on static banks of problems, AI-powered systems will dynamically generate problem sets using models trained on diverse pedagogical corpora (Christ et al., 2024). This approach can help educators differentiate instruction more effectively, which allows them to meet students at their individual levels while maintaining curricular relevance. These systems will incorporate information about a learner's domain preferences, prior progress, and even career aspirations to create tasks that are both challenging and personally meaningful. For example, a student exploring algebra might engage with data-driven models related to space exploration, while another studying statistics could analyze social media trends or climate projections. By grounding abstract concepts in real-world applications, these generative systems will foster engagement and support knowledge transfer across disciplines. This evolution will transform problem-solving from a procedural activity into a cognitively rich and contextually grounded experience.

Narrative-Driven and Game-Based Instruction

The fusion of AI with interactive storytelling engines will give rise to narrative-based mathematics instruction, where students engage with mathematical content through evolving plots and immersive simulations (Moore et al., 2024). These

AI-driven platforms will construct dynamic stories that adapt in real time based on learner performance, decision-making, and emotional engagement. This approach holds pedagogical importance for both digital game-based and serious game applications in the mathematics classroom, where narrative contexts can drive sustained attention, critical thinking, and meaningful learning outcomes (Arif et al., 2025; Hui & Mahmud, 2023; Hussein et al., 2022). Each mathematical challenge will become part of a broader narrative arc, prompting learners to apply concepts to navigate a fictional scenario, solve a mystery, or complete a mission. This instructional shift toward narrative structure will increase motivation and deepen conceptual understanding by embedding mathematics in emotionally resonant and problem-rich environments. Rather than viewing mathematics as a series of isolated exercises, students will experience it as a tool for exploration and resolution within a cohesive story. The ability of AI to modify the storyline based on learner behavior ensures that every experience remains personalized, immersive, and pedagogically aligned.

Creativity Augmentation and Mathematical Inquiry

Future AI systems will extend their role from scaffolding known concepts to co-participating in the creative processes of mathematics. As one of the first major applications of AI in creativity, these tools will support learners in exploring open-ended questions and engaging in mathematical discovery. These systems will be capable of engaging in conjecture generation, symbolic reasoning, and proof exploration in collaboration with learners (Berson et al., 2023). In the classroom, this methodology can facilitate inquiry-based learning environments where students work alongside AI to explore mathematical ideas. Using models trained on formal logic and advanced symbolic manipulation, AI will help students formulate original problems, visualize abstract relationships, and examine multiple pathways to a solution. This approach will empower students to participate in mathematical creativity, moving beyond consumption toward the generation of new ideas. Instead of merely solving teacher-assigned problems, learners will propose their own conjectures, iterate on hypotheses, and explore the underlying structure of mathematical principles. AI will act not as a replacement for human creativity but as a catalyst that extends the learner's capacity for invention and abstraction (Garcia, 2024).

AI-Driven Policy, Curriculum, and Teacher Development

AI will also play a transformative role in shaping mathematics education at the systemic level. National education systems and school networks will increasingly integrate AI-powered learning analytics into their curriculum development and assessment frameworks (Mishra et al., 2024; Okewu et al., 2021). These systems will provide continuous, data-informed insights into learner progress, concept mastery, and engagement patterns, allowing for agile adjustments to curriculum content and instructional priorities. Simultaneously, teacher development will become more personalized through AI-driven feedback systems that analyze classroom discourse, track instructional efficacy, and recommend targeted interventions. Teachers will receive actionable guidance on student misconceptions, effective pedagogical strategies, and differentiated support pathways. By embedding AI into teacher training and curriculum evaluation (Sperling et al., 2024; Tan et al., 2025), educational institutions will be better positioned to align instruction with the evolving demands of STEM-oriented economies and the needs of diverse learners.

A Redefined Landscape for Mathematics Education

The cumulative impact of these developments suggests a fundamental redefinition of mathematics education in the age of AI (Richard et al., 2022; Zreik, 2024). Instruction will no longer proceed through static, one-size-fits-all pathways but will instead unfold within responsive ecosystems that adapt to each learner's cognitive, emotional, and contextual profile. AI will serve as both a mentor and a collaborator that shapes instruction, augments insight, and supports the co-construction of knowledge. This reimagined paradigm will position mathematics as a dialogic, exploratory, and socially relevant discipline. The integration of neuroadaptive interfaces, immersive media, generative problem design, intelligent feedback, and AI-driven policies will produce learning environments that are rigorous yet humane, scalable yet personalized. As these technologies mature, they will offer educators and learners tools not just for mastering mathematics but for experiencing it as a deeply meaningful and creative pursuit. Regardless of background, ability, or learning style, this transformation promises greater access, deeper engagement, and a renewed sense of agency in the mathematical journey for all.

CONCLUSION

As AI continues to transform the educational landscape, its strategic integration into mathematics instruction offers profound opportunities to reimagine how students engage with one of the most foundational disciplines in the curriculum. As this chapter has demonstrated, AI possesses the capacity to rehumanize mathematics instruction by adapting to individual cognitive needs, personalizing learning trajectories, and transforming abstract content into deeply interactive experiences. These developments signal a pedagogical recalibration where mathematical thinking is no longer confined to symbolic procedures but cultivated through adaptive dialogue, multimodal representation, and creative inquiry. The implications of these innovations are both immediate and long-term. First, students must develop the metacognitive skills needed to engage critically with feedback, question algorithmic authority, and build resilience in navigating complex, adaptive learning environments. For mathematics educators, it is essential to develop critical competencies in AI literacy to understand how these systems shape feedback, structure learning experiences, and influence students' mathematical identities. Researchers must also interrogate the assumptions embedded within AI systems and examine their implications for equity, access, and epistemological diversity in mathematics education. Finally, policymakers must craft frameworks that support responsible innovation while safeguarding the disciplinary integrity and humanistic aims of mathematics instruction. If guided by pedagogical intentionality and ethical foresight, the integration of AI can fundamentally redefine what it means to learn mathematics in a connected and human-centered world.

REFERENCES

Acut, D. P., Gamusa, E. V., Pernaa, J., Yuenyong, C., Pantaleon, A. T., Espina, R. C., & Garcia, M. B. (2025). AI Shaming Among Teacher Education Students: A Reflection on Acceptance and Identity in the Age of Generative Tools. In *Pitfalls of AI Integration in Education: Skill Obsolescence, Misuse, and Bias*. IGI Global., DOI: 10.4018/979-8-3373-0122-8.ch005

Almusaed, A., Almssad, A., Yitmen, I., & Homod, R. Z. (2023). Enhancing Student Engagement: Harnessing "AIED"'s Power in Hybrid Education—A Review Analysis. *Education Sciences*, *13*(7), 1–24. DOI: 10.3390/educsci13070632

Alt, D. (2023). Assessing the Benefits of Gamification in Mathematics for Student Gameful Experience and Gaming Motivation. *Computers & Education*, *200*, 1–15. DOI: 10.1016/j.compedu.2023.104806

Arif, Y. M., Nugroho, F., Aini, Q., Fauzan, A. C., & Garcia, M. B. (2025). A Systematic Literature Review of Serious Games for Physical Education: Technologies, Implementations, and Evaluations. In *Global Innovations in Physical Education and Health*. IGI Global., DOI: 10.4018/979-8-3693-3952-7.ch001

Arif, Y. M., & Nurhayati, H. (2022). Learning Material Selection for Metaverse-Based Mathematics Pedagogy Media Using Multi-Criteria Recommender System. *International Journal of Intelligent Engineering and Systems*, *15*(6), 541–551. DOI: 10.22266/ijies2022.1231.48

Armani, F., Daly, I., Vernitski, A., Gillmeister, H., & Scherer, R. (2023). Maths Anxiety and Cognitive State Monitoring for Neuroadaptive Learning Systems Using Electroencephalography. *2023 IEEE International Conference on Metrology for eXtended Reality, Artificial Intelligence and Neural Engineering (MetroXRAINE)*. https://doi.org/DOI: 10.1109/MetroXRAINE58569.2023.10405694

Berson, I. R., Berson, M. J., Luo, W., & He, H. (2023). Intelligence Augmentation in Early Childhood Education: A Multimodal Creative Inquiry Approach. In *Communications in Computer and Information Science* (pp. 756-763). Springer Nature Switzerland. https://doi.org/DOI: 10.1007/978-3-031-36336-8_116

Bozkurt, A., Xiao, J., Farrow, R., Bai, J. Y. H., Nerantzi, C., Moore, S., & Asino, T. I. (2024). The Manifesto for Teaching and Learning in a Time of Generative AI: A Critical Collective Stance to Better Navigate the Future. *Open Praxis*, *16*(4), 487–513. DOI: 10.55982/openpraxis.16.4.777

Bulut, N., Cevikbas, M., & Kaiser, G. (2024). Teaching Mathematics Through Augmented, Virtual, and Mixed Reality: An Analysis of Recent Advancements. In F. Dilling & I. Witzke (Eds.), *Augmented and Virtual Reality in Mathematics Education: International Symposium on Augmented and Virtual Reality 2022* (pp. 11-35). Springer Fachmedien Wiesbaden. https://doi.org/DOI: 10.1007/978-3-658-45271-1_2

Busuttil, L., & Calleja, J. (2025). Teachers' Beliefs and Practices About the Potential of ChatGPT in Teaching Mathematics in Secondary Schools. *Digital Experiences in Mathematics Education, 11*(1), 140–166. DOI: 10.1007/s40751-024-00168-3

Chaiarwut, S., Srikoon, S., Siritaratiwat, A., & Kwangmuang, P. (2025). Enhancing Executive Mathematics Problem-Solving Through a Constructivist Digital Learning Platform: Design, Development and Evaluation. *Social Sciences & Humanities Open, 11*, 1–15. DOI: 10.1016/j.ssaho.2025.101338

Chen, M.-F., Chen, Y.-C., Zuo, P.-Y., & Hou, H.-T. (2023). Design and Evaluation of a Remote Synchronous Gamified Mathematics Teaching Activity That Integrates Multi-Representational Scaffolding and a Mind Tool for Gamified Learning. *Education and Information Technologies, 28*(10), 13207–13233. DOI: 10.1007/s10639-023-11708-6 PMID: 37361748

Christ, B. R., Kropko, J., & Hartvigsen, T. (2024). MATHWELL: Generating Educational Math Word Problems Using Teacher Annotations. *Findings of the Association for Computational Linguistics.*

Damaševičius, R., & Sidekerskienė, T. (2023a). Designing Gamified Augmented Reality-Based Escape Rooms. *International Workshop on Gamification and Motivational Technologies.*

Damaševičius, R., & Sidekerskienė, T. (2023b). Designing Metaverse Escape Rooms for Microlearning in STEM Education. In Queirós, R., Cruz, M., Pinto, C., & Mascarenhas, D. (Eds.), *Fostering Pedagogy Through Micro and Adaptive Learning in Higher Education: Trends, Tools, and Applications* (pp. 192–211). IGI Global., DOI: 10.4018/978-1-6684-8656-6.ch009

Elmawati, E., Martadiputra, B. A. P., & Samosir, C. M. (2023). Gamification Research Focus in Learning Mathematics. *Proceedings of the 2023 5th World Symposium on Software Engineering*. https://doi.org/DOI: 10.1145/3631991.3632012

Engelbrecht, J., & Borba, M. C. (2024). Recent Developments in Using Digital Technology in Mathematics Education. *ZDM Mathematics Education, 56*(2), 281–292. DOI: 10.1007/s11858-023-01530-2

Espinosa-Pinos, C. A., Mazaquiza-Paucar, A. M., & Sánchez Benítez, C. A. (2024). *The Use of Gamification in Mathematics Education: Enhancing Geometry Comprehension with High School Students*. Learning and Collaboration Technologies., DOI: 10.1007/978-3-031-61685-3_2

Foshee, C. M., Elliott, S. N., & Atkinson, R. K. (2016). Technology-Enhanced Learning in College Mathematics Remediation. *British Journal of Educational Technology*, *47*(5), 893–905. DOI: 10.1111/bjet.12285

Gantalao, L. C., Calzada, J. G. D., Capuyan, D. L., Lumantas, B. C., Acut, D. P., & Garcia, M. B. (2025). Equipping the Next Generation of Technicians: Navigating School Infrastructure and Technical Knowledge in the Age of AI Integration. In *Pitfalls of AI Integration in Education: Skill Obsolescence, Misuse, and Bias*. IGI Global., DOI: 10.4018/979-8-3373-0122-8.ch009

Gaona, J., Reguant, M., Valdivia, I., Vásquez, M., & Sancho-Vinuesa, T. (2018). Feedback by Automatic Assessment Systems Used in Mathematics Homework in the Engineering Field. *Computer Applications in Engineering Education*, *26*(4), 994–1007. DOI: 10.1002/cae.21950

Garcia, M. B. (2024). The Paradox of Artificial Creativity: Challenges and Opportunities of Generative AI Artistry. *Creativity Research Journal*, •••, 1–14. DOI: 10.1080/10400419.2024.2354622

Garcia, M. B., de Almeida, R. S., Acut, D. P., de Almeida, R. P. P., Garcia, P. S., & Stefani, E. (2025). Teaching Medicine With Generative Artificial Intelligence (GenAI): A Review of Practices, Pitfalls, and Possibilities in Medical Education. In *Teaching in the Age of Medical Technology* (pp. 123-156). IGI Global. https://doi.org/DOI: 10.4018/979-8-3373-1519-5.ch005

Garcia, M. B., Rosak-Szyrocka, J., Yılmaz, R., Metwally, A. H. S., Acut, D. P., Ofosu-Ampong, K., & Bozkurt, A. (2025). Rethinking Educational Assessment in the Age of Generative AI: Actionable Strategies to Mitigate Academic Dishonesty. In *Pitfalls of AI Integration in Education: Skill Obsolescence, Misuse, and Bias*. IGI Global., DOI: 10.4018/979-8-3373-0122-8.ch001

Gómez Niño, J. R., Patricia, Á. D. L., Andrés, C., & Ortega González, E. (2024). Gamifying Learning with AI: A Pathway to 21st-Century Skills. *Journal of Research in Childhood Education*, •••, 1–16. DOI: 10.1080/02568543.2024.2421974

Grant, M. J., & Booth, A. (2009). A Typology of Reviews: An Analysis of 14 Review Types and Associated Methodologies. *Health Information and Libraries Journal*, *26*(2), 91–108. DOI: 10.1111/j.1471-1842.2009.00848.x PMID: 19490148

Gravemeijer, K., Stephan, M., Julie, C., Lin, F.-L., & Ohtani, M. (2017). What Mathematics Education May Prepare Students for the Society of the Future? *International Journal of Science and Mathematics Education*, *15*(1), 105–123. DOI: 10.1007/s10763-017-9814-6

Greenhalgh, T., Thorne, S., & Malterud, K. (2018). Time to Challenge the Spurious Hierarchy of Systematic over Narrative Reviews? *European Journal of Clinical Investigation*, *48*(6), 1–6. DOI: 10.1111/eci.12931 PMID: 29578574

Hamady, S., Mershad, K., & Jabakhanji, B. (2024). Multi-Version Interactive Assessment Through the Integration of GeoGebra with Moodle. *Frontiers in Education*, *9*, 1–15. DOI: 10.3389/feduc.2024.1466128

Hasanah, N. A., Aziza, M. R., Junikhah, A., Arif, Y. M., & Garcia, M. B. (2025). Navigating the Use of AI in Engineering Education Through a Systematic Review of Technology, Regulations, and Challenges. In *Pitfalls of AI Integration in Education: Skill Obsolescence, Misuse, and Bias*. IGI Global., DOI: 10.4018/979-8-3373-0122-8.ch016

Huang, X., Wild, F., & Whitelock, D. (2021). Design Dimensions for Holographic Intelligent Agents: A Comparative Analysis. *1st International Workshop on Multimodal Artificial Intelligence in Education.*

Hui, H. B., & Mahmud, M. S. (2023). Influence of Game-Based Learning in Mathematics Education on the Students' Cognitive and Affective Domain: A Systematic Review. *Frontiers in Psychology*, *14*, 1–15. DOI: 10.3389/fpsyg.2023.1105806 PMID: 37057144

Hussein, M. H., Ow, S. H., Elaish, M. M., & Jensen, E. O. (2022). Digital Game-Based Learning in K-12 Mathematics Education: A Systematic Literature Review. *Education and Information Technologies*, *27*(2), 2859–2891. DOI: 10.1007/s10639-021-10721-x

Hwang, G.-J., & Tu, Y.-F. (2021). Roles and Research Trends of Artificial Intelligence in Mathematics Education: A Bibliometric Mapping Analysis and Systematic Review. *Mathematics*, *9*(6), 1–19. DOI: 10.3390/math9060584

Izquierdo-Álvarez, V., & Jimeno-Postigo, C. (2025). Challenges and Opportunities of Integrating Generative Artificial Intelligence in Higher Education: A Systematic Review. In *Pitfalls of AI Integration in Education: Skill Obsolescence, Misuse, and Bias*. IGI Global., DOI: 10.4018/979-8-3373-0122-8.ch017

Kabudi, T., Pappas, I., & Olsen, D. H. (2021). Ai-Enabled Adaptive Learning Systems: A Systematic Mapping of the Literature. *Computers and Education: Artificial Intelligence*, *2*, 1–12. DOI: 10.1016/j.caeai.2021.100017

Kovari, A. (2025). A Systematic Review of AI-Powered Collaborative Learning in Higher Education: Trends and Outcomes from the Last Decade. *Social Sciences & Humanities Open*, *11*, 1–13. DOI: 10.1016/j.ssaho.2025.101335

Kulkarni, A., Albright, C., Kamble, P., & Chu, S. L. (2024). Investigating Situated Learning Theory Through an Augmented Reality Mobile Assistant for Everyday STEM Learning. *2024 IEEE Conference on Virtual Reality and 3D User Interfaces Abstracts and Workshops (VRW)*. https://doi.org/DOI: 10.1109/vrw62533.2024.00274

Lai, J. W., & Cheong, K. H. (2022). Adoption of Virtual and Augmented Reality for Mathematics Education: A Scoping Review. *IEEE Access : Practical Innovations, Open Solutions*, *10*, 13693–13703. DOI: 10.1109/ACCESS.2022.3145991

Lee, D., & Yeo, S. (2022). Developing an AI-Based Chatbot for Practicing Responsive Teaching in Mathematics. *Computers & Education*, *191*, 1–17. DOI: 10.1016/j.compedu.2022.104646

Lee, J. Y., Pyon, C. U., & Woo, J. (2023). Digital Twin for Math Education: A Study on the Utilization of Games and Gamification for University Mathematics Education. *Electronics (Basel)*, *12*(15), 1–19. DOI: 10.3390/electronics12153207

Lenz, K., Reinhold, F., & Wittmann, G. (2024). Transitions Between Conceptual and Procedural Knowledge Profiles. Patterns in Understanding Fractions and Indicators for Individual Differences. *Learning and Individual Differences*, *116*, 1–12. DOI: 10.1016/j.lindif.2024.102548

Liu, J., Sun, D., Sun, J., Wang, J., & Yu, P. L. H. (2025). Designing a Generative AI Enabled Learning Environment for Mathematics Word Problem Solving in Primary Schools: Learning Performance, Attitudes and Interaction. *Computers and Education: Artificial Intelligence*, *9*, 1–11. DOI: 10.1016/j.caeai.2025.100438

Luque-Sánchez, F., & Montejo-Gámez, J. (2023). *A Virtual Escape Room for the Enhancement of Mathematical Communication in Secondary Education*. Technology, Knowledge and Learning., DOI: 10.1007/s10758-023-09706-1

Maher, D. (2024). Embracing AI in the Classroom. In *AI in Education* (pp. 41–44). TLN Journal.

Mangubat, J. C., Mangubat, M. R., Uy, T. B. L., Acut, D. P., & Garcia, M. B. (2025). Safeguarding Educational Innovations Amid AI Disruptions: A Reassessment of Patenting for Sustained Intellectual Property Protection. In *Pitfalls of AI Integration in Education: Skill Obsolescence, Misuse, and Bias*. IGI Global., DOI: 10.4018/979-8-3373-0122-8.ch013

Mishra, N., Garcia, P. S., Habal, B. G. M., & Garcia, M. B. (2024). Harnessing an AI-Driven Analytics Model to Optimize Training and Treatment in Physical Education for Sports Injury Prevention. *Proceedings of the 8th International Conference on Education and Multimedia Technology*. https://doi.org/DOI: 10.1145/3678726.3678740

Mohamed, A. M., Shaaban, T. S., Bakry, S. H., Guillén-Gámez, F. D., & Strzelecki, A. (2024). Empowering the Faculty of Education Students: Applying AI's Potential for Motivating and Enhancing Learning. *Innovative Higher Education*, *50*(2), 587–609. DOI: 10.1007/s10755-024-09747-z

Moore, D. E., Moore, S. R. R., Ireen, B., Iskandar, W. P., Artazyan, G., & Murnane, E. L. (2024). Teaching Artificial Intelligence in Extracurricular Contexts Through Narrative-Based Learnersourcing. *Proceedings of the CHI Conference on Human Factors in Computing Systems*. https://doi.org/DOI: 10.1145/3613904.3642198

Morris, W., Holmes, L., Choi, J. S., & Crossley, S. (2024). Automated Scoring of Constructed Response Items in Math Assessment Using Large Language Models. *International Journal of Artificial Intelligence in Education*. Advance online publication. DOI: 10.1007/s40593-024-00418-w

Muhamad Fadzil, N., & Osman, S. (2025). Scoping the Landscape: Comparative Review of Collaborative Learning Methods in Mathematical Problem-Solving Pedagogy. *International Electronic Journal of Mathematics Education*, *20*(2), 1–13. DOI: 10.29333/iejme/15935

Mustafa, A. N. (2024). The Future of Mathematics Education: Adaptive Learning Technologies and Artificial Intelligence. *International Journal of Science and Research Archive*, *12*(1), 2594–2599. DOI: 10.30574/ijsra.2024.12.1.1134

Mustafa, A. S., Alkawsi, G. A., Ofosu-Ampong, K., Vanduhe, V. Z., Garcia, M. B., & Baashar, Y. (2022). Gamification of E-Learning in African Universities: Identifying Adoption Factors Through Task-Technology Fit and Technology Acceptance Model. In Portela, F., & Queirós, R. (Eds.), *Next-Generation Applications and Implementations of Gamification Systems* (pp. 73–96). IGI Global., DOI: 10.4018/978-1-7998-8089-9.ch005

Na, H., & Sung, H. (2025). Learn Math Through Motion: A Technology-Enhanced Embodied Approach with Augmented Reality for Geometry Learning in K-12 Classrooms. *Interactive Learning Environments*, •••, 1–14. DOI: 10.1080/10494820.2025.2450663

Nguyen, A., Ngo, H. N., Hong, Y., Dang, B., & Nguyen, B.-P. T. (2023). Ethical Principles for Artificial Intelligence in Education. *Education and Information Technologies*, *28*(4), 4221–4241. DOI: 10.1007/s10639-022-11316-w PMID: 36254344

Ningsih, Y. L., Octaria, D., Nopriyanti, T. D., & Jumroh, J. (2024). Development of a Desmos-Assisted Planar Analytic Geometry Textbook to Support High Order Thinking Skills. [Jurnal Teori dan Aplikasi Matematika]. *JTAM*, *8*(2), 1–11. DOI: 10.31764/jtam.v8i2.20775

Nortvedt, G. A., & Buchholtz, N. (2018). Assessment in Mathematics Education: Responding to Issues Regarding Methodology, Policy, and Equity. *ZDM*, *50*(4), 555–570. DOI: 10.1007/s11858-018-0963-z

Okewu, E., Adewole, P., Misra, S., Maskeliunas, R., & Damasevicius, R. (2021). Artificial Neural Networks for Educational Data Mining in Higher Education: A Systematic Literature Review. *Applied Artificial Intelligence*, *35*(13), 983–1021. DOI: 10.1080/08839514.2021.1922847

Owusu, R., Bonyah, E., & Arthur, Y. D. (2023). The Effect of GeoGebra on University Students' Understanding of Polar Coordinates. *Cogent Education*, *10*(1), 1–16. DOI: 10.1080/2331186x.2023.2177050

Pepin, B., Buchholtz, N., & Salinas-Hernández, U. (2025). A Scoping Survey of ChatGPT in Mathematics Education. *Digital Experiences in Mathematics Education*, *11*(1), 9–41. DOI: 10.1007/s40751-025-00172-1

Pinto, C. M. A., Nikolopoulos, C., Cruz, M., Queirós, R., & Petridis, K. (2024). Empowering Engineering Students' Math Literacy with Digital Escape Rooms. *2024 IEEE World Engineering Education Conference (EDUNINE)*. https://doi.org/DOI: 10.1109/EDUNINE60625.2024.10500542

Pope, D. (2022). Using Desmos and GeoGebra to Engage Students and Develop Conceptual Understanding of Mathematics. In *Advances in Educational Technologies and Instructional Design* (pp. 104-129). IGI Global. https://doi.org/DOI: 10.4018/978-1-6684-5920-1.ch006

Richard, P. R., Vélez, M. P., & Vaerenbergh, S. V. (2022). *Mathematics Education in the Age of Artificial Intelligence: How Artificial Intelligence can Serve Mathematical Human Learning*. Springer Cham., DOI: 10.1007/978-3-030-86909-0

Rozgonjuk, D., Kraav, T., Mikkor, K., Orav-Puurand, K., & Täht, K. (2020). Mathematics Anxiety Among STEM and Social Sciences Students: The Roles of Mathematics Self-Efficacy, and Deep and Surface Approach to Learning. *International Journal of STEM Education*, *7*(1), 1–11. DOI: 10.1186/s40594-020-00246-z

Saborío-Taylor, S., & Rojas-Ramírez, F. (2024). Universal Design for Learning and Artificial Intelligence in the Digital Era: Fostering Inclusion and Autonomous Learning. *International Journal of Professional Development. Learners and Learning*, *6*(2), 1–8. DOI: 10.30935/ijpdll/14694

Sangwin, C. J., & Köcher, N. (2016). Automation of Mathematics Examinations. *Computers & Education*, *94*, 215–227. DOI: 10.1016/j.compedu.2015.11.014

Santos, W. D. M. Q. D., Peretti, A., Teixeira, J. M. X. N., Peres, F. F. F., Mauricio, C. R. M., & Silva, M. M. O. D. (2025). Mixed Reality as a Tool to Enhance Mathematics Education in Elementary School. *2025 IEEE Conference on Virtual Reality and 3D User Interfaces Abstracts and Workshops (VRW)*. https://doi.org/DOI: 10.1109/VRW66409.2025.00055

Saranya, K., & Sankaradass, V. (2023). Hyperpersonalization of Educational Content Through Multimodal Deep Learning and Gamification. *2023 International Conference on Data Science, Agents & Artificial Intelligence (ICDSAAI)*. https://doi.org/DOI: 10.1109/icdsaai59313.2023.10452428

Sarkar, S., & Bhatia, G. (2021). Writing and Appraising Narrative Reviews. *Journal of Clinical and Scientific Research*, *10*(3), 169–172.

Schukajlow, S., Rakoczy, K., & Pekrun, R. (2023). Emotions and Motivation in Mathematics Education: Where We Are Today and Where We Need to Go. *ZDM Mathematics Education*, *55*(2), 249–267. DOI: 10.1007/s11858-022-01463-2 PMID: 36684477

Shimizu, Y., & Vithal, R. (2023). *Mathematics Curriculum Reforms Around the World: The 24th ICMI Study*. Springer Cham., DOI: 10.1007/978-3-031-13548-4

Sidekerskienė, T., & Damaševičius, R. (2023). Out-of-the-Box Learning: Digital Escape Rooms as a Metaphor for Breaking Down Barriers in STEM Education. *Sustainability*, *15*(9), 1–33. DOI: 10.3390/su15097393

Sperling, K., Stenberg, C.-J., McGrath, C., Åkerfeldt, A., Heintz, F., & Stenliden, L. (2024). In Search of Artificial Intelligence (AI) Literacy in Teacher Education: A Scoping Review. *Computers and Education Open*, *6*, 1–13. https://doi.org/https://doi.org/10.1016/j.caeo.2024.100169

Stohlmann, M. S. (2023). Mathematical Digital Escape Rooms. *School Science and Mathematics*, *123*(1), 26–30. DOI: 10.1111/ssm.12564

Sukhera, J. (2022). Narrative Reviews: Flexible, Rigorous, and Practical. *Journal of Graduate Medical Education*, *14*(4), 414–417. DOI: 10.4300/jgme-d-22-00480.1 PMID: 35991099

Tan, D. Y., & Cheah, C. W. (2021). Developing a Gamified Ai-Enabled Online Learning Application to Improve Students' Perception of University Physics. *Computers and Education: Artificial Intelligence*, *2*, 1–10. DOI: 10.1016/j.caeai.2021.100032

Tan, X., Cheng, G., & Ling, M. H. (2025). Artificial Intelligence in Teaching and Teacher Professional Development: A Systematic Review. *Computers and Education: Artificial Intelligence*, *8*, 1–19. DOI: 10.1016/j.caeai.2024.100355

Trigka, M., Dritsas, E., & Mylonas, P. (2024). New Perspectives in e-Learning: EEG-Based Modelling of Human Cognition Individual Differences. *IFIP Advances in Information and Communication Technology*. Advance online publication. DOI: 10.1007/978-3-031-63227-3_20

Trindade, M. A. M., Edirisinghe, G. S., & Luo, L. (2025). Teaching Mathematical Concepts in Management with Generative Artificial Intelligence: The Power of Human Oversight in AI-Driven Learning. *International Journal of Management Education*, *23*(2), 1–18. DOI: 10.1016/j.ijme.2024.101104

Valderama, A. M. C., Tuazon, J. B. D., & Garcia, M. B. (2022). Promoting Student Thinking and Engagement Through Question-Based and Gamified Learning. *2022 IEEE 14th International Conference on Humanoid, Nanotechnology, Information Technology, Communication and Control, Environment and Management (HNICEM)*. https://doi.org/DOI: 10.1109/HNICEM57413.2022.10109470

Vintere, A., Safiulina, E., & Panova, O. (2024). AI-Based Mathematics Learning Platforms in Undergraduate Engineering Studies: Analyses of User Experiences. *Engineering for Rural Development*, *23*, 1042–1047. DOI: 10.22616/ERDev.2024.23.TF216

Walter, Y. (2024). Embracing the Future of Artificial Intelligence in the Classroom: The Relevance of AI Literacy, Prompt Engineering, and Critical Thinking in Modern Education. *International Journal of Educational Technology in Higher Education*, *21*(1), 1–29. DOI: 10.1186/s41239-024-00448-3

Xia, Q., Weng, X., Ouyang, F., Lin, T. J., & Chiu, T. K. F. (2024). A Scoping Review on How Generative Artificial Intelligence Transforms Assessment in Higher Education. *International Journal of Educational Technology in Higher Education, 21*(1), 1–22. DOI: 10.1186/s41239-024-00468-z

Xiao, J., Bozkurt, A., Nichols, M., Pazurek, A., Stracke, C. M., Bai, J. Y. H., & Themeli, C. (2025). Venturing into the Unknown: Critical Insights into Grey Areas and Pioneering Future Directions in Educational Generative AI Research. *TechTrends*, •••, 1–16. DOI: 10.1007/s11528-025-01060-6

Yeo, S., Moon, J., & Kim, D. (2024). Transforming Mathematics Education with AI: Innovations, Implementations, and Insights. *The Mathematics Educator, 63*(2), 386–392. DOI: 10.7468/mathedu.2024.63.2.387

Zakariya, Y. F. (2022). Improving Students' Mathematics Self-Efficacy: A Systematic Review of Intervention Studies. *Frontiers in Psychology, 13*, 1–13. DOI: 10.3389/fpsyg.2022.986622 PMID: 36225698

Zreik, M. (2024). Redefining Mathematics Education in the Age of Artificial Intelligence: Challenges and Opportunities. In Njurai, E., & Uworwabayeho, A. (Eds.), *Impacts of Globalization and Innovation in Mathematics Education* (pp. 19–40). IGI Global Scientific Publishing., DOI: 10.4018/979-8-3693-2873-6.ch002

KEY TERMS AND DEFINITIONS

Adaptive Learning: Refers to the use of AI systems that dynamically adjust instructional content and pacing based on student performance and behavior.

Artificial Intelligence in Education (AIEd): Encompasses the application of AI technologies to enhance teaching, learning, and assessment across educational contexts.

Automated Assessment: Involves AI-powered tools that evaluate student work, provide real-time feedback, and support scalable grading in mathematics education.

Digital Escape Rooms: Interactive learning environments where students solve AI-supported mathematical challenges to progress through narrative-based scenarios.

Gamification: Refers to the integration of game elements into learning experiences, often supported by AI to personalize challenges and sustain student engagement.

Mathematics Education: Focuses on the discipline-specific study of teaching and learning mathematical concepts with emphasis on cognitive, technological, and pedagogical strategies.

Personalized Learning: Involves tailoring instructional experiences to individual learner profiles using AI to adapt content, feedback, and learning trajectories.

Chapter 7
Prospective Teachers' Perceived Affordances and Constraints of Using ChatGPT in Mathematical Problem Posing

Fadime Ulusoy
https://orcid.org/0000-0003-3393-8778
Kastamonu University, Turkey

ABSTRACT

This qualitative study explores prospective mathematics teachers' (PMTs) perceived affordances and constraints of using ChatGPT in mathematical problem posing. Data were collected from 23 PMTs through reflection papers, which documented their experiences using ChatGPT to pose real-life mathematical problems with varying cognitive demand levels. The study employed qualitative content analysis using both deductive and inductive approaches to examine PMTs' experiences with ChatGPT. The findings reveal that PMTs value ChatGPT for its immediate feedback, contextual diversity, and ability to provide personalized learning paths. Additionally, PMTs highlighted its potential as an assessment tool for evaluating the quality of posed problems. However, significant constraints were also identified, such as ChatGPT's limited ability to generate diverse and novel problems, difficulties in producing realistic and contextually rich problems, and mathematical inaccuracies. Additionally, PMTs noted ChatGPT's poor visualization and complex language use, particularly in higher cognitive demand tasks.

DOI: 10.4018/979-8-3373-1998-8.ch007

INTRODUCTION

In recent years, artificial intelligence (AI)-powered chatbots have attracted considerable scholarly attention for their potential to enhance pedagogical practices and learning outcomes (Hwang & Chang, 2021; Kuhail et al., 2023). These tools facilitate personalized learning, scaffold complex tasks, and promote interactive engagement through adaptive dialogue (Winkler & Söllner, 2018). Their integration into teacher education has shown particular promise, offering educators dynamic platforms for individualized instruction and flexible pedagogical experimentation (Han & Lee, 2022; Lee & Yeo, 2022). However, despite these advantages, further empirical investigation is necessary to optimize their systematic adoption in teacher training programs (Hwang & Chang, 2021).

Within mathematics education, chatbots such as ChatGPT are increasingly employed to augment teachers' problem-solving skills, conceptual mastery, and lesson design (Brouitin, 2024; Ergene & Ergene, 2024; Tunç, 2024). Yet, their application in *mathematical problem posing*—a cognitively demanding practice essential for fostering creativity, critical thinking, and deeper conceptual understanding—remains under-researched (Biton & Segal, 2025; Kim, Park, & Joung, 2025). Problem posing, defined as the generation or reformulation of mathematical problems, constitutes a cornerstone of mathematical cognition (Silver, 1994). Empirical studies have consistently highlighted its efficacy in advancing students' mathematical competencies, including problem-solving proficiency, conceptual fluency, and academic achievement (Cai et al., 2015; Zhang et al., 2024). Moreover, teachers' capacity to craft pedagogically sound problems directly influences instructional quality and student outcomes (Cai & Hwang, 2020; Cai & Rott, 2024). As both an assessment and pedagogical strategy, problem posing enables educators to diagnose misconceptions, evaluate comprehension, and stimulate higher-order engagement with mathematical content (Stoyanova & Ellerton, 1996; Zhang et al., 2024).

Despite its pedagogical value, problem posing is often perceived as a complex practice, distinct from conventional problem-solving due to its open-ended nature. Given its significance and the documented challenges teachers face in problem-posing tasks, this study examines the affordances and limitations of AI chatbots in this domain from the perspective of preservice mathematics teachers. Specifically, it addresses the following research question:

What are the perceived affordances and constraints of ChatGPT in generating context-based mathematical problems, as reported by prospective mathematics teachers?

The Necessity and Significance of the Study

The accessibility and intuitive interface of ChatGPT have contributed to its widespread adoption in educational settings, with both students and educators leveraging its capabilities (Jeon & Lee, 2023; Rahman & Watanobe, 2023). However, the educational application of chatbots presents both opportunities and challenges, as their output is contingent upon the quality and specificity of user prompts (Rospigliosi, 2023). This variability raises concerns about potential cognitive impacts, including the dissemination of misinformation, the acquisition of incomplete or flawed conceptual understanding (Wardat et al., 2023), and the provision of superficial explanations (Javaid et al., 2023; Zhang et al., 2023).

Existing literature has extensively examined the affordances and limitations of ChatGPT in education (Javaid et al., 2023; Kasneci et al., 2023; Rasul et al., 2023; Tlili et al., 2023). The tool demonstrates utility in addressing both routine and non-routine problems, alongside performing diverse educational tasks (Sánchez-Ruiz et al., 2023; Wardat et al., 2023). For teachers, ChatGPT offers support in lesson planning, instructional material development, differentiated content creation, and the design and evaluation of assessments (Javaid et al., 2023; Kasneci et al., 2023; Rasul et al., 2023; Tlili et al., 2023). Nevertheless, concerns persist regarding its propensity to generate inaccurate or misleading information (Javaid et al., 2023; Lucy & Bamman, 2021; Rasul et al., 2023) and the risk of fostering overreliance, potentially stifling creativity among learners and instructors alike (Javaid et al., 2023; Kasneci et al., 2023).

A recent research by Kim et al. (2025) investigated preservice mathematics teachers' (PMTs) experiences with ChatGPT-mediated problem-posing activities. Participants identified several advantages, including (i) step-by-step guidance, (ii) immediate feedback and interactivity, (iii) exposure to diverse examples and strategies, and (iv) personalized learning pathways. However, they also noted limitations, such as incorrect responses and issues with the clarity and simplicity of presented solutions. The current study extends these findings by exploring PMTs' perceptions of ChatGPT's affordances and constraints in the context of posing real-life, cognitively stratified problems related to area measurement. This investigation provides insights into ChatGPT's capacity to simulate authentic scenarios while managing cognitive load—a crucial consideration in problem-posing tasks. Furthermore, this study examines ChatGPT's potential as a collaborative partner in problem posing, wherein iterative dialogue facilitates the co-construction and refinement of mathematical problems. Despite these promising applications, significant constraints remain, particularly regarding the tool's limitations in generating novel, open-ended problems that demand higher-order thinking. These findings underscore the necessity of a balanced approach to integrating chatbots into problem-posing activities—one that preserves pedagogical integrity while harnessing technological innovation.

PMTs' perspectives are especially valuable, as they will ultimately shape the future of mathematics instruction. Their insights can inform the development of AI-driven educational tools, teacher training programs, and policies aimed at optimizing the role of technology in mathematics education. By elucidating the affordances and constraints of ChatGPT in problem posing, this study contributes to a more nuanced understanding of how AI can be effectively leveraged to enhance learning outcomes. The implications of this research extend to instructional design, teacher preparation, and the broader discourse on technology integration in mathematics education.

THEORETICAL BACKGROUND

The literature review is organized into three thematic areas. First, recent research on AI in education is explained with a focus on generative AI and its role in teaching and learning. Second, the body of work on mathematical problem posing is reviewed by highlighting its cognitive, creative, and pedagogical dimensions. Third, research on teacher preparation on problem posing is discussed to highlight the gap in the recent literature.

AI in Education

The integration of Artificial Intelligence (AI) technologies into educational contexts has rapidly reshaped traditional pedagogical practices, offering new affordances for personalized learning, intelligent tutoring, formative assessment, and administrative support (Luckin & Cukurova, 2019; Holmes et al., 2022). Among these innovations, generative AI tools—particularly large language models such as ChatGPT—have gained prominence for their ability to simulate human-like dialogue, respond to open-ended questions, and generate educational content across disciplines. These capabilities make AI tools particularly attractive in teacher education, where flexibility, individualization, and immediate feedback are vital for developing professional competencies (Hwang & Chang, 2021; Kasneci et al., 2023). However, meaningful integration of AI in education necessitates not just technical adoption but also pedagogical vision, ethical awareness, and curricular alignment.

In the context of teacher education, AI tools have been employed to support various instructional functions, such as lesson planning (Broutin, 2024), generating problem-based tasks (Wardat et al., 2023), and providing real-time feedback on pedagogical decisions (Gill et al., 2024). These applications have opened new possibilities for adaptive learning environments, where pre-service teachers can experiment with teaching scenarios, analyze AI-generated outputs, and develop critical reflection skills (Ng et al., 2021). Moreover, AI has shown potential in scaffolding complex cognitive tasks, such as mathematical problem posing, by offering iterative support and promoting conceptual variation (Kim et al., 2025). Nevertheless, studies also highlight significant challenges, including inaccuracies in AI-generated content, overreliance on machine-generated materials, and concerns regarding fairness, privacy, and data ethics (Javaid et al., 2023; Tlili et al., 2023).

Given these affordances and limitations, recent scholarship calls for a more deliberate and theory-informed integration of AI tools into teacher education programs. Frameworks such as Technological Pedagogical Content Knowledge (TPACK) (Mishra & Koehler, 2006) and AI literacy models (Long & Magerko, 2020) provide conceptual scaffolds for analyzing how teachers interact with AI, design prompts, and evaluate educational outputs. Ethical guidelines from global institutions such as UNESCO (2023) and the OECD (2023) emphasize the importance of fostering teacher autonomy, safeguarding digital equity, and developing critical AI literacy among educators. As AI continues to evolve, its transformative potential in education will depend largely on how teacher educators design learning experiences that balance innovation with ethical responsibility and pedagogical rigor.

Use of ChatGPT in Mathematics Teacher Education

ChatGPT has emerged as a valuable tool in educational contexts owing to its accessibility and intuitive interface. Consequently, education researchers and practitioners have rapidly incorporated it into various pedagogical applications (Busuttil & Calleja, 2025; Jeon & Lee, 2023; Rahman & Watanobe, 2023; Ali et al., 2023; Gill et al., 2024; Memarian & Doleck, 2023; Meyer et al., 2023; Zamfroiu et al., 2023). Current research presents a complex picture, portraying ChatGPT simultaneously as a transformative educational asset and a source of substantial ethical, practical, and academic integrity challenges. While demonstrating potential to enhance personalized learning and improve educational accessibility, scholars emphasize the necessity for judicious implementation and skilled prompt engineering to avoid ethical dilemmas, privacy issues, misinformation dissemination, over-dependence, and skill degradation (Azaria et al., 2024; Tlili et al., 2023; Wardat et al., 2023). For instance, Ali et al. (2023) note ChatGPT's constraints in delivering truly individualized instruction due to its lack of comprehensive student profiling. Conversely, other researchers (e.g., Gill et al., 2024) underscore its effectiveness in facilitating personalized learning through diverse educational resources and immediate feedback. This dichotomy underscores the importance of comprehensively understanding AI's capabilities while acknowledging its limitations to create meaningful educational innovations.

The incorporation of AI chatbots like ChatGPT into teacher education programs has grown increasingly imperative as these technologies transform contemporary pedagogical approaches (MacDowell & Korchinsk, 2023). These tools provide comprehensive support for educators, ranging from assessment design and lesson planning to automating administrative functions such as grading, report generation, and mathematical problem formulation. Furthermore, ChatGPT assists in analyzing problem difficulty, tracking student progress, and providing formative assessments (Celik et al., 2022). Given these multifaceted applications, integrating ChatGPT into preservice teacher education becomes essential for developing future educators' technological competencies.

In mathematics teacher education, ChatGPT has been employed in several distinct capacities. A primary application involves its use as a problem-solving aid (Ergene & Ergene, 2024; Noster et al., 2024). Noster et al. (2024) investigated eleven prospective teachers' use of ChatGPT to solve mathematical problems, examining their mathematical fidelity, prompting strategies, and AI interaction patterns. The study revealed participants' tendency to uncritically accept ChatGPT's incorrect solutions and identified varied prompting approaches (including zero-shot prompting, task-specific questioning, and few-shot prompting). Notably, participants exhibited particular difficulty identifying errors in ChatGPT's solutions to more complex mathematical problems. Similarly, Wardat et al. (2023) documented instances of incomplete or inaccurate mathematical responses from ChatGPT, particularly noting its limited geometric understanding and inability to visually represent geometric properties through diagrams.

Another significant application involves lesson plan and instructional material development (e.g., Broutin, 2024; Gurl et al., 2025; Tunç, 2024). Gurl et al. (2025) conducted a qualitative study examining prospective teachers' use of ChatGPT for microteaching lesson plans, focusing on mathematical accuracy and pedagogical effectiveness. Findings indicated that while participants competently evaluated the pedagogical aspects of ChatGPT-generated plans - frequently critiquing their lack of student-centered approaches - they recognized the tool's value in providing conceptually aligned starting points. However, participants unanimously reported requiring substantial modifications before implementation. The study also revealed participants' challenges in accurately assessing the mathematical validity of ChatGPT's solutions within lesson plans. These findings suggest that while ChatGPT offers numerous benefits for educators, it also presents notable concerns (Pepin et al., 2025). The current study extends this research by investigating prospective mathematics teachers' experiences using ChatGPT as a problem-posing assistant, thereby contributing to scholarship on artificial intelligence applications in mathematics education.

Mathematical Problem Posing

Mathematical problem posing refers not only to the act of solving a problem but also to the formulation, adaptation, and creation of problems themselves (Brown & Walter, 1983; Silver, 1994). While problem solving has dominated mathematics education research for decades, problem posing has emerged more recently as a critical and distinct area of investigation (Cai et al., 2013). The pedagogical benefits of problem posing are well-documented, including its capacity to:

1. **Foster mathematical creativity** through the exploration of novel ideas and representations (Sadak et al., 2022; Ulusoy et al., 2025; Yuan & Sriraman, 2011);
2. **Deepen conceptual understanding** by encouraging learners to reframe knowledge in new contexts (Chen & Cai, 2020); and
3. **Enhance reading comprehension and interpretative skills** through engagement with mathematical language and structure (Rosenshine, Meister, & Chapman, 1996).

Notably, problem posing imposes greater cognitive demands than problem solving (Cai & Hwang, 2002), as it requires sophisticated reasoning processes, flexible thinking, and meta-cognitive awareness. These demands vary according to task characteristics, context, and the level of scaffolding provided (Cai et al., 2013). Engaging learners in problem posing contributes significantly to the development of cognitive abilities, mathematical communication skills, and problem-solving strategies, making it a cornerstone of mathematical thinking and an essential component of high-quality instruction (Brown & Walter, 1983; Silver & Cai, 1996).

The conceptualization of problem posing has evolved across multiple theoretical perspectives. Leung (1993) defines it as either generating original problems or reformulating existing ones, while Silver (1994) characterizes it as constructing new problems to explore mathematical situations or modifying problems during the solution process. These definitions underscore the dual nature of problem posing as both a creative and adaptive endeavor, requiring learners to navigate between innovation and modification. Scholars have developed various classification frameworks for problem posing activities (Christou et al., 2024; Silver, 1994; Stoyanova & Ellerton, 1996). Silver's (1994) model distinguishes three temporal phases:

1. **Pre-solution posing** (before solving a problem),
2. **Within-solution posing** (during the problem-solving process), and
3. **Post-solution posing** (after solving a problem).

Alternatively, Stoyanova and Ellerton (1996) proposed a structural taxonomy comprising:

- **Structured problem posing**, which involves modifying given problems;
- **Free problem posing**, which entails creating problems without explicit constraints; and
- **Semi-structured problem posing**, which requires generating problems within specified contextual parameters.

Semi-structured problem posing, in particular, holds significant pedagogical value. It demands the identification of underlying mathematical structures, the application of prior knowledge, and the use of relational reasoning (Yuan & Sriraman, 2011). This approach often integrates multiple representational formats—such as numerical expressions, diagrams, graphs, and tables—thereby enriching mathematical reasoning (Bonotto & Santo, 2015).

Research consistently shows that both in-service and preservice teachers tend to perform better in structured problem posing contexts compared to free-form tasks (Silver & Cai, 2017; Stickles, 2011). Consequently, semi-structured problem posing is widely used in empirical studies (Bonotto & Santo, 2015; Ulusoy & Kepceoğlu, 2018; Ulusoy, 2023, 2025; van Harpen & Sriraman, 2013) because it balances creative exploration with cognitive support. For teacher education, this approach provides a scaffolded environment in which preservice teachers can practice generating mathematically sound, contextually relevant, and pedagogically appropriate problems. The present study adopts a semi-structured problem posing framework to investigate how prospective mathematics teachers formulate area measurement problems. This choice reflects both the documented efficacy of semi-structured approaches in fostering higher-order thinking and the alignment of such tasks with the complex cognitive processes involved in mathematics teaching and learning.

Problem Posing in Teacher Education

Extensive research underscores the critical role of problem posing in mathematics education for both students and teachers. As a pedagogical practice, problem posing has been shown to deepen conceptual understanding, strengthen problem-solving skills, and nurture mathematical creativity (Bonotto & Santo, 2015; Van Harpen & Sriraman, 2013). In teacher education, problem posing serves dual purposes: as an instructional goal in itself and as a means to develop mathematical and pedagogical content knowledge (Kilic, 2015; Lee et al., 2018). Recognizing problem posing as equally fundamental as problem solving (Cai et al., 2023), scholars emphasize that teachers' proficiency in formulating contextually meaningful problems significantly influences students' mathematical development and perceptions of the discipline (Crespo, 2015; NCTM, 1991). Despite this importance, opportunities for teachers to engage in problem posing during their formative education—whether in pre-service training or professional development—remain limited, with instruction predominantly focused on solving pre-existing problems (Crespo & Sinclair, 2008).

In response to this gap, recent research has increasingly focused on developing professional programs to enhance teachers' problem-posing competencies. Studies demonstrate that targeted interventions can effectively transform teachers' problem-posing approaches. Crespo (2003) documented how prospective teachers progressed from posing basic computational problems to formulating more complex, open-ended tasks through structured course activities. Similarly, Leavy and Hourigan (2019) observed significant evolution in 415 pre-service teachers' conceptions of mathematical problems, from viewing them as single-solution exercises to recognizing their potential for multiple solution pathways and representations. These findings collectively highlight the transformative potential of systematic training in reshaping teachers' problem-posing practices and pedagogical perspectives.

The current study extends this line of inquiry by examining problem posing within an innovative ChatGPT-mediated environment. This investigation carries substantial implications for both teacher education and AI integration in mathematics learning. Unlike traditional problem-posing contexts, ChatGPT offers dynamic interaction, immediate feedback, and adaptive problem variation, creating unique opportunities for: (i) enhanced pedagogical skill development through AI-assisted refinement of problem-posing techniques, (ii) exploration of diverse problem formulations in real-time, (iii) development of AI-integration competencies for future classrooms. Methodologically, this study breaks new ground by: (i) investigating AI's role in fostering cognitive flexibility and creativity in problem posing, (ii) analyzing the quality and characteristics of AI-mediated mathematical problems and (iii) bridging the research gap between artificial intelligence applications and teacher professional development. By focusing on prospective teachers' experiences with ChatGPT, this research contributes to a nuanced understanding of how emerging technologies can transform mathematical thinking and instructional practices. The findings promise to inform both the design of AI-enhanced teacher education programs and the development of effective strategies for technology integration in mathematics classrooms.

Theoretical Framework: TPACK

The Technological Pedagogical Content Knowledge (TPACK) framework (Mishra & Koehler, 2006) offers a comprehensive lens for analyzing how teachers integrate technology into pedagogical practices while maintaining a strong link to subject matter expertise. Within TPACK, technological knowledge (TK) refers to the ability to use and adapt technological tools; pedagogical knowledge (PK) concerns instructional methods and strategies; and content knowledge (CK) relates to the understanding of the subject matter. The intersections—technological pedagogical knowledge (TPK), technological content knowledge (TCK), and pedagogical content knowledge (PCK)—represent increasingly integrated forms of teacher knowledge, with TPACK at the center as the full synthesis. Applying this framework to AI-supported mathematical problem posing allows for a nuanced examination of how preservice mathematics teachers draw on and integrate these forms of knowledge when engaging with generative AI tools such as ChatGPT. In the present study, TPACK provides a theoretical basis for interpreting both the affordances and constraints identified in participants' use of ChatGPT, highlighting how strengths often emerge from effective integration of TK, PK, and CK, while constraints can be traced to gaps in one or more of these domains.

METHODOLOGY

Participants

This qualitative study involved 23 prospective mathematics teachers (PMTs) (8 male, 15 female) enrolled in an elective course within a Grades 5-8 Mathematics Teacher Training Program. Following approval by the University Institutional Review Board and obtaining informed consent from all voluntary participants, the study was conducted with PMTs who had completed foundational content courses (e.g., calculus, geometry) and the majority of their pedagogical training (e.g., mathematics teaching methods). The research was implemented while participants were concurrently enrolled in a compulsory problem-solving and posing course. Data collection occurred after instruction on evaluating problem quality based on multiple components, including realism, solvability, and cognitive load levels, had been delivered in both courses. For this study, PMTs worked individually with ChatGPT to generate area measurement problems, applying their developing understanding of problem analysis and construction

Data Collection and Analysis Procedures

As illustrated in Figure 1, this study's data collection process comprised three sequential phases within an elective course framework. During the initial phase, prospective mathematics teachers (PMTs) developed competencies in evaluating mathematical problems across multiple dimensions, including cognitive demand levels, real-world contextualization, linguistic clarity, and procedural complexity.

This phase involved rigorous examination of established cognitive taxonomies (e.g., Smith & Stein's framework, Bloom's taxonomy) to distinguish between low, medium, and high cognitive-level tasks. Subsequently, PMTs applied this analytical framework to assess the cognitive load of problems observed during their school internship placements as part of their field experience requirements.

Figure 1. Data collection procedure

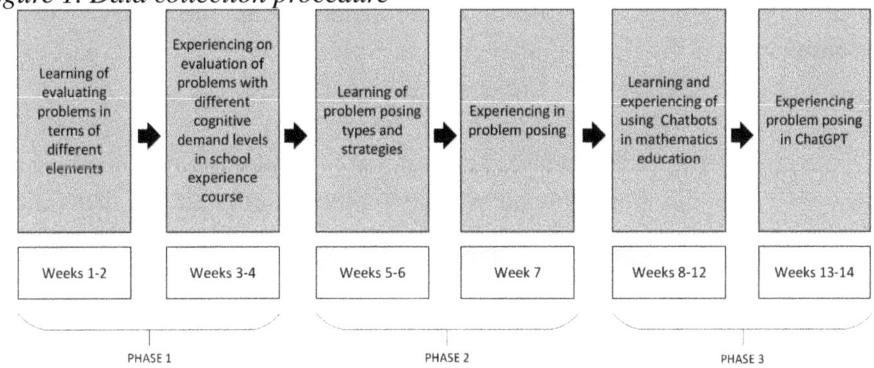

The second instructional phase introduced PMTs to the taxonomy of problem posing (structured, semi-structured, and free-form approaches) along with quality assessment criteria for posed problems. Through this training, participants acquired evaluative skills focusing on key dimensions: solvability, linguistic precision, contextual realism, and mathematical sophistication. In the seventh week of implementation, PMTs completed an individual problem-posing activity without time constraints, adhering to three specific requirements: (i) incorporation of authentic real-world contexts, (ii) representation of varied cognitive loads (low, medium, high), and (iii) alignment with area measurement concepts for grades 5-8. This intensive task required approximately two hours for completion, after which participants submitted their problem sets to the researchers. Complementing their problem formulations, PMTs produced reflective narratives addressing four critical aspects: 1) Methodological approach to determining problem difficulty levels, 2) Rationale for selecting specific real-world contexts, 3) Challenges encountered during the problem-posing process and 4) Self-evaluation of their problem-posing competencies.

The third phase of data collection involved implementing a five-week instructional program focusing on AI applications in mathematics education. Initially, participants' pre-existing attitudes and expectations regarding AI in mathematics were assessed. These preliminary data revealed substantially limited prior knowledge and experience with AI technologies in mathematical contexts. Then, in-class information and discussions on the use of AI in mathematics education were held for two weeks. The subsequent weeks focused on practical applications, where participants: (i) engaged with chatbot interfaces for mathematical problem solving and (ii) developed prompt-writing skills for lesson planning scenarios. These activities were conducted in a computer laboratory under researcher supervision, providing hands-on experience with educational chatbot functionality and applications. Following this training phase, participants received copies of their manually constructed problems from Phase Two. They were asked to pose problems using ChatGPT again by focusing on the same components in the problem posing task. They submitted their problems and the prompts they used in a word document. Each participant also wrote a reflection paper to answer the following questions:

1. Time investment: Estimated average duration for AI-assisted problem posing
   a. How long did it take you on average to pose the problems by using the AI tools?
2. Comparative analysis: Critical evaluation of self-posed versus AI-generated problems
   a. You were given photocopies of the problems you had previously posed. At this point, Evaluate the problems you have posed previously in comparison with the problems posed by AI. Explain the advantages and disadvantages of AI in problem posing.
3. Process evaluation
   a. What were the difficulties you encountered while constructing problems with AI tools? What caused this situation?
   b. How well do you think the AI tool supported your efforts to create meaningful real-life connections in the problems?
   c. How did you determine the cognitive load level of the problems when constructing problems with AI tools? What/how was the role/limitations/potential of artificial intelligence in this regard?
   d. How did you decide that the problems generated by AI are mathematically correct and pedagogically appropriate?
   e. Have you revised/changed the problems/solutions produced by AI tools? What did you revise and why? Please explain with detailed examples.

They submitted their problems, prompt flows, and reflection papers to Google classroom. In this study, the problems posed by PMTs and ChatGPT and PMTs' written responses especially for the second question in Figure 2 were used as data sources.

PMTs' perceived affordances and constraints of using ChatGPT in problem posing in reflection papers were examined through qualitative content analysis (Hsieh & Shannon, 2005). Both deductive and inductive approaches were utilized in the analysis of data. In the inductive approach, themes and categories arise from the data through the researcher's meticulous analysis and continuous comparison. In the deductive approach, initial coding is based on a theory or pertinent research findings. To determine initial codes, previous studies regarding teachers' perceived affordances and constraints in problem solving and problem posing with chatbots were examined. In the literature, the following affordances were frequently cited: Immediate feedback and interactivity, diversity of responses, individualized learning paths (e.g., Kim et al., 2025; Memarian & Doleck, 2023; Meyer et al., 2023), and an assessment tool (Wardat et al, 2023), linguistic clarity (Ergene & Ergene, 2025; Pelton & Pelton, 2023). Besides, the following constraints were frequently cited: incorrect responses, concerns with clarity and simplicity in solutions and language (Kim et al., 2025; Ergene & Ergene, 2025), and limited visual ability (e.g., Wang, Zhang & Wang, 2024). After deductive analysis, the researcher and a mathematics educator, who specializes in problem posing, scrutinized 23 PMTs' written responses to the task question: "*Explain the advantages and disadvantages of AI in problem posing*." In this inductive analysis, two coders read all responses multiple times, identifying themes throughout. During the initial reading, we identified twelve preliminary themes. Some of these themes had a connection to the affordances, while others were associated with the constraints of ChatGPT use in problem posing. Following a discussion, we grouped these themes into two overarching categories: *PMTs' perceived affordances of using ChatGPT in problems posing* and *PMTs' perceived constraints of using ChatGPT in problems posing*. Two raters independently coded the PMTs' responses within an Excel document for each theme, assigning a code of 1 if the PMTs mentioned it in their response and 0 if not. In the reflection papers, we obtained 63 statements regarding the affordances of using ChatGPT. We were in agreement on 55 of these statements (91%). We also obtained 84 statements related to the constraints of using ChatGPT. We were in agreement on 72 of these statements (%86). To reach a consensus, we discussed the non-matching responses and finalized the codes.

RESULTS

The results are presented in two sections. In the first section, PMTs' perceived affordances of using ChatGPT in problem posing and in the second section, the constraints are presented. A summary of the results obtained is given in Figure 2.

Figure 2. PMTs' perceived affordances and constraints

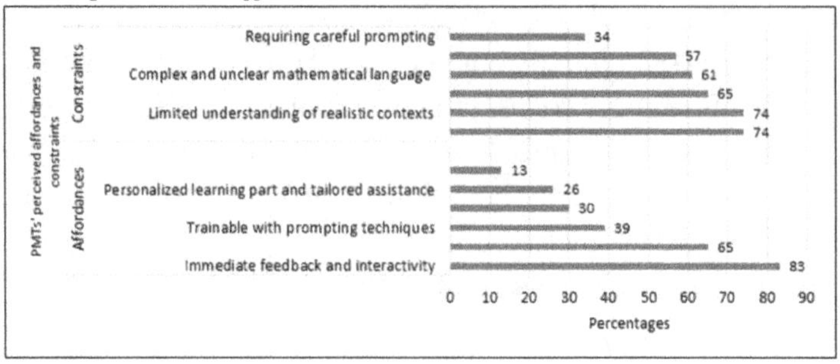

Prospective Teachers' Perceived Affordances of Using ChatGPT in Problem Posing

Immediate Feedback and Interactivity

The most frequently mentioned affordance of using ChatGPT in problem posing is the immediate feedback and interactivity of the platform. 19 PMTs out of 23 (83%) cited the immediate support and interactive nature of ChatGPT. Written reflections say that this feature helps with real-time learning because it lets PMTs see the results of their work right away and change them to fit the needs of the problem-posing task. The PMTs commented on the significance of this aspect in their experience as follows: "It saves time both in creating problems and correcting mistakes in the problems (PMT14)"; "I appreciate engaging in real-time dialogue with the AI. The immediate feedback allowed me to revise the posed problems (PMT6"); "When I tell the AI that I don't like the problem and want to change it, it can still produce different and new style problems within seconds (PMT22)" and so on.

Diversity in Contextual Examples

15 PMTs out of 23 (65%) acknowledged the value of contextual diversity in AI-posed problems. According to written reflections, this contextual diversity gave them the chance to choose more appropriate and intriguing contexts for the students when posing problems. Moreover, this diversity helped them both to expand their repertoire of real-life contexts and to prepare problems according to students' levels or specific needs. The platform's capacity to offer various real-life contexts to a problem or diverse examples for a single concept (area measurement) facilitates a more thorough problem-posing experience, as evidenced by the PMTs' remarks, including: "ChatGPT generates various real-life contexts for problems in

any mathematical topic and verbalizes them correctly. It is a very useful tool for posing many problems that I could not think of at first (PMT6)." ; "AI can make connections between different mathematical fields such as algebra, geometry, and numbers to produce problems that combine these fields. It broadened my mind (PMT17)," and "AI could create problems according to different grade levels and cognitive demand levels. This diversity can help teachers prepare individualized learning opportunities for their students (PMT17)."

Trainable with Prompting Techniques

As another affordance of AI, 15 PMTs (39%) cited training the model as a way to increase the chances of receiving a desired response in the problem-posing process. Their explanation showed that they were aware that the accuracy of responses depends on the quality and specificity of their prompts. For example, these PMTs noted that it is necessary to provide examples and definitions about the cognitive demand of levels because they claimed that AI could not differentiate medium and high cognitive demand levels without training. Moreover, some PMTs also found AI's ability to be trained useful to increase the chances of receiving a suitable problem in real-life contexts. The problem-posing task requires posing problems related to real-life contexts. In this regard, PMTs described the five main aspects of realistic problems in detail: the event, the question, the existence of information, and the purpose and specificity of the information (Vicente & Manchado, 2017). The PMTs commented on the importance of these aspects in their experience as follows:

PMT4: First of all, I asked the AI to derive the Bloom taxonomy. I asked it to separate the levels it derived according to low-level, medium-level, and high-level cognitive load levels. To be completely sure of the levels, I asked it to recreate the same taxonomy and the same cognitive levels (in a different conversation), and when I noticed that they were the same, I started to create the questions according to the cognitive demand levels it created.

PMT14: ChatGPT is a pre-trained language model. Previous training has limited its capabilities. In my experience, I recognized that ChatGPT did not differentiate cognitive demand levels. For this reason, I provided information about cognitive demand levels to AI in advance. The information I provided included the definition of cognitive demand levels and examples of problems for each level. AI used this information accurately while posing problems.

A potential Assessment Tool

Seven PMTs (30%) mentioned ChatGPT as a potential assessment tool in the problem-posing process. In this regard, they first posed the problems without using

ChatGPT and then asked AI to evaluate them. They claimed that AI's evaluations deepen their understanding and support assessment skills. Hence, they noted that they could revise their problems based on AI's plausible suggestions. To be more illustrative, PMT12's process was presented below. First, PMT12 checked how ChatGPT produced problems based on cognitive load levels. Then, he decided to ask ChatGPT to evaluate the problem and revise it according to this evaluation. Table 1 presents PMT12's problem that he posed without using ChatGPT, the dialogic process between PMT12 and ChatGPT, and the final version of the posed problem. PMT12 presented the final version of the problem as revised by AI because he found AI's criticisms and suggestions about clarity, complexity, context, and language reasonable.

According to PMT12's reflections, "Using ChatGPT as an assessment tool is one of the biggest advantages of AI because it explains my mistakes in my problems and gives me ideas, and I have gained a different perspective." Moreover, instead of asking the chatbot to pose a problem, some PMTs in particular chose a different approach. They presented their own posed problems and asked the model to verify or falsify their cognitive demand levels. For instance, PMT21 expressed, "When I asked the AI to assess the cognitive demand levels of my problems, I was pleased that the results aligned with the difficulty level I had determined." Hence, they utilized ChatGPT to double-check the problems to ensure their accuracy and appropriateness.

Table 1. PMT12's use of ChatGPT as an assessment tool to evaluate his posed problem Personalized Learning Paths and Tailored Assistance

<table>
<tr><td>PMT12's prompt: I wrote a low cognitive demand problem and I would like you to evaluate what I did wrong in the problem.
Problem written by PMT12
Mrs. Nurten, who wants to buy a house, sees that the gross area of a house she likes at the real estate agency is 110 m^2. Upon checking the catalog information for the house, she notices that the elevator and stairwell take up 40 m^2. She wants to find the net area of the house. What is the net area of the house? (The elevator and stairwell space are not included in the net area calculation.)</td></tr>
<tr><td>ChatGPT's response
Strengths:
1. Real-Life Connection: The problem is based on a real-life scenario, such as purchasing a house, which students may encounter in their daily lives. This can capture their interest.
2. Relationship Between Net and Gross Area: The problem addresses a concept that students may have heard of but might not fully understand. This helps them see how mathematics applies in real-world situations.
Weaknesses and Suggestions:
1. Clarity in Presenting Data:
o The problem mentions the "elevator and staircase space," but it is not explicitly stated whether this space is inside or outside the apartment. This ambiguity might cause confusion for students.
o Suggestion: The statement could be made clearer as follows: "The elevator and staircase space inside the apartment covers 40 m^2 and is not included in the net area calculation."
2. Mathematical Complexity:
o The problem only involves a simple subtraction operation (110 - 40), which results in a low cognitive load. A more complex problem could be designed.
o Suggestions: Additional information or steps can be incorporated, such as:
▪ "If the apartment with a net area of 70 m^2 costs 5,000 TL per square meter, what is the total cost?"
▪ Alternatively, different apartment options could be provided, and students could be asked to make comparisons.
3. Enhancing Contextual Relevance:
o While mentioning the elevator and staircase space makes sense, adding more details about the apartment's general characteristics could create a more realistic context.
o Suggestion: Additional information, such as the presence of a balcony, number of rooms, or total price, could help students develop a deeper mathematical understanding.
4. Use of Relevant Terms:
o Terms like "net area" and "gross area" might be unfamiliar to some students. A brief explanation of these terms could be beneficial.
Suggestion: A short clarification can be added: "Gross area refers to the total size of the apartment, including walls, while net area represents the usable living space."</td></tr>
<tr><td>PMT12's prompt: Can you revise the problem again based on your suggestions. I believe using a visual would be more effective, so revising the question with a visual would be more suitable for me.</td></tr>
</table>

continued on following page

Table 1. Continued

The problem revised by ChatGPT

Mrs. Nurten likes an apartment with a gross area of 110 m^2 at the real estate agency. However, the elevator and staircase space occupy a total of 40 m^2. Wanting to find out the usable net area of the apartment, Mrs. Nurten asks the following questions:

1. What is the net area of the apartment in square meters?
2. If the price per net square meter is 5,000 TL, can you calculate the total cost of the apartment?
3. The same real estate agent suggests another apartment with a gross area of 120 m^2 and an elevator and staircase space of 35 m^2. Which apartment has a larger net area?

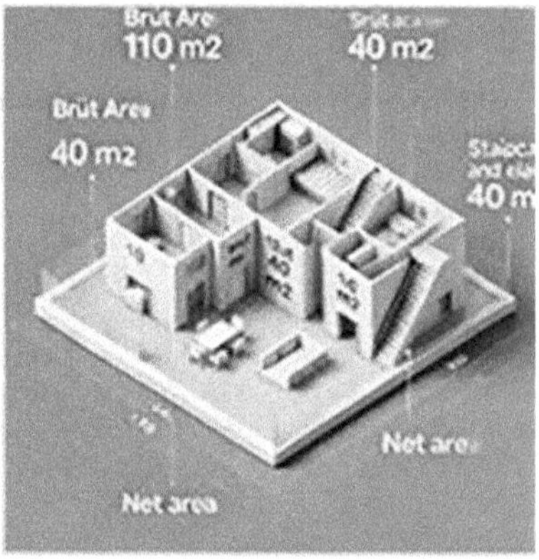

Six PMTs (26%) cited the platform's capacity to customize learning sessions as a significant affordance in problem posing. They identified personalized learning paths and customized assistance as beneficial features that address their needs, thereby improving their problem-posing experience through adaptive interactions, including prompts such as “Can you reconsider real-life context based on grades 5-8?” and “Provide another problem for the middle cognitive demand level.” The PMTs' remarks clearly illustrate this, stating that the system provides personalized learning opportunities through sessions it stores. This feature made my job much easier in terms of continuing where I left off and reviewing what I did before (PMT1”), “a unique learning opportunity to pose problems through the flow of prompts (PMT19),” and “personalized answers are useful to create correct and appropriate mathematical problems through interactive revision aids (e.g., change the context of the problem, make the problem more difficult, etc.) (PMT20).” Hence, PMTs' comments reflect a shared hope for ChatGPT's capacity to provide personalization and support in education.

Linguistic Clarity

Three PMTs (13%) noted the clarity of ChatGPT’s use of language in posed problems as another affordance. Their reflections indicated that they found AI better at using language correctly in syntactic and semantic structures than they were. These PMTs mainly compared their problem-posing process and ChatGPT's problem-posing process in terms of using language. Through this comparison, they concluded that AI uses clear language for problem posing. The following excerpts illustrate their views:

PMT19: The solvability of ChatGPT's problems is better than mine. In the class activity of problem posing, I recognized that my problems were unsolvable when I tried to solve my problem. However, ChatGPT could immediately pose a solvable problem. I was not sure if my problem was understandable during the class activity. I realize the clarity of my problem when I ask someone else to solve it, but ChatGPT demonstrated superior understanding.

PMT17: It was really difficult to write a problem categorized at a high cognitive demand level in terms of language use and present it in a way that students could understand. The AI generates well-structured and clear sentences for the problems. Our AI was good at writing such problems because the information, language, and story were all appropriate for students.

These explanations indicated that some PMTs focused on ChatGPT's potential to generate grammatically correct and somewhat relevant text in a problem-posing context.

Prospective Teachers' Perceived Constraints of Using ChatGPT in Problem Posing

Limited Diversity in Problem Types

74% of the PMTs (n=17) stated that AI can produce stereotypical problems about area measurement. They emphasized that this situation limits the diversity of mathematical problems that can be posed. Specifically, PMTs reported that ChatGPT produced simple problems involving finding the area of regular shapes or problems limited to subtracting the area of two regular shapes from each other. Despite the contextual diversity and the ability to present a large number of problems in seconds, they stated that the AI could not come across area measurement problems that would support students to make inferences about the concept of area. The following sentences illustrate PMTs' perceived constraints about AI in terms of limitations in posing different problem types.

PMT5: The AI does not offer different problem types. The problems it posed are too easy or too difficult, failing to engage learners and potentially reducing their motivation.

PMT10: Because when I asked the AI to create a shape, it created a problem of creating a regular shape according to the features I wanted and always using the same regular shapes (circle, square, rectangle). However, we can also calculate areas in irregular shapes.

PMT22: A serious disadvantage of AI when compared to a human is that it sometimes produces repetitive or similar problems. I don't think it is possible to compete with human creativity and originality. In particular, AI may have difficulty producing open-ended problems that require higher-level thinking skills. It is necessary to give well-structured prompts to generate more effective solutions.

In conclusion, they criticized ChatGPT's performance in posing various types of area measurement problems, citing its negative impact on students' reasoning and motivation for problem solving. Finally, some PMTs (PMT22) also showed that they were aware that the reason for this limited type of problem generation might be related to the quality of the prompts that they provided.

Limited Understanding of Realistic Contexts

As another constraint of AI, 17 PMTs (74%) cited limitations in ChatGPT's understanding of reality-based mathematical tasks. In this regard, most of the PMTs utilized Vicente and Manchado's (2017) five main aspects, as defined by Palm and Burman (2002)—event, question, existence of information, purpose, and specificity of the information—to assess the reality of problems posed by ChatGPT. They criticized the platform's limited capacity to generate reality-based problems, which may diminish students' motivation and interest in problem-solving, as evidenced by the PMTs' comments, including, "…AI only dresses up problems with objects and events that exist in real life. It does not set up problems from the perspective of 'Would I feel the need to make this calculation in this situation?' (PMT1)," "… GPT added only a ceramic tile object to a simple mathematical procedure. This is not a problem that a student would need to solve (PMT11)." "Mostly, AI poses problems of fencing and field division. Since most of the population lives in cities today, fencing is not a meaningful real-life context for the students (PMT22)," and so on. They also mentioned that it is necessary to provide more accurate prompts to the platform to achieve the desired results.

Incorrect Responses

A significant concern was noted by 15 PMTs out of 23 (65%), who recognized errors in posed problems in terms of cognitive demand levels, the solutions of the problems, and alignment with students' grade levels. Several comments indicated that the platform assigned incorrect cognitive demand levels to the problems, which led to confusion. The actual and ChatGPT-determined cognitive demand levels problems were found to be inconsistent, which raised concerns about the accuracy of responses. Moreover, this inconsistency required extra time to provide many prompts associated with different levels of cognitive demands. For example, PMT7 claimed that the problem with a medium cognitive load was at the same level as the problem with a low cognitive load. Another PMT14 also noted that “the AI could not differentiate between a high and medium level of cognitive demand in problems. For difficult questions, the platform simply increases the number of steps (e.g., calculating two areas and subtracting the result from each other) or adds additional questions that need to be answered in the problem (e.g., calculating perimeter-area, not just area”). A number of criticisms suggested that since ChatGPT sometimes provided incorrect solutions, teachers should control the problems generated by the platform: “When calculating the area of a circle, it used the number π incorrectly or used the radius instead of the diameter. Hence, teachers should check AI-generated problems in terms of pedagogical, mathematical, contextual, and curricular aspects (PMT22”). “The AI does not always produce mathematically correct responses. It fails when producing high cognitive demanding problems because they included an operational structure and mathematical misconceptions, and it took me too much time to correct them (PMT21).” In a similar vein, PMT17 emphasized the need to check and evaluate the problems artificial intelligence produces. Because occasionally it can give inappropriate data and give incorrect solutions to the problems.” Moreover, some PMTs criticized ChatGPT in terms of using inputs incorrectly in the solutions of the problems. For example, in a problem, a PMT asked to calculate the area of a circle; the platform incorrectly used the radius instead of the diameter.

Complex and Unclear Mathematical Language

61% of the PMTs (n=14) evaluated ChatGPT’s use of language and mathematical terminology as a constraint in the problem-posing process. According to these PMTs, the platform sometimes provides unexpected results that did not align with mathematical structures and students’ previous learning. For example, although some PMTs explicitly asked the platform to pose problems for the middle school level (5th–8th grade), ChatGPT could pose problems on topics such as ellipses and Heron's theorems, which are not in the middle school mathematics curriculum. This situation creates complexity in the mathematical language of the posed problems. In this sense, some PMTs’ comments are as follows: “Although it was a 7th-grade outcome, there was a problem, including an ellipse, and I tried to make it compatible with middle school by asking it to be turned into a circle” (PMT 22). “Although I wrote it as a 6th-grade student, ChatGPT generated a problem that included topics not covered at the 6th-grade level, such as Heron's area formula and the Pythagorean theorem” (PMT2). These PMTs also stated that ChatGPT cannot prepare problems with clear mathematical language because it does not have information about students' prior learning and level of readiness, what happened in the classroom, and what students experienced. Another criticism proposed by PMTs was the mathematical complexity of language in high cognitive demand problems. According to these reflections, when a problem with high cognitive load is requested, ChatGPT generates both linguistically longer and computationally more complex questions. This leads to ambiguity and complexity in the language of the problem. The PMTs commented on this aspect in their experience as follows: "...In problems with high cognitive load, the language used in the question was not understandable (PMT14)." Sometimes, the AI prepares problems that are too lengthy for medium and high cognitive demands. It creates difficulty in understanding the problem (PMT13)". PMT13 provided the following example to show how ChatGPT prepared too long for a problem (see Table 2). For this problem, PMT13 provided additional prompts to clarify the language of the problem by shortening it.

Table 2. PMT13's example for a linguistically complex problem created by ChatGPT

PMT13's prompt: "The floor of Mrs Elif's kitchen will be covered with tiles. The tiles are square with one side of 60 cm. The floor of Mrs Elif's kitchen takes the exact number of tiles.12 tiles are used for the floor and 14 tiles are used for the floor. How many square metres is the floor of Mrs. Elif's kitchen?" Make this question into a question format that will make the student think more in terms of meaning by narrating this question.
ChatGPT's response: Mrs Elif decided to renovate the kitchen of her newly moved house. The kitchen floor was old and Elif decided to lay tiles to make it more stylish and modern. However, she had to carefully calculate the size of the tiles because the number of tiles and the total area of her kitchen were interconnected. The tiles will be arranged in a square shape with a side of 60 cm and will completely cover the floor of her kitchen. Mrs Elif measured the length and width of her kitchen. The length of her kitchen was exactly 14 rows of tiles, while the width was 12 rows of tiles. In this case, Mrs Elif wants to find the total area of her kitchen, but she must also calculate the area of the tiles. In order to find the total area of Mrs Elif's kitchen, you need to solve the following questions: 1. Calculate the area of a tile (Calculate the area of a square tile with a side of 60 cm). 2. Calculate the total area of the number of tiles in Mrs Elif's kitchen. (Since the dimensions of her kitchen are 12 x 14 tiles, find how many tiles will be used in total and the area to be covered with these tiles.) 3. Calculate the total area of Mrs Elif's kitchen in square metres.

Poor Visualization Ability

13 PMTs out of 23 (57%) considered the poor visualization ability of ChatGPT as a constraint in problem posing. According to written reflections, PMTs commented on the role of poor visualization in posing problems as follows: "The AI does not fully respond to the data related to creating images and graphics (PMT3)," "Since it could not pose the problem including geometric shapes, it limits my problems in textual format (PMT20)," "Using a text-only form of input and output affects the complexity of language in posed problems (PMT10), and so on. To be more

illustrative, Table 3 shows PMT10's prompting process in problem posing. As seen in Table 3, although PMT10 provided many prompts about visual creation for his problem in ChatGPT, the relationship of the visuals with the problem was weak. As a result, PMT10 decided not to use any visuals produced by ChatGPT.

Table 3. PMT10's prompts about visual creation in problem posing

PMT10's problem: Ayşe is taking part in a treasure hunt. The treasure is hidden in a rectangular park. The park has a long side of 100 metres and a short side of 80 metres. In the south-west corner of the park there is a square playground with sides of 30 metres. The treasure map indicates that the treasure is hidden only in the area outside the playground. What is the size of this area that Ayşe has to explore to find the treasure?
PMT10's prompts **Prompt 1:** Instead of giving a description of the green area, an image can be given in the problem. I want you to create this image. The image should be from a bird's eye view (i.e. it should be like looking at a rectangular park from the air). The side lengths of the geometric shapes given in the visual should not be given. **Prompt 2:** The visual should not contain an image from real life. Let it be like a sketch map. **Prompt 3:** Remove the trees from the visual. Let it be a rectangular park. The playground should also be square. **Prompt 4:** I want you to draw a simple sketch, you don't need to use different colors and materials, just like the construction of a park is done according to a sketch. **Prompt 5:** OK, now remove everything unnecessary from this sketch and make it just a rectangular area. Also, let there be a square playground inside this rectangular area. **Prompt 6:** I want you to remove the details from the picture and give a square playground inside the rectangular park in accordance with the problem you have given. **Prompt 7:** You have given the square playground well, but the shape is not rectangular. I would also like you to add the word 'playground' to the square playground area. **Prompt 8:** There is no writing. the rectangle is nice but the square inside is not square. **Prompt 9:** Give the park a rectangular shape and the playground a square shape.
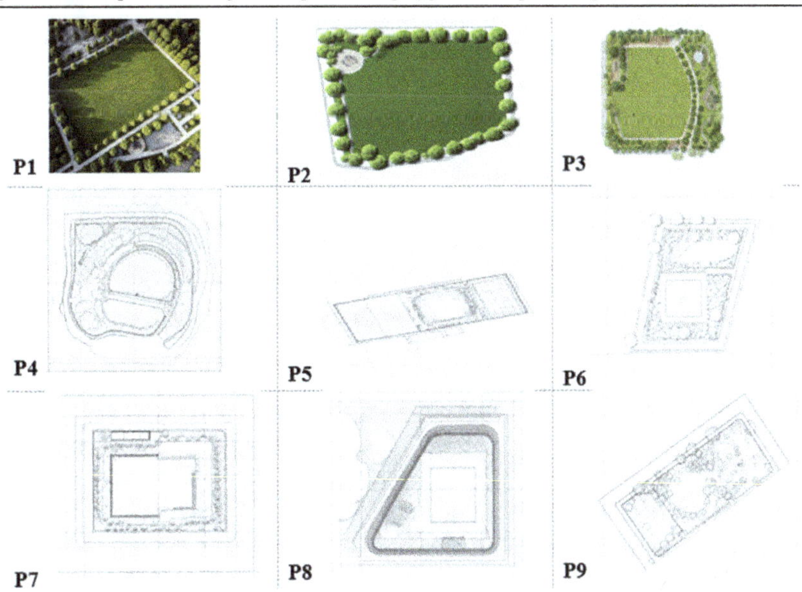

Similarly, another prospective teacher (PMT6) asked ChatGPT to create a visual suitable for her problem. Her problem, prompts, visuals created are given in Table 4. PMT6 stated that his attempt to have a suitable visual produced in ChatGPT for the problem resulted in failure. PMT6 commented on her experience on producing visuals with ChatGPT in problem posing as follows: "One of the biggest disadvantages of AI is creating visuals. No matter how many prompts we give, the visuals never turn out the way we want them to. The visuals are too artificial, not appropriate for the problem, or the texts in the visuals usually use foreign languages, which makes it difficult for students to understand. Therefore, it is not possible to prepare questions with visuals."

Table 4. PMT6's prompts to ChatGPT while creating visuals

<table>
<tr><td colspan="2">Problem: Teacher Zeynep is planning to prepare a race track for students for a sports event to be organized in the school garden. Since there is limited space in the garden, teacher Zeynep wants to design a running track in the form of parallel sides with no sharp corners. This area will allow students to run safely and compete in an organized way during the event. Teacher Zeynep wants to order a line drawing paint suitable for the floor by calculating the area of the track. She learnt that 250 milliliters of paint is needed for 1 square meter area. She wants to buy exactly as much paint as she needs to avoid wasting paint.
Prompt 1: Create a visual suitable for this problem. Students should be able to understand the question when they look at the visual. The visual should evoke the question and not be complicated. Information: In the runway design, a parallelogram has a base of 12 meters and a corresponding height of 8 meters. An empty safety strip 1-meter-wide must be left around the perimeter of the runway. The area of the safety strip will not be included in the calculation, only the part of the runway to be painted will be taken into account
Prompt 2: Make all text in the image in Turkish</td></tr>
<tr><td>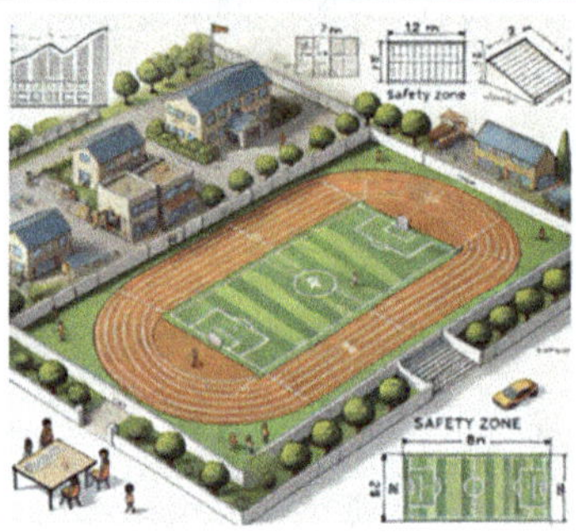

P1</td><td>

P2</td></tr>
</table>

Requiring Careful Prompting

Although it is possible to reach the desired answers with prompts in ChatGPT, some pre-service teachers (35%) stated that giving many prompts to the platform took longer than posing the problem themselves. They stated that this situation could be considered an obstacle for teachers to use time effectively. They also stated that although they gave many prompts, they still could not reach the desired results and inferred that they should be more careful in terms of prompting. PMT10's attempts in Table 3 can be an example of this situation. Many PMTs wrote in their reflection papers that they were able to reach the desired problems (especially for the problems with a high cognitive demand level) with many prompts given cautiously and consecutively. PMT6 and PMT19 provided the following examples:

> *PMT6: ChatGPT had difficulty in creating problems that require multi-stage or advanced mathematics in terms of cognitive level... Therefore, I revised and organized the problems again and again. It is possible to produce as many problems as we want, but it still takes time to obtain the problem with the quality we want.*
>
> *PMT19: If we provide more specific and detailed prompts to the ChatGPT, it may remain superficial... When I asked for a problem at a higher cognitive level, I did not find it sufficient even though I provided the details of using reasoning. I asked the platform to give me feedback and improve it, and in its second answer it posed a problem that was satisfactory to its cognitive level.*

CONCLUSION

This study explored prospective mathematics teachers' (PMTs) perceptions of the affordances and constraints of using ChatGPT in mathematical problem posing. While ChatGPT provides immediate feedback, diverse contextual examples, and opportunities for adaptive learning, it also presents challenges related to problem originality, realistic contextualization, and mathematical accuracy. The implications of these findings contribute to the broader discourse on AI integration in mathematics education, particularly in fostering problem-posing skills among future educators.

The findings reveal that PMTs perceive several advantages of using ChatGPT in problem solving, including immediate feedback and interactivity, diversity in contextual examples, trainability through prompting techniques, and its potential as an assessment tool. These affordances align with previous research on the benefits of AI in education, particularly in providing personalized learning experiences and scaffolding complex tasks (Kim et al., 2025; Hwang & Chang, 2021; Lee & Yeo, 2022; Memarian & Doleck, 2023). The immediate feedback and interactivity offered by ChatGPT were particularly valued by PMTs, as they allowed for real-time revisions and iterative problem refinement. This feature enhances the efficiency of problem posing and supports PMTs in developing a more profound understanding of how to construct meaningful and pedagogically appropriate problems. While the immediacy and efficiency of ChatGPT in supporting mathematical problem posing present clear pedagogical advantages, these affordances must be considered alongside broader ethical, pedagogical, and socio-technical implications. Risks such as over-reliance on AI-generated content, potential deskilling of teachers, inequitable access to advanced AI tools, and data privacy concerns have been widely noted in recent educational policy documents (UNESCO, 2023; OECD, 2023). Addressing these issues in pre-service mathematics teacher education requires explicit instruction on responsible AI use, critical evaluation of AI outputs, and strategies for maintaining pedagogical autonomy. Such an approach ensures that future educators can integrate AI tools effectively without diminishing their own professional expertise.

ChatGPT's ability to generate various real-life contexts enabled PMTs to expand their problem-posing repertoire, enhancing their ability to create meaningful and pedagogically relevant tasks for diverse student needs. This aligns with the literature on the importance of context-rich problems in mathematics education, which can enhance students' engagement and understanding (Cai et al., 2015; Silver, 1994). Moreover, the ability of ChatGPT to generate problems tailored to specific grade levels and cognitive demands further underscores its potential as a tool for differentiated instruction, allowing teachers to address the diverse needs of their students. Another significant affordance identified was ChatGPT's potential as an assessment tool. Several PMTs leveraged the platform to evaluate their posed problems, receiving constructive feedback that deepened their understanding of cognitive demand levels and problem quality. This study suggests that AI tools can play a valuable role in self-regulated learning by enabling prospective teachers to critically analyze their own instructional materials (Wardat et al., 2023). This was in line with what other studies have found about how important it is for AI-generated educational content to be clear and precise in mathematical language (Ergene & Ergene, 2025; Pelton & Pelton, 2023): the model's language was clear and precise, which made it easier to make well-structured and understandable problems.

Despite these benefits, PMTs also identified several constraints that limit the efficacy of ChatGPT in problem posing. A primary concern was the model's tendency to produce stereotypical and repetitive problems that lacked the complexity and creativity required for higher-order thinking. Many PMTs noted that ChatGPT frequently generated conventional area measurement problems, often relying on simple geometric calculations rather than fostering deeper mathematical reasoning. This finding is consistent with concerns raised in the literature about the potential for AI to generate superficial or formulaic responses, particularly in open-ended tasks that require creativity and originality (Javaid et al., 2023; Kasneci et al., 2023; Dao & Lee, 2023; Wang et al., 2024). The results indicated that PMTs proposed ChatGPT's inability to generate authentic real-life contexts that align with students' lived experiences as another constraint. PMTs observed that while the platform could insert real-world objects into problem scenarios, it often failed to capture the complexity of real-world scenarios. This limitation highlights the importance of carefully crafting prompts to guide ChatGPT in generating contextually rich and meaningful problems. However, even with detailed prompts, PMTs found that

ChatGPT struggled to produce problems that aligned with students' lived experiences and prior knowledge, which are crucial for fostering engagement and motivation in mathematics learning (Palm & Burman, 2002; Vicente & Manchado, 2017).

Incorrect responses and mathematical inaccuracies were also a significant concern, particularly in problems with higher cognitive demand levels. PMTs reported that ChatGPT sometimes provided incorrect solutions or misaligned cognitive demand levels, requiring additional time and effort to correct these errors. PMTs reported difficulties in refining problem complexity through ChatGPT, as the platform often equated higher cognitive demand with increased procedural steps rather than deeper conceptual engagement. This issue necessitated extensive prompt engineering, with PMTs providing multiple refinements to obtain more meaningful outputs. While this iterative prompting process showcases the adaptability of AI tools, it also implies a challenging learning curve for educators who aim to fully utilize AI's potential in problem posing (Kim et al., 2025). This finding underscores the need for teachers to critically evaluate AI-generated problems and solutions, particularly in terms of their mathematical accuracy and pedagogical appropriateness. While ChatGPT can serve as a valuable tool for generating ideas and scaffolding problem posing, it should not replace the teacher's role in ensuring the quality and rigor of mathematical tasks. It is important to note that ChatGPT may not consistently provide the most effective or efficient solutions; therefore, it is advisable to verify the results using an alternative source or calculator to confirm their accuracy (Wardat et al., 2023). These results also reveal that AI developers need to focus on developing models' ability to distinguish between routine and non-routine problem structures, enhancing their capacity to generate open-ended and creative mathematical problems. More research may look into how machine learning techniques can be used to improve AI's ability to pose problems based on repeated user input and criteria that are specific to the domain. Finally, the study highlighted the challenges associated with ChatGPT's poor visualization ability and complex mathematical language. PMTs found that the tool struggled to generate clear and concise problems, particularly at higher cognitive demand levels, where the language often became overly complex and difficult to understand. Additionally, ChatGPT's inability to produce effective visuals for geometric problems was considered a significant limitation, particularly in mathematics education, where visual representations play a crucial role in supporting students' understanding of abstract concepts in geometry. These results were similar to the results of some studies in the literature (Dao & Lee, 2023; Remoto, 2024). For example, Dao and Lee (2023) found that while ChatGPT solved low-difficulty problems correctly to a great extent (83%), the rate of solving high-difficulty level problems was around 10%. Similarly, they reported that the platform was successful in solving exponential and logarithmic functions, but its performance was low in subjects such as spatial geometry and calculus. At this point, it must be recognized that the accuracy or performance of ChatGPT depends on many different factors: the nature and quality of the input, the complexity of the topic, and the scope and relevance of the language modeling with its training data (Wardat et al., 2023).

Interpreting the findings through the lens of TPACK further illuminates the interplay between technology, pedagogy, and content in AI-supported mathematical problem posing (Kim et al. 2025). The identified affordances—such as generating diverse problem contexts, refining questions through iterative prompting, and incorporating multiple representations—often reflected integrated TPACK competencies, where participants successfully combined technological skills with pedagogical adaptability and strong mathematical content knowledge. Conversely, several constraints—including difficulties in crafting precise prompts, overreliance on AI-generated structures, and limited capacity to detect mathematical inaccuracies—can be understood as gaps in specific TPACK components, particularly in the integration of TK with CK or PK. This theoretical framing not only deepens the analytical interpretation of the results but also enhances the transferability of the study's implications to other contexts in teacher education where AI tools are increasingly present. Overall, the findings reveal that the integration of ChatGPT into mathematical problem-posing tasks offers significant pedagogical benefits while posing notable challenges. These insights extend beyond individual teacher practices, highlighting the need for targeted support from curriculum designers, program coordinators, and institutional leaders. For example, embedding AI literacy modules into preservice teacher education can help educators critically evaluate AI outputs, integrate AI tools with subject-specific pedagogies, and maintain professional autonomy in instructional decision-making. Additionally, program-level policies could promote balanced use of AI to avoid overreliance, encourage ethical engagement with technology, and ensure equitable access to AI resources across diverse educational contexts.

Limitations and Recommendations

This study provides valuable insights into prospective teachers' perceptions and applications of ChatGPT in mathematical problem posing. There were several limitations to this study. However, these limitations create important implications for mathematics teacher education.

The content and nature of the task's prompts may be a limitation. The prompts in a problem-posing task shape learners' engagement with the task (Cai et al., 2023). In the current study, the prompts asked PMTs to pose a problem in a real-world context at each cognitive demand level. Moreover, the problem-posing task was limited to area measurement. This study shows some problems with using ChatGPT to pose problems that are different from the study that looked at how prospective teachers used ChatGPT to pose fraction problems (Kim et al., 2025). This means that mathematical topics might affect how PMTs think about these problems. The study's focus on area measurement provides valuable insight into PMTs' use of ChatGPT in a specific mathematical domain. However, other content areas—such as algebra, geometry, and statistics—may pose distinct cognitive and representational challenges. Comparative studies across different content areas may also reveal how cognitive demand and task structure influence the effectiveness of AI integration. Beyond the classroom, these findings have implications for the design of teacher education curricula, particularly in developing competencies in AI-augmented pedagogy. Collaboration between teacher educators, instructional designers, and policymakers will be essential to establish guidelines for responsible AI use in mathematics education. Such efforts can ensure that AI integration not only enhances instructional quality but also supports the long-term professional growth of teachers.

The current study looked at PMTs' perceptions by using self-reported data instead of directly observing how they came up with problems through ChatGPT. However, the prompts they wrote in ChatGPT were used as supporting data. Future research should focus on their problem-posing process through individualized interviews to get detailed data about their actual difficulties in problem posing while using ChatGPT. Moreover, PMTs' written comments showed that understanding the prompting strategies is crucial to capturing the role of using chatbots in the problem-posing process in depth. PMTs' reflection papers indicated that many of them were aware that it is crucial to train the model to increase the chances of getting desired responses in the problem-posing process. In the current study, some PMTs explored that it is possible by providing a small number of examples and explanations, which is frequently referred to as a few-shot setting (Noster et al., 2024; Snell et al., 2017). They also corrected errors in ChatGPT-posed problems through re-prompting. However, most of the PMTs relied merely on the previous training for the language model and just submitted the prompt with the problem-posing task. This difference highlights the role of prompting in the quality of posed problems in terms of ensuring desired features. Future studies can examine the prompting approaches and the quality of posed problems by considering different elements such as solvability, cognitive demand level, reality, and language use. This study is limited to PMTs' use of ChatGPT in a short time. In the future, researchers should look into the long-term effects of using AI to help with math problems on teacher development and find ways to make it easier for humans and AI to work together on math problems. As AI technologies continue to evolve, their integration into teacher education must be guided by evidence-based practices that ensure their effective and meaningful use. By critically engaging with AI in educational settings, mathematics educators can foster a more nuanced and informed approach to leveraging technology in problem-posing activities, ultimately enhancing both teaching and learning experiences.

Implications for Future Studies

The findings suggest several actionable strategies for embedding ChatGPT into pre-service mathematics education. Teacher education curricula could incorporate structured modules on AI-mediated problem posing, combining theoretical foundations with hands-on practice. These modules should cover prompt engineering techniques, critical evaluation of AI outputs, ethical use principles, and alignment with curricular goals. Teacher educators themselves require professional development on AI affordances, constraints, and integration strategies, enabling them to model best practices. Assessment of AI-mediated problem-posing activities could combine rubric-based evaluations of problem quality with reflective journals documenting the reasoning behind prompt choices and AI modifications.

While this study focuses on the perspectives of prospective mathematics teachers, the impact of AI-generated problems on student engagement, motivation, and learning outcomes remains an important area for future research. Understanding how students interpret, interact with, and learn from AI-mediated problems will be crucial in evaluating the broader pedagogical value of such tools. Future studies could adopt a dual-perspective design, capturing both teacher and student experiences to provide a holistic picture of AI integration in mathematics education. To conclude, beyond the practical affordances and constraints identified in this study, the integration of AI tools like ChatGPT into teacher education raises a range of ethical, pedagogical, and institutional considerations that warrant careful attention. Teacher autonomy emerges as a critical issue, as the reliance on AI-generated problem ideas may shift decision-making power from educators to algorithms, potentially constraining creative agency. Similarly, overreliance on AI-generated content poses risks of diminishing teachers' independent problem-posing capacity, leading to gradual deskilling if reflective and critical engagement with AI outputs is not deliberately fostered. From a digital equity perspective, unequal access to reliable AI tools, language models, and relevant training could exacerbate existing disparities among teacher candidates, particularly in under-resourced contexts. These challenges are echoed in recent policy and guidance documents from UNESCO (2023) and the OECD (2023), which emphasize the necessity of embedding AI literacy into teacher preparation programs while safeguarding professional judgment, ensuring equitable access, and promoting culturally responsive use. Aligning with emerging AI literacy frameworks (e.g., Long & Magerko, 2020; Ng et al., 2021) can help teacher education programs design learning experiences that both leverage the strengths of AI and critically interrogate its limitations, thereby cultivating a balanced, ethically informed integration into pedagogical practice.

REFERENCES

Ali, O., Murray, P., Momin, M., & Al-Anzi, F. (2023). The knowledge and innovation challenges of ChatGPT: A scoping review. *Technology in Society*, *75*(102402).

Azaria, A., Azoulay, R., & Reches, S. (2024). ChatGPT is a remarkable tool: For experts. *Data Intelligence*, *6*(1), 240–296. DOI: 10.1162/dint_a_00235

Biton, Y., & Segal, R. (2025). Learning to craft and critically evaluate prompts: The role of generative AI (ChatGPT) in enhancing pre-service mathematics teachers' TPACK and problem-posing skills. [IJEMST]. *International Journal of Education in Mathematics, Science, and Technology*, *13*(1), 202–223.

Bonotto, C., & Santo, D. L. (2015). On the relationship between problem posing, problem solving, and creativity in the primary school. In Singer, F. M., Ellerton, N. F., & Cai, J. (Eds.), *Mathematical problem posing: From research into effective practice* (pp. 103–123). Springer.

Broutin, M. S. T. (2024). Exploring Mathematics Teacher Candidates' Instrumentation Process of Generative Artificial Intelligence for Developing Lesson Plans. *Yükseköğretim Dergisi*, *14*(1), 165–176.

Brown, S. I., & Walter, M. I. (1983). *The art of problem posing*. Franklin Institute Pres.

Busuttil, L., & Calleja, J. (2025). Teachers' beliefs and practices about the potential of ChatGPT in teaching Mathematics in secondary schools. *Digital Experiences in Mathematics Education*, *11*, 140–166.

Cai, J., & Hwang, S. (2002). Generalized and generative thinking in US and Chinese students' mathematical problem solving and problem posing. *The Journal of Mathematical Behavior*, *21*(4), 401–421. DOI: 10.1016/S0732-3123(02)00142-6

Cai, J., & Hwang, S. (2020). Learning to teach through mathematical problem posing: Theoretical considerations, methodology, and directions for future research. *International Journal of Educational Research*, *102*, 101391.

Cai, J., Hwang, S., Jiang, C., & Silber, S. (2015). Problem-posing research in mathematics education: Some answered and unanswered questions. In Cai, J., Ellerton, N., & Singer, F. M. (Eds.), *Mathematical problem posing: From research to effective practice* (pp. 3–34). Springer.

Cai, J., Moyer, J. C., Wang, N., Hwang, S., Nie, B., & Garber, T. (2013). Mathematical problem posing as a measure of curricular effect on students' learning. *Educational Studies in Mathematics, 83*(1), 57–69. DOI: 10.1007/s10649-012-9429-3

Cai, J., Ran, H., Hwang, S., Ma, Y., Han, J., & Muirhead, F. (2023). Impact of prompts on students' mathematical problem posing. *The Journal of Mathematical Behavior, 72*, 101087.

Cai, J., & Rott, B. (2024). On understanding mathematical problem-posing processes. *ZDM Mathematics Education, 56*(1), 61–71.

Celik, I., Dindar, M., Muukkonen, H., & Järvelä, S. (2022). The promises and challenges of artifcial intelligence for teachers: A systematic review of research. *TechTrends, 66*(4), 616–630.

Chen, T., & Cai, J. (2020). An elementary mathematics teacher learning to teach using problem posing: A case of the distributive property of multiplication over addition. *International Journal of Educational Research, 102*, 101420.

Christou, C., Pitta-Pantazi, D., & Chimoni, M. (2024). Teachers' mathematical problem posing: The role of processes and complexity levels in posing problems on the fraction part-whole concept. *The Journal of Mathematical Behavior, 73*, 101134.

Crespo, S. (2003). Learning to pose mathematical problems: Exploring changes in preservice teachers' practices. *Educational Studies in Mathematics, 52*, 243–270.

Crespo, S. (2015). A collection of problem-posing experiences for prospective mathematics teachers that make a difference. In Singer, F. M., Ellerton, N. F., & Cai, J. (Eds.), *Mathematical problem posing: From research into effective practice* (pp. 493–511). Springer.

Crespo, S., & Sinclair, N. (2008). What makes a problem mathematically interesting? Inviting prospective teachers to pose better problems. *Journal of Mathematics Teacher Education, 11*, 395–415.

Ergene, O., & Ergene, B. C. (2025). AI ChatBots' solutions to mathematical problems in interactive e-textbooks: Affordances and constraints from the eyes of students and teachers. *Education and Information Technologies, 30*(1), 509–545.

Gill, S. S., Xu, M., Patros, P., Wu, H., Kaur, R., Kaur, K., & Buyya, R. (2024). Transformative effects of ChatGPT on modern education: Emerging Era of AI Chatbots. *Internet of Things and Cyber-Physical Systems, 4*, 19–23.

Gurl, T. J., Markinson, M. P., & Artzt, A. F. (2025). Using ChatGPT as a lesson planning assistant with preservice secondary mathematics teachers. *Digital Experiences in Mathematics Education, 11*(1), 114–139.

Han, S., & Lee, M. K. (2022). FAQ chatbot and inclusive learning in massive open online courses. *Computers & Education, 179*, 104395.

Holmes, W., Porayska-Pomsta, K., Holstein, K., Sutherland, E., Baker, T., Shum, S. B., & Koedinger, K. R. (2022). Ethics of AI in education: Towards a community-wide framework. *International Journal of Artificial Intelligence in Education, 32*(3), 504–526.

Hsieh, H. F., & Shannon, S. E. (2005). Three approaches to qualitative content analysis. *Qualitative Health Research, 15*(9), 1277–1288. PMID: 16204405

Hwang, G., & Chang, C. (2021). A review of opportunities and challenges of chatbots in education. *Interactive Learning Environments, 31*(7), 4099–4112.

Javaid, M., Haleem, A., Singh, R. P., Khan, S., & Khan, I. H. (2023). Unlocking the opportunities through ChatGPT Tool towards ameliorating the education system. *BenchCouncil Transactions on Benchmarks. Standards and Evaluations, 3*(2), 100115.

Jeon, J., & Lee, S. (2023). Large language models in education: A focus on the complementary relationship between human teachers and ChatGPT. *Education and Information Technologies, 28*(12), 15873–15892.

Kasneci, E., Seßler, K., Küchemann, S., Bannert, M., Dementieva, D., Fischer, F., & Kasneci, G. (2023). ChatGPT for good? On opportunities and challenges of large language models for education. *Learning and Individual Differences, 103*, 102274.

Kilic, C. (2015). Analyzing pre-service primary teachers' fraction knowledge structures through problem posing. *Eurasia Journal of Mathematics, Science and Technology Education, 11*(6), 1603–1619.

Kim, Y. R., Park, M. S., & Joung, E. (2025). Exploring the integration of artificial intelligence in math education: Preservice Teachers' experiences and reflections on problem-posing activities with ChatGPT. *School Science and Mathematics*. Advance online publication. DOI: 10.1111/ssm.18336

Kuhail, M. A., Alturki, N., Alramlawi, S., & Alhejori, K. (2023). Interacting with educational chatbots: A systematic review. *Education and Information Technologies, 28*(1), 973–1018.

Leavy, A., & Hourigan, M. (2019). Posing mathematically worthwhile problems: Developing the problem-posing skills of prospective teachers. *Journal of Mathematics Teacher Education*, •••, 1–21. DOI: 10.1007/s10857-018-09425-w

Lee, D., & Yeo, S. (2022). Developing an AI-based chatbot for practicing responsive teaching in mathematics. *Computers & Education, 191*, 104646.

Lee, Y., Capraro, R. M., & Capraro, M. M. (2018). Mathematics teachers' subject matter knowledge and pedagogical content knowledge in problem posing. *International Electronic Journal of Mathematics Education, 13*(2), 75–90.

Leung, S. S. (1993). *The relation of mathematical knowledge and creative thinking to the mathematical problem posing of prospective elementary school teachers on tasks differing in numerical information content.* University of Pittsburgh.

Long, D., & Magerko, B. (2020, April). What is AI literacy? Competencies and design considerations. In *Proceedings of the 2020 CHI conference on human factors in computing systems* (pp. 1-16).

Luckin, R., & Cukurova, M. (2019). Designing educational technologies in the age of AI: A learning sciences-driven approach. *British Journal of Educational Technology*, *50*(6), 2824–2838.

Lucy, L., & Bamman, D. (2021). Gender and representation bias in GPT-3 generated stories. In Akoury, N., Brahman, F., Chaturvedi, S., Clark, E., Iyyer, M., & Martin, L. J. (Eds.), *Proceedings of the third workshop on narrative understanding* (pp. 48–55). Association for Computational Linguistics. https://doi.org/DOI: 10.18653/v1/2021.nuse-1.5

MacDowell, P., & Korchinsk, K. (2023). A collaborative future: New roles of students and teachers learning and creating with generative AI. In Bauchard, S., Rao, A., Shah, P., & Shryock, C. (Eds.), *CHAT (GPT): Navigating the impact of generative AI technologies on educational theory and practice* (pp. 590–507). Pedagogy Ventures LLC.

Memarian, B., & Doleck, T. (2023). ChatGPT in education: Methods, potentials, and limitations. *Computers in Human Behavior: Artificial Humans, 1*(2), 100022.

Meyer, J. G., Urbanowicz, R. J., Martin, P. C., O'Connor, K., Li, R., Peng, P. C., & Moore, J. H. (2023). ChatGPT and large language models in academia: Opportunities and challenges. *BioData Mining, 16*(1), 20. PMID: 37443040

Mishra, P., & Koehler, M. J. (2006). Technological pedagogical content knowledge: A framework for teacher knowledge. *Teachers College Record, 108*(6), 1017–1054.

National Council of Teachers of Mathematics. (1991). *Professional standards for teaching mathematics*. Author.

Ng, D. T. K., Leung, J. K. L., Chu, S. K. W., & Qiao, M. S. (2021). Conceptualizing AI literacy: An exploratory review. *Computers and Education: Artificial Intelligence*, *2*, 100041.

Noster, N., Gerber, S., & Siller, H. S. (2024). Pre-Service Teachers' Approaches in Solving Mathematics Tasks with ChatGPT. *Digital Experiences in Mathematics Education*, *10*(3), 543–567.

OECD Digital Education Outlook 2023. (2023). OECD. https://doi.org/DOI: 10.1787/c74f03de-en

Palm, T., & Burman, L. (2002). Reality in mathematics assessment–an analysis of task-reality concordance in Finnish and Swedish national assessments.

Pelton, T., & Pelton, L. F. (2023, March). Adapting ChatGPT to support teacher education in mathematics. In *Society for Information Technology & Teacher Education International Conference* (pp. 1662-1670). Association for the Advancement of Computing in Education (AACE).

Pepin, B., Buchholtz, N., & Salinas-Hernández, U. (2025). A scoping survey of ChatGPT in mathematics education. *Digital Experiences in Mathematics Education*, •••, 1–33.

Rahman, M. M., & Watanobe, Y. (2023). ChatGPT for education and research: Opportunities, threats, and strategies. *Applied Sciences (Basel, Switzerland)*, *13*(9), 5783.

Rasul, T., Nair, S., Kalendra, D., Robin, M., de Oliveira Santini, F., Ladeira, W. J., & Heathcote, L. (2023). The role of ChatGPT in higher education: Benefits, challenges, and future research directions. *Journal of Applied Learning and Teaching*, *6*(1), 41–56.

Remoto, J. P. (2024). ChatGPT and other AIs: Personal relief and limitations among mathematics-oriented learners. *Environment and Social Psychology*, *9*(1), 1–13.

Rosenshine, B., Meister, C., & Chapman, S. (1996). Teaching students to generate questions: A review of the intervention studies. *Review of Educational Research*, *66*(2), 181–221.

Rospigliosi, P. A. (2023). Artificial intelligence in teaching and learning: What questions should we ask of ChatGPT? *Interactive Learning Environments*, *31*(1), 1–3.

Sadak, M., Incikabi, L., Ulusoy, F., & Pektas, M. (2022). Investigating mathematical creativity through the connection between creative abilities in problem posing and problem solving. *Thinking Skills and Creativity*, *45*, 101108.

Sánchez-Ruiz, L. M., Moll-López, S., Nuñez-Pérez, A., Moraño-Fernández, J. A., & Vega-Fleitas, E. (2023). ChatGPT challenges blended learning methodologies in engineering education: A case study in mathematics. *Applied Sciences (Basel, Switzerland)*, *13*(10), 6039.

Silver, E. A. (1994). On mathematical problem posing. *For the Learning of Mathematics*, *14*(1), 19–28.

Silver, E. A., & Cai, J. (1996). An analysis of arithmetic problem posing by middle school students. *Journal for Research in Mathematics Education*, *27*(5), 521–539.

Snell, J., Swersky, K., & Zemel, R. (2017). Prototypical networks for few-shot learning. *Advances in Neural Information Processing Systems*, •••, 30.

Stickles, P. R. (2011). An analysis of secondary and middle school teachers' mathematical problem posing. *Investigations in Mathematics Learning*, *3*(2), 1–34.

Stoyanova, E., & Ellerton, N. F. (1996). A framework for research into students' problem posing in school mathematics. In Clarkson, P. (Ed.), *Technology in mathematics education* (pp. 518–525). MERGA.

Tlili, A., Shehata, B., Adarkwah, M. A., Bozkurt, A., Hickey, D. T., Huang, R., & Agyemang, B. (2023). What if the devil is my guardian angel: ChatGPT as a case study of using chatbots in education. *Smart Learning Environments*, *10*(1), 15.

Tunç, M. P. (2024). Examining Pre-service Mathematics Teachers' Purposes of Using ChatGPT in Lesson Plan Development. *Sakarya University Journal of Education*, *14*(2), 391–406.

Ulusoy, F. (2023). Middle Level Mathematics Teachers' Problems on Linear Relationships in a Semi-Structured Problem Posing Situation. *RMLE Online: Research in Middle Level Education*, *46*(10), 1–19.

Ulusoy, F. (2025). Using general-mathematical and content-specific elements to assess the quality of prospective mathematics teachers' problems in a problem-posing context. *Journal of Mathematics Teacher Education*, •••, 1–33. DOI: 10.1007/s10857-025-09697-z

Ulusoy, F., & Kepceoğlu, İ. (2018). İlköğretim matematik öğretmen adaylarının yarıyapılandırılmış problem kurma bağlamında oluşturdukları problemlerin bağlamsal ve bilişsel yapısı. *Kırşehir Eğitim Fakültesi Dergisi*, *19*(3), 1910–1936.

Ulusoy, F., Sadak, M., Incikabi, L., & Pektas, M. (2025). Exploring Gender Differences in Mathematical Creativity: Linking Problem Posing and Problem Solving. *Psychology in the Schools*. Advance online publication. DOI: 10.1002/pits.70060

UNESCO. (2023). ChatGPT and artificial intelligence in higher education: quick start guide. UNESCO International Institute for Higher Education in Latin America and the Caribbean. https://unesdoc.unesco.org/ark:/48223/pf0000385146

Van Harpen, X. Y., & Sriraman, B. (2013). Creativity and mathematical problem posing: An analysis of high school students' mathematical problem posing in China and the USA. *Educational Studies in Mathematics*, *82*(2), 201–221.

Vicente, S., & Manchado, E. (2017). Dominios de contenido y autenticidad: Un análisis de los problemas aritméticos verbales incluidos en los libros de texto españoles. *PNA. Revista de Investigación en Didáctica de la Matemática*, *11*(4), 253–279.

Wang, P., Zhang, Q., Zhang, W., & Sun, J. (2024). The application of ChatGPT in nursing: A bibliometric and visualized analysis. *Frontiers in Medicine*, *11*, 1521712. PMID: 39744533

Wardat, Y., Tashtoush, M., AlAli, R., & Jarrah, A. (2023). ChatGPT: A revolutionary tool for teaching and learning mathematics. *Eurasia Journal of Mathematics, Science and Technology Education, 19*(7), (#2286). https://doi.org/DOI: 10.29333/ejmste/13272

Winkler, R., & Söllner, M. (2018, July). Unleashing the potential of chatbots in education: A state-of-the-art analysis. In *Academy of management proceedings* (Vol. 2018, No. 1, p. 15903). Briarcliff Manor, NY 10510: Academy of Management.

Yuan, X., & Sriraman, B. (2011). An exploratory study of relationships between students' creativity and mathematical problem-posing abilities. *The elements of creativity and giftedness in mathematics*, 5-28.

Zhang, L., Stylianides, G. J., & Stylianides, A. J. (2024). Enhancing mathematical problem posing competence: A meta-analysis of intervention studies. *International Journal of STEM Education*, *11*, 48.

Zhang, R., Zou, D., & Cheng, G. (2023). Chatbot-based learning of logical fallacies in EFL writing: Perceived effectiveness in improving target knowledge and learner motivation. *Interactive Learning Environments*. Advance online publication. DOI: 10.1080/10494820.2023.2220374

KEY TERMS AND DEFINITIONS

AI Tools in Education: They are technologies that apply machine learning, natural language processing, and adaptive algorithms to support learning, teaching, and assessment. Generative AI tools such as ChatGPT are particularly relevant in teacher education, as they can provide diverse problem contexts, immediate feedback, and iterative refinement opportunities for pre-service teachers (Kasneci et al., 2023; Kim et al., 2025).

Free Problem Posing: Free problem posing occurs when learners generate problems without any predefined structure, conditions, or constraints (Stoyanova & Ellerton, 1996). This type of task maximizes student creativity and autonomy, allowing for highly original mathematical thinking.

Problem Posing: It refers to the process of generating new mathematical problems or reformulating existing ones (Silver, 1994). It plays a central role in mathematics education by fostering creativity, critical thinking, and deeper conceptual understanding.

Semi-Structured Problem Posing: It involves creating new problems within given conditions, contexts, or parameters determined by the teacher or researcher (Stoyanova & Ellerton, 1996).

Structured Problem Posing: It refers to the reformulation of a given mathematical problem or situation by making small modifications or variations (Silver, 1994).

TPACK (Technological Pedagogical Content Knowledge): TPACK is a theoretical framework describing the knowledge teachers need to effectively integrate technology into their teaching. It emphasizes the intersection of three domains: content knowledge (CK), pedagogical knowledge (PK), and technological knowledge (TK) (Mishra & Koehler, 2006).

Chapter 8
Student and Teacher Perceptions of AI-Supported Mathematics Education:
Perspectives From Cambodia

Rany Sam
https://orcid.org/0000-0003-3266-5974
National University of Battambang, Cambodia

Sinath No
https://orcid.org/0009-0001-1644-8702
National University of Battambang, Cambodia

Kamrang Tith
https://orcid.org/0009-0007-2736-5455
National University of Chea Sim Kamchaymear, Cambodia

Pisith Chin
https://orcid.org/0009-0003-4784-717X
National University of Chea Sim Kamchaymear, Cambodia

Sinoeurn Kheuy
https://orcid.org/0009-0000-2828-7435
National University of Battambang, Cambodia

Ngorntheng Thol
National University of Chea Sim Kamchaymear, Cambodia

Vuthea Da
https://orcid.org/0009-0003-3185-0999
National University of Battambang, Cambodia

Sereyrath Em
https://orcid.org/0000-0002-6803-195X
National University of Cheasim Kamchaymear, Cambodia

Hak Yoeng
https://orcid.org/0000-0003-4145-0350
National University of Battambang, Cambodia

Sarith Chiv
https://orcid.org/0009-0000-0239-5307
National Meanchey University, Cambodia

DOI: 10.4018/979-8-3373-1998-8.ch008

ABSTRACT

The Royal Government of Cambodia has introduced a range of educational and strategic policies to advance educational technology and strengthen digital literacy across the national education system. Integrating Artificial Intelligence (AI) into teaching and learning is among the most widely adopted innovations. While AI in mathematics education has gained increasing traction regionally and globally, its impact on Cambodian students' and teachers' experiences remains underexplored. This study seeks to address this gap by examining the perceptions of university students and mathematics teachers regarding AI-supported mathematics education, with particular attention to perceived benefits, challenges, and its potential to enhance learning outcomes. Using a qualitative research approach, in-depth interviews were conducted with 30 participants from various high schools, providing insights into the opportunities and constraints of AI integration in the Cambodian context.

1. INTRODUCTION

As artificial intelligence (AI) has improved, it has changed many parts of education, including how teachers teach, how students stay interested, and how well lessons work (Chen et al., 2020). AI-powered tools could change traditional math classrooms by offering personalized learning paths, instant feedback, and advanced analytics (Xu & Ouyang, 2022; Crompton & Burke, 2023; Opesemowo, & Adewuyi, 2024; Göktepe Yıldız & Göktepe Körpeoğlu, 2025; Hossein-Mohand et al., 2025). These tools provide teachers with data-driven insights and help them address everyday problems in math teaching, such as meeting the needs of students who learn at different speeds or filling in gaps in their basic knowledge (UNESCO, 2023; Sam et al., 2025). In light of this, it is important to understand how technology, pedagogy, and cultural contexts affect each other to judge the role of AI-powered solutions in improving teaching and learning. Cambodia is a rapidly developing country that is placing increasing emphasis on modernizing its education system. This makes it important to study these dynamics.

It is important to pay special attention to the views of students and teachers, which are key to the success of any educational intervention (Zou et al., 2025). In Cambodia, where traditional rote-learning methods are often used, AI in math classes may lead to new problems and challenges (MoEYS, 2022). For example, rural schools do not have much digital infrastructure, students have different levels of exposure to technology, and teachers have different ideas about how to teach, which may affect how people see the role of AI. The Cambodian government's push for digital literacy and the rise of localized tech solutions show how AI could affect the country (Chea et al, 2022). This study looks at how students and teachers feel about AI-supported math education to better understand the complex relationship between innovation and educational equity in a sociocultural setting where resources and access are not equal. This study aims to gather important information to help shape policies and practices that create fair AI-driven learning environments in Cambodia (World Bank, 2023). It does this by looking into people's hopes, obstacles, and what is possible. This introduction sets the stage for an investigation into the technical aspects of AI-supported education and the human factors that affect its use and long-term viability in schools in Cambodia.

Research Question:

How do students and teachers in Cambodia perceive the integration of AI-supported tools in mathematics education, and what are the key opportunities, challenges, and implications for equitable implementation?

Research Objectives:

1. To examine the perceptions of Cambodian students and teachers regarding the use of AI in mathematics education, including their attitudes, acceptance, and concerns.
2. To identify the opportunities offered by AI-supported mathematics education, such as personalized learning, real-time feedback, and enhanced engagement.
3. To explore the challenges hindering effective AI integration, including infrastructural limitations, digital literacy gaps, and teacher preparedness.

2. LITERATURE REVIEW

2.1. Overview of Cambodia's Education System

Cambodia's education system is entrenched in a historical context shaped by the nation's tumultuous past and its contemporary aspirations toward modernization and reform. Following the devastating impact of the Khmer Rouge regime, which decimated the country's educational infrastructure and human capital, Cambodia has undertaken extensive efforts to rebuild its education sector (Tan, 2007). The Ministry of Education, Youth and Sport (MoEYS) is the principal authority in this endeavor and is tasked with policy formulation, curriculum development, and the implementation of national education reforms (MoEYS, 2024).

The Cambodian education system has three main levels: primary, secondary, and higher education. Primary education, encompassing grades one through six, focuses on foundational literacy and numeracy for children aged six to eleven. Secondary education is divided into lower secondary (grades 7–9) and upper secondary (grades 10–12) education, offering a more diverse curriculum that includes sciences, humanities, and technical subjects (UNESCO, 2023). Higher education, offered through universities and technical institutes, has seen steady growth driven by increasing demand for skilled labor and socioeconomic development (World Bank, 2023). Despite expanding public and private institutions, challenges remain regarding equitable access, quality assurance, and teacher capacity. Geographic and socioeconomic disparities continue to impact educational equity. Rural areas often experience limited infrastructure, shortages of qualified teachers, and reduced access to technological resources, which impedes the delivery of high-quality education (Yem, 2025.). In response, the Cambodian government, in collaboration with international partners, has initiated reforms aimed at inclusive education, improved teacher training, and integrated digital tools to bridge the urban–rural divide (Asian Development Bank [ADB], 2023). As the education sector evolves, understanding the existing system's structure and constraints is critical for effectively implementing innovative solutions such as artificial intelligence (AI) in classrooms.

2.2. Integration of AI in Cambodian Schools

The integration of artificial intelligence (AI) in Cambodian schools represents a significant milestone in the nation's educational modernization efforts. Recent initiatives by the government and development partners have introduced AI-powered educational tools in selected schools, particularly to enhance mathematics instruction (UNESCO, 2021; MoEYS, 2023). These tools aim to personalize learning, increase student engagement, and provide real-time feedback, aligning with global trends in education technology (Luckin et al., 2016; Chhay et al., 2024). AI integration in Cambodia is motivated by its potential to tailor learning pathways, cater to diverse student needs, and facilitate differentiated instruction. Early evidence suggests that AI can improve student comprehension and encourage self-directed learning (Fu & Weng, 2024; Holmes & Porayska-Pomsta, 2022; Holmes et al., 2022; Saing et al., 2023; Run et al., 2025). However, successful implementation remains uneven due to infrastructural limitations, especially in rural schools. Many institutions face challenges such as unreliable electricity, inadequate internet connectivity, and outdated hardware, which restrict AI deployment (World Bank, 2023).

A key concern among educators is the lack of training and professional development opportunities necessary to effectively incorporate AI into teaching practices (OECD, 2021; Vong & Kao, 2022). Without adequate support, teachers may struggle with the technical and pedagogical aspects of AI integration, potentially undermining its effectiveness. Furthermore, concerns about depersonalization, reduced teacher agency, and the ethical implications of data-driven education persist (Williamson & Eynon, 2020; UNICEF, 2023). Equity also poses a significant challenge, as disparities in technology access threaten to widen achievement gaps between socioeconomic groups. Policymakers must prioritize frameworks that ensure equitable access to AI-enhanced education while upholding inclusive values (NGO Education Partnership [NEP], 2024).

Mathematics education, which emphasizes problem-solving and logical reasoning, benefits significantly from AI innovations (VanLehn, 2022; Henkel et al., 2024). AI systems can provide adaptive feedback, identify learning gaps, propose targeted interventions, and support teachers and students (VanLehn, 2022; Chea et al, 2022; Saing et al., 2023; Pum & Sok, 2024; Pen & Morrell, 2024; Run et al., 2025; Sok, et al, 2025). In Cambodia, where educational disparities persist, AI-powered tools such as interactive math visualizations could democratize access to quality resources (UNESCO, 2023; MoEYS, 2024). However, the success of AI depends on user perceptions. Digital literacy, perceived relevance, and ease of use influence adoption (Venkatesh et al., 2003; Pen & Morrell, 2024). In Cambodia, where edtech adoption is nascent, understanding teacher and student attitudes is critical for effective implementation (Pen & Morrell, 2024; Pum & Sok, 2024).

2.3. AI in Education

Artificial intelligence (AI) represents a transformative force in the realm of education, reshaping traditional pedagogies and unlocking new dimensions of learning (Luckin et al., 2022; Sam et al., 2025). Within the educational landscape, AI introduces tools and systems designed to augment teaching and enhance student experiences (Fu & Weng, 2024; Holmes & Porayska-Pomsta, 2022; Holmes et al., 2022). These tools range from intelligent tutoring systems and personalized learning platforms to automated grading and AI-driven content creation (Zawacki-Richter et al., 2019). The core advantage of incorporating AI into education lies in its capacity to offer personalized learning experiences, adapting instructional materials to suit the individual learning pace and style of each student (Khine, 2024). By employing advanced algorithms, educational AI can analyze vast quantities of data regarding student performance, thereby aligning educational strategies with individual needs and optimizing learning outcomes (Chen et al., 2020; Sam et al., 2025).

The integration of AI in education further extends to facilitating administrative efficiency and enriching teaching methodologies (VanLehn, 2022). For educators, AI systems provide valuable insights and analytics that can inform teaching strategies, highlighting areas where students may require additional support or alternative instructional approaches (VanLehn, 2022). This data-driven support aids teachers in fostering an inclusive learning environment while managing diverse student needs effectively (UNESCO, 2023). Additionally, AI can empower teachers with advanced tools such as virtual assistants and interactive learning modules, enriching the pedagogical process and allowing educators to focus more on in depth, creative interactions with students (Chea et al, 2022; Saing et al., 2023; Pum & Sok, 2024; Pen & Morrell, 2024; Run et al., 2025; Sok, et al, 2025). However, the deployment of AI in education is not without its challenges; ethical considerations, digital literacy, and access disparities are pivotal issues that necessitate careful deliberation to ensure equitable and responsible utilization (Tamilmani et al., 2021; Scherer et al., 2021).

Moreover, AI-supported education embodies the promise of reducing educational inequities, particularly in regions with limited access to traditional resources (World Bank, 2023). In regions where educational infrastructure may vary significantly across urban and rural areas, AI can serve as a catalyst for democratizing education, making high-quality learning resources available to a broader audience (Chea et al, 2022). Collaborative initiatives, technological investment, and policy frameworks are essential to overcoming barriers to AI integration and fostering an environment where both students and teachers can fully harness the benefits of AI (Selwyn, 2022). While AI in education offers substantial opportunities, it also demands a conscientious approach that prioritizes equity, accessibility, and ethical governance to facilitate a progressive and beneficial educational experience for all stakeholders (Venkatesh et al., 2003).

2.4. Mathematics Education

Mathematics education, a fundamental component of academic curricula worldwide, plays a critical role in equipping students with problem-solving skills and logical reasoning capabilities (Simms, 2016). In Cambodia, as in many other countries, the structure of mathematics education has been designed to form a sturdy base upon which students can build further understanding in the sciences and engineering disciplines (Ministry of Education, Youth and Sport [MoEYS], 2019). Historically, mathematics instruction in Cambodia has been traditional, relying heavily on rote learning and memorization techniques (Tan, 2007). This approach, while effective in certain contexts, has been criticized for not adequately fostering deep understanding or promoting critical thinking skills among students (Tan, 2010). In recent years, however, there has been a concerted effort to reform mathematics education and make it more engaging and innovative (MoEYS, 2021).

Pedagogical shifts are encouraged to include more student-centered approaches, problem-based learning, and the integration of real-world scenarios into mathematics lessons (Saing et al., 2023; Run et al., 2025). These changes aim to shift the learning paradigm from procedural to conceptual understanding, encouraging students to explore mathematical concepts actively and develop a more intuitive and comprehensive grasp of the subject matter (Xu & Ouyang, 2022; Crompton & Burke, 2023; Opesemowo, & Adewuyi, 2024; Göktepe Yıldız & Göktepe Körpeoğlu, 2025;

Hossein-Mohand et al., 2025). Furthermore, with the advancement of educational technologies, new opportunities have emerged to enhance mathematics instruction through digital tools that offer interactive and adaptive learning experiences (Chea et al, 2022). The national curriculum in Cambodia has begun to reflect these changes, with modifications intended to enhance students' analytical skills and appreciation for the discipline (MoEYS, 2022).

Teacher professional development programs are also being implemented, with a focus on increasing teachers' instructional capabilities and their ability to integrate technology effectively (Benzer et al., 2025). These efforts highlight the growing recognition of the need to evolve traditional mathematics education frameworks to meet the demands of a rapidly changing world (World Bank, 2023). In this transitional phase, there is an essential emphasis on balancing foundational knowledge with the flexibility to adjust pedagogical practices that incorporate innovative teaching methodologies, preparing Cambodian students for the global stage (UNESCO, 2022).

2.5. Challenges faced

Despite its promise, the integration of AI-supported mathematics education in Cambodia presents a host of complex challenges that must be addressed systematically. Chief among these is the persistent digital divide. Many rural and underresourced schools lack the foundational infrastructure such as stable internet connectivity, digital devices, and reliable electricity required to implement AI technologies effectively. This digital disparity reinforces existing educational inequalities, limiting the ability of students in marginalized areas to benefit from AI-enhanced learning environments.

In addition to infrastructure issues, there are significant pedagogical and institutional hurdles. Many educators face difficulties adapting to AI-based instruction, particularly in the absence of adequate training and support. Professional development opportunities focused on digital pedagogy and AI literacy remain scarce, leaving teachers ill equipped to integrate these tools confidently and effectively into their teaching. Additionally, resistance to change among educators, who may view AI as a threat to traditional teaching practices, further impedes adoption. This resistance is often rooted in concerns about diminished teacher agency and the potential loss of meaningful teacher–student interactions.

Another critical challenge is the lack of alignment between AI tools and the national curriculum. Without clear frameworks guiding the pedagogical use of AI, educators may struggle to incorporate these technologies in ways that are educationally coherent and contextually relevant. Moreover, many AI systems are designed for global markets and may not reflect Cambodia's linguistic, cultural, or curricular realities. Content that fails to consider the local language and cultural nuances can hinder student engagement and comprehension, undermining the effectiveness of AI-based instruction. Ethical concerns also arise, particularly regarding data privacy and security. AI systems typically collect and analyze large volumes of student data, raising important questions about how this information is stored, shared, and protected. In the absence of strong data governance policies, the use of AI in education could expose students to risks related to surveillance, consent, and misuse of personal information. Addressing these multifaceted challenges requires a holistic and collaborative approach. Investment in digital infrastructure must be matched by strategic policy development, culturally relevant content creation, and robust teacher training programs. Establishing regulatory frameworks that uphold ethical standards and safeguard student data is equally crucial. Only through sustained, coordinated efforts can Cambodia overcome these barriers and harness the full potential of AI to create an inclusive, equitable, and forward-looking educational system.

2.6 Perceptions of Technology

The integration of technology in education has been shaped by diverse and often multifaceted perceptions, which influence its adoption, utility, and effectiveness in different contexts (Scherer et al., 2019). Perceptions of technology are rooted in cultural, social, and individual factors, and they often dictate the ways in which technological advancements are embraced or resisted within educational systems (Selwyn, 2019). In the Cambodian context, these perceptions are deeply entwined with historical patterns of access to technology, existing infrastructure, and broader societal attitudes toward modernization (Chea et al, 2022). Specifically, the role of digital tools in education is frequently viewed through the lens of their perceived ability to bridge gaps in resources or exacerbate educational inequalities (MoEYS, 2022). Such perceptions are especially critical in shaping stakeholder confidence, particularly among students and teachers, whose attitudes determine the success of technology integration in classrooms (Venkatesh & Davis, 2000).

Teachers, as primary agents of implementation, often assess technology on the basis of its potential to enhance instructional strategies and streamline teaching processes (Ertmer et al., 1999). However, perceptions within this group are not uniform and vary widely depending on technological literacy, prior exposure, and professional support (Xu & Ouyang, 2022; Crompton & Burke, 2023; Opesemowo, & Adewuyi, 2024; Göktepe Yıldız & Göktepe Körpeoğlu, 2025; Hossein-Mohand et al., 2025). For example, educators who feel adequately trained to use technology in pedagogical settings tend to express greater optimism about its impact, whereas those who perceive it as complex or time-consuming may exhibit hesitancy (Benzer et al., 2025; Chea et al., 2022). In Cambodia, where professional development opportunities related to educational technology remain limited in some regions, this difference in perception can be pronounced (World Bank, 2018). Furthermore, teachers may view technology either as a tool for democratizing education by reaching underserved populations or as an intrusion that complicates traditional methods of instruction (Saing et al., 2023; Run et al., 2025).

Similarly, students' perceptions of technology are shaped by factors such as prior access, familiarity, and the relevance of technological tools to their learning goals (Chea et al, 2022; Saing et al., 2023; Pum & Sok, 2024; Pen & Morrell, 2024; Run et al., 2025; Sok, et al, 2025). When students perceive technology as a means to foster engagement, provide interactive learning opportunities, or simplify abstract concepts such as those often encountered in mathematics, their receptiveness to its integration increases significantly (Chen et al., 2020; Esteban & Cruz, 2021). Conversely, if technology is seen as inaccessible, unintuitive, or irrelevant to their educational context, it may be regarded with skepticism or disinterest (Tan, 2010). In Cambodia, where socioeconomic disparities continue to affect access to digital tools, students' perceptions often reflect these unequal opportunities, thereby reinforcing the complex interplay between optimism for innovation and mistrust of its efficacy (UNESCO, 2022). Consequently, understanding these perceptions is pivotal for creating policies and programs that navigate cultural and logistical challenges, ensuring that technology serves as an enabler rather than a barrier in reshaping mathematics education (MoEYS, 2023).

2.7. Context of the Study

The context of this study is set against the backdrop of Cambodia's evolving educational landscape, where traditional methodologies are increasingly meeting groundbreaking technological advancements. In particular, the Cambodian education system has been undergoing significant reforms aimed at improving quality and accessibility, driven by governmental ambition and international support (UNESCO, 2020). Historically, the system has faced numerous challenges, such as limited resources, high student-to-teacher ratios, and a need for modern pedagogical strategies (Ministry of Education, Youth and Sport [MoEYS], 2019). These factors, alongside initiatives to align with international standards, underscore the complexity and urgency of educational transformation in the nation. Within this framework, the integration of artificial intelligence (AI) into Cambodian schools represents a pivotal development that seeks to redefine educational paradigms. AI technologies offer the potential to tailor learning experiences to individual student needs, enhance resource allocation, and streamline administrative processes (Luckin et al., 2016). The incorporation of such technologies, however, is not without its challenges. It requires substantial infrastructure investment, teacher training, and a cultural shift in pedagogical approaches (Fu & Weng, 2024; Holmes & Porayska-Pomsta, 2022;

Holmes et al., 2022). There is also a discernible gap between urban and rural areas concerning access to technology, exacerbating existing disparities and necessitating policies that promote equitable resource distribution (UNESCO, 2021).

These factors culminate in a unique environment where both students and educators are adapting to rapidly changing conditions. Understanding their perceptions of AI-supported education is crucial in assessing the effectiveness and inclusivity of such innovations. The Cambodian context thus serves as a microcosm of broader global trends in technological integration in education, highlighting both the opportunities and hurdles inherent in adopting AI within traditional schooling structures. As such, the study promises to contribute valuable insights into how educational systems can effectively navigate the intersection of heritage, innovation, and equity.

3. METHODOLOGY

To establish a methodology for exploring student and teacher perceptions of AI-supported mathematics education in Cambodia, a systematic approach has been employed to ensure comprehensive and insightful findings. This section elaborates upon the strategies that underpin the research design, participants, data collection methods, and data analysis, each contributing to a robust framework tailored to the study's unique cultural and educational context. The research design adopted in this study is a qualitative research approach. This dual strategy facilitates a nuanced understanding of perceptions and experiences while allowing for statistically significant results (Creswell & Plano Clark, 2018; Angrosino, 2007). Qualitative data are gathered through interviews, capturing detailed narratives and personal insights. Participant selection is a critical aspect of the methodology, involving a purposeful sampling technique to recruit teachers and students from various educational settings across Cambodia. This deliberate selection ensures representation from diverse demographic backgrounds, including urban and rural schools, to capture a wide range of experiences with AI technologies in mathematics education (Palinkas et al., 2015; Bryman, 2016). Both educators and learners are engaged in this study, allowing for a comparative analysis that considers both instructional and learning perspectives. Ethical considerations are meticulously addressed, with informed consent obtained from all participants, emphasizing the voluntary nature of participation and the confidentiality of responses (Israel & Hay, 2006). Data collection methods are carefully chosen to align with the research objectives and to facilitate comprehensive acquisition of information. semi structured interviews and focus groups offer rich qualitative data, encouraging participants to articulate their experiences and reflections in their own voices (Merriam & Tisdell, 2016). This integrative strategy ensures a detailed examination of both the statistical and narrative dimensions of perceptions. Finally, data analysis involves a methodical approach, employing coding techniques for qualitative data. Thematic analysis is used to identify recurring themes and insights in narrative data (Braun & Clarke, 2006).

3.1. Research Design

The study design incorporates a qualitative research approach to explore student and teacher perceptions in AI-supported mathematics education and aligns well with established educational research methodologies. Qualitative research in education focuses on capturing rich, descriptive data about participants' experiences and perspectives, using methods such as interviews, observations, and document analysis (Merriam & Tisdell, 2016; Delve, 2024). This approach allows researchers to understand the deeper context, motivations, and cultural factors influencing educational phenomena beyond quantitative measures like test scores (Delve, 2024). Creswell and Plano Clark (2018) emphasize that qualitative research is particularly valuable when the aim is to explore multiple perspectives and gain a comprehensive, contextually rich understanding of complex educational issues. The qualitative approach enables in-depth exploration of lived experiences, empowering participants by giving them a voice in the research process. Thus, utilizing a qualitative research approach to study perceptions of AI-supported mathematics education in Cambodia is appropriate to capture students' and teachers' nuanced views and experiences in this emerging educational context.

3.2. Participants

The study participants were meticulously selected to provide a comprehensive perspective on AI-supported mathematics education within the Cambodian context. 30 Participants included both 15 students and 15 teachers from high schools in Cambodia, ensuring a broad spectrum of insights into the intersection of AI and mathematics education. Participation has focused primarily on individuals actively engaged in mathematics instruction or learning, thereby offering valuable first-hand experiences and perceptions related to the integration of AI technologies in educational settings. The teachers involved in the study were chosen from diverse subject specialties and educational backgrounds, facilitating an understanding of how AI tools could enhance pedagogical practices across different mathematical domains. Their involvement aimed to highlight the facilitators of and barriers to adopting AI-driven educational resources, as well as to elucidate their perceptions concerning the impact of AI on teaching efficacy, curriculum adaptation, and student engagement (Creswell & Poth, 2018). Additionally, the diversity among teacher participants allowed an exploration of how institutional characteristics, such as urban versus rural settings, might influence AI adoption and utility in mathematics education (Palinkas et al., 2015).

On the student side, participants were drawn from various socioeconomic backgrounds, allowing for a nuanced exploration of how AI-supported education may affect learners differently depending on their access to technology and prior computing experience (OECD, 2021). The inclusion of students from different academic levels provided a cross-sectional view of the student interface with AI tools, potentially generating insights into age-related or stage-related differences in AI integration within mathematical instruction. This approach was intended to capture a more holistic view of the educational challenges and opportunities presented by AI, enriching the overall understanding of how these technologies could be tailored to meet diverse learning needs and objectives within Cambodia's educational landscape.

3.3. Data collection methods

The study participants were carefully selected to provide a comprehensive understanding of AI-supported mathematics education in the Cambodian context. The sample included 30 participants, including 15 students and 15 teachers from various educational institutions, spanning primary, secondary, and tertiary levels, as shown in Tables 1 and 2. This diversity ensured a broad spectrum of insights into the integration of AI in mathematics education. The participants were specifically chosen for their active involvement in either teaching or learning mathematics, offering valuable first-hand experiences and perspectives on the use of AI technologies in educational settings. The teacher participants represented various subject specialties and educational backgrounds, allowing the study to examine how AI tools might enhance pedagogical practices across different areas of mathematics. Their inclusion aimed to shed light on both the facilitators of and barriers to adopting AI-driven educational resources and their perceptions regarding AI's impact on teaching effectiveness, curriculum adaptation, and student engagement (Creswell & Poth, 2018). Additionally, the diversity of institutional contexts, such as urban versus rural schools, has enabled an exploration of how these factors may influence the implementation and effectiveness of AI in mathematics instruction (Palinkas et al., 2015).

Table 1. Teachers' profiles

Code	Age	Sex	School Location	Years of Experiences	Educational Background
T1	34	M	Battambang	10 years	B.Sc.
T2	42	M	Battambang	12 years	M.Sc.
T3	48	M	Battambang	18 years	B.Sc.
T4	35	M	Battambang	11 years	B.Sc.
T5	42	M	Banteay Meanchey	16 years	B.Sc.
T6	37	M	Banteay Meanchey	13 years	B.Sc.
T7	34	M	Banteay Meanchey	10 years	B.Sc.
T8	32	M	Banteay Meanchey	8 years	M.Sc.
T9	42	M	Pursat	14 years	B.Sc.
T10	51	M	Pursat	22 years	M. Ed.
T11	45	M	Pursat	16 years	B.Sc.
T12	43	M	Pursat	18 years	B.Sc.
T13	34	M	Oddor Meanchey	12 years	B.Sc.
T14	38	M	Oddor Meanchey	13 years	B.Sc.
T15	43	M	Oddor Meanchey	14 years	B.Sc.

Table 2. Students' profile

Code	Age	Sex	Grade	High School Location
S1	18	F	12	Battambang
S2	18	F	12	Battambang
S3	18	F	12	Battambang
S4	17	M	11	Banteay Meanchey
S5	17	M	11	Banteay Meanchey
S6	17	M	11	Banteay Meanchey
S7	18	F	12	Pursat
S8	18	F	12	Pursat
S9	18	F	12	Pursat

continued on following page

Table 2. Continued

Code	Age	Sex	Grade	High School Location
S10	18	M	12	Oddor Meanchey
S11	18	M	12	Oddor Meanchey
S12	17	M	11	Oddor Meanchey
S13	17	F	11	Battambang
S14	17	F	11	Battambang
S15	17	F	11	Battambang

On the student side, participants come from various socioeconomic backgrounds, enabling a nuanced analysis of how AI-supported education may affect learners differently on the basis of their access to technology and prior experience with digital tools (OECD, 2021). The inclusion of students from different academic levels provided a cross-sectional view of how learners interact with AI tools at various stages, potentially revealing age- or grade-related differences in engagement and effectiveness. This inclusive approach aims to offer a holistic perspective on the challenges and opportunities of integrating AI into Cambodian mathematics education, contributing to a deeper understanding of how such technologies can be adapted to diverse educational needs and goals.

3.4. Data analysis

In the examination of student and teacher perceptions of AI-supported mathematics education in Cambodia, the data analysis process serves as a cornerstone for distilling meaningful insights from the collected data. Qualitative data obtained from in-depth interviews were analyzed through thematic analysis. This involved a systematic coding process to identify recurrent themes and subthemes that captured the essence of participant experiences and attitudes (Braun & Clarke, 2006). Qualitative data analysis software was employed to manage and organize the data, ensuring accuracy and consistency in identifying themes such as enthusiasm for innovative educational tools, apprehension regarding the adequacy of AI in addressing specific educational needs, and the perceived impact on teacher roles. This comprehensive approach to data analysis not only illuminates the multidimensional nature of stakeholder perceptions but also provides a robust foundation for formulating strategic recommendations to enhance the implementation of AI in mathematics education in Cambodia, ensuring that it is both effective and contextually relevant.

4. FINDINGS

The study of AI-supported mathematics education in Cambodian schools yielded several key findings that reflect both optimism and concern among students and teachers. From the students' perspective, the reception of AI tools was largely positive. Many students reported that AI-enhanced platforms improved their understanding of mathematical concepts by offering interactive content and personalized feedback. The ability to learn at one's own pace and receive immediate responses to questions fostered greater engagement and motivation.

However, the students also highlighted persistent barriers such as limited access to devices and varying levels of digital literacy. These challenges are particularly pronounced among students from rural or low-income backgrounds, indicating the continuing digital divide within Cambodia's educational landscape. This disparity underscores the need for targeted interventions to ensure that all students can benefit from technological advancements. Teachers expressed more measured enthusiasm toward AI integration. While many acknowledged the potential of AI to enhance teaching through adaptive instruction and workload reduction, they also voiced concerns about their readiness to use such technologies effectively. The lack of comprehensive training and ongoing support has emerged as a significant impediment to implementation. Teachers are also wary of the potential reduction in meaningful teacher–student interactions and the possibility of technology replacing rather than complementing human instruction. These perspectives reveal a clear dichotomy: students are generally eager to embrace AI tools, whereas teachers adopt a more cautious stance shaped by practical and ethical concerns. Both groups, however, recognized the transformative potential of AI in mathematics education. The findings suggest that for AI to be successfully and sustainably integrated into Cambodian schools, efforts must address infrastructure, capacity building, and equity considerations. Strategic planning and inclusive dialog among stakeholders are critical to ensuring that AI serves as a tool for educational enhancement rather than exacerbating existing challenges.

4.1. Findings Based on Research Objective One: to Examine the Perceptions of Cambodian Students and Teachers Regarding the Use of AI In Mathematics Education, Including Their Attitudes, Acceptance, and Concerns

In exploring student perceptions of AI-supported mathematics education in Cambodia, it is evident that a complex interplay of technological access, trust, and cultural factors influences learners' engagement with artificial intelligence tools. One prominent factor is the accessibility and user-friendliness of AI-based educational platforms, which significantly impact student motivation and academic participation. For many Cambodian students, particularly those in urban areas where digital infrastructure is relatively more developed, AI tools are seen as offering enhanced learning through personalized feedback and adaptive content delivery. These systems enable learners to proceed at their own pace, reinforcing understanding and increasing confidence in mastering mathematical concepts. One of the students shared that:

> *"My teachers introduced our class to AI platforms such as ChatGPT, Gemini, and Microsoft Copilot to help us with mathematics. These tools are handy when I need a different explanation than the one provided in class. I regularly use them to work through exercise problems assigned for homework.*
>
> *Unfortunately, it is difficult for me to take full advantage of these resources. I have trouble accessing them due to my slow internet service and an old smartphone. Despite these challenges, I am very pleased with how AI supports my learning in class, after school, and during self-study." (S3).*

However, this optimism is not uniformly distributed. Students in rural or underserved regions often report limited access to devices, unreliable internet connectivity, and insufficient exposure to digital tools. Such disparities risk entrenching the digital divide, thereby exacerbating existing educational inequalities. This concern highlights the critical need for policies that prioritize equitable technology distribution and digital literacy training. Students' perceptions are also shaped by the degree of trust they place in AI systems. While some learners' express confidence in the accuracy and usefulness of AI-driven feedback, others harbor skepticism, often rooted in a lack of understanding of how AI functions. One teacher explained:

> *"As strongly emphasized by our Minister of Education, Dr. Hang Chuon Naron, teachers need to understand artificial intelligence (AI), which is rapidly transforming teaching and learning. AI supports classroom instruction and plays a key role in enhancing students' personal growth, social development, and employability skills. Mathematics teachers are encouraged to integrate AI tools into their teaching methodologies and classroom activities in this context. While many of us have only basic knowledge of these technologies, we recognize the importance of continuous professional training to keep pace with these changes. By building our capacity and adapting to this new educational landscape, we can better prepare students for the challenges and opportunities of the twenty-first century". (T10).*

This gap suggests a need for foundational education on digital technologies and AI literacy to promote more informed and critical engagement with these tools. Additionally, Cambodia's historically teacher-centered educational model influences how students perceive the legitimacy of AI as a learning facilitator. The traditional reliance on rote learning and face-to-face instruction may create initial resistance to technology-mediated learning environments. Addressing these cultural dynamics through student orientation programs and hybrid instructional models could ease the transition and foster more widespread acceptance of AI-enhanced education.

4.2. Findings Based on Research Objective Two: to Identify the Opportunities Offered by AI-Supported Mathematics Education, Such as Personalized Learning, Real-Time Feedback, and Enhanced Engagement in Cambodia

Understanding teacher perceptions is central to the successful implementation of AI in Cambodian mathematics classrooms, as teachers play a pivotal role in adopting, mediating, and sustaining technological innovations. The findings indicate that many Cambodian teachers perceive AI tools as valuable resources for enhancing teaching efficacy and supporting differentiated instruction. AI-enabled platforms that identify student weaknesses, automate assessments, and provide curated learning resources are viewed as promising tools to support more student-centered learning practices. Despite recognizing these benefits, teachers also express significant reservations regarding the practical and pedagogical challenges associated with AI integration. Key concerns include limited infrastructure, insufficient access to reliable digital devices, and the absence of ongoing technical support, particularly in rural schools. Moreover, the majority of teachers reported feeling underprepared to utilize AI effectively, citing a lack of professional development in both technical competencies and pedagogical strategies aligned with AI use. One teacher shared the following:

> *"AI's most significant benefit in education is its support for individual students. I teach Grade 12 in high school, and my class has 45 students. With so many learners, giving each learner the personal attention, they need is nearly impossible. If an AI tool can quickly identify which students are struggling with topics such as algebra or fractions, I can focus my time on helping them directly. AI could also save me hours in grading quizzes and tests, allowing me to use that time to plan more effective lessons. My primary concern, however, is reliability. Electricity cuts out often, and the internet is very slow, especially during the rainy season. If I plan a whole lesson around an AI tool and the internet fails, the entire lesson can be disrupted. This may become one more responsibility added to teachers without enough training or support. We already carry heavy workloads, especially when preparing students for national high school exams, so proper training and reliable infrastructure are crucial if AI is to be truly useful" (T3).*

There is also apprehension about the potential depersonalization of the teaching process. Some educators worry that an overreliance on algorithm-driven instruction might diminish their role in shaping critical thinking, empathy, and social interaction, skills often nurtured through traditional teacher–student engagement. While these concerns are valid, they are generally accompanied by a willingness to adapt, adequate training, institutional support, and inclusive decision-making. Teachers call for a more consultative approach to policy development, emphasizing the importance of recognizing local contexts and giving educators a voice in shaping the role of AI in their classrooms. When supported by tailored capacity-building initiatives, teacher receptiveness suggests strong potential for successful and sustainable AI integration in Cambodia's educational landscape.

4.3. Findings Based on Research Objective Three: To Explore the Challenges Hindering Effective AI Integration, Including Infrastructural Limitations, Digital Literacy Gaps, and Teacher Preparedness in Cambodia

Integrating AI into Cambodian mathematics classrooms is critically hindered by profound infrastructural limitations, which reflect and exacerbate broader systemic inequities between urban and rural regions. Schools in remote areas often face chronic issues, including unreliable electricity, inadequate internet bandwidth, and a severe shortage of digital devices that prevent the deployment and sustained use of AI-powered tools. These gaps restrict access to technology and negatively shape teachers' and students' perceptions of its feasibility and value. The participants from rural schools emphasized that technological scarcity forces them to rely on traditional methods, despite recognizing the potential benefits of AI. Even in urban settings with better infrastructure, intermittent connectivity and outdated equipment remain persistent barriers. This stark disparity reveals a fundamental misalignment between the promise of AI-driven education and the on-the-ground realities of its implementation, thereby reinforcing existing educational inequalities and stifling innovation at the grassroots level. Another teacher shares that:

> *"For most teachers in my school, the most significant barrier is the lack of reliable electricity and internet. We often hear about the promise of AI in education, but our reality is very different. I once spent a week preparing a lesson using an adaptive online math game, only to have the power cut for the entire morning. The whole lesson collapsed, disappointing the students and frustrating them. Experiences such as this make technology feel unreliable. AI integration remains theoretical without investment in stable infrastructure, electricity, the internet, or proper devices. Rural students' risk being left behind while innovation benefits only urban schools" (T15).*

Beyond infrastructure, two deeply interconnected challenges emerged: significant digital literacy gaps and insufficient teacher preparedness. Educators across all levels reported feeling inadequately equipped to use AI tools, as their training excluded AI literacy and ongoing pedagogical support for technology integration. A lack of professional development and school-based technical assistance worsened this sense of unpreparedness. Many teachers also expressed anxiety about their evolving roles, worrying that AI could diminish their instructional agency or weaken teacher–student relationships. Furthermore, students with limited prior exposure to digital environments often struggle to use AI platforms effectively, requiring extensive guidance to navigate interfaces and interpret automated feedback. This disconnect between user capability and technological demand underscores the need for holistic capacity building. The findings strongly suggest that teachers and students cannot harness AI benefits without targeted investments in digital literacy and pedagogical support. Ultimately, stakeholders stressed that success depends on technical readiness and the cultural adaptation of AI tools to align with local teaching traditions, linguistic preferences, and classroom realities. Addressing these multilayered challenges is essential to ensure that AI is a bridge toward more equitable and practical learning rather than a barrier deepening the digital divide. Most importantly, one teacher explained the following:

> *"The most effective teacher training would not be a one-day workshop in Phnom Penh. We genuinely need continuous, practical, and context-specific support. First, we need to see AI in action. The best training begins with a master teacher demonstrating a lesson with our students in our classrooms. We want to observe how they use an AI tool to generate practice problems, manage the class, and provide clear explanations. Seeing it in a real setting makes it meaningful. Second, training must be in Khmer and aligned with our national curriculum. For example, we need to learn how to use AI tools to create exercises that match the Grade 11 mathematics textbook, not just generic activities from a global platform. Relevance is key if AI is to support our actual teaching needs. Finally, we need ongoing support. A WhatsApp group with a dedicated trainer or a teacher community where we can ask questions, share tips, and solve problems together would be invaluable. This sustained help builds confidence and ensures that teachers do not feel abandoned. AI can be a powerful teaching assistant but cannot replace the wisdom, encouragement, and relationships that only teachers provide" (T12).*

5. DISCUSSION AND IMPLICATIONS

5.1. Discussions

The exploration of AI-supported mathematics education in Cambodia reveals a rich tapestry of insights, illustrating both promising advancements and noteworthy challenges. Central to this discussion is the nuanced interaction between teachers and students with technology-driven educational tools (Chea et al, 2022; Saing et al., 2023; Pum & Sok, 2024; Pen & Morrell, 2024; Run et al., 2025; Sok, et al, 2025). As AI technology has been progressively integrated into classrooms, it has reshaped traditional teaching paradigms, prompting reevaluations of pedagogical methods. Teachers express dual perceptions: on the one hand, AI capabilities offer dynamic, personalized learning experiences that can adapt to the unique needs of each student; on the other hand, they face the hurdle of aligning these technological tools with existing curricula and assessment standards (UNESCO, 2021; OECD, 2021, Keng, 2022). This dichotomy underscores a pressing need for targeted professional development to ensure that educators are equipped with the skills and confidence to harness AI effectively (Luckin et al., 2016; Sok et al., 2025). From the students' perspective, AI tools foster enthusiasm and engagement in mathematics, transforming abstract concepts into interactive and relatable scenarios. These tools facilitate culturally relevant content, integrating local contexts and languages, which enhances understanding and retention. However, the disparity in access to these technologies highlights a crucial obstacle, as not all students reap the benefits equally. Socioeconomic factors contribute significantly to this inequity, raising concerns about perpetuating existing divides. Addressing these disparities requires a strategic focus on equitable technological deployment and supportive infrastructures, ensuring that AI-driven benefits are inclusively accessible. Moving forward, the role of AI in education necessitates ongoing dialog between educational stakeholders, policymakers, and technology developers (Crompton & Burke, 2023; Opesemowo, & Adewuyi, 2024; Göktepe Yıldız & Göktepe Körpeoğlu, 2025; Hossein-Mohand et al., 2025). Establishing clear frameworks for AI integration, which include ethical considerations and data privacy, is imperative. Education systems must evolve in tandem with technological advancements, continually adapting curricula and pedagogical strategies to maximize educational outcomes. This evolution demands collaborative efforts to enrich teaching practices, overcome barriers, and explore innovative pathways for future educational excellence. Through continued exploration and refinement, Cambodia has the potential to lead exemplary AI-supported educational practices, benefiting both learners and educators alike (Fu & Weng, 2024; Holmes & Porayska-Pomsta, 2022; Holmes et al., 2022).

The comparative examination of student and teacher perceptions presents a layered understanding of the opportunities and challenges surrounding AI-supported mathematics education in Cambodia. Students tend to express enthusiastic support for AI integration, particularly appreciation for the interactivity, personalization, and real-time feedback offered by AI systems. These features align well with their desire for autonomy and engagement, helping them navigate complex mathematical content more confidently and effectively (Luckin et al., 2016). In contrast, teachers adopt a more measured stance, balancing optimism with caution. While acknowledging AI's capacity to transform instructional practices, educators are attuned to the logistical and philosophical barriers to its adoption. Their reservations primarily revolve around inadequate training, concerns over educational equity, and uncertainties about how AI fits into established pedagogical frameworks. The variability in perceptions among teachers is also linked to disparities in institutional support and digital infrastructure, which affect their readiness to integrate AI tools meaningfully (OECD, 2021).

The comparative analysis underscores the importance of harmonizing stakeholder perspectives through inclusive planning and support structures. Whereas students appear ready to embrace AI as a learning enhancer, teachers require targeted investments in professional development and infrastructural improvements to feel equally empowered. Bridging this perceptual gap is crucial for achieving synergy between instructional innovation and pedagogical integrity. Ultimately, the success of AI-supported mathematics education in Cambodia depends on strategic alignment between student enthusiasm and teacher preparedness. Policymakers must design integration strategies that are not only technologically sound but also pedagogically and culturally responsive. This dual focus will be essential in fostering a learning environment where AI complements, rather than competes with, human instruction.

5.2. Implications for Teaching Practice

5.2.1. Implications for Teaching Practice

Artificial intelligence (AI) is poised to redefine teaching practices in mathematics education, particularly in resource-constrained contexts such as Cambodia. As AI technologies become more prevalent in classrooms, they provide opportunities for educators to shift from traditional, teacher-centered models toward more adaptive, student-centered instruction. AI-driven platforms can analyze real-time student performance data, offering valuable insights into learners' strengths and areas for improvement. These insights enable educators to deliver differentiated instruction, tailor interventions, and adjust pedagogical approaches to better accommodate diverse learning styles and needs.

Beyond improving instructional precision, AI tools support formative assessment practices, enabling teachers to make evidence-based decisions about curriculum pacing and content delivery. This capability is especially valuable in Cambodia, where large class sizes and varied student abilities present persistent challenges. Through the integration of AI, teachers are better equipped to manage these complexities, fostering more inclusive and responsive classroom environments. Moreover, the integration of AI encourages a pedagogical shift toward collaborative, inquiry-based learning—moving away from rote memorization toward higher-order thinking skills such as problem-solving and critical analysis. In a Cambodian context, where educational equity remains a concern, AI can help bridge resource gaps by offering standardized access to high-quality instructional materials and adaptive learning experiences. However, realizing these benefits requires a significant transformation in teaching roles. Educators must transition from being primary knowledge transmitters to facilitators of learning, guiding students through technology-enhanced educational journeys.

This transformation necessitates robust, ongoing professional development. Teachers must be empowered with both technical competencies and pedagogical strategies for effectively integrating AI into lesson planning and classroom activities. Furthermore, curricular reforms are essential to ensure coherence between AI-enhanced instruction and national educational goals. Emphasizing digital literacy, critical thinking, and adaptability in the curriculum will better prepare students for the demands of a technology-driven future. Ultimately, the implications of AI integration extend beyond individual classrooms to the broader educational ecosystem. Cultivating a teaching workforce that is adaptable, technologically competent, and pedagogically innovative is essential for leveraging AI's full potential to improve educational outcomes in Cambodia.

5.2.2. Recommendations

The integration of AI-supported mathematics education in Cambodia presents both opportunities and challenges, necessitating a multifaceted approach to ensure its successful implementation. As we delve into the recommendations for optimizing this educational transformation, it becomes essential to consider policy-level adjustments alongside practical strategies for educators.

First, policy recommendations must address the foundational infrastructure requirements and equitable access to AI technologies. The Cambodian government, in collaboration with educational institutions, should invest in the development of digital infrastructure to facilitate the seamless integration of AI tools in classrooms across urban and rural areas alike. This includes ensuring that schools possess the required hardware, software, and internet connectivity to support AI applications. Furthermore, policy frameworks should encompass comprehensive training programs for teachers, enabling them to harness the potential of AI effectively. Such training should focus not only on technical skills but also on adapting pedagogical strategies that complement AI tools, thereby enhancing teaching and learning processes. Additionally, policymakers need to develop guidelines that safeguard data privacy and ethical use of AI in educational settings, thus fostering trust among stakeholders.

In parallel, suggestions for educators emphasize the adoption of a learner-centered approach to maximize the benefits of AI in teaching mathematics. Educators should be encouraged to explore adaptive learning platforms that tailor educational content according to individual student needs, promoting personalized learning experiences. To facilitate this, educators can employ AI-driven analytics tools to gain insights into student performance and learning patterns, enabling them to identify areas where students may require further assistance or enrichment. Moreover, fostering a collaborative learning environment in which students can engage with AI tools collectively can enhance peer-to-peer interaction and problem-solving skills. Teachers should also be proactive in fostering a culture of curiosity and continuous learning, preparing students to navigate an increasingly AI-driven world. By equipping students with critical thinking skills and digital literacy, educators can ensure that learners are not only passive recipients of knowledge but also active participants in their educational journeys. Through a synergistic combination of robust policy frameworks and innovative educational practices, Cambodia can harness the power of AI to transform mathematics education, ultimately paving the way for a more inclusive and effective learning experience. This approach will require ongoing collaboration among government agencies, educational institutions, and technology providers to continually assess and refine AI integration strategies.

5.2.3. Policy recommendations

In light of the transformative potential of AI-supported mathematics education, especially within the Cambodian context, strategic policy interventions are essential to ensure equitable access, enhanced learning outcomes, and sustainability. A primary recommendation involves the integration of AI tools into the national curriculum. This not only necessitates a revision of existing educational frameworks to accommodate cutting-edge technologies but also requires the establishment of standardized guidelines for AI assisted learning. This can foster consistency across educational institutions while meeting the diverse needs of Cambodian students. Moreover, policies must prioritize digital infrastructure development, particularly in rural and underserved regions, to bridge the digital divide and ensure that technological advancements benefit all students, irrespective of their geographic location. Additionally, teacher training and professional development must be reimagined to encompass AI literacy. Policymakers should advocate for comprehensive training programs that equip teachers with the skills necessary to effectively leverage AI tools in the classroom. Such programs should focus on enhancing teachers' understanding of AI capabilities and limitations, as well as integrating AI methodologies into pedagogical strategies. Furthermore, the establishment of collaborative networks among educators can facilitate the sharing of best practices and resources, fostering a community of learning and innovation. Policymakers should also consider partnerships with technology firms and educational institutions to ensure access to the latest AI advancements and facilitate ongoing research on the impact of AI in educational settings. Equally crucial is the protection of data privacy and ethical considerations in AI implementation. Policies should be devised to safeguard student data, applying stringent data protection measures aligned with international standards. Ethical guidelines must underscore the importance of transparency, accountability, and inclusivity in AI systems. By addressing these critical aspects through well-crafted policies, Cambodia can lead the way in effectively integrating AI in mathematics education, ultimately enhancing the educational landscape and preparing students for a technology-driven future.

5.2.4. Suggestions for educators

In light of the evolving landscape of AI-supported mathematics education in Cambodia, educators play a pivotal role in facilitating seamless integration and fostering an environment conducive to student engagement and learning. To harness the full potential of AI tools, educators must first cultivate a deep understanding of the technological resources available and adapt their pedagogical approaches accordingly. By remaining informed about the latest advancements in AI-driven educational tools, educators can better identify appropriate software and applications that align with curriculum goals and enhance instructional delivery. Moreover, educators should emphasize the critical need for a balanced pedagogical approach that incorporates AI tools without overshadowing traditional teaching methodologies. While AI can provide personalized learning experiences and instant feedback, foundational teaching and human interaction remain indispensable for developing critical thinking and problem-solving skills. As such, teachers should be encouraged to blend AI tools with conventional teaching practices, creating hybrid models that cater to diverse learning styles and facilitate comprehensive understanding. Additionally, continuous professional development is paramount for educators to integrate AI effectively into their teaching repertoire. Schools and educational institutions should invest in regular training workshops and collaborative learning sessions, where teachers can exchange insights and learn from peer experiences. By creating an inclusive learning community, educators can collectively overcome challenges associated with AI integration, such as addressing technological disparities and fostering digital literacy among students. Ultimately, a proactive approach to professional development will empower educators to unlock the transformative potential of AI in enriching the mathematics education landscape in Cambodia.

5.2.5. Future Directions

In considering future directions for AI-supported mathematics education in Cambodia, it becomes essential to analyze emerging trends and advancements in educational technology that could underpin transformative shifts in pedagogical methodologies. As AI continues to extend its reach, educators and policymakers are prompted to pursue strategies that optimize AI's role in the mathematics curriculum, ensuring that it not only enhances learning outcomes but also promotes equitable access. Future endeavors should focus on expanding AI-enhanced initiatives with the potential for personalized learning experiences, catering to the diverse needs and proficiencies of students. Sophisticated adaptive learning software can tailor instruction, providing real-time feedback and support, thus cultivating an environment conducive to individualized progress and discovery. Parallel to these innovations, teacher training and professional development must evolve to support this AI integration. Developing competencies in effectively employing AI tools in the classroom is paramount; therefore, investment in training programs that equip educators with the necessary skills and understanding of the potential and limitations of AI is crucial. Such initiatives could include workshops, collaborative platforms, and continued education courses, all aimed at bridging the gap between traditional teaching practices and modern technological facilitation. As educators become proficient with AI applications, their role transitions from being information providers to facilitators, guiding students through AI-assisted problem-solving processes. Furthermore, discussions surrounding ethical implications and digital equity must progress. Establishing policies that safeguard data privacy and implement measures to counteract the digital divide will become increasingly critical. Initiatives might encompass infrastructural investments to ensure that every student can access and benefit from AI technologies while also encouraging inclusivity. At the broader policy level, stakeholders should coalesce around creating frameworks that foster ethical AI usage and the shared responsibility of stewardship over educational data. By addressing these elements, Cambodia can confidently navigate the complexities of integrating AI in mathematics education, paving the way for a future where AI not only supports but also enhances educational systems sustainably.

6. LIMITATIONS OF THE STUDY

In exploring the limitations of this study on AI-supported mathematics education in Cambodia, it is crucial to acknowledge several factors that may affect the generalizability and applicability of its findings. First, a significant limitation arises from the demographic constraints within the study sample. Participants, primarily drawn from urban areas, may not reflect the diverse educational environments and socioeconomic spectra across Cambodia, which could significantly influence perceptions regarding AI in education. The disparity between urban and rural schools, often highlighted by differing access to technology and varying levels of teacher preparedness, underscores the need for caution when extrapolating results to the wider Cambodian landscape.

Moreover, the technological infrastructure, a pivotal component of AI integration in educational settings, presents considerable variability in Cambodian schools. Poor or inconsistent internet connectivity and limited access to advanced computing resources in several regions can undermine the optimal utilization of AI tools intended for enhancing educational practices. These infrastructural limitations suggest that the experiences and perceptions collected within the study may not fully capture the challenges faced by less resourced schools, potentially skewing the overall representation of AI integration efficacy in Cambodian mathematics education. Another key limitation pertains to the scope and depth of the qualitative methodologies employed. While these methods offer valuable insights into perceptions, they might not fully encompass the complexities of educational practices influenced by cultural, pedagogical, and familial factors. The reliance on surveys and interviews, primarily focusing on perceptual data, could inadvertently lead to an oversimplification of nuanced educational dynamics that are critical in this context. To ensure a robust understanding of AI's role, future research might consider incorporating longitudinal studies or mixed-method approaches to capture the evolving nature of AI integration over time, taking a more comprehensive view of the impacts and intricacies involved. Thus, while this study provides foundational insights, these limitations must be recognized to inform subsequent research that aims for a more holistic understanding of AI-supported mathematics education in Cambodia.

7. CONCLUSION

In summary, the exploration of students' and teachers' perceptions of AI-supported mathematics education in Cambodia offers enlightening insights into the contemporary educational landscape. Throughout the analysis, several compelling themes emerged, underscoring the transformative potential and inherent challenges of integrating artificial intelligence into educational settings. Cambodian classrooms, while embracing technological advancements, must also navigate cultural sensitivities and infrastructural constraints. AI can bolster mathematical understanding, providing personalized learning experiences and immediate feedback, which are crucial for fostering academic growth. However, the study also revealed varying degrees of preparedness among educators, who expressed concerns about their proficiency in using AI applications effectively. Furthermore, the integration of AI into mathematics education has highlighted disparities in technology access, raising pertinent questions about equity and inclusion across different educational settings. While urban schools exhibit readiness to adopt AI tools, rural and underserved areas face limitations due to insufficient resources and training opportunities. These challenges necessitate strategic policy interventions aimed at bridging the digital divide and fostering an inclusive environment conducive to AI adoption. Stakeholders must collaborate to ensure that AI systems are designed with an understanding of local educational contexts and cultural nuances. This will facilitate relevant and engaging educational experiences for Cambodian students.

As the study concludes, it reflects an overarching optimism toward AI's potential to catalyze a shift in pedagogical paradigms, fostering a dynamic and interactive learning atmosphere. The findings call for a balanced approach, where AI is viewed not as a panacea but as a complementary tool that enriches traditional teaching methodologies. By investing in capacity-building initiatives for teachers and enhancing infrastructural support across the country, Cambodia can fully leverage the benefits of AI in mathematics education. The road ahead requires a concerted effort to address existing barriers while capitalizing on the opportunities AI presents to redefine and reenergize the educational experiences of Cambodian learners in mathematics.

REFERENCES

ADB. (2023). *Cambodia education sector assessment: Strategy and road map.* Asian Development Bank. https://www.adb.org/publications/cambodia-education-sector-assessment

Angrosino, M. (2007). *Doing ethnographic and observational research.* SAGE Publications., DOI: 10.4135/9781849208932

Benzer, R., Benzer, S., & Doğan, T. (2025). Assessing science teachers' digital literacy with survey-based machine learning. *Information Development.* Advance online publication. DOI: 10.1177/02666669251350669

Braun, V., & Clarke, V. (2006). Using thematic analysis in psychology. *Qualitative Research in Psychology, 3*(2), 77–101. DOI: 10.1191/1478088706qp063oa

Bryman, A. (2016). *Social research methods* (5th ed.). Oxford University Press.

Chea, P., Bo, C., & Minami, R. (2022). Cambodian Secondary School Teachers' Readiness for Online Teaching During the Covid-19 Pandemic (CDRI Working Paper Series No. 134). Cambodia Development Research Institute. https://doi.org/ DOI: 10.64202/wp.134.202205

Chen, H., Park, H. W., & Breazeal, C. (2020). Teaching and learning with children: Impact of reciprocal peer learning with a social robot on children's learning and emotive engagement. *Computers & Education, 150*, 103836. DOI: 10.1016/j.compedu.2020.103836

Chen, L., Chen, P., & Lin, Z. (2020). Artificial intelligence in education: A review. *IEEE Access : Practical Innovations, Open Solutions, 8*, 75264–75278. DOI: 10.1109/ACCESS.2020.2988510

Creswell, J. W., & Plano Clark, V. L. (2018). *Designing and conducting mixed methods research* (3rd ed.). SAGE Publications.

Creswell, J. W., & Poth, C. N. (2018). *Qualitative inquiry and research design: Choosing among five approaches* (4th ed.). SAGE Publications.

Crompton, H., & Burke, D. (2023). Artificial intelligence in higher education: The state of the field. *International Journal of Educational Technology in Higher Education, 20*(1), 22. DOI: 10.1186/s41239-023-00392-8

Delve, Ho. L., & Limpaecher, A. (2024b, July 08). Understanding Qualitative Research In Education. https://delvetool.com/blog/qualitative-research-education

Ertmer, P. A., Addison, P., Lane, M., Ross, E., & Woods, D. (1999). Examining teachers' beliefs about the role of technology in the elementary classroom. *Journal of Research on Computing in Education*, *32*(1), 54–72. https://www.learntechlib.org/p/89775/

Esteban, A. M.Jr, & Cruz, M. J. P. (2021). Digital divide in times of pandemic among teacher education students. *OAlib*, *8*, e7323. DOI: 10.4236/oalib.1107323

Fu, Y., & Weng, Z. (2024). Navigating the ethical terrain of AI in education: A systematic review on framing responsible human-centered AI practices. *Computers and Education: Artificial Intelligence*, *7*, 100306. DOI: 10.1016/j.caeai.2024.100306

Göktepe Yıldız, S., & Göktepe Körpeoğlu, S. (2025). Trends and insights of AI in mathematics education: A bibliometric analysis. *International Electronic Journal of Mathematics Education*, *20*(3), em0837. Advance online publication. DOI: 10.29333/iejme/16401

Henkel, O., Horne-Robinson, H., Kozhakhmetova, N., & Lee, A. (2024). *Effective and Scalable Math Support: Evidence on the Impact of an AI-Tutor on Math Achievement in Ghana*. arXiv. https://doi.org//arXiv.2402.09809DOI: 10.48550

Holmes, W., & Porayska-Pomsta, K. (Eds.). (2022). *The ethics of artificial intelli gence in education: Practices, challenges, and debates* (1st ed.). Routledge., DOI: 10.4324/9780429329067

Holmes, W., Porayska-Pomsta, K., Holstein, K., Sutherland, E., Baker, T., Buckingham Shum, S., Santos, O. C., Rodrigo, M. T., Cukurova, M., Bittencourt, I. I., & Koedinger, K. R. (2022). Ethics of AI in education: Toward a community-wide framework. *International Journal of Artificial Intelligence in Education*, *32*, 504–526. DOI: 10.1007/s40593-021-00239-1

Hossein-Mohand, H., Hossein-Mohand, H., Albanese, V., & Olmos Gómez, M. D. C. (2025). AI in mathematics education: A bibliometric analysis of global trends and collaborations (2020-2024). *Eurasia Journal of Mathematics, Science and Technology Education*, *21*(2), em2576. Advance online publication. DOI: 10.29333/ejmste/15915

Israel, M., & Hay, I. (2006). *Research ethics for social scientists: Between ethical conduct and regulatory compliance*. SAGE Publications., DOI: 10.4135/9781849209779

Keng, C. (2022). The digital divide and the challenges of education equity in rural Cambodia. *Cambodia Education Review*, *5*(1), 34–45.

Khine, M. S. (2024). Educational data mining and learning analytics. In Khine, M. S. (Ed.), *Artificial intelligence in education* (pp. 1–20). Springer., DOI: 10.1007/978-981-97-9350-1_1

Luckin, R., George, K., & Cukurova, M. (2022). *AI for school teachers* (1st ed.). CRC Press., DOI: 10.1201/9781003193173

Luckin, R., Holmes, W., Griffiths, M., & Forcier, L. B. (2016). *Intelligence unleashed: An argument for AI in education*. Pearson Education.

Merriam, S. B., & Tisdell, E. J. (2016). *Qualitative research: A guide to design and implementation* (4th ed.). Jossey-Bass.

Ministry of Education. Youth and Sport. (2019). *Education strategic plan 2019–2023*. Royal Government of Cambodia.

Ministry of Education, Youth and Sport. (2019). *National curriculum framework for basic education*. MoEYS.

Ministry of Education, Youth and Sport. (2021). *Education reform strategic plan 2021–2025*. MoEYS.

Ministry of Education, Youth and Sport. (2022). *Mathematics curriculum guidelines*. MoEYS.

Ministry of Education, Youth and Sport. (2023). *Cambodia digital education policy framework*. MoEYS.

Ministry of Education. Youth and Sport. (2024). *Annual education congress report*. MoEYS.

Ministry of Education. Youth and Sport. (2024). *Education strategic plan 2024–2028*. https://www.moeys.gov.kh/en/policies-and-strategies

OECD. (2021). *21st-century readers: Developing literacy skills in a digital world*. OECD Publishing., DOI: 10.1787/a83d84cb-

OECD. (2021). *Teachers and technology: The role of digital technology in supporting teaching*. OECD Publishing., DOI: 10.1787/f5d50f16-

Opesemowo, O. A. G., & Adewuyi, H. O. (2024). A systematic review of artificial intelligence in mathematics education: The emergence of 4IR. *Eurasia Journal of Mathematics, Science and Technology Education*, *20*(7), em2478. Advance online publication. DOI: 10.29333/ejmste/14762

Palinkas, L. A., Horwitz, S. M., Green, C. A., Wisdom, J. P., Duan, N., & Hoagwood, K. (2015). Purposeful sampling for qualitative data collection and analysis in mixed method implementation research. *Administration and Policy in Mental Health, 42*(5), 533–544. DOI: 10.1007/s10488-013-0528-y PMID: 24193818

Pen, S., & Morrell, P. D. (2024). Perceptions and challenges of technological use in teaching among late-career teachers: A case study in Cambodia. *Discover Education, 3*(1), 211. DOI: 10.1007/s44217-024-00265-w

Pum, M., & Sok, S. (2024). Leveraging AI in education in Cambodia: A review of perceived concerns and associated benefits. *Asian Journal of Distance Education, 19*(2). https://asianjde.com/ojs/index.php/AsianJDE/article/view/794

Run, N., Tep, P., Mot, N., & Phuong, C. (2025). Reviewing challenges of curriculum implementation in Cambodian teacher education and possibilities for improvement. *Journal of Multidisciplinary Research, 4*(1). Advance online publication. DOI: 10.56943/jmr.v4i1.735

Saing, C. H., Chea, P., & Song, S. (2023). *Assessing technology readiness of students and teachers in Cambodian higher education during COVID-19: Implications for digital learning* [Working paper]. Cambodia Development Research Institute., DOI: 10.64202/wp.143.202311

Sam, R., Li, X., Sok, K., Tieng, M., & Yoeng, H. (2025). Effective Turnaround Leadership Practices in Cambodia: Perspectives from School Principals. In Liu, P., & Thien, L. M. (Eds.), *Turnaround Leadership in Southeast Asian Countries*. Springer., DOI: 10.1007/978-981-96-7894-5_5

Sam, R., Sok, K., Tieng, M., Yoeng, H., Chiv, S., Thay, S., & Saorann, S. (2025). Examining principal leadership in Cambodian high schools: A case study approach. *European Journal of Educational Management, 8*(1), 13–29. DOI: 10.12973/eu-jem.8.1.13

Sam, R., Tieng, M., Yoeng, H., Chiv, S., Thay, S., & Saing, S. (2025). Exploring school principal leadership: A case study of upper secondary school in North-western Cambodia. *Multidisciplinary Reviews, 8*(10), 2025311. DOI: 10.31893/multirev.2025311

Scherer, R., Siddiq, F., & Tondeur, J. (2021). Teacher's attitudes toward the use of artificial intelligence (AI) applications in education. *Computers in Human Behavior, 115*, 106612. DOI: 10.1016/j.chb.2020.106612

Scherer, R., Tondeur, J., & Siddiq, F. (2019). The importance of attitudes toward technology for preservice teachers' technological, pedagogical, and content knowledge. *Computers & Education, 137*, 1–12. DOI: 10.1016/j.compedu.2019.04.002

Selwyn, N. (2019). *Should robots replace teachers? AI and the future of education.* Polity Press.

Selwyn, N. (2022). *Education and technology: Key issues and debates* (3rd ed.). Bloomsbury.

Simms, V. (2016). [Review of the book *Mathematical mindsets: Unleashing students' potential through creative math, inspiring messages and innovative teaching*, by J. Boaler]. *Research in Mathematics Education, 18*(3), 317–320. DOI: 10.1080/14794802.2016.1237374

Sok, S., Heng, K., & Pum, M. (2025). Investigating high school students' attitudes toward the use of AI in education: Evidence from Cambodia. *SAGE Open, 15*(3). Advance online publication. DOI: 10.1177/21582440251353575

Tamilmani, K., Rana, N. P., Wamba, S. F., & Dwivedi, R. (2021). The extended Unified Theory of Acceptance and Use of Technology (UTAUT2): A systematic literature review and theory evaluation. *International Journal of Information Management, 57*, 102269. DOI: 10.1016/j.ijinfomgt.2020.102269

Tan, C. (2007). Education reforms in Cambodia: Issues and concerns. *Educational Research for Policy and Practice, 6*(1), 15–24. DOI: 10.1007/s10671-007-9020-3

Tan, P. L. (2010). Toward a culturally sensitive and deeper understanding of "rote learning" and memorization of adult learners. *Journal of Studies in International Education, 15*(2), 124–145. DOI: 10.1177/1028315309357940

UNESCO. (2020). *Cambodia education sector snapshot.* https://unesdoc.unesco.org

UNESCO. (2021). *AI and education: Guidance for policy-makers.* UNESCO. https://unesdoc.unesco.org/ark:/48223/pf0000376704

UNESCO. (2022). *Digital learning for all in Cambodia.* UNESCO., DOI: 10.54675/UNES2022.KH

UNESCO. (2022). *Education transformation in Cambodia.* UNESCO., DOI: 10.54675/UNES2022.CAM

UNESCO. (2023). *AI and education in the Global South.* UNESCO., DOI: 10.54675/UNES2023.AIED

UNESCO. (2023). *AI for equitable education*. UNESCO. https://doi.org/DOI: 10.7890/unesco-ai-2023

UNESCO. (2023). *Global education monitoring report: Cambodia country profile*. https://www.unesco.org/gem-report/cambodia

VanLehn, K. (2022). Intelligent tutoring systems for STEM education. *AI Magazine*, *43*(1), 34–50. DOI: 10.1609/aimag.v43i1.19118

Venkatesh, V., & Davis, F. D. (2000). A theoretical extension of the technology acceptance model: Four longitudinal field studies. *Management Science*, *46*(2), 186–204. DOI: 10.1287/mnsc.46.2.186.11926

Venkatesh, V., Morris, M. G., Davis, G. B., & Davis, F. D. (2003). User acceptance of information technology: Toward a unified view. *Management Information Systems Quarterly*, *27*(3), 425–478. DOI: 10.2307/30036540

Williamson, B., & Eynon, R. (2020). Historical threads, missing links, and future directions in AI in education. *Learning, Media and Technology*, *45*(3), 223–235. DOI: 10.1080/17439884.2020.1798995

World Bank. (2018). *Higher education in Cambodia: Vision and roadmap 2030*. World Bank. https://www.worldbank.org

World Bank. (2023). *Cambodia digital human capital development report*. World Bank. https://doi.org/DOI: 10.1596/978-1-4648-1987-6

World Bank. (2023). *Cambodia education sector review*. World Bank. https://doi .org/DOI: 10.1596/978-1-4648-1987-6

World Bank. (2023). *Cambodia higher education expansion and employability*. World Bank. https://www.worldbank.org/en/country/cambodia/publication/higher -education-expansion

World Bank. (2023). *Digital transformation in Cambodian education*. World Bank. https://doi.org/DOI: 10.1596/978-1-4648-1987-6

World Bank. (2023). *Education technology in Southeast Asia*. World Bank., DOI: 10.1596/wb-edtech-2023

Xu, W., & Ouyang, F. (2022). The application of AI technologies in STEM education: A systematic review from 2011 to 2021. *International Journal of STEM Education*, *9*(1), 59. DOI: 10.1186/s40594-022-00377-5

Yem, B. (2025). From social disparities to educational disparities: An academic reflection and discussion in the Cambodian education system. *Studies in Empowering Education*, *6*(1), 1–8. DOI: 10.3943/siee.77

Zawacki-Richter, O., Marín, V. I., Bond, M., & Gouverneur, F. (2019). Systematic review of research on artificial intelligence applications in higher education – Where are the educators? *International Journal of Educational Technology in Higher Education*, *16*(1), 39. DOI: 10.1186/s41239-019-0171-0

Zou, Y., Kuek, F., Feng, W., & Cheng, X. (2025). Digital learning in the 21st century: Trends, challenges, and innovations in technology integration. *Frontiers in Education*, *10*, 1562391. DOI: 10.3389/feduc.2025.1562391

KEY TERMS AND DEFINITION

Artificial Intelligence (AI): Refers to computer systems that simulate aspects of human intelligence, such as learning, problem solving, and decision making. In education, AI is increasingly used to personalize learning, provide real-time feedback, and automate tasks such as grading. AI can adapt content for mathematics education to individual learning levels, making abstract concepts more accessible. However, it raises concerns about ethics, data privacy, and equitable access, especially in Cambodia, where infrastructure and teacher readiness vary widely.

Educational Technology: Refers to digital tools and platforms designed to improve teaching and learning processes. This includes learning management systems and interactive simulations of advanced AI-driven platforms. In mathematics education, such tools can foster a deeper understanding through adaptive exercises and instant feedback. In Cambodia, educational technology is viewed as an opportunity to expand access and a challenge since disparities in infrastructure, training, and cultural adaptation may limit effectiveness. Its integration requires careful planning to ensure inclusivity.

Student Perceptions: Learners' attitudes, beliefs, and feelings about educational practices and technologies. In the Cambodian study, many students expressed positive views of AI-supported mathematics education, valuing features such as personalized feedback, interactivity, and self-paced learning. However, perceptions are shaped by access to devices, digital literacy, and cultural expectations. Students in rural areas often face barriers that influence their confidence in AI tools, highlighting the importance of equitable implementation strategies.

Teacher Perceptions: Reflect educators' views and attitudes toward integrating new tools, such as AI, into their teaching practices. In Cambodia, while some teachers recognize the potential benefits of AI for enhancing mathematics instruction, others are cautious. Concerns include insufficient training, reduced teacher–student interaction risks, and infrastructure challenges in under resourced schools. Teachers' acceptance is crucial because they mediate between technology and learners. Supporting teachers with professional development and context-relevant AI tools is vital for successful integration.

The Digital Divide: Describes unequal access to digital technologies, infrastructure, and skills across different populations. This divide is most visible in Cambodian education between urban and rural schools. Urban students are more likely to access AI tools, whereas rural learners face barriers such as unreliable electricity, limited internet, and scarce devices. This inequality risks widening educational gaps instead of reducing them. Addressing the digital divide requires investments in infrastructure, digital literacy, and culturally responsive technology to ensure fairness.

Chapter 9
Sustaining Mathematics Education in the AI Era:
Opportunities, Challenges, and Future Directions

Ahmet Oğuz Akçay
https://orcid.org/0000-0003-2109-976X
Elementary Education Department, Education Faculty, Eskisehir Osmangazi University, Eskişehir, Turkey

Emel Çilingir Altıner
https://orcid.org/0000-0002-8085-553X
Elementary Education Department, Education Faculty, Çukurova University, Adana, Turkey

ABSTRACT

This chapter investigates the role of artificial intelligence (AI) in mathematics education by leveraging established theoretical frameworks such as constructivism and socio-cultural learning theory. AI-powered tools, including intelligent tutoring systems and adaptive learning technologies, which support individualized instruction tailored to learners' cognitive profiles, enhancing conceptual understanding and problem-solving skills. While AI presents opportunities for personalized learning and can help bridge educational inequalities, significant challenges arise, including issues of digital accessibility, algorithmic bias, and ethical considerations regarding data use. The chapter emphasizes the need for a critical assessment of AI's pedagogical implications and urges careful planning to ensure that these technologies foster inclusive and equitable learning environments. Furthermore, it explores the broader societal effects of AI on educational practices and the necessity for educators to adapt to these changes while maintaining human interaction in the learning process.

DOI: 10.4018/979-8-3373-1998-8.ch009

1. INTRODUCTION

Artificial Intelligence (AI) is increasingly shaping the education field, making AI literacy a critical competency for both learners and educators (Long & Magerko, 2020). AI technologies in education have initiated a radical transformation in terms of access to information and academic productivity. While AI tools offer significant opportunities to personalize learning experiences, increase productivity, and provide democratic access to information (Dwivedi et al., 2023). AI advancements have significantly transformed mathematics education by reshaping traditional pedagogical practices and introducing new forms of personalized, data-informed, and technology-mediated instruction. Integrating AI into mathematics classrooms has altered how students engage with mathematical content and how teachers design and deliver instruction. Technologies such as intelligent tutoring systems, automated assessment tools, and adaptive learning platforms offer opportunities for tailoring instruction to individual learning needs, thereby promoting deeper conceptual understanding and learner autonomy (Baker & Smith, 2019; Zawacki-Richter et al., 2019). Although AI's short-term impact on student engagement and achievement is evident, it is crucial to examine its long-term, sustainable effects.

These developments reflect a broader paradigm shift—from standardized instruction to personalized, learner-centered approaches—driven by AI's capacity to analyze large volumes of learning data in real-time. AI systems can provide adaptive feedback, scaffold complex tasks, and facilitate differentiated instruction, thus enhancing the teaching and learning of mathematics at the primary school level. AI also provides logistical support for educators by automating grading and tracking progress, allowing teachers to focus on higher-order instructional goals, such as reasoning, problem-solving, and fostering metacognition (Holmes et al., 2019). Adaptive learning platforms offer a personalized learning experience that enhances student engagement and outcomes by tailoring content to each student's individual needs. By offering real-time feedback and assistance, intelligent tutoring systems help students grasp challenging mathematical concepts. By improving the speed and precision of student performance evaluation, automated assessment systems free up teachers to concentrate on more strategic facets of teaching. Many teachers are not ready for AI-powered education, despite being largely aware of the potential benefits that AI can bring to education (Wang et al., 2023). However, there is still a serious issue regarding teachers' readiness for AI integration.

Beyond the classroom, there are broader ethical and societal implications for the sustainability of AI in mathematical education. Students' interactions with mathematical content are shaped by AI technologies, which also impact digital literacy (Zeeshan et al., 2024) and computational thinking (Celik, 2023; Zeeshan et al., 2024), two abilities crucial to 21st-century citizenship. The sustainability of AI in mathematics instruction is the department's top priority. It investigates the equitable and sustainable integration of AI technologies into educational institutions. Data privacy, algorithmic decision-making transparency, and the potential of AI to replace human contact in educational settings are among the ethical issues addressed. The long-term benefits of AI in developing the critical thinking and problem-solving skills essential for lifelong learning are also explored. Although a growing body of research has explored AI's short-term benefits—such as increased engagement, improved learning analytics, and enhanced performance on assessments (Luckin et al., 2016; Holmes et al., 2019; Baker & Smith, 2019)—relatively few studies have systematically examined its long-term pedagogical consequences, ethical risks, and sustainable implementation strategies in mathematics education (Williamson & Eynon, 2020; Akgün & Greenhow, 2022; Zawacki-Richter et al., 2019).

This chapter fills this gap by providing an interdisciplinary and forward-looking analysis. AI is presented not simply as a tool but as a catalyst for educational transformation—one that requires careful design, ongoing evaluation, and a commitment to social justice. As such, this chapter provides a timely and necessary contribution for educators, researchers, and policymakers navigating the complex intersection of mathematics education and artificial intelligence.

2. THEORETICAL FOUNDATIONS OF AI IN MATHEMATICS EDUCATION

Integrating artificial intelligence (AI) into mathematics education is not merely a technological advancement but a pedagogical evolution rooted in established learning theories. To ensure the meaningful and sustainable implementation of AI tools, it is critical to situate them within robust theoretical frameworks. This section examines national context and three key perspectives—constructivism, socio-cultural learning theory, and digital pedagogy—to illuminate how AI can support and transform mathematics teaching and learning.

2.1 Constructivism and AI: Facilitating Active, Inquiry-Based Learning

Constructivist learning theory, primarily associated with Jean Piaget and later expanded by scholars such as Jerome Bruner and Ernst von Glasersfeld, posits that learners actively construct knowledge through interaction with their environment rather than passively receiving information (Piaget, 1954; Bruner, 1961; von Glasersfeld, 1995). AI-powered educational tools align closely with this perspective by providing personalized, exploratory learning environments that adapt to individual learners' cognitive development and prior knowledge.

Intelligent Tutoring Systems and adaptive learning platforms leverage real-time data to provide scaffolding, timely feedback, and problem-solving opportunities tailored to each student's learning trajectory (Villegas-Ch et al., 2025). Intelligent Tutoring Systems use artificial intelligence, educational science, and psychology to create personalized learning experiences (Bagheri, 2015). These systems give students instant feedback, similar to one-on-one instruction, and include a subject area model, a student model, a teaching model, and a user interface (Lin et al., 2023). This setup helps the system choose what and how to teach. Adaptive Learning Systems are a newer type of educational technology that aims to fix the problems found in Intelligent Tutoring Systems. Adaptive learning aims to analyze students' learning behaviors and offer a dynamic learning path according to their strengths and weaknesses (Lin et al., 2023). Adaptive Learning Systems enhance learning by adapting lessons and teaching methods to suit each student's knowledge, learning style, and individual needs. These systems analyze how students interact with the material to create personalized learning paths and adjust their teaching methods accordingly (Bagheri, 2015). For example, platforms such as Carnegie Learning and Squirrel AI utilize machine learning algorithms to diagnose student misconceptions and dynamically adjust content, thereby promoting a deeper conceptual understanding (Koedinger & Corbett, 2006). Moreover, constructivist AI applications encourage active engagement by presenting learners with open-ended tasks, simulations, and virtual manipulatives—especially effective in developing number sense and spatial reasoning in mathematics (Papert, 1980). Such tools enable learners to test hypotheses, reflect on outcomes, and iteratively improve their understanding, consistent with the inquiry-based approaches advocated by constructivist theory.

2.2 Socio-Cultural Learning Theories: AI as a Mediator of Collaborative Learning

Building upon Vygotsky's socio-cultural theory of learning, which emphasizes the importance of social interaction, language, and cultural tools in cognitive development, AI technologies are increasingly designed to facilitate collaborative and dialogic learning (Vygotsky, 1978; Mercer, 2000). Within this framework, AI serves not only as an individualized tutor but also as a mediator of peer interaction, community engagement, and co-construction of knowledge. For instance, AI-enhanced learning environments such as AI chatbots and collaborative problem-solving platforms (e.g., MathSpring, Classkick) promote dialogic engagement by prompting students to explain their reasoning, justify their answers, and provide feedback to peers (Rosé et al., 2008; Holmes et al., 2019). These features are aligned with the principles of socially shared regulation and intersubjectivity that underpin socio-cultural learning processes (Hadwin et al., 2018).

In multilingual or diverse classrooms, AI tools with natural language processing (NLP) capabilities can translate content, scaffold vocabulary development, and facilitate inclusive participation, thereby supporting the social construction of meaning across linguistic and cultural boundaries (Luckin et al., 2016; Akgün & Greenhow, 2022). When used strategically, such tools contribute to equitable participation in mathematics discourse and help reduce opportunity gaps.

2.3 Digital Pedagogy and AI: Aligning with Contemporary Teaching Practices

Digital pedagogy refers to the thoughtful integration of digital tools into teaching and learning processes in ways that are pedagogically sound and contextually relevant (Selwyn, 2016). AI aligns with digital pedagogy by offering dynamic, data-driven instructional designs that support differentiated instruction, formative assessment, and learning analytics.

AI-based platforms, such as DreamBox and ALEKS, exemplify the synergy between digital pedagogy and algorithmic personalization. These platforms continuously collect learner data, analyze patterns of engagement and performance, and adjust instructional content to optimize learning pathways (VanLehn, 2011; Zawacki-Richter et al., 2019). Moreover, AI systems contribute to teacher professional development by generating insights into student learning behaviors, enabling more targeted pedagogical interventions (Holmes et al., 2019). Furthermore, AI supports digital pedagogical principles by fostering learner agency, offering multiple representations of mathematical concepts (e.g., visual, symbolic, verbal), and enabling multimodal learning experiences (Clark-Wilson et al., 2020). In this way, AI enhances educators' pedagogical repertoire and aligns with the principles of the Universal Design for Learning (UDL), ensuring that learning is accessible, engaging, and effective for all students (CAST, 2018).

2.4 National Context: AI and Mathematics Education in Türkiye

While global advancements in AI-powered education tools are significant, understanding how these technologies align with the national curriculum and educational reforms is equally critical. Türkiye has taken progressive steps in integrating AI and digital tools into primary and secondary education, particularly under the umbrella of the "Türkiye Century Education Model - Türkiye Yüzyılı Maarif Modeli" introduced by the Ministry of National Education (MEB, 2023). This model emphasizes equity, digital competence, and skill-based learning, aligning closely with the above theoretical foundations.

One prominent example is the enhancement of the Education Information Network - Eğitim Bilişim Ağı (EBA) platform with AI capabilities. EBA's recommendation system offers personalized learning resources to students, supporting constructivist principles through adaptive content that matches the learner's pace and prior knowledge. This feature is especially relevant for mathematics education, where students can receive customized practice questions and video content to support conceptual learning (MoNE Innovation and Educational Technologies General Directorate-MEB Yenilik ve Eğitim Teknolojileri Genel Müdürlüğü, 2023).

From a socio-cultural perspective, Türkiye has also piloted AI-supported collaborative learning environments in selected schools as part of TÜBİTAK-funded projects. For instance, AI-driven classroom response systems and intelligent group-matching algorithms have been tested to foster student interaction, peer tutoring, and formative assessment in mathematics problem-solving activities (TÜBİTAK, 2022). These initiatives align with Vygotsky's principles, emphasizing the importance of mediated interaction and scaffolding within the zone of proximal development (ZPD).

Digital pedagogy in Türkiye has gained momentum through the Digital Literacy for Teachers programs. These initiatives aim to enhance teachers' capacities to integrate AI tools effectively in line with curricular goals and ethical standards (MEB, 2022). Moreover, the new curriculum emphasizes data literacy, algorithmic thinking, and problem-solving, placing AI as a content area and a pedagogical tool in mathematics education. The AI-based evaluation systems explored for formative assessment align with digital pedagogy principles, enabling teachers to interpret learning analytics and adjust instruction accordingly.

Table 1. The Theoretical Lens

Theoretical Lens	**AI Contribution**	**Example from Türkiye**
Constructivism	Personalized learning paths, interactive simulations, and dynamic feedback	AI-enhanced EBA content, adaptive math modules
Socio-Cultural Theory	Collaborative platforms and AI chatbots facilitate peer discussion	tools TÜBİTAK-supported AI collaborative
Digital Pedagogy	Real-time analytics, multimodal content delivery, learner agency	MEB's teacher training on AI tools, curriculum-integrated AI systems

3. INCLUSION, EQUITY, AND ETHICAL CONSIDERATIONS

The spread of educational technologies, aided by AI, increases learning opportunities and risks widening digital disparities. Students who live in rural areas, come from low-income families, or lack access to proper equipment and technology are particularly disadvantaged when using AI-based systems. Government regulations and educational establishments should prioritize the advancement of technology infrastructure and the fulfillment of fundamental requirements, such as access to devices and the internet. The objective of giving every student equal access to digital resources has motivated programs like One Laptop per Child (OLPC) and the Fatih Project in Türkiye. The Ministry of National Education prepared a project named the Movement of Enhancing Opportunities and Improving Technology project (FATIH). This project aims to ensure equality of opportunity in education and training, as well as to enhance the technology in schools (Çiftçi et al., 2013; Demir, 2024). It seeks to provide equal opportunities for all students. The "One Laptop per Child" (OLPC) project is a global initiative that aims to provide affordable laptops and digital devices to students in low-income countries (Doğan et al., 2016). These projects aim to accelerate digital transformation in education, support teachers with technology, and increase students' digital literacy. However, infrastructure gaps, teacher training, and content development have challenged the implementation of these projects in many countries (Doğan et al., 2016). An examination of the FATIH project shows that technology integration is ineffective in the classroom without adequate teacher training (Demir, 2024). Similarly, due to infrastructure deficiencies, OLPC did not achieve the expected success in some regions (Pouezevara et al., 2013). These findings suggest that ensuring equality of opportunity in education is possible by deploying technological tools and a comprehensive instructional strategy.

It is of great importance to increase participation in education during the digital transformation era in order to ensure equal opportunities and the effective inclusion of disadvantaged groups in learning processes (UNESCO, 2022). However, these projects must be adapted to current technologies and continuously developed to be effective and sustainable. In recent years, the increasing use of artificial intelligence technologies in education has transformed learning processes with applications such as learning analytics, adaptive learning systems, and individualized educational content (Holmes et al., 2019). Accordingly, providing access to AI-based educational tools, especially for disadvantaged student groups, is critical to reducing the digital divide. AI-supported learning environments foster self-learning skills by enabling individuals to learn at their own pace and according to their needs, thereby contributing to educational sustainability (Zawacki-Richter et al., 2019). Therefore, integrating artificial intelligence in educational policies and practices with an equal opportunity perspective not only keeps pace with technological development but also serves to ensure social justice.

Artificial intelligence systems require the collection and analysis of a wide range of student data to function effectively. However, concerns about digital security, student rights, and data privacy become more prominent during this process. Adopting ethical guidelines prohibiting the sharing of students' academic and personal information with outside parties is essential.

4. AI APPLICATIONS IN MATHEMATICS EDUCATION

Teachers must understand artificial intelligence, apply it in a pedagogical context, and critically evaluate it to successfully integrate it into learning environments. To achieve this, educators must receive in-service training and professional development opportunities, as well as basic literacy in AI, data analytics, and ethical use of these technologies. By automating time-consuming administrative tasks, such as recording student performance, checking homework, and taking attendance, artificial intelligence (AI) systems can free up teachers to focus more on pedagogical activities. As a result, educators have more time to engage with students and foster their personal growth.

Artificial intelligence can be helpful in the classroom only if it is intended to support instruction rather than replace teachers. By offering individualized learning experiences with artificial intelligence systems operating under the direction of the teacher, hybrid models can enhance the quality of instruction in this situation. By analyzing the data from artificial intelligence, the teacher enhances instruction as a guide who is aware of the student's cognitive, affective, and social needs.

AI-powered learning software can be integrated into the next generation of educational technology projects to deliver content tailored to individual student needs. For instance, Socrat.ai offers educators a platform to design personalized learning experiences, which can enhance student engagement and improve academic performance. This AI-driven tool is handy in subjects such as mathematics, where it can monitor students' responses to problem-solving tasks, provide immediate feedback, and adjust instruction based on individual learning patterns. By automating processes like tracking assignments, checking homework, and taking attendance, Google Classroom and Microsoft Teams reduce the workload for teachers. AI can evaluate a student's assignment, provide comments, and notify the teacher when something “requires intervention” occurs. This allows the teacher to devote more time to students needing attention. Carnegie Learning (USA) is an AI-powered math platform that provides teachers with comprehensive analysis reports, which evaluate student answers and offer customized exercises. For instance, the teacher utilizes AI recommendations to plan each student's study time while also directly addressing conceptual errors. As a result, rather than competing with the technology, the teacher works in conjunction with it.

Students with various learning profiles, such as attention deficit hyperactivity disorder, autism spectrum disorders, or learning disabilities, may benefit from personalized learning experiences made possible by artificial intelligence. For students with special education needs, language barriers, or those who are immigrants, it also enhances accessibility and provides supportive learning pathways. In this regard, incorporating AI into inclusive education can improve the flexibility and equity of learning environments. AI-powered programs, such as Ghotit Real Writer and Kurzweil 3000, were created for students who struggle with writing and have dyslexia. When a student makes a spelling error, these systems automatically identify it and offer pertinent feedback. When an immigrant student who does not speak Turkish uses Duolingo to learn the language, artificial intelligence can identify the language structures that the student finds challenging and offer extra practice. As a result, both motivation and learning speed may rise.

Educators and software developers alone cannot achieve successful and long-lasting AI integration. To develop reliable and student-centered solutions, an interdisciplinary approach involving educators, software developers, psychologists, ethicists, and policymakers is required. Through this collaboration, systems that balance technicality and pedagogy can be developed. Incorporating AI into group learning processes rather than solitary learning is becoming increasingly important. AI-enabled systems that analyze student interactions can be used to assign group roles and track the learning process in real time.

Furthermore, software developers and metacognitive prompts that assist students in planning and evaluating their work cannot successfully and sustainably integrate AI independently. Reliable, student-centered solutions require an interdisciplinary approach involving educators, software developers, psychologists, ethicists, and legislators. Systems that successfully balance pedagogy and technology may result from this partnership. Moreover, it is increasingly important to integrate AI into collaborative learning processes rather than focusing solely on individual learning. AI-enabled systems can help organize group roles and monitor the learning process in real time by analyzing student interactions.

Additionally, metacognitive prompts can help students assess and plan their learning, thereby enhancing their overall educational experience. Learning can deepen learning. Using short-term results alone to assess the impact of artificial intelligence-supported teaching methods on students is insufficient. Long-term monitoring of the effects on high-level cognitive processes, including learning retention, abstract thinking abilities, problem-solving, analytical thinking, and creative productivity, is necessary. Such studies are crucial for assessing the long-term viability and educational impact of artificial intelligence.

5. OPPORTUNITIES AND ADVANTAGES OF AI IN MATHEMATICS EDUCATION

Artificial intelligence (AI) presents transformative potential in mathematics education by enabling more inclusive, responsive, and effective learning experiences. One of the most promising applications lies in personalizing learning processes. AI-powered adaptive learning systems can analyze students' prior knowledge, pace, and misconceptions to deliver individualized content and feedback (Luckin et al., 2016). This allows for differentiated instruction, where advanced learners can access enriched content while those experiencing difficulties receive targeted support to bridge learning gaps. Differentiated instruction matches content to students' proficiency levels, utilizes varied strategies and assessments, and fosters a flexible, inclusive classroom environment.

On the other hand, teachers can adapt the teaching process to suit students' readiness levels, interests, and learning styles. Moreover, AI technologies facilitate immediate feedback mechanisms, transforming learning into a more dynamic and interactive process. Students can recognize and correct their errors in real-time, strengthening formative assessment practices and encouraging self-regulated learning (Holmes et al., 2019). By continuously monitoring learners' progress, AI systems enhance academic performance and foster metacognitive awareness, a crucial component of mathematical reasoning.

AI-enhanced learning environments also support the development of higher-order cognitive skills such as problem-solving, critical thinking, and mathematical modeling. Intelligent tutoring systems and open-ended problem-solving platforms allow students to explore multiple solution strategies and engage with non-routine problems (Bower, 2019). These environments encourage a deeper understanding of mathematical concepts by promoting inquiry and flexibility in thinking. In addition, AI contributes to the advancement of equitable and accessible education. With multimodal interfaces, multilingual options, and assistive technologies, AI tools can accommodate diverse learners, including those with disabilities or those from linguistically and culturally diverse backgrounds (Akgün & Greenhow, 2022). This inclusiveness positions AI as a technological aid and a means to reduce educational inequities.

For teachers, AI offers significant support in classroom management, student performance tracking, and assessment design. Data-driven insights generated by AI systems enable educators to make informed decisions, tailor instruction, and identify at-risk students early (Zawacki-Richter et al., 2019). Furthermore, AI-powered professional development platforms can provide teachers with customized learning pathways, keeping them engaged in continuous improvement and lifelong learning. Ultimately, integrating AI into mathematics education not only reconfigures students' learning experiences but also redefines the teacher's role and reshapes pedagogical practices. These innovations, however, must be aligned with sound educational theories, ethical considerations, and sustainable infrastructure to ensure that the benefits of AI are equitably realized across diverse educational contexts.

6. CURRENT STUDY

The case study examines the effect of artificial intelligence (AI) enhanced mathematics instruction on the problem-solving strategies of third-grade primary school students. Fifteen students and their teachers participated in a qualitative case study. Students initially solved mathematical problems using traditional methods, followed by sessions utilizing AI tools such as Chatbots and Copilots. Data were collected through student work, screen recordings, and semi-structured interviews, and were analyzed thematically. The authors first reviewed all transcripts to become familiar with the data. During the initial coding cycle, meaningful units related to the research questions were identified and grouped according to their similarity. In the second cycle, these categories were refined and synthesized into broader themes. To ensure reliability, two researchers coded the data independently and resolved any discrepancies through discussion. This iterative process led to the emergence of four major themes: guidance, speed and accessibility, motivation, and sustainability in learning.

The integration of AI in education has shown promise in enhancing personalized learning experiences, particularly in mathematics education. AI tools can adapt to individual students' learning paces and styles, providing tailored support that traditional methods may not offer (Jaiswal & Arun, 2021). While artificial intelligence (AI) has garnered increasing attention in education, most existing research focuses on its implementation in higher education or secondary schooling (Zawacki-Richter et al., 2019; Holmes et al., 2019). These studies emphasize AI's potential to personalize learning, support assessment, and enhance learner engagement. However, the application of AI in primary education, particularly in mathematics teaching, remains significantly underexplored (Chen et al., 2020). Current literature often highlights intelligent tutoring systems (ITS) and learning analytics for older students, with limited empirical evidence on how younger learners interact with AI technologies in problem-solving contexts (Tuomi, 2018). Moreover, studies that include primary students tend to focus on general digital learning environments rather than evaluating

AI-supported tools such as chatbots or copilots and their impact on cognitive and affective learning outcomes. The scoping review by Yim and Su (2024) highlights this gap. Although various AI tools are implemented in K–12 settings, research involving primary students primarily addresses general pedagogical strategies and digital platforms. Few studies assess the impact of intelligent agents or AI-supported tools on cognitive and affective learning outcomes.

This lack of focus on the early grades is a critical omission, especially given that foundational mathematical skills and positive attitudes toward mathematics were developed mainly during this period (National Mathematics Advisory Panel, 2008). There is an urgent need to understand how AI can scaffold these early learning experiences and address challenges such as math anxiety, limited conceptual understanding, and individual learning differences among young children. Additionally, few studies take a qualitative approach to investigate the lived experiences of students and teachers during AI-supported learning, making it challenging to capture the nuanced, context-rich perspectives needed for effective classroom integration (Lee & Kwon, 2024). As AI becomes more prevalent in educational settings, research must address ethical, pedagogical, and developmental concerns unique to early learners (Holmes et al., 2022). Therefore, this study contributes to filling an important gap by focusing on the problem-solving processes of third-grade students with AI tools and offering insight into how these technologies can support cognitive development and motivational factors in early mathematics education.

The primary aim of this study is to investigate the impact of AI-supported teaching practices on the mathematical problem-solving skills of third-grade students. Specifically, it aims to investigate the impact of AI tools on students' cognitive strategies, motivation, long-term learning retention, and teachers' perceptions of integrating AI into classroom instruction. The research problems of this study were determined as follows:

- How do AI-supported tools influence the mathematical problem-solving processes of third-grade students?
- In what ways do students and teachers perceive AI as supportive or limiting in their learning experience?

6.1 Case Study

This section presents successful application examples to illustrate the practical applications of AI in mathematics education in primary schools. The case study offers educators and policymakers valuable insights, highlighting best practices and lessons learned through pilot initiatives and practical applications. An application was carried out to examine the effect of artificial intelligence-supported mathematics teaching on the problem-solving processes of 3rd-grade primary school students. The application was planned and conducted within a qualitative research design framework.

6.2 Sampling

Simple random sampling was used to select the participants. "In this method, every individual has an equal chance of being selected in the sample from the population" (Acharya et al., 2013, p. 330). The study was conducted with 15 3rd-grade students from two classes and their teachers. The students' names are anonymous and coded as S1, S2, ..., and S15, while the names of two teachers are coded as T1 and T2.

6.3 Process

The mathematical problem-solving processes of students were initially observed using classical methods. Each participant independently solved eight problems involving mathematical operations. Observers systematically recorded the problem-solving strategies, the sequence of procedural steps, errors, and specific difficulties encountered. In the subsequent phase, students utilized an artificial intelligence-supported application, such as ChatGPT, Chatbot, Gemini, or Copilot, to address comparable mathematical problems. Observers documented the nature of students' interactions with the artificial intelligence system, the types of feedback or hints provided, and the influence of these elements on students' solution strategies. The observation protocol included an analysis of alternative solution approaches suggested by the artificial intelligence, students' evaluations of these strategies, and modifications in decision-making processes relative to the traditional approach. This structured observation was designed to assess the extent to which artificial intelligence support diversifies and enhances students' problem-solving abilities.

6.4 Data Collecting and Analysis

Data were collected through student products and semi-structured interviews. The researchers developed eight mathematical problems as a data collection tool and semi-structured interview forms for students and teachers. Expert opinions were obtained to evaluate the linguistic clarity, appropriateness for students' cognitive levels, and alignment with the curriculum of mathematical problems. The necessary revisions were made based on the feedback received, and the problems were finalized accordingly.

While developing the interview forms, the relevant literature was first reviewed. Accordingly, a draft form consisting of open-ended questions was prepared. The prepared form was presented to three academicians who are experts in their fields, and the content validity, comprehensibility, and suitability of the questions for the research were evaluated. In line with the expert opinions, some statements were simplified, and some questions were restructured. The finalized semi-structured interview forms were used in one-to-one interviews with the students and teachers.

The qualitative data obtained were analyzed using the descriptive analysis method. In the descriptive analysis process, the data were organized in line with the predetermined themes, based on the research questions, and interpreted using direct quotations from the participants' statements. Two separate researchers independently analyzed the data during the coding and theme identification processes, and the findings were compared to calculate the consensus rate and ensure reliability (Miles & Huberman, 1994). To increase the validity of the data, case studies were incorporated into the context of the responses obtained from the participants.

6.5 Findings

In this section, the experiences of students who participated in the artificial intelligence-supported mathematics problem-solving application were evaluated using a thematic coding method within the scope of qualitative data analysis. Four main themes were revealed in line with student opinions and solution examples: (1) Guidance, (2) Speed and Accessibility, (3) Increased Motivation, and (4) Sustainability in Learning.

Guidance

The study demonstrated that artificial intelligence aids students in progressing through problem-solving, particularly in multi-step operations. Students stated they saw the solution paths more clearly when working with artificial intelligence. S1 stated that AI provided easy guidance for him. This response demonstrates that the student arrived at the correct result and gained the necessary experience to understand the logic of the solution process. S2 and S8 stated that the AI explained the solution to the problem in detail and provided visual support for the answers.

AI explains all the details and provides the visuals. S2

Artificial intelligence has also provided me with various solutions. This made me look at it from a different perspective. S8

Below is the teacher's opinion that artificial intelligence is guiding students, especially in basic computational skills, and supporting conceptual understanding.

Some students were making mistakes, especially in the order of operations. Artificial intelligence guided their thought process. This was something I could not do one-on-one in the classroom. T1

When the answers of students and artificial intelligence tools are examined, unlike the student's response, which focuses solely on calculations, the answer generated by ChatGPT includes detailed reasoning and a clear explanation of both methods, offering a more comprehensive understanding of the problem (see Appendix).

Speed and Accessibility

Students mentioned the rapid response feature of artificial intelligence as an important advantage. When comparing the solution process with the teacher with the one with artificial intelligence, they stated that receiving instant feedback supports the learning process.

Artificial intelligence solves the problem faster. S1

He responds very fast. I do not have to wait. S3

This statement indicates that the student prioritizes efficiency and progress, avoiding time wastage during problem-solving. This is a crucial supportive factor, particularly for students with short attention spans. A teacher's observation also supports this finding:

Some students either give up or are interested in something else while waiting for their turn in class. When they ask the AI, they receive an instant answer, thereby sustaining their attention. T2

In this context, when artificial intelligence presents problems with different solutions comparatively, students can choose the appropriate strategies. For example, when the problem of serving 3 or 4 cookies to a class of 24 students was presented, the artificial intelligence presented both solution options, and the student was able to evaluate the options against each other. This situation allowed the student to encounter different strategies and demonstrate problem-solving flexibility.

Motivation

Working with artificial intelligence increased students' interest and desire for problem-solving. The solutions' understanding gave students confidence. S1's first experience left a positive impression, and the student was eager to solve the following problems.

When the AI helped me, I felt very successful. I can now solve even more difficult questions. S1

The teacher mentioned the increase in students' motivation with the following words:

Some students who were previously intimidated by mathematics found that they could solve questions more easily when working with artificial intelligence. They experienced less anxiety. T1

This finding indicates that the student developed a positive affective attachment to the mathematics problem-solving process. Artificial intelligence applications support not only the cognitive but also the affective domain. However, some students stated that solving problems with artificial intelligence is cheating and decreases their motivation.

It is like cheating. S5

I feel like I am cheating because it seems all done by the AI. S13

T1 stated that students were confused about the ways of using artificial intelligence to solve problems. The statements of the teacher coded T1 as an example of this situation are given below:"

Since AI solves problems quickly, students often perceive it as a virtual tool for cheating. Students using AI without fully understanding how to utilize it can be perceived as cheating. T1

Sustainability in Learning

It was determined that the artificial intelligence-supported solution process had a positive impact on students' learning retention. Students were able to re-examine the solutions they learned, reinforcing their learning.

It would be easier, and I would like to use this tool in future learning processes. S7

This student's response demonstrates that artificial intelligence fosters a positive habit in the learning process and supports its continuity. At the same time, the student's verbal statement, *"I understood the solutions by rereading them,"* reveals that it strengthens the repeatability of learning and metacognitive awareness. Additionally, students could reinforce the learning they obtained with the support of artificial intelligence, apply similar strategies to new problems, and recall the solution processes more effectively. S6 and T2 explained this process as follows:

I solved a question I once did not understand with the help of artificial intelligence. Then I solved a similar problem on my own .S9

Artificial intelligence can be utilized in mathematics education to clarify subjects that are not understood more clearly, particularly in individual learning, and to explore various solutions to problem-solving questions. T2

Another student used the following statement:

I initially did not understand, but it stuck with me when I reread the examples provided by artificial intelligence. S11

These findings reveal that AI-supported learning environments provide a structured environment that supports instructive and sustainable learning for primary school students. Students can evaluate solution methods based on their learning speeds and gain permanent learning by comprehending the solution processes.

7. DISCUSSION

The study's findings indicate that AI tools significantly contributed to students' problem-solving processes, particularly in tasks requiring multi-step operations. Students reported that AI helped them understand solution paths more clearly, and teachers observed that AI supported students' conceptual understanding, particularly in areas like the order of operations. At the same time, teachers observed that AI support enhanced students' conceptual understanding—especially in topics such as the order of operations. These results are consistent with previous research that emphasizes the role of AI in providing personalized scaffolding to facilitate cognitive development (Luckin et al., 2016). This difference highlights the potential of artificial intelligence as a powerful educational tool that supports sustainable learning by offering deeper explanations and guiding students beyond mere calculations. Such qualities position AI as a valuable and enduring component of the learning environment, enabling students to move beyond rote computation toward a deeper understanding of mathematics.

Students expressed their satisfaction with the rapid feedback provided by AI tools and stated that this instant feedback helped them maintain their attention during the problem-solving process. Teachers emphasized that this instant feedback supported continuous participation in the learning process, especially for students with short attention spans. These findings are consistent with studies highlighting AI's potential to enhance learning efficiency and accessibility (Holmes et al., 2019). AI-supported teaching systems can provide a more effective learning experience by adapting to students' learning pace (Yi et al., 2025).

Working with artificial intelligence has increased students' interest and self-confidence in mathematics. Students who previously experienced mathematics anxiety reported feeling more comfortable and motivated when interacting with artificial intelligence tools. However, some students approached these technologies cautiously, stating that excessive reliance on artificial intelligence could be perceived as a form of "cheating." This dual attitude reflects the complex relationship between the use of technology in education and student motivation (Williamson & Eynon, 2020). The literature emphasizes that artificial intelligence-supported learning systems can enhance student motivation and foster sustainable learning models by tailoring to individual needs (Miao et al., 2021). In this study, it was observed that the artificial intelligence-supported learning process had a positive impact on students' long-term retention of mathematical concepts. Albahli (2025) states that artificial intelligence-based teaching systems can provide a more effective learning experience by adapting to students' learning speed. The ability of students to repeatedly examine solutions generated by AI reinforced conceptual understanding and allowed them to apply these strategies to solve similar problems. This suggests that

AI tools can promote sustainable learning by supporting metacognitive awareness and self-regulated learning approaches (Luckin et al., 2016).

8. CONCLUSION

This study examined the sustainability of learning in artificial intelligence-supported problem-solving processes among elementary school students. The findings indicated that AI made a positive contribution to students' learning processes across both cognitive and affective domains. The implementation of AI-supported environments fostered a greater diversity in students' thinking patterns and promoted both process-oriented and result-oriented approaches to problem-solving. These outcomes suggest that AI can serve as a significant tool in promoting sustainable mathematics learning. However, certain variables—such as students' age, the language used in the AI application, and the extent of teacher facilitation—emerged as critical factors that must be carefully considered in the design and implementation of AI-supported learning environments.

The concluding section of the chapter offers recommendations for future research and practical applications. It underscores the importance of collaboration among educational stakeholders and presents actionable ideas for integrating AI into institutional and national education systems. Additionally, the chapter points to emerging trends and future research directions, including the development of AI tools that support collaborative learning and the application of AI technologies to address global educational challenges.

REFERENCES

Acharya, A. S., Prakash, A., Saxena, P., & Nigam, A. (2013). Sampling: Why and how of it. *Indian Journal of Medical Specialties*, *4*(2), 330–333. DOI: 10.7713/ijms.2013.0032

Akgün, S., & Greenhow, C. (2022). Artificial intelligence in education: Addressing ethical challenges in K-12 settings. *AI and Ethics*, *2*, 431–440. DOI: 10.1007/s43681-021-00096-7 PMID: 34790956

Albahli, S. (2025). Advancing sustainable educational practices through AI-driven prediction of academic outcomes. *Sustainability*, *17*(3), 1087. DOI: 10.3390/su17031087

Bagheri, M. M. (2015). Intelligent and adaptive tutoring systems: How to integrate learners. *International Journal of Education*, *7*(2), 1–16.

Baker, T., & Smith, L. (2019). *Educ-AI-tion rebooted? Exploring the future of artificial intelligence in schools and colleges*. Nesta. https://www.nesta.org.uk/report/education-rebooted/

Bower, M. (2019). *Design of technology-enhanced learning: Integrating research and practice*. Emerald Publishing Limited.

Bruner, J. S. (1961). The act of discovery. *Harvard Educational Review*, *31*, 21–32.

CAST. (2018). Universal design for learning guidelines version 2.2. CAST. http://udlguidelines.cast.org

Celik, I. (2023). Exploring the determinants of artificial intelligence (AI) literacy: Digital divide, computational thinking, cognitive absorption. *Telematics and Informatics*, *83*. Advance online publication. DOI: 10.1016/j.tele.2023.102026

Chen, X., Xie, H., Zou, D., & Hwang, G.-J. (2020). Application and theory gaps during the rise of artificial intelligence in education. *Computers and Education: Artificial Intelligence*, *1*, 100002. DOI: 10.1016/j.caeai.2020.100002

Çiftçi, S., Taşkaya, S. M., & Alemdar, M. (2013). The opinions of classroom teachers about the FATIH project. *Elementary Education Online*, *12*(1), 227–240.

Clark-Wilson, A., Robutti, O., & Thomas, M. (2020). Teaching with digital technology. *ZDM Mathematics Education*, *52*, 1223–1242. DOI: 10.1007/s11858-020-01196-0 PMID: 33133297

Demir, Ö. (2024). Another brick in the wall of ed-tech failures? A systematic literature review of the FATIH project in Turkey from the perspective of in-service teachers. *Learning, Media and Technology*, *49*(1), 20–34. DOI: 10.1080/17439884.2023.2233424

Doğan, D., Çınar, M., & Seferoğlu, S. S. (2016). "One Laptop per Child" projects and FATIH project: A comparative examination. *SDU International Journal of Educational Studies*, *3*(1), 1–26.

Dwivedi, Y. K., Kshetri, N., Hughes, L., Slade, E. L., Jeyaraj, A., Kar, A. K., & Wright, R. (2023). Opinion Paper: "So what if ChatGPT wrote it?" Multidisciplinary perspectives on opportunities, challenges and implications of generative conversational AI for research, practice and policy. *International Journal of Information Management*, *71*, 102642.

Hadwin, A. F., Bakhtiar, A., & Miller, M. (2018). Challenges in online collaboration: Effects of scripting shared task perceptions. *International Journal of Computer-Supported Collaborative Learning*, *13*(3), 301–329. DOI: 10.1007/s11412-018-9279-9

Holmes, W., Bialik, M., & Fadel, C. (2019). *Artificial Intelligence in Education: Promises and Implications for Teaching and Learning*. Center for Curriculum Redesign., https://www.researchgate.net/publication/332180327_Artificial_Intelligence_in_Education_Promise_and_Implications_for_Teaching_and_Learning

Holmes, W., Porayska-Pomsta, K., Holstein, K., Sutherland, E., Baker, T., & Santos, O. C. (2022). Ethics of AI in education: Towards a community-wide framework. *International Journal of Artificial Intelligence in Education*, *32*, 538–566. DOI: 10.1007/s40593-021-00239-1

Jaiswal, A., & Arun, C. J. (2021). Potential of Artificial Intelligence for transformation of the education system in India. [IJEDICT]. *International Journal of Education and Development Using Information and Communication Technology*, *17*(1), 142–158.

Koedinger, K. R., & Corbett, A. (2006). Cognitive tutors: Technology bringing learning sciences to the classroom. In Sawyer, R. K. (Ed.), *The Cambridge Handbook of the Learning Sciences* (pp. 61–77). Cambridge University Press., DOI: 10.1017/CBO9780511816833.006

Lee, S. J., & Kwon, K. (2024). A systematic review of AI education in K-12 classrooms from 2018 to 2023: Topics, strategies, and learning outcomes. *Computers and Education: Artificial Intelligence*, *6*, 100211. DOI: 10.1016/j.caeai.2024.100211

Lin, C. C., Huang, A. Y., & Lu, O. H. (2023). Artificial intelligence in intelligent tutoring systems toward sustainable education: a systematic review. *Smart learning environments, 10*(1), 41. https://doi.org/DOI: 10.1186/s40561-023-00260-y

Long, D., & Magerko, B. (2020, April). What is AI literacy? Competencies and design considerations. In *Proceedings of the 2020 CHI conference on human factors in computing systems* (pp. 1-16).

Luckin, R., Holmes, W., Griffiths, M., & Forcier, L. B. (2016). *Intelligence Unleashed: An argument for AI in education*. Pearson Education. https://static.googleusercontent .com/media/edu.google.com/tr//pdfs/Intelligence-Unleashed-Publication.pdf

Mercer, L. S. (2000). Measuring the use and value of electronic journals and books. *Issues in science and technology librarianship, 25*(Winter).

Miao, F., Holmes, W., Huang, R., & Zhang, H. (2021). *AI and education: A guidance for policymakers*. UNESCO Publishing.

Miles, M. B., & Huberman, A. M. (1994). *Qualitative data analysis: An expanded sourcebook* (2nd ed.). Sage Publications.

Ministry of National Education (MEB). (2022). *Öğretmenler için dijital okuryazarlık eğitim materyalleri (Digital literacy training materials for teachers)*. MEB Yayınları.

Ministry of National Education (MEB). (2023). *Türkiye Yüzyılı Maarif Modeli*. Talim ve Terbiye Kurulu Başkanlığı.

National Mathematics Advisory Panel. (2008). *Foundations for Success: The Final Report of the National Mathematics Advisory Panel*. U.S. Department of Education.

Papert, S. (1980). *Mindstorms: Children, computers, and powerful ideas*. Basic Books.

Piaget, J. (1954). *The construction of reality in the child* (Cook, M., Trans.). Basic Books.

Pouezevara, L., Dincer, G., Kipp, S., & Sener, U. (2013). *Turkey's FATIH Project: A plan to conquer the digital divide or a technological leap of faith?* RTI International.

Rosé, C., Wang, Y. C., Cui, Y., Arguello, J., Stegmann, K., Weinberger, A., & Fischer, F. (2008). Analyzing collaborative learning processes automatically: Exploiting the advances of computational linguistics in computer-supported collaborative learning. *International Journal of Computer-Supported Collaborative Learning, 3*(3), 237–271.

Selwyn, N. (2016). *Is technology good for education?* John Wiley & Sons.

TÜBİTAK. (2022). *Yapay zekâ destekli öğrenme ortamlarının geliştirilmesi ve pilot uygulaması: Matematik derslerinde işbirliğine dayalı öğrenme örnekleri (Development and pilot application of artificial intelligence-supported learning environments: Examples of collaborative learning in mathematics lessons).* TÜBİTAK Proje Raporu.

Tuomi, I. (2018). The Impact of Artificial Intelligence on Learning, Teaching, and Education: Policies for the Future. *European Commission Report.* https://doi.org/. https://publications.jrc.ec.europa.eu/repository/handle/JRC113226DOI: 10.2766/16182

UNESCO. (2022). *Reimagining our futures together: A new social contract for education.* Paris: UNESCO. https://unesdoc.unesco.org/ark:/48223/pf0000379707.locale=en

VanLehn, K. (2011). The relative effectiveness of human tutoring, intelligent tutoring systems, and other tutoring systems. *Educational Psychologist, 46*(4), 197–221. DOI: 10.1080/00461520.2011.611369

Villegas-Ch, W., Buenano-Fernandez, D., Navarro, A. M., & Mera-Navarrete, A. (2025). Adaptive intelligent tutoring systems for STEM education: Analysis of the learning impact and effectiveness of personalized feedback. *Smart Learning Environments, 12*(1), 1–31. DOI: 10.1186/s40561-025-00389-y

von Glasersfeld, E. (1995). *Radical constructivism: A way of knowing and learning.* Falmer Press.

Vygotsky, L. S. (1978). *Mind in society: The development of higher psychological processes.* Harvard University Press.

Wang, X., Li, L., Tan, S. C., Yang, L., & Lei, J. (2023). Preparing for AI-enhanced education: Conceptualizing and empirically examining teachers' AI readiness. *Computers in Human ehavior, 146.* 107798. https://doi.org/DOI: 10.1016/j.chb.2023.107798

Williamson, B., & Eynon, R. (2020). Historical threads, missing links, and future directions in AI in education. *Learning, Media and Technology, 45*(3), 223–235. DOI: 10.1080/17439884.2020.1798995

Yi, L., Liu, D., Jiang, T., & Xian, Y. (2025). The effectiveness of AI on K-12 students' mathematics learning: A systematic review and meta-analysis. *International Journal of Science and Mathematics Education, 23*, 1105–1126. DOI: 10.1007/s10763-024-10499-7

Yim, I. H. Y., & Su, J. (2024). Artificial intelligence (AI) learning tools in K-12 education: A scoping review. *Journal of Computers in Education*, *12*, 93–131. DOI: 10.1007/s40692-023-00304-9

Zawacki-Richter, O., Marín, V. I., Bond, M., & Gouverneur, F. (2019). Systematic review of research on artificial intelligence applications in higher education – where are the educators? *International Journal of Educational Technology in Higher Education*, *16*(1), 1–27. DOI: 10.1186/s41239-019-0171-0

Zeeshan, K., Hämäläinen, T., & Neittaanmäki, P. (2024). Computational thinking and AI coding for kids to develop digital literacy. *International Journal of Education*, *12*(3), 55–74. DOI: 10.5121/ije2024.12305

KEY TERMS AND DEFINITIONS

Adaptive Learning Systems: Educational platforms that use algorithms to adjust the learning content and instructional path in real-time, based on each student's performance, learning style, and needs.

Algorithmic Bias: Systematic and unfair discrimination embedded in the outcomes of AI systems, often caused by biases in training data or algorithm design, which can lead to unequal treatment of students.

Artificial Intelligence (AI): The capability of machines or software to simulate human intelligence processes, such as learning, reasoning, and problem-solving. In mathematics education, AI often refers to digital tools that adapt to students' needs or provide automated feedback.

Digital Divide: The gap between individuals who have easy access to digital technologies and those who do not, often due to socioeconomic, geographic, or infrastructural disparities.

Digital Pedagogy: The strategic and purposeful use of digital tools, resources, and technologies to enhance teaching and learning processes, focusing on both technological and pedagogical effectiveness.

Intelligent Tutoring Systems (ITS): AI-powered computer programs designed to provide personalized guidance, feedback, and instructional support to learners, often mimicking the role of a human tutor.

Learning Analytics: The collection and analysis of data about learners and their contexts, for the purpose of understanding and optimizing learning and the environments in which it occurs.

Personalized Learning: Instructional approaches and technologies that tailor learning experiences to the individual abilities, preferences, and needs of each student.

Sustainable Education: Addressing current educational requirements while preparing individuals to effectively engage with future social, cultural, and environmental challenges.

Universal Design for Learning (UDL): An educational framework that aims to optimize teaching and learning for all people by providing multiple means of representation, engagement, and expression.

APPENDIX

Example of Students and AI solutions

Figure 1. S3 solution

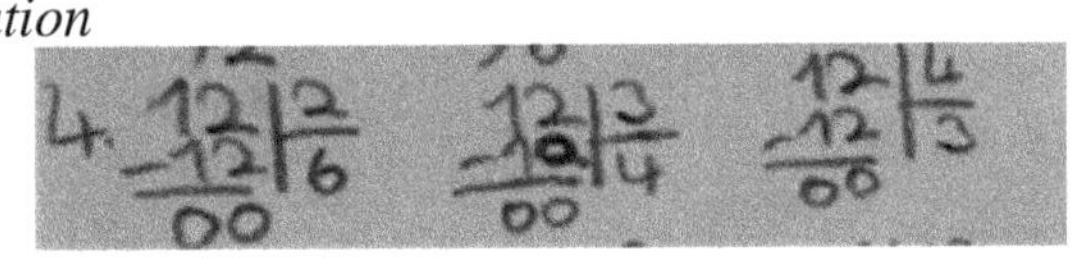

Table 1. ChatGPT Solution

Method 1: Presentation in Packages of 3
There are three cookies in each package.
To distribute equally to 24 people, 24 people × 3 cookies = 72 cookies.

A total of 72 cookies / 3 = 24 packages are prepared.
Everyone receives 1 package (3 cookies).
There is no waste.

Method 2: Presentation on Plates of 4
There are 4 cookies on each plate.
Total number of people: 24
The total number should be divisible by 4 to distribute the cookies evenly.
Total number of cookies:
1 plate for 24 people = 24 plates × 4 = 96 cookies
However, if each person gets a plate, there will be too many cookies.
Should we share the plates?
If there are 4 cookies on each plate, we need a total number that is a multiple of 4 to distribute them equally among 24 people.
Let us say everyone gets 2 cookies: 24 people × 2 = 48 cookies
48 cookies / 4 = 12 plates
In this case, each plate is shared by 2 people.
That is to say:
12 plates are prepared.
Each plate has 4 cookies.
Each plate is shared by 2 people.
There is no waste.

Comparison and Recommendation
Method Total Cookies Method of Presentation Wastage per Person Number of Servings
3 Pack 72 24 packs 3 cookies None 24
4 Plates 48 12 plates (2 people share) 2 cookies None 12

Conclusion and Recommendation:
If you want to make fewer cookies:
● The 4-plate method is better (48 cookies are enough).
If everyone is asked to take their own portion:
● The 3-pack method is suitable (1 pack without sharing with anyone).

Chapter 10
Understanding the Role of AI in Mathematics Education:
A Q Methodological Inquiry

Bayram Özer
https://orcid.org/0009-0001-0649-4473
Ondokuz Mayıs University, Turkey

Volkan Duran
https://orcid.org/0000-0003-0692-0265
Iğdır University, Turkey

ABSTRACT

This chapter explores the integration of Artificial Intelligence in mathematics education, highlighting its potential to personalize learning, enhance conceptual understanding, and support instruction through technologies such as intelligent tutoring systems, adaptive platforms, and tools like GeoGebra and ChatGPT. Using Q-methodology, the study analyzes mathematics teacher candidates' perceptions, revealing two primary viewpoints: those who support AI's motivational benefits but are concerned about shallow learning and reduced human interaction, and those who value face-to-face engagement while supporting AI's personalized feedback. Results emphasize the irreplaceable role of teachers in providing emotional and cognitive support. The findings advocate for a balanced, ethically aware implementation of AI—one that ensures equitable access, protects data integrity, and maintains pedagogical values, while enhancing mathematics learning through collaborative, human-centered approaches.

DOI: 10.4018/979-8-3373-1998-8.ch010

INTRODUCTION

Artificial Intelligence (AI) is becoming a transformative technology in education generally and for mathematics instruction in particular. AI-powered technologies and tools are proliferating in mathematics education to provide problem-solving support, personalize learning and develop conceptual understanding. Examples of AI-powered technologies include intelligent tutoring systems, AI adaptive learning platforms and interactive AI tools like ChatGPT and GeoGebra, that provide instant feedback that engage students and adapt to students' individual learning pathways (Canonigo, 2024; Torres-Peña et al., 2024).

AI-powered strategies substantially improved student motivation, student understanding of mathematics, and the ability to visualize complex mathematical concepts and, instantaneously, identify a valid method of problem-solving (Torres-Peña et al., 2024). Additionally, meta-analyses have determined that AI systems result in a modest increase in math performance as compared to the first form of task of instruction (Yi et al., 2024). Evidence shows there are consistent improvements in math performance, particularly when AI systems are able to adapt in real time to students' inputs (Yi et al., 2024). The challenges of moving toward AI-enhanced learning are ample. Issues of equitable access, AI bias, the de-skilling of teachers, and the need to ensure that AI enhances human instruction rather than replace it (Canonigo, 2024; Choi, 2022) remain issues. Therefore, effective implementation will still require deliberate planning, teacher education, and ethical considering of how best use the data available and what our pedagogical intentions are. Framing AI within the context of mathematics education means more than simply framing the deployment of technological tools, it means re-imagining instruction, equity, and engagement in a data- and AI-driven age. If used mindfully, AI may present new ways to make mathematics more available, personal, and engaging for all learners.

The integration of artificial intelligence (AI) into educational contexts has its origins in the foundational developments of symbolic AI and rule-based systems, which were pivotal in the early evolution of computing and mathematics. These systems, rooted in the pioneering work of computer scientists, established the theoretical underpinnings of computation and logic that enabled the subsequent development of AI technologies (Garrido, 2012). Turing's work on formalizing computation through the Turing Machine and von Neumann's contributions to computer architecture and logic systems provided a framework that allowed for the creation of intelligent systems capable of processing and reasoning over structured data. These early advancements laid the groundwork for AI's eventual application in educational settings by demonstrating the potential for machines to emulate logical reasoning and problem-solving processes.

The application of artificial intelligence in educational settings has expanded significantly during the past three decades. It progressed from being nothing more than concepts to being actual, practical instruments that promote learning. One significant shift is the development of Intelligent Tutoring Systems, sometimes known as ITS. Each student's learning style is taken into account when these systems are modified. They are utilized rather frequently in fields such as mathematics, which need students to answer issues. Artificial intelligence is used by ITS to monitor how well a student is performing, and then to modify the teachings in order to better match the learner's requirements (Fu, 2024). These systems provide a particular strategy for the learner by adapting to their needs as they acquire more knowledge. Students are able to improve their abilities and fill in the gaps in their knowledge that they do not understand. This method of instruction has the potential to do more for each individual student than traditional classroom settings often do. Unlike old systems, today's AI uses deep learning to handle lots of data, making answers that feel like human thought and fit different learning settings. For instance, these systems can check math work, offer new ways to think about problems, and push for new ideas by asking open questions or giving new scenes. A study done from 2020 to 2024 shows a quick rise in using these AI tools in schools around the world, noting a big jump in use during those years (Hossein-Mohand et al., 2025). This boost shows the growing trust in AI's power to change how we teach, making it more active and fun.

Before individual learning, AI has largely contributed to the enhancement of collaborative educational environments. Mixed-method studies combining qualitative and quantitative approaches have shown that collaborative AI-mediated programming of lessons can greatly enhance both teaching methods and student outcomes when it comes to mathematics. AI tools enable teachers to design lessons that are more interactive and address the needs of their students, creating a classroom ambiance that thrives on active participation. AI-enabled lesson planning affords teachers more time to work with students, discuss with them, or grade assignments; however, the studies by Zakaria et al. (2024) also suggest that a more engaging classroom environment is also created, in which teachers use AI to modify content on the basis of students' reasoning and learning styles. For example, AI can detect patterns in student responses to common errors and provide suggestions for interventions that are most relevant, thereby elevating the effectiveness of instruction.

If artificial intelligence is to properly support the educational framework, researchers recommend instructional design models that balance the use of AI as a tool with human reasoning, creativity, and logical problem-solving. In other words, overusing AI reduces human agency in the educational process, whereas failure to use it to the maximum would be a disservice to its potentials. Instructional design models that work with AI should encourage student engagement and average conceptual understanding through collaborative learning where students interact with each other while working with AI tools. Such models best encourage active engagement, critical thinking, and logical reasoning in collaborative contexts so that AI could assist in instruction rather than replace persons in instructing (Gao et al., 2024). In this sense, AI woul d bring much gain to the teaching process, which in turn fosters creativity and problem-solving skills that take a front seat in the success of every student.

Artificial Intelligence's (AI) ecosystem is having varying degrees of impact on the teaching of mathematics. It goes beyond being just under History and Sciences. There are varied formats of its working to bear down on personalizing, motivating, and engaging ways of learning mathematics. Intelligent Tutoring Systems (ITS) such as Edmentum Exact Path and Sofia have offered adaptive feedback while also keeping track of the general progress of the student, thus furthering engagement and achievement (Khazanchi et al., 2024; Fu, 2024). Virtual tutors and AI-powered chatbots such as ChatGPT, MathGPT, and Wolfram Alpha offer just-in-time assistance to strengthen the pedagogically sound instructional materials through interactive problem solving of mathematical concepts (Torres-Peña et al., 2024). The most presentative form of AI technologies are adaptive learning systems, which generate instructional content and pacing to meet students' needs in real time. In particular, adaptive learning systems seem to be effective in different genres of environments throughout the K-12 educational system (Yi et al., 2024).

Generative AI tools advocate learning with real-time and step-by–step guidance, and signal a reduction in students' math anxiety while promoting independence for the student (Inoferio et al., 2024). Gamified and immersive artificial intelligence styled environments grow from the subjects normalized in K–12 settings using simulations and interacting tasks that developed both conceptual understanding and students' self-efficacy (Canonigo, 2024). AI's impact on evaluation has drastically altered the game; teachers can and are making decisions based on data that affects teaching (Yadav & Bhardwaj, 2024), while also gathering and aggregating student data in real-time. Finally, AI tools are being included into curriculum design and task generation, therefore improving how math is taught and practiced in classrooms (Park & Lim, 2023). Together, these technologies are modernizing conventional teaching methods and matching instruction with individual learning demands, hence transforming mathematics education.

The utilization of all kinds of artificial intelligence (AI) as a means of facilitating conceptual understanding continues to rise within education and scientific practice by directing abstract concepts to students, scientists, and researchers with the advantages of being interactive, accessible, and personalized. Educational tools such as GeoGebra and ChatGPT have been shown to enhance students' conceptual understanding and self-efficacy in mathematics while also fostering conversational and collaborative learning through adaptive platforms and intelligent tutoring systems (Canonigo, 2024).

While some students perceive and engage with AI primarily as a digital or technological phenomenon, many younger learners are beginning to recognize it as a socio-cultural phenomenon of learning and to reflect on the ethical implications of AI-based applications (Heeg & Avraamidou, 2024). Beyond this shift in perception, AI technology also holds considerable potential to reduce educational inequalities by enabling personalized learning pathways and fostering inclusivity, as shown in studies from diverse and resource-constrained contexts (Adeniyi et al., 2024). More broadly, situating conceptual modeling in relation to AI is promising for the future: the integration of explainable knowledge representation with knowledge generated by machine learning and data analysis may open new avenues for human–machine collaboration (Bork et al., 2023). In this way, AI tools complement traditional methods by supporting deeper understanding while simultaneously expanding equitable access to knowledge.

Artificial Intelligence (AI) is rapidly reshaping the educational landscape by offering personalized, efficient, and inclusive learning experiences. One of AI's most transformative impacts lies in personalized learning, where adaptive systems analyze student performance data to tailor instruction to individual needs, improving engagement and outcomes (Trivedi, 2023; Woolf, 2015; Harry, 2023; Ge, 2024). Additionally, AI automates routine administrative tasks such as grading and attendance tracking, freeing educators to focus on student mentorship and interaction (Woolf, 2015). Intelligent tutoring systems and real-time feedback further enhance instructional quality by offering timely, customized support (Mishra, 2024; Yu & Lu, 2021). AI also improves accessibility by adapting educational content for students with disabilities or those in underserved areas (Gonzalez & Hernández, 2025; Prasad, 2025; Naseri & Abdullah, 2025). In specialized fields like medicine and IT, AI-powered simulations offer hands-on training in complex scenarios, better preparing students for real-world applications (Babur, 2025; Bushuyev et al., 2024). Moreover, AI enables large-scale data analysis, aiding curriculum development and policy-making (Jaakkola et al., 2020; Kay, 2012). Despite these advancements, challenges remain—particularly around data privacy, bias, and the risk of diminishing human interaction in education (Gillani et al., 2023; Mishra, 2024; Mindzak, 2024). Overall, while AI offers powerful tools to enhance education, its implementation must be guided by ethical considerations and a focus on equity.

Learning and assessment with support from artificial intelligence (AI) will influence education and documents and provide a more effective and personalized learning experience with higher levels of engagement and performance. AI assessment and feedback tools (e.g., adaptive learning technologies, smart tutoring systems, and automatic grading platforms) make it easier for learners to receive real-time, individual feedback to optimize motivation and learning outcomes (Salameh, 2025), (Saputra et al., 2024). The report and evidence from new technologies will reduce ongoing workloads, as they allow automatic grading and feedback, enhance quicker turnaround, and assist instructors so they can focus on higher value-adds of teaching (Mahamuni et al., 2024; Agbarakwe & Chibueze, 2024). In some environments, actual performance of generative AI tools like ChatGPT achieves accuracy levels that are to be comparable to human feedback, especially when incorporating supplemental components or features like embeddings for optimised feedback (Kuzminykh et al., 2024; Herb & Lloyd, 2024). Student opinions related to AI-generated feedback have been mixed. Given heads up or thought of the source of feedback stemming from AI students still may wish to have human-generated feedback be provided during the learning process if provided that option (Nazaretsky et al., 2024; Roe et al., 2024). For remote language or writing activities, AI-enhanced feedback through natural language processing and speech processing (e.g., recorded audio) has been shown to improve assessments of grammar and vocabulary, and overall ability to communicate in written and oral communication (Evenddy, 2024; Youn et al., 2025). While these benefits and potential will move assessment and feedback forward into the future, there are still challenges and barriers such as algorithmic bias, ethically using data, infrastructure challenges, and unequal technology access (Yakkala, 2024; Bulut & Wongvorachan, 2022). In conclusion, while the potential for AI to help educational assessment and feedback is strong, thoughtful implementation to and engagement with its potential and shortcomings will be crucial.

Artificial Intelligence (AI) is drastically changing our understanding of teachers and their role in the modern classroom. Instead of being only knowledge providers, teachers are increasingly facilitating students' learning in AI-driven platforms that move beyond one-size-fits-all standards toward personalized and adaptive instruction (Fitria, 2023; Truong, 2024). In this context, AI creates opportunities for teachers to act as co-teachers by utilizing intelligent tools that complete routine administrative tasks such as grading, monitoring student growth, and adjusting lessons in real time (Taufikin et al., 2024; Zhang & Zhang, 2024). These functions allow teachers to focus more on supporting learners directly, especially in cases where students struggle with feedback or engagement, since AI can detect disengagement early and provide data-driven signals for timely intervention (Karumbaiah et al., 2023).

Nevertheless, these capabilities of AI do not replace teaching and learning, nor can they substitute for the empathy and social intelligence that educators provide—qualities that AI has yet to replicate (Nikitina & Ishchenko, 2024). For this reason, teachers must integrate digital and AI literacies into their practice not only to employ emerging tools but also to ensure equitable access and ethical opportunities for students (Bekdemir, 2024). Ultimately, the educator's role is essential for maintaining the humanistic and ethical dimensions of education while guiding AI integration in ways that serve, rather than undermine, the purpose of teaching (Shen & Su, 2020; Ramakrishnan et al., 2024). In this evolving landscape, the teacher's position is shifting toward a multifaceted role that blends coaching or consultancy, digital fluency, and emotional intelligence in partnership with AI technologies.

At the same time, the integration of AI into education—and society more broadly—brings a range of challenges and ethical dilemmas. Data privacy and security remain foremost concerns, as AI systems rely on sensitive personal data that is vulnerable to misuse and breaches (Abimbola et al., 2024; Wang, 2024; Syifa, 2024). Algorithmic bias constitutes another major challenge, since biased training data can reinforce existing inequalities (Ciriaco & Marín, 2023; Purwanto et al., 2024; Thakre et al., 2023). Transparency and explainability also raise concerns, as many AI technologies function as opaque "black boxes," limiting user trust (Osasona et al., 2024; Prajapati, 2025). Moreover, automation driven by AI intensifies worries about job displacement, especially in routine tasks, exacerbating inequality unless large-scale reskilling efforts are undertaken (Adesoga et al., 2024; Abhulimen & Ejike, 2024). Questions of accountability remain pressing as well, particularly in high-risk fields such as healthcare and finance, where responsibility for AI-driven decisions is often unclear (Lehmann, 2021; Islam, 2025). A further overarching issue is the inconsistency of ethical frameworks across regions and sectors, even though principles like fairness, transparency, and accountability are widely endorsed (Shukla, 2024; Shah et al., 2025).

To navigate these opportunities and challenges, education systems must establish strong ethical safeguards, adopt inclusive governance models, and continuously adapt policies in line with the pace of technological change. Only by balancing AI's technical power with human-centered values can we ensure that the educational mission—supporting student learning and development—remains intact.

In closing, the introduction of artificial intelligence into mathematics classrooms represents a watershed moment in mathematics teaching and learning. AI-driven tools are changing the landscape of learning and teaching in mathematics by personalizing, democratizing, and engaging classrooms as well as providing relevant and timely assessments and adapted support for students in real time. But with this great possibility comes important responsibilities, and as professionals, we need to think about issues of equity (certain students benefit more), ethical use of data (how their data is used), and algorithmic bias (also known as machine learning bias, is a type of bias in artificial intelligence algorithms). It's our mission as educators to harness technology in a positive way that doesn't exacerbate existing inequities—especially for our students who have been historically marginalized. But one thing is for sure: teachers will always be important—not only in the role of seeking to facilitate learning opportunities and mentorship but acting as an ethical decision-maker and an important human context in an ever-evolving technological landscape.

The most successful approaches to the integration of AI into math classrooms will find a happy medium between the benefits of technological innovation with the values of human-centered education. As research and practice develop, there must be thoughtful, collaborative approaches to realize the potential of AI in math education, while maintaining the integrity, equity, and quality of learning for students now and in the future.

This Q-methodological study systematically explored math teacher candidates' perspectives on AI in mathematics education. The methodology created a rich Q-set, gathered data from Q-sorts, and analyzed them by mean scores, PCA, and qualitative information to delineate and describe perspectives—simultaneous excitement for the potential of AI visuals and ambivalence regarding the effects on human relationships, empathy, and critical thinking. The methodology can offer a strong basis to the findings of the study, and inform suggestions for thoughtful integration of AI's possibilities into mathematics education.

METHODOLOGY

This research applied Q-methodology to explore the beliefs of 10 math teacher candidates about the relevance of artificial intelligence (AI) to mathematics education. Q method is great for looking at deep belief systems as it mixes both talking and number-based ways to show what people think (Brown, 1980; Stephenson, 1953). Q-methodology employs a mixed-methods approach consisting of qualitative methods to connect with participants' subjective beliefs quantitatively, and it is best suited to highlight common perspectives within the group by asking participants to rank a set of statements (Q-sorting). At each of the steps, quantitative approaches such as principal component analysis were utilized to highlight different beliefs toward AI in teaching mathematics.

The study consisted of 10 math teacher candidates who were purposefully chosen to participate due to their involvement in the field of mathematics education and potential as future educators. These teacher candidates will likely be in a teacher education program and have different experiences with AI technologies. The use of convenience sampling presumes the participants are motivated to participate in the study and fit within the scope of the research, which provided a small but specific subset of participants who will have experiences to share on learning and potentially demonstrate mathematical practices/methods for the integration of AI in the classroom.

A Q-set of 40 statements were designed to reflect a variety of perspectives on the role of AI in mathematics education. The statements were developed from a detailed review of the existing literature about AI, specifically themes related to visualization, the interactions between teacher and students, the ethics of AI, and the focus on skill development questions. Informal consultations with educators and AI experts refined and reworked the statements in the statement pool, considering what statements would be of most relevance and those likely to show the broadest range of opinions. A pilot test with representatives from both groups confirmed the wording and breadth of the statements. Therefore, the final Q-set comprised of 40 statements was organized, accounting for AI's pedagogical value, risks, and implications for education. Each statement was then translated into English.

The data collection for this study utilized the method of Q-sorting. In the Q-sorting process participants ranked the 40 statements within a forced distribution grid that allowed participants to specify their level of agreement with a statement by assigning a score on a scale of -4 (most disagree) to +4 (most agree). The grid was quasi-normal distribution, which means the forced assigned scores had to identify what statements they agreed or disagreed with the most. Participants were given instructions regarding the purpose of the study, how to sort the statements, and that they were not really correct or incorrect answers. Each participant sorted the statements, either a physical or digital grid, and the ranking for each statement was operationalized numerically as rows and columns identifying the assigned score.

The Q-sort data analysis employed a mixed-methods approach to identify collective perspectives and their implications. The quantitative stage began with computing a mean score for each statement across the 10 participants, followed by an analysis of overall agreement or disagreement. In line with established Q-methodology standards (Watts & Stenner, 2012), the top five and bottom five statements (based on mean scores) were highlighted as most representative of consensus or divergence. To reduce dimensionality, all rankings were subjected to Principal Components Analysis (PCA), a widely applied procedure in Q-method studies (Brown, 1980). PCA eigenvalues greater than 1.0 and factors explaining at least 40–50% of the variance were retained, in line with methodological conventions. The two-dimensional factor solution was plotted on a bi-axial scatter plot titled, "Q-Method PCA: Distribution of Statements in Factor Space," with Factor 1 and Factor 2 representing broad shared perspectives. Standardized z-scores (±1.00 as a common threshold for distinguishing salient items) were calculated for each statement to indicate stronger associations with one factor over another. Factor 1 was labelled "AI enthusiasts, but apprehensive about human depth and interaction," whereas Factor 2 was labelled "defenders of human interaction, personalized supporters of AI."

The qualitative stage complemented these results by thematically analyzing participant comments recorded during the sorting process, especially around extreme rankings (most agreed/disagreed statements). This step ensured that quantitative findings were contextualized with participant reasoning, thereby strengthening interpretation.

To maximize rigor and reproducibility, the Q-set was carefully constructed to represent a balance of viewpoints while minimizing bias, following guidelines by Watts and Stenner (2012). Standardized instructions were used to reduce procedural variance. PCA and z-score calculations were performed using established Q-methodology software (e.g., PQMethod 2.35; Schmolck, 2014), which automatically reports eigenvalues, explained variance, and correlation matrices. Triangulation was achieved by combining mean score analysis, PCA loadings, and qualitative thematic analysis, thereby enhancing validity and credibility.

Ethical safeguards included obtaining informed consent, ensuring anonymity in reporting, and maintaining voluntary participation without incentives. Limitations include the small sample size (a common feature in Q-method studies, which are designed for depth rather than breadth), the inherently subjective nature of Q-sorting, and potential cultural/educational background effects, which were not fully captured.

FINDINGS

Q-Methodological Analysis: Artificial Intelligence in Mathematics Education

This response elaborates on and renders the results of a Q-methodological analysis that examined perceptions of artificial intelligence (AI) in mathematics education. The analysis used Q-sort data collection technique involving 10 participants who ranked 40 statements related to AI's role in mathematics education from -4 (most disagree) to +4 (most agree). By calculating the mean Q-scores per statement we can see the group's collective view focusing on the five statements they agreed the most and the five statements they disagreed the most. In the following, we provide a fuller account, interpretation, and implications of the results.

Overview of the Q-Sort Data

40 statements on various issues such as AI in mathematics education, the use of AI to support interactions with students, ethical issues, and the potential for AI to substitute for more traditional ways when working with students.

10 mathematics teacher candidates rated all 40 statements against the scale of agreement to disagreement.

The ranking scale for the statements ranged from -4 to 0 (representing neutral) to +4. The mean for each statement was calculated by taking an average of all 10 people's scores to compare the group's stance on AI in mathematics education.

RESULTS

Most Agreed-Upon Statements

The top five statements with the highest mean scores reflect the ideas that participants most strongly endorsed. These statements highlight both the perceived benefits of AI and significant concerns about its limitations.

Table 1. Top 5 Most Agreed-Upon Statements

Statement Number	Statement (English Translation)	Mean Score
5	AI applications cannot replace face-to-face interaction with a teacher.	2.8
21	AI helps visualize abstract mathematical concepts, making them easier to understand.	2.5
8	Accepting AI-proposed solutions without questioning can make students passive.	2.2
24	Over-reliance on AI weakens my own problem-solving skills.	1.9
26	AI-based courses reduce collaboration with classmates.	1.6

Interpretation of Most Agreed-Upon Statements

This indicator ("AI applications cannot replace having face-to-face interaction with a teacher") received the highest level of agreement among participants, which was evidenced by a mean score of 2.8. This indicates that there was widespread agreement that human interaction with human teachers is critical in mathematics education. Participants, in large part educators and stakeholders, appreciate the multifaceted role that teachers fulfill during both instructional and non-instructional time that go beyond aspects of instruction or teaching. For example, human teachers are able to provide personalized feedback, emotional encouragements, and inspire motivation that artificial intelligence, despite its technological advancement, cannot offer because it lacks empathy and human interactions. This overwhelming support for human engagement demonstrates the view that human interactions and relationships are an essential building block of learning, particularly in mathematics. Knowledge and understanding necessarily depend on relationships, through conversation or dialogue, with other people. Therefore, as useful as AI can be to support the educational process, it is not seen as a replacement for teaching, but simply as a supplementary tool. This provides clear evidence that people support the concept of blended learning models, where learners may use AI in the educational experience, but nothing can replace face-to-face engagement with human teachers, including most of the relational aspects that result in growth and understanding.

The mean score of 2.5 on the statement “AI makes abstract mathematical concepts easier to visualize, which helps students understand them better” reveals that participants strongly endorsed the idea that AI could facilitate better learning in mathematics via visualization. Abstract concepts such as geometric proofs, algebraic functions, or calculus concepts can be difficult to understand, particularly for those students who do not relate to a traditional mathematical explanation that is clearly defined textually or symbolically. AI can take these abstract concepts through providing visual representations using interactive graphs, 3D models, or dynamic simulations and turn them into concrete concepts. This finding indicates a strong awareness of the potential of AI to support different learners that might benefit from a visual understanding rather than abstract reasoning (i.e., students who relate better to the visual skill consideration). Essentially, AI can take something complex and increase its explicitness through visualization to assist student outcomes. Ultimately, this means that using AI could enhance students' mathematics learning, particularly about those students who might disengage otherwise, and thus increase the reach and inclusiveness of mathematics education.

The perceived “Accepting solutions AI suggests without question makes students passive” received a mean score of 2.2, which illustrates a clear area of concern for participants with the possibility of over reliance on AI in learning. In mathematics education, which is heavily reliant on critical thinking and working through problems actively, the fear expressed is that students will be become passive consumers of AI produced solutions rather than active thinkers working through problem themselves. The concern is compounded by the speed and ease with which AI is able to output a correct solution, often veering students away from investigating the important concepts relevant to the problem and ultimately developing their thinking capabilities and validating answers. Participants tend to favour inquiry processes equally to inquiry outcomes, which suggests perhaps that educational experiences should focus more heavily on exploration which can then lead to deeper understanding rather than simply on efficiency. In order to realize this quite logical expectation behaviourally, teaching staff must encourage students to not only question outputs of AI, but to also use those outputs as starting points for discussion, analysis and investigation. The implication seems apparent: that while the teacher can rely on AI to make their tasks easier, the teacher's behaviour in terms of integrating AI in ways that reinforce critical thinking should remain a fundamental part of the learning experience.

The item “Over-reliance on AI weakens my own problem-solving skills,” scored a mean of 1.9. This rating indicates a very common fear; the fear that using AI too much would undercut an overarching goal of mathematics teaching in particular:

independent problem-solving. In fact, participants see problem-solving broadly as not just a mathematical skill, but more broadly as a life skill, which is essential for critical thinking and creativity. There is fear that if students continually go to AI to find answers—whether that be homework, proofs, or computations—they miss a key piece of developing persistence and analytical ability when using no technological support to challenge them. This points to the essential balance; AI can support but cannot do the heavy lifting required to learn mathematics. The implication is that when designing AI tools, we hope aide the development of skill—perhaps allowing students to explain their reasoning or to solve a problem step-by-step—the software allows the student to develop independent thinking, rather than just supplanting it altogether.

The response of "AI-based courses lead to less collaboration with classmates," with a mean of 1.6, is an important caution regarding the possible isolating nature of AI-based education. Participants value the social aspect of learning and the value of collaborating with peers as part of their learning, both from an understanding of mathematics perspective and from the perspective of gaining important soft skills (e.g., communication, teamwork, collaborative solving of problems), which are often valued in real-world situations. AI-based courses, particularly self-paced AI-based courses, are generally designed for learners to progress at their own pace and can create an isolating learning experience for students by limiting collaborative opportunities with their classmates. The moderate agreement level suggests while the concern is real, it may not be as strongly felt as other concerns, I believe it is still an important consideration. To address this concern, AI platforms will need to incorporate collaborative components, such as virtual group projects, peer review opportunities, and discussion forums so that students can engage with and benefit from the perspectives and supports of their classmates. The expectation is that technology will not replace the social aspects of education, but rather enhance them, and the same peer-to-peer richness of education can be preserved.

The most widely accepted statements from this Q-methodological analysis were related to a balanced and nuanced appreciation for AI's role in mathematics education. All participants viewed their appreciation for incorporating AI into their learning experiences positively, especially with AI-enhanced visualizations that improved the learning experience by making abstract ideas tangible. Nonetheless, there was a notable wariness and understanding of the downsides: the irreplaceable function of a human teacher, the need for critical thinking and problem-solving, and the necessity of collaboration (in many forms) among students. Our findings offer a clear urging for integration—AI may be integrated to complement traditional education, but must enhance and not take away the experience that undermines current human education and its best values of knowing. There is a vision for the future of added technology, and more importantly, communication – between that and the intention related to the professional form of human mathematics education.

Most Disagreed-Upon Statements

The five statements with the lowest mean scores represent the ideas that participants least accepted. These statements revealed many participants' ideas about limitations or inappropriate use in AI in mathematics education.

Table 2. Top 5 Most Disagreed-Upon Statements

Statement Number	Statement (English Translation)	Mean Score
23	AI should completely replace standard textbooks.	-3.0
38	AI should consider cultural differences in mathematics teaching.	-2.3
16	AI tools add extra workload to the teacher's lesson planning.	-1.8
30	Time spent on AI-supported platforms is more productive than traditional studying.	-1.5
39	In the future, AI literacy will be mandatory for math teachers.	-1.3

An examination of the statements with the greatest amount of disagreement indicates a clear preference for traditional educational materials and a cautious appraisal of the role AI could play in mathematics education. For Statement 23, "AI should take the place of standard textbooks," participants had the greatest disagreement with a mean of -3.0 in the dataset. This finding reflects the degree in which participants value a textbook as an established, systematic, and comprehensive resource, attributes they perceive AI currently does not offer in depth and coherence. The overwhelming consensus is not to envisage AI as simply replacing textbooks, but instead, participants advocated for an additive process, for example, augmenting the textbook with interactive activities or digital functions that exist within the CE framework to enrich learning without taking away from a trusted medium.

The case was similar in relation to Statement 38, "AI should recognize cultural differences in teaching mathematics," which was rated to be hugely contentious responder had a mean score of -2.3. Participants probably regard mathematics as a universal subject based on objective principles, while disciplines like history or literature may be viewed with more concern for cultural context. Disagreement with this statement suggests that AI tools in mathematics may produce culturally neutral content to be standardized. Favoring clarity and authenticity in mathematics education, AI has the potential to strengthen at least a degree of standardization and consistency based on the universal nature of mathematics, and avoid unique differences based on cultural contexts.

In comparison to concern for added teacher consultants, Statement 16 ("AI tools add to the teacher's workload during lesson planning"), participants rated AI tools positively based on a mean score of -2.3 in terms of the release in lesson planning. Participants perceived how AI could save time in tasks such as creating practice problems for students and monitoring student progress, suggesting that AI could create efficiencies by allowing teachers to engage finitely more effort into the instruction and the students - and improving their unit of KARMA.

Skepticism resurfaced in Statement 30, "Time spent on AI-supported platforms is more productive than traditional, face-to-face studying," with an average score of -1.5. Participants questioned whether AI platforms are any more productive than standard practices like lectures, textbooks, or group study, and whether they add more depth to learning. This skepticism corresponds to a wider hesitancy to overstate the value of AI, and suggests a preferred stance in which AI canbe acknowledged while simultaneously keeping AI's contribution into perspective along with existing traditional practices to ensure it results in true and meaningful learning.

Finally, in Statement 39, "In the future to teach math teachers will have to have AI literacy," participants reported a mean score of -1.3. The participants resisted the idea of putting technological skills above pedagogical delivery. They acknowledged AI was present and that technology is here to stay, but stressed that "old fashioned" pedagogical abilities along with subject expertise were more important than technology in delivering math content effectively. Overall, by emphasizing the idea that AI literacy might be a useful OPTIONAL curriculum enhancement skill, but not a require capability, participants expressed a view that in math teaching and learning, technology should serve as an enhancement not as a replacement to "traditional" qualifications of a math teacher.

Overall, these disagreements indicate a conservative stance regarding AI in mathematics education. Participants were consistently more favorable to traditional source materials such as textbooks, expressed doubts about AI's potential productivity and transformational claims, and resisted adapting AI to cultural contexts or requiring related adapted skills of teachers. The inclination toward an established tradition, even while cautiously experimenting with AI as a supplement instead of a potentially transformative replacement, is clear.

The PCA Diagram and Results

The PCA scatter plot, titled "Q-Method PCA: Distribution of Statements in Factor Space," provides a glimpse into a Q-study concerning attitudes towards artificial intelligence (AI) in mathematics teaching. This diagram plots out 38 statements along an x-axis labeled Factor 1 (-10.0 to 10.0) and a y-axis labeled Factor 2 (-6.0 to 6.0). Each statement is represented on the plot by an orange "x" with a corresponding number from 1 to 38, and the x's location reflects how participants ranked the statement in their Q-sorts, wherein individuals sort statements into a distribution along a continuum based on their agreement or disagreement with the statement. The PCA process examines the various rankings to reveal common perspectives (factors) between participants. The section interprets and expands the diagram to provide additional insights in combination with the factor analysis and summary of participant perspectives to discuss educators and stakeholders perceptions of the role of AI in mathematics education.

Figure 1. Q method PCA

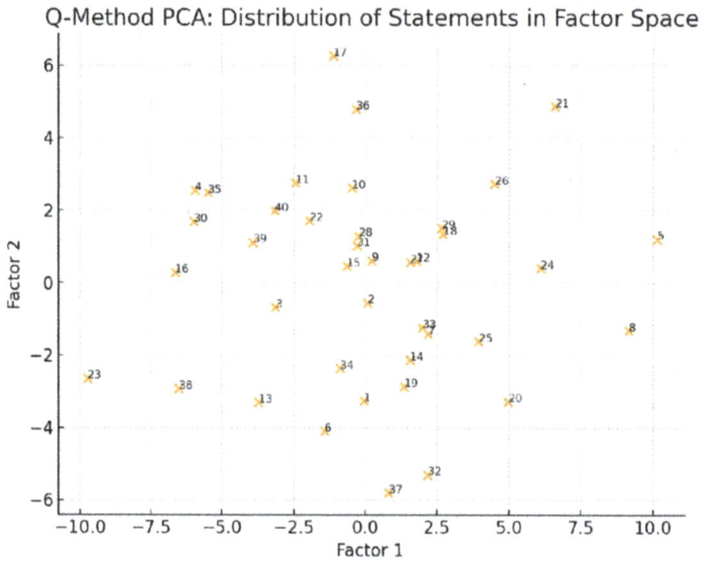

Understanding the PCA Diagram

PCA identifies different perspectives and viewpoints within Q-methodology through analyzing statement rankings, composite factor analysis reveals that factors represent the opinions of groups or individuals with related perspectives, and the loadings of factors represent the extent to which the statements map on positive or negative association in relation to shared perspectives. Statements farther from the "origin" or (0,0) define a factor clearly, while statements closer to the origin are more neutral or consensual, therefore they provide a representation or visual map of preferences and attitudes toward AI in education.

Factor 1: AI Enthusiasts, But Cautious About Depth and Human Interaction

Factor 1 (X-axis) represents "'AI enthusiasts, but cautious about depth and the need for human interaction." This group sees the potential for motivation, future horizon, objective nature, and multimedia enhancement of AI, yet unsure about surface level learning, dangers of being passive in learning, and replacing human educators. The also cited systematic factors leaving confused about the system to be maintained by AI.

Table 3. Factor 1 Defining Statements

	Statement Num	Z-Score	Statement Summary
1	4	1.82	AI makes my study process more motivating.
2	17	1.80	AI will make math lessons more attractive in the future.
3	35	1.69	Maintenance and updating of AI-based systems are challenging for institutions.
4	11	1.35	AI evaluates my mistakes more objectively than a human teacher.
5	36	1.33	AI enriches learning materials visually and audibly.

Table 4. Factor 1 Defining Statements continued

Rank	Statement Num	Z-Score	Statement Summary
1	37	-1.86	AI tools direct students to answers rather than deep learning.
2	8	-1.83	Accepting AI solutions without question may make students passive.
3	32	-1.67	AI is of limited benefit in teaching advanced math topics.
4	20	-1.55	Automatic AI graders can harm students if they produce errors.
5	5	-1.18	AI applications cannot replace face-to-face teacher interaction.

Factor 1, illustrated along the X-axis, exemplifies the perspective of "AI Enthusiasts, but Worried About Shallow Learning and Human Interaction." These people are excited about AI because it motivates students, makes math lessons exciting, evaluates students objectively, and supports students' learning through multimedia. However, they are concerned that AI promotes shallow learning in students, makes them passive, and that it will never take the place of human teachers. They also acknowledge institutional obstacles to maintaining the AI. The statements that defines

Factor 1's viewpoint are centered around priority to Study Least: AI makes studying more motivating to students (Statement 4, Z-Score 1.82), it is going to make math lessons more exciting in the future (Statement 17, Z-Score 1.80), that institutions have to maintain and update (Statement 35, Z-Score 1.69), evaluates mistakes more objectively - AI is less biased than human teachers (Statement 11, Z-Score 1.35), and that it enhanced the visual and audial qualities of learning materials (Statement 36, Z-Score 1.33).

Conversely, this group doesn't believe AI tools support deep learning, merely guiding students to answers (Statement 37, Z-Score -1.86), suggests that unquestioned solutions provided by AI could make students passive (Statement 8, Z-Score -1.83), questioned AI's ability to teach advanced math topics (Statement 32, Z-Score -1.67), warns errant automatic AI graders can harm students (Statement 20, Z-Score -1.55), and believes AI cannot replace face-to-face teacher-student interaction (Statement 5, Z-Score -1.18). In summary, this perspective reflects a balanced positive belief in AI's potential in education, while at the same time believing the need exists for deep learning and human interaction, and being aware of pragmatic challenges of implementation.

Factor 2: Human Interaction Defenders, Personalized AI Supporters

Factor 2 (Y-axis) represents "Human Interaction Defenders, Personal AI Supported." It emphasizes a need to prioritize human teachers, supports personalized AI adaptations, and values reducing achievement gaps and cultural considerations, however, they have skepticism surrounding AI's objectivity, benefits of creativity, and the possibility of infrastructure.

Table 5. Factor 2 Defining Statements

Rank	Statement Num	Z-Score	Statement Summary
1	5	1.68	AI applications cannot replace face-to-face teacher interaction.
2	1	1.59	AI adapts math learning to my individual needs.
3	13	1.44	AI-based learning reduces achievement gaps among students.
4	38	1.39	AI should consider cultural differences in math teaching.
5	34	1.06	Data-driven adaptivity improves exam performance.

Table 6. Factor 2 Defining Statements continued

Rank	Statement Num	Z-Score	Statement Summary
1	28	-2.21	Thanks to AI, teachers can spend more time on creative strategies.
2	11	-1.82	AI evaluates my mistakes more objectively than a human teacher.
3	37	-1.71	AI tools direct students to answers rather than deep learning.
4	14	-1.62	Weak internet infrastructure makes AI-based lessons inefficient.
5	16	-1.51	AI tools add extra workload to lesson planning.

Factor 2, shown on the Y-axis, is the viewpoint of "Human Interaction Defenders, Personalized AI Supporters" - these individuals prioritize acknowledging the pricelessness of human teachers, while at the same time, engage in the functionality of AI as a means for personalized learning, as well as a means of reducing achievement gaps in math education. They express skepticism towards the ability of AI to provide more objectivity, the ability to truly foster creativity within the learning process and its ability to provide the infrastructure to support the learning process. The defining statements for Factor 2 showcase its priorities: that AI cannot substitute the experience of face-to-face interaction with a teacher (Statement 5, Z-Score 1.68), that math learning must be adaptive to individuals (Statement 1, Z-Score 1.59), that it helps to reduce educational gaps (Statement 13, Z-Score 1.44), it needs to be culturally sensitive (Statement 37, Z-Score 1.39), and it finds the adaptivity will help improve exam performance by using data to inform adaptation (Statement 34, Z-Score 1.06). Factor 2 also disagrees that AI will allow teachers to use more creative strategies (Statement 28, Z-Score -2.21), that it objectively evaluates mistakes (Statement 11, Z-Score -1.82), or actually promotes deep learning (Statement 37, Z-Score -1.71), as well as expresses concern about the weak internet infrastructure (Statement 14, Z-Score -1.62) and the large amount of extra work (Statement 16, Z-Score -1.51). Here, these statements are positioned in proximity to one another. On the teacher-centered aspect on the right (Factor 1; 5.0 - 7.5) are statements such as 17 (7.5, 6.0) and 5 (7.5, 2.0), focusing on human interaction, while the left aspect (Factor 1: -2.0 to -5.0) includes statements like 23 (-2.0, -2.0) and 37 (-5.0; 6.0), which highlight openness to the use of AI but with a sense of risk. Although the top statements convey a sense of optimism or 'good' associated with AI's benefits, the bottom statements, including 32 at -5.0, -6.0, illustrate some sort of hesitancy or caution. There are statements that are publicly neutral, located near the origin, including Statement 2 (0.0, 0.0) that illustrate broader values that may be shared such as the promotion of 'critical thinking'. Within this analysis, we see areas of agreement with respect to values associated with human interaction (right-side of the diagram) and agreeing with the risk of AI overstepping its usefulness (bottom left); it seems we agree when we say Factor 1 will favour tradition, or Factor 2 will balance innovation with caution! Overall, the diagram illustrates that there are mostly teacher-centered perspectives, a small portion of folks that are open to using AI, and seen a muddled optimism and caution, and some consensus on an overall regard to core educational values.

DISCUSSION

This study, using a Q-methodology approach, reveals a careful negotiation between excitement about the use of artificial intelligence (AI) in math instruction and a worry about protecting key human aspects of teaching. These findings align well with existing research, which acknowledges AI's ability to improve learning but also warns against becoming overly dependent on it and losing the human connection.

A common idea among those involved in the study was that human teachers are indispensable, especially for providing emotional encouragement, inspiration, and a connection to social and cultural contexts. This viewpoint is consistent with the arguments made by Fitria (2023) and Nikitina and Ishchenko (2024), who emphasize that AI cannot duplicate the empathy and social awareness of teachers. Similarly, Shen and Su (2020) argue that the humanistic roles of teachers become even more important as AI is used more widely. This supports the overall agreement in the study that AI should enhance, rather than replace, in-person teaching.

However, participants also strongly supported AI's ability to help students understand complex math ideas visually. This echoes the results of Torres-Peña et al. (2024) and Canonigo (2024), who show that smart tutoring systems and adaptable visualization tools can greatly improve understanding and motivation in math. These results suggest that future teachers see AI as a tool to improve teaching, particularly in making challenging concepts easier to grasp. This is consistent with research showing small but meaningful improvements in performance when AI is used to provide personalized feedback (Yi et al., 2024).

Despite the promising aspects, some notable concerns also arose. Worries about students becoming too passive and losing their ability to solve problems reflect a wider concern in academic research that AI could hinder independent thought (Choi, 2022; Gao et al., 2024). Participants also feared that AI might negatively impact teamwork among students, aligning with research by Zakaria et al. (2024), who suggest that AI-driven individualized learning could reduce social interaction unless collaboration is specifically designed into the learning environment. This highlights the need for future AI tools to be carefully integrated with teaching methods that encourage investigation and teamwork to preserve the social and critical aspects of learning math.

Disagreement with the idea of AI replacing textbooks or automatically improving productivity also suggests a leaning towards familiar teaching methods. The value participants placed on textbooks as reliable and consistent resources mirrors the findings of Park and Lim (2023), who found that educators often prefer combining AI with traditional materials rather than replacing them entirely. Similarly, hesitation about making AI literacy mandatory for all teachers indicates a preference for prioritizing teaching skills over purely technical abilities, supporting Bekdemir's (2024) argument that teacher training should focus on the ethical and educational integration of AI rather than just technical expertise.

The factor analysis further supports these ideas, identifying two main viewpoints: one group is enthusiastic about AI but cautious about its impact on in-depth learning and human connection, while the other champions human interaction and supports personalized AI. This division reflects broader debates within the field, between those who see AI primarily as a tool for motivation and adaptation (Fu, 2024; Hossein-Mohand et al., 2025) and those who insist that human relationships, inclusivity, and cultural sensitivity remain essential (Heeg & Avraamidou, 2024; Adeniyi et al., 2024). Importantly, both groups agree that AI is most effective as a tool to support teachers, rather than replace them.

Overall, these findings support the growing academic agreement that AI in mathematics education should be implemented in a balanced, fair, and ethical manner. As the study participants emphasized, AI has the potential to make math more accessible, interesting, and personalized, but only if its use is guided by thoughtful teaching practices, attention to social interaction, and an understanding of the essential role of human teachers.

CONCLUSION

This research suggests that when incorporating AI into math education, we should take a careful, focused, and sensible approach, keeping in mind how future teachers feel about it.

Firstly, since most participants strongly believed that AI can't take the place of human interaction, math teacher training programs should clearly present AI tools as tools to help, not replace, traditional classroom teaching. Training sessions can show future teachers how to use what AI provides—like visuals or automatic feedback—to start discussions, encourage exploration, and ask important questions, rather than treating them as the final answers.

Secondly, considering that participants saw the benefit of AI in showing abstract math ideas, those creating AI tools and educators should focus on AI applications that improve understanding through lively representations. They should also include ways for students to question and double-check what the AI produces. This addresses concerns about students becoming too passive and losing problem-solving skills.

Thirdly, because participants thought AI-based lessons might decrease teamwork, AI platforms should be used in ways that keep and even improve student interaction. For example, AI-powered tasks could be combined with group talks, looking for errors together, or having students review each other's work. This would ensure that the social and communication aspects of learning math are not lost.

Finally, the doubts about AI replacing textbooks and the hesitation about requiring AI literacy for everyone suggest a gradual and cautious approach is best. Educators and leaders should promote a mix of resources—like textbooks improved with AI-generated examples or feedback—and see AI literacy as a chance for professional development for teachers, rather than a mandatory skill for everyone. In conclusion, the recommendations from this study all point to the same idea: AI should make math education better by enhancing, not reducing, the human, collaborative, and critical-thinking elements.

REFERENCES

Abhulimen, A., & Ejike, O. (2024). Ethical considerations in AI use for SMEs and supply chains: Current challenges and future directions. *International Journal of Applied Research in Social Sciences.* https://doi.org/DOI: 10.51594/ijarss.v6i8.1391

Abimbola, C., Eden, C., Chisom, O., & Adeniyi, I. (2024). *Integrating AI in education: Opportunities, challenges, and ethical considerations.* Magna Scientia Advanced Research and Reviews., DOI: 10.30574/msarr.2024.10.2.0039

Adeniyi, I., Edeni, C., & Adeleye, O. (2024). *The role of AI-enhanced tools in overcoming socioeconomic barriers in education: A conceptual analysis.* World Journal of Advanced Research and Reviews., DOI: 10.30574/wjarr.2024.21.3.0780

Adesoga, T., Ojo, C., Obani, O., Nwafor, K., & Rasul, O. (2024). *AI integration in business development: Ethical considerations and practical solutions.* GSC Advanced Research and Reviews., DOI: 10.30574/gscarr.2024.20.1.0282

Babur, M. N. (2025). AI in education: A luxury or a necessity for developing nations? *Journal of Biological and Allied Health Sciences, 5*(1), 1–2. DOI: 10.56536/jbahs.v5i1.111

Bekdemir, Y. (2024). The urgency of AI integration in teacher training: Shaping the future of education. *Journal of Research in Didactical Sciences.* https://doi.org/DOI: 10.51853/jorids/15485

Bork, D., Ali, S., & Roelens, B. (2023). Conceptual modeling and artificial intelligence: A systematic mapping study. *arXiv.* https://doi.org//arXiv.2303.06758DOI: 10.48550

Brown, S. R. (1980). *Political subjectivity: Applications of Q methodology in political science.* Yale University Press.

Bulut, O., & Wongvorachan, T. (2022). *Feedback generation through artificial intelligence.* The Open/Technology in Education, Society, and Scholarship Association Conference., DOI: 10.18357/otessac.2022.2.1.125

Bushuyev, S. D., Bushuyev, S. D., Igbal, A. B., & Elams, C. (2024). The AI revolution in IT education: Революция искусственного интеллекта в ИТ-образовании. *International Journal of Information and Communication Technology, 5*(2[18]), 8–22. DOI: 10.54309/IJICT.2024.18.2.001

Canonigo, A. (2024). Levering AI to enhance students' conceptual understanding and confidence in mathematics. *Journal of Computer Assisted Learning*, *40*, 3215–3229. DOI: 10.1111/jcal.13065

Choi, I. (2022). *Exploring teaching and learning methods using artificial intelligence (AI) in the mathematics classroom: Focusing on the development of middle school statistic scenarios*. Korean School Mathematics Society., DOI: 10.30807/ksms.2022.25.2.003

Evenddy, S. (2024). *Investigating AI's automated feedback in English language learning*. FLIP Foreign Language Instruction Probe., DOI: 10.54213/flip.v3i1.401

Fitria, T. (2023). The use of artificial intelligence in education (AIED): Can AI replace the teacher's role? *Epigram (e-journal)*. https://doi.org/DOI: 10.32722/epi.v20i2.5711

Fu, A. (2024). *Investigation of recent advances related to AI in mathematics education*. Applied and Computational Engineering., DOI: 10.54254/2755-2721/37/20230476

Gao, W., Gao, S., Malomo, O., Allagan, J., Eyob, E., Challa, C., & Su, J. (2024). Exploring the interplay between AI and human logic in mathematical problem-solving. *Online Journal of Applied Knowledge Management*. https://doi.org/DOI: 10.36965/ojakm.2024.12(1)73-93

Garrido, A. (2012). AI and mathematical education. *Education Sciences*, *2*, 22–32. DOI: 10.3390/EDUC2010022

Ge, S. (2024). The contribution of AI to the development of teaching. *Transactions on Economics. Business and Management Research*, *8*, 85–87. DOI: 10.62051/0ckgra56

Gillani, N., Eynon, R., Chiabaut, C., & Finkel, K. (2023). Unpacking the "black box" of AI in education. *arXiv*. https://arxiv.org/abs/2301.01602

Harry, A. (2023). Role of AI in education. [INJURITY]. *Interdisciplinary Journal and Humanity*, *2*(3), 260–268. DOI: 10.58631/injurity.v2i3.52

Heeg, D., & Avraamidou, L. (2024). Young children's understanding of AI. *Education and Information Technologies*. Advance online publication. DOI: 10.1007/s10639-024-13169-x

Herb, A., & Lloyd, C. (2024). *The future of feedback*. ASCILITE Publications., DOI: 10.14742/apubs.2024.1386

Hossein-Mohand, H., Hossein-Mohand, H., Albanese, V., & Del Carmen Olmos Gómez, M. (2025). AI in mathematics education: A bibliometric analysis of global trends and collaborations (2020–2024). *Eurasia Journal of Mathematics, Science and Technology Education*. Advance online publication. DOI: 10.29333/ejmste/15915

Inoferio, H., Espartero, M., Asiri, M., Damin, M., & Chavez, J. (2024). *Coping with math anxiety and lack of confidence through AI-assisted learning*. Environment and Social Psychology., DOI: 10.54517/esp.v9i5.2228

Islam, A. (2025). Ethical challenges and opportunities in AI-driven healthcare. *Journal of AI-Powered Medical Innovations*. https://doi.org/DOI: 10.60087/japmi.vol.03.issue.01.id.007

Jaakkola, H., Henno, J., Henno, J., Lahti, A., & Makela, J. (2020, September). Artificial intelligence and education. In *2020 43rd International Convention on Information, Communication and Electronic Technology (MIPRO)* (pp. xxx–xxx). IEEE. https://doi.org/DOI: 10.23919/MIPRO48935.2020.9245329

Karumbaiah, S., Borchers, C., Shou, T., Falhs, A., Liu, P., Nagashima, T., Rummel, N., & Aleven, V. (2023). A spatiotemporal analysis of teacher practices in supporting student learning and engagement in an AI-enabled classroom, 450–462. https://doi.org/DOI: 10.1007/978-3-031-36272-9_37

Kay, J. (2012). AI and education: Grand challenges. *IEEE Intelligent Systems*, *27*, 66–69.

Khazanchi, R., Di Mitri, D., & Drachsler, H. (2024). The effect of AI-based systems on mathematics achievement in rural context: A quantitative study. *Journal of Computer Assisted Learning*. Advance online publication. DOI: 10.1111/jcal.13098

Kuzminykh, I., Nawaz, T., Shenzhang, S., Ghita, B., Raphael, J., & Xiao, H. (2024). Personalised feedback framework for online education programmes using generative AI. *arXiv*. https://doi.org//arXiv.2410.11904DOI: 10.48550

Laverde Gonzalez, J. S., & Rodríguez Hernández, L. A. (2025). AI and education: Combination to enhance knowledge. *Seminars in Medical Writing and Education*, *4*, 37. DOI: 10.56294/mw202537

Lehmann, L. (2021). Ethical challenges of integrating AI into healthcare. *Artificial Intelligence in Medicine*. Advance online publication. DOI: 10.1007/978-3-030-58080-3_337-1

Mahamuni, A. P., & Tonpe, S. (2024). Enhancing educational assessment with artificial intelligence: Challenges and opportunities. *2024 International Conference on Knowledge Engineering and Communication Systems (ICKECS), 1,* 1–5. https://doi.org/DOI: 10.1109/ICKECS61492.2024.10616620

Mindzak, M. (2024). Beyond work: AI and educational labour. *Brock Education Journal, 33*(3). Advance online publication. DOI: 10.26522/brocked.v33i3.1174

Mishra, S. (2024). Transformative impact of AI on education: Personalizing learning and addressing challenges. *International Journal for Research in Applied Science and Engineering Technology, 12*(8), 1183–1190. https://www.ijraset.com

Naseri, R. N. N., & Abdullah, R. N. R. (2025). Transforming education with AI: Insights from developed countries. [IJRISS]. *International Journal of Research and Innovation in Social Science, 9*(3), 3877–3886. DOI: 10.47772/IJRISS.2025.90300308

Nazaretsky, T., Mejia-Domenzain, P., Swamy, V., Frej, J., & Käser, T. (2024). AI or human? Evaluating student feedback perceptions in higher education, 284–298. https://doi.org/DOI: 10.1007/978-3-031-72315-5_20

Nikitina, I., & Ishchenko, T. (2024). *The impact of AI on teachers: Support or replacement?* Scientific Journal of Polonia University., DOI: 10.23856/6511

Osasona, F., Amoo, O., Atadoga, A., Abrahams, T., Farayola, O., & Ayinla, B. (2024). *Reviewing the ethical implications of AI in decision making processes.* International Journal of Management & Entrepreneurship Research., DOI: 10.51594/ijmer.v6i2.773

Park, M., & Lim, W. (2023). AI-integrated mathematics education: A review of literature in the Korean context. *The Korean Society of Educational Studies in Mathematics – Journal of Educational Research in Mathematics.* https://doi.org/DOI: 10.29275/jerm.2023.33.3.771

Prajapati, S. (2025). *Ethical considerations in AI design and deployment.* World Journal of Advanced Research and Reviews., DOI: 10.30574/wjarr.2025.25.1.0270

Prasad, A. (2025, February). Role of AI in modern education. In *Transforming Knowledge: A Multidisciplinary Research on Integrative Learning Across Disciplines* (pp. xxx–xxx). https://doi.org/DOI: 10.51767/ic250459

Purwanto, A., Fauzan, M., Widya, T., & Azzaky, N. (2024). Ethical implications and challenges of AI implementation in business operations. *TechComp Innovations. Journal of Computer Science and Technology.* Advance online publication. DOI: 10.70063/techcompinnovations.v1i2.52

Ramakrishnan, S., Bishnoi, M., Joghee, S., Jijitha, S., & Kumar, A. (2024). Social engineering: Role of teachers in cohabitation of AI with education. *2024 2nd International Conference on Cyber Resilience (ICCR),* 1–6. https://doi.org/DOI: 10.1109/ICCR61006.2024.10532897

Roe, J., Perkins, M., Singapore, D., Vietnam, B., & V., V. (2024). Understanding student and academic staff perceptions of AI use in assessment and feedback. *arXiv.* https://doi.org/DOI: 10.70770/rzzz6y35

Salameh, W. (2025). *Exploring the impact of AI-driven real-time feedback systems on learner engagement and adaptive content delivery in education.* International Journal of Science and Research Archive., DOI: 10.30574/ijsra.2025.14.2.0299

Saputra, I., Kurniawan, A., Yanita, M., Putri, E., & Mahniza, M. (2024). *The evolution of educational assessment: How artificial intelligence is shaping the trends and future of learning evaluation.* The Indonesian Journal of Computer Science., DOI: 10.33022/ijcs.v13i6.4465

Schmolck, P. (2014). *PQMethod (Version 2.35) [Computer software].* http://schmolck.org/qmethod

Shah, K., Joshi, H., & Joshi, H. (2025). Integrating moral values in AI: Addressing ethical challenges for fair and responsible technology. *Journal of Informatics and Web Engineering.* https://doi.org/DOI: 10.33093/jiwe.2026.4.1.16

Shen, L., & Su, A. (2020). The changing roles of teachers with AI. In *Revolutionizing Education in the Age of AI and Machine Learning.* https://doi.org/DOI: 10.4018/978-1-5225-7793-5.ch001

Shukla, S. (2024). Principles governing ethical development and deployment of AI. *International Journal of Engineering Business Management.* Advance online publication. DOI: 10.22161/ijebm.8.2.5

Stephenson, W. (1953). *The study of behavior: Q-technique and its methodology.* University of Chicago Press.

Syifa, A. (2024). *Ethics in the age of AI: Principles and guidelines for responsible implementation in workplace.* International Journal of Advanced Technology and Social Sciences., DOI: 10.59890/ijatss.v2i2.1398

Taufikin, M., S., Azifah, N., Nikmah, F., Kuanr, J., & P., P. (2024). The impact of AI on teacher roles and pedagogy in the 21st century classroom. *2024 International Conference on Knowledge Engineering and Communication Systems (ICKECS), 1,* 1–5. https://doi.org/DOI: 10.1109/ICKECS61492.2024.10617236

Thakre, P., Niveditha, P., Jain, P., Soni, D., & Vishwakarma, M. (2023). *Exploring the ethical dimensions of AI in decision-making processes*. International Journal of Innovative Research in Computer and Communication Engineering., DOI: 10.15680/ijircce.2023.1110048

Torres-Peña, R., Peña-González, D., Chacuto-López, E., Ariza, E., & Vergara, D. (2024). Updating calculus teaching with AI: A classroom experience. *Education Sciences*. Advance online publication. DOI: 10.3390/educsci14091019

Trivedi, N. B. (2023). AI in education—a transformative force. *2023 1st DMIHER International Conference on Artificial Intelligence in Education and Industry 4.0 (IDICAIEI)*.

Truong, U. (2024). Writing classes in the AI era: Redefining English teachers' roles. *2024 6th International Workshop on Artificial Intelligence and Education (WAIE)*, 50–55. https://doi.org/DOI: 10.1109/WAIE63876.2024.00016

Wang, Y. (2024). Ethical considerations of AI in financial decision. *Computers and Artificial Intelligence*. Advance online publication. DOI: 10.59400/cai.v2i1.1290

Watts, S., & Stenner, P. (2012). Doing Q methodological research: Theory, method and interpretation. *Sage (Atlanta, Ga.)*.

Woolf, B. (2015). AI and education: Celebrating 30 years of marriage.

Yadav, I., & Bhardwaj, R. (2024). AI integrated model design for education system for analytical computation (mathematics). *2024 4th International Conference on Advance Computing and Innovative Technologies in Engineering (ICACITE)*, 1412–1417. https://doi.org/DOI: 10.1109/ICACITE60783.2024.10616503

Yakkala, K. (2024). *AI-powered assessment tools for e-learning: Enhancing feedback and grading systems*. World Journal of Advanced Engineering Technology and Sciences., DOI: 10.30574/wjaets.2024.13.1.0497

Yi, L., Liu, D., Jiang, T., & Xian, Y. (2024). The effectiveness of AI on K-12 students' mathematics learning: A systematic review and meta-analysis. *International Journal of Science and Mathematics Education*. Advance online publication. DOI: 10.1007/s10763-024-10499-7

Youn, C., Salam, A., & Rahman, A. (2025). *AI-driven tools in providing feedback on students' writing*. International Journal of Research and Innovation in Social Science., DOI: 10.47772/ijriss.2025.903sedu0006

Yu, S., & Lu, Y. (2021). Frontiers of AI in education. In *An Introduction to Artificial Intelligence in Education*.

Zakaria, R., Herwanis, D., Wahyuni, S., Abadi, A. S., Umar, A., Mandasari, L., Agama, I., & Takengon, I. (2024). *AI in English and math education: Bridging the gap between theory and practice*. Communications on Applied Nonlinear Analysis., DOI: 10.52783/cana.v31.1101

Zhang, J., & Zhang, Z. (2024). AI in teacher education: Unlocking new dimensions in teaching support, inclusive learning, and digital literacy. *Journal of Computer Assisted Learning*, *40*, 1871–1885. DOI: 10.1111/jcal.12988

KEY TERMS AND DEFINITIONS

Adaptive Learning Platforms: Educational technologies that analyze learners' progress and tailor content pacing, difficulty, and feedback accordingly.

AI Literacy: The knowledge, skills, and critical awareness needed to use, evaluate, and integrate AI technologies effectively and ethically in education.

Algorithmic Bias: Systematic errors in AI decision-making caused by biased training data, which may reinforce social inequities.

Artificial Intelligence (AI): Computer-based systems that simulate human intelligence to perform tasks such as problem-solving, reasoning, and adaptive learning.

Intelligent Tutoring Systems (ITS): AI-powered instructional systems that adapt learning materials and strategies to individual students' needs in real time.

Principal Component Analysis (PCA): A statistical technique used in Q-methodology to reduce data dimensionality and identify factors (shared perspectives) among participants.

Q-Methodology: A mixed-methods research approach combining qualitative and quantitative techniques to study subjective viewpoints by ranking statements (Q-sorting).

Visualization in Mathematics Education: The use of dynamic, often AI-enhanced tools (e.g., GeoGebra, ChatGPT) to transform abstract mathematical concepts into interactive and comprehensible visual representations.

Chapter 11
Using Artificial Intelligence in Primary School Mathematics Teaching

Adem Doğan
https://orcid.org/0000-0001-6952-7415
Faculty of Education, Kahramanmaraş Sütçü İmam University, Turkey

ABSTRACT

Artificial Intelligence (AI) is transforming primary school mathematics education by offering adaptive learning experiences, personalized instruction, and real-time feedback for students. AI-powered tools, automated assessment platforms, and data-driven learning analytics, enable teachers to address diverse student needs effectively. One of AI's key contributions is adaptive learning, where algorithms analyse student performance and adjust lesson complexity accordingly. AI enhances automated assessment, reducing teacher workload by providing instant feedback and identifying learning gaps. However, successful AI integration in primary mathematics education requires teacher training and ethical considerations, including data privacy and fair AI implementation. Teachers must be equipped with the necessary digital skills to effectively utilize AI tools while maintaining a balance between technology and human-centered pedagogy. AI has the potential to revolutionize primary mathematics education, making learning more inclusive, engaging, and effective for young learners.

DOI: 10.4018/979-8-3373-1998-8.ch011

INTRODUCTION

The acceleration of scientific and technological progress has a profound impact on educational and social systems. Information and technology play a pivotal role in the advancement of the educational process, while also contributing to the dynamism of the economy. The rapid evolution of information technology has led to profound changes in social structures and the emergence of information societies. In addition to monitoring the developments in science and technology that affect social order, it has become imperative to adapt these developments to the social sphere (Gurol, 1990). Another factor affecting social life is the rapid increase in the number of students. This situation has made it necessary to change the educational process and quality, and to integrate information technologies into educational environments. The integration of Artificial Intelligence (AI) in primary school mathematics education is an important area of research, emphasizing its capacity to enhance teaching methodologies, boost student engagement, and improve learning outcomes. AI technologies, particularly machine learning and interactive platforms, are increasingly being utilized to customize educational experiences to meet the diverse needs of students, thus fostering inclusive and effective learning environments.

AI applications in education can provide personalized learning experiences, which have proven beneficial in improving mathematical competencies among primary school students. For example, studies suggest that incorporating AI-driven tools, including learning management systems, facilitates personalized feedback and adaptive learning pathways tailored to individual student needs. This has been evidenced by the utilization of Google Apps for Education (GAFE), which proves effective in enhancing communication skills and supporting mathematics education for preservice teachers in primary settings. Additionally, research indicates that mobile learning technologies combined with AI can lead to applications designed to increase student engagement through customized problem-solving scenarios.

The motivation and confidence of students in mathematics is another critical area where AI can significantly contribute. Research has documented that students' self-concept and performance in mathematics are positively affected by interventions that enhance their competency beliefs, a factor especially crucial for marginalized groups, such as Indigenous students in Australia (Han, 2019).

Moreover, it is essential to recognize the role of teacher training and professional development in the effective use of AI technologies. The competencies of educators directly influence students' academic achievements (Saenz et al., 2023). As the educational landscape evolves with AI, professional development must focus on training teachers in both AI utilization and blended learning approaches that incorporate technology-enhanced instructional strategies. Addressing teachers' anxiety around teaching mathematics is also crucial, as it can adversely affect student performance.

AI is important in elementary school mathematics teaching for the following reasons. It supports individual learning and offers personalized content for each student. It develops mathematical thinking skills. It concretizes problem-solving and abstract concepts. It supports teachers and analyzes student data, saving time. It provides access to students from different regions through technology. It fosters digital skills: It encourages interaction with technology at an early age.

In this section, the benefits of AI in primary school mathematics education such as Personalized Learning, Instant Feedback and Assessment, Adaptive Learning, Interactive and Fun Learning, Data Analytics and Insights will be emphasized. In addition, Application Areas (Mathematics Applications and Games, Smart Tutoring Systems, Voice Assistants) and Challenges and Considerations (Accessibility, Data Privacy and Security, Teacher Education) will also be discussed.

BENEFITS OF USING AI IN PRIMARY SCHOOL

1. Personalized Learning

The integration of AI into primary school education offers numerous benefits, particularly in fostering personalized learning experiences. One of the most significant advantages of AI in educational settings is its capacity to tailor learning experiences to individual student needs. This capability is achieved through advanced algorithms that analyze a student's strengths and weaknesses, allowing the learning material to adapt accordingly. For instance, highlight the design of AI-based learning man agement systems that provide highly personalized learning experiences, adapting content to match each student's unique learning pace and style. Similarly, Jauhiainen and Guerra's study on the application of generative AI in classroom settings emphasizes that personalized learning can significantly enhance student engagement by tailoring content based on individual knowledge and interests (Jauhiainen & Guerra, 2023). This alignment between content and student abilities is crucial for optimizing learning outcomes.

Based in Ankara University in Türkiye, the website (https://solorota.com), which offers individualized teaching from primary school to the last grade of high school and even for university preparation, offers more than online education with curriculum-appropriate content. SoloRota is an AI-based digital learning platform specializing in educational technologies. Our comprehensive education solutions, ranging from primary school to high school, are developed with scientific pedagogical approaches and advanced technology integration. By analyzing students' individual learning styles and needs, the platform offers personalized education programs, optimizes academic performance and maximizes learning efficiency. Our data analytics system provides measurable results and transparently reports student progress to parents and educators. Our interactive learning methods increase student motivation and engagement, while our content, which is fully compatible with the Turkish National Education curriculum, supports exam success. With SoloRota, your students grow up as individuals who are equipped with the skills required by the digital age, academically equipped and ready for the future.

The significance of AI in promoting personalized learning outcomes is evidenced by the work of Agbong-Coates, which elucidates how the integration of tools like ChatGPT can substantially boost learning outcomes by aligning educational content with student preferences and learning styles (Agbong-Coates, 2024). Additionally, reinforce the importance of personalized content delivery in e-learning systems, demonstrating that AI-based adaptive learning systems can markedly improve student engagement and knowledge retention. By customizing educational experiences in this manner, AI holds the potential not only to improve academic performance but also to effectively address diverse learning needs.

2. Instant Feedback and Assessment

The integration of AI into elementary mathematics education has emerged as a transformative approach that fosters immediate feedback and assessment, significantly enhancing student learning experiences. These AI systems are designed to provide instant feedback, allowing students to recognize and correct errors promptly, which promotes a culture of continuous improvement in their mathematical skills.

Research indicates that the employment of AI in education can substantially bolster mathematics achievement among elementary students. A meta-analysis by Hwang highlights how AI-assisted learning tools can lead to measurable improvements in students' mathematics performance, illustrating its potential to positively affect educational outcomes during formative learning years (Hwang, 2022). Hidayat et al. also assert that the introduction of AI-based teaching methodologies can effectively enhance foundational mathematics education, suggesting that such systems improve both immediate learning outcomes and provide a framework for future success in mathematics (Hidayat et al., 2022).

Moreover, the adaptability of AI technologies allows for personalized learning experiences. Capinding discusses AI-driven tools, such as Photomath, that cater to individual learning needs by offering personalized tutorials and tailored exercises based on students' performance levels (Capinding, 2023). Such tools are essential for fostering an environment where students can engage with tasks suited to their capabilities, thus promoting greater engagement and reducing math anxiety.

Immediate feedback mechanisms are critical in maximizing learning retention and conceptual understanding in mathematics. The Immediate Feedback Assessment Technique (IFAT) has been shown to enhance the learning process through timely responses to students' inquiries, providing opportunities for reflection and correction (Gürkan, 2018). This aligns with findings from Sperling et al., which indicate that machine learning applications can facilitate individualized feedback, allowing educators to effectively address student misunderstandings during lessons (Sperling et al., 2022).

Furthermore, AI's role extends beyond mere calculation assistance; it plays a vital part in developing crucial problem-solving skills and mathematical reasoning. The use of visual learning environments, as identified by Gürefe et al., allows students to visualize complex mathematical concepts through AI-enhanced tools, thus supporting spatial reasoning and comprehension in geometry (Gürefe et al., 2024). This visual component is particularly beneficial as it caters to diverse learning styles and strengthens conceptual understanding through interactive engagement.

Another significant aspect is the positive correlation between teachers' attitudes towards AI and the effective implementation of these technologies in classrooms. Li and Noori's research substantiates that when teachers exhibit a favorable attitude towards AI, it significantly influences their intent to incorporate AI tools in their teaching practices, highlighting the importance of instructor preparedness and perception in the successful deployment of AI in educational settings.

3. Adaptive Learning

AI systems can monitor students' performance in real-time, allowing for dynamic adjustments in the difficulty of tasks and the customization of learning materials to fit individual abilities and needs. This adaptive learning framework not only makes learning more effective by catering to distinct learning rates but also fosters increased engagement by presenting relevant and appropriately challenging materials tailored for each student.

Recent studies emphasize the importance of contextual factors in facilitating AI adoption among teachers. For instance, Li and Noori indicate that contextual factors play a significant role in how primary mathematics teachers engage with AI tools, suggesting that supportive school environments can ease the integration process (Li & Noori, 2024). Consequently, adaptive learning environments driven by AI can significantly improve not only student learning outcomes but also teachers' instructional practices, allowing for more individualized and effective pedagogical approaches (Tashtoush et al., 2024).

Moreover, the relationship between teaching methodologies and AI integration becomes crucial, especially in early education where cognitive capacities are still developing. Teachers must adapt their instructional strategies to leverage AI capabilities, thereby utilizing the technology to foster mathematical understanding at a foundational level (Liu, 2023). Studies highlight that while traditional teaching styles may dominate, integrating differentiated methods paired with AI can activate student engagement and promote deeper comprehension of mathematical concepts (Jehlička & Rejsek, 2018).

The movement toward adaptive learning necessitates robust frameworks for continuous feedback and assessment. Tools enabled by AI not only provide real-time insights into student performance but also suggest modifications in instructional strategies based on data-driven analysis (Tashtoush et al., 2024). This adaptive framework can effectively enhance mathematical vocabulary and general comprehension by ensuring that learning activities resonate with students' current understanding and interest levels, thereby optimizing their educational journey.

4. Interactive and Entertaining Learning

The integration of AI-supported interactive tools in primary school mathematics education has been shown to enhance the learning experience by making it more engaging and enjoyable for students. AI-powered applications and games foster an environment where mathematics can be understood as a fun activity rather than a chore. This notion is supported by several studies that articulate the significance of realistic and child-friendly learning models in mathematics instruction.

One significant method is Realistic Mathematics Education (RME), which emphasizes the use of real-life contexts to aid students in understanding abstract mathematical concepts. The RME approach enables students to visualize and relate mathematical tasks to their everyday lives, creating a more engaging learning atmosphere. The application of RME has demonstrated effectiveness not only in improving students' mathematical problem-solving abilities but also in fostering independence during learning. The positive effects of contextual and relatable teaching methods align with findings that demonstrate increased motivation among students when learning mathematics through enjoyable and relatable frameworks (Nurhayati & Rasyid, 2019).

Furthermore, playful learning strategies, such as those incorporated in gamified educational apps, play a crucial role in enhancing students' motivation and interest in mathematics. The concept of gamification integrates elements of game design into educational settings, encouraging children to engage with mathematical concepts enthusiastically. Research highlights that gamified learning tools, like Quizizz, create a dynamic and interactive space where competition and cooperation take place, effectively boosting students' engagement and learning outcomes (Sundari & Hertuti, 2022). These technologies not only reduce the perception of mathematics as a challenging subject but also foster a collaborative learning environment where students can explore mathematical concepts interactively (Setiawan & Fitria, 2024).

5. Data Analytics and Insights

AI plays a transformative role in primary school mathematics education by providing teachers with critical data analytics and insights into student learning progress. This capability enables educators to implement tailored teaching strategies that foster student understanding and skills in mathematics.

AI-driven analytics can help identify learners' strengths and weaknesses, thereby allowing for differentiated instruction. For instance, Han emphasizes the importance of understanding students' self-concept in mathematics, which correlates with their academic achievement. When teachers use data analytics to track students' beliefs about their competencies, they can actively design interventions to bolster students' confidence and performance in mathematics, particularly among underrepresented groups like female and Indigenous students (Han, 2019). This targeted approach ensures that instruction is not only data-driven but also sensitive to cultural and gender-related discrepancies in performance.

Moreover, the relationship between teacher anxiety and student achievement in mathematics underscores the importance of AI tools that can facilitate emotional and pedagogical supports for educators. Teachers experiencing high levels of mathematics anxiety may inadvertently communicate low expectations to students, negatively impacting their learning outcomes (Ramirez et al., 2018). AI tools can aid in the professional development of teachers by promoting effective instructional strategies that focus on a growth mindset, thereby reducing anxiety and fostering a positive learning environment. For example, insights generated by AI can guide teachers in adopting interactive teaching methods that discourage rote memorization and emphasize conceptual understanding.

Furthermore, the incorporation of AI-generated insights into classroom practices can enhance methodologies employed in teaching mathematics. Strategies like flipped classrooms and visual aids have proven effective in increasing student engagement and comprehension (Wardat et al., 2022; Hai et al., 2023). Such methodologies are aligned with active learning, where students are encouraged to explore mathematical concepts collaboratively, thus nurturing their communicative competencies in a supportive community setting.

AI APPLICATION AREAS IN PRIMARY SCHOOL MATHEMATICS TEACHING

1. Math Apps and Games

AI is increasingly utilized in education, particularly in primary school mathematics, to enhance learning through interactive applications and games. Research indicates that AI-supported math apps can significantly improve student engagement and understanding of fundamental mathematical concepts. For instance, a study conducted by Outhwaite et al., demonstrated that using well-designed interactive math apps effectively raises early math achievement in children aged 4-5 years. The randomized control trial indicated that students receiving instruction through these apps performed better in assessments, underscoring the potential of technology in educational contexts (Outhwaite et al., 2019).

Math games, when integrated with AI features, have been found to be instrumental in developing problem-solving skills. Properly designed math games promote meaningful interactions and practice, ultimately enhancing children's math skills. Game mechanics, such as rewards for successful participation, can guide students' cognitive processes and improve their problem-solving strategies. Ke et al. further elaborate that engaging students through game-based tasks effectively correlates with increased math ability, suggesting that in-game incentives structure their learning experiences positively (Ke et al., 2024).

However, the effectiveness of these tools can vary among students due to individual responsiveness to digital learning interventions. Salminen et al. highlight that some students exhibit atypical developmental trajectories in their mathematical skills, suggesting a careful approach to implementing these apps to ensure all students, including those with learning difficulties, benefit from such innovations (Salminen et al., 2015). Therefore, monitoring individual progress and utilizing adaptive learning features within apps are essential for catering to diverse learning needs. AI applications in primary school mathematics through interactive apps and games foster a dynamic educational environment where students can engage deeply with mathematical concepts, enhance their problem-solving skills, and enjoy the learning process.

2. Intelligent Tutoring Systems

Intelligent Tutoring Systems (ITSs) have emerged as transformative tools in primary school mathematics education, offering personalized learning experiences tailored to the unique needs of each student. These systems leverage AI to analyze individual learner profiles and adapt instructional materials accordingly, significantly enhancing the educational process (Maity & Deroy, 2024; Pappas & Drigas, 2016; Yan & Song, 2015). One of the primary advantages of ITSs is their capacity to provide immediate feedback and tailored exercises, which are critical for primary school students who may require different levels of support to master foundational mathematical concepts (Rodrigues et al., 2010).

Research indicates that ITSs not only support cognitive development but can also enhance students' engagement in mathematics. For instance, the interactive nature of these systems encourages active participation from students, which is a vital component of effective learning (Santos & Jorge, 2013; Chen et al., 2020). The technological framework of ITSs is supported by advanced features such as knowledge tracing and adaptive learning models that monitor student progress and adjust learning paths dynamically. This ability to tailor learning experiences is vital, considering the diversity in comprehension levels found within primary school classrooms (Noguchi et al., 2015). Additionally, the emphasis on personalized instruction in these systems helps bridge educational gaps, allowing all students, regardless of their starting point, to achieve better mathematics outcomes (Gadanidis, 2017).

Moreover, the integration of generative AI into ITSs is enhancing their ability to provide micro-learning experiences tailored specifically to learners' immediate requirements (Maity & Deroy, 2024). Recent advancements enable these systems to not only adapt to individual learning needs but also to generate new content based on student performance. This development underscores the potential of ITSs to provide a continually evolving learning environment that optimally engages students (Pappas & Drigas, 2016).

In conclusion, the application of Intelligent Tutoring Systems in primary school mathematics fundamentally reshapes educational practices by embracing the tenets of personalized learning. By leveraging AI, these systems represent a significant step toward providing quality education that caters to the unique needs of every student, ensuring all learners have the opportunity to succeed in mathematics.

3. Voice Assistants

The integration of AI into voice assistants can significantly enhance math education for primary school students, fostering their independent learning skills. There are many voice-activated AI assistants available, such as Siri, Alexa, Google Assistant, Cortana, Bixby, and Xiaodu, and children can start talking and communicating with them as early as primary school. Research highlights that AI-based voice assistants can respond to students' inquiries and provide contextual information, facilitating deeper understanding and engagement in mathematical concepts. For instance, the implementation of technology in mathematics education has been associated with improved student engagement and conceptual understanding (Akçay et al., 2021).

Specifically, AI tools can offer personalized feedback and targeted assistance based on each student's unique learning path, thus catering to diverse learning needs.

Several studies underscore the importance of educational technology in mathematics, suggesting that the integration of digital devices can positively influence students' learning outcomes. For example, the use of educational technologies, including voice assistants, can lead to significant gains in student achievement in mathematics (Akçay et al., 2021). These technologies not only provide on-demand help but also encourage self-regulated learning- a vital skill for independent learning. Additionally, the support that voice assistants offer can help demystify complex mathematical concepts, enabling students to engage more freely with materials at their own pace without immediate dependence on teachers.

CHALLENGES AND CONSIDERATIONS IN PRIMARY MATHEMATICS EDUCATION

Primary mathematics education faces several challenges and considerations that affect teaching methodologies and learning outcomes. These challenges range from curriculum design and pedagogical approaches to socio-cultural factors and teacher preparedness.

One significant challenge is the adequacy of the mathematics curriculum itself. Research indicates that many mathematics textbooks heavily emphasize problem-solving while neglecting the process of problem posing, which is essential for developing a deeper understanding of mathematical concepts. Mínguez et al. postulate that comprehensive curricular projects should integrate both problem-solving and problem-posing tasks to enhance learning experiences across different educational levels (Mínguez et al., 2021). This idea aligns with the sentiment expressed by Schuck on the need for evolving pedagogical frameworks that leverage mobile technologies to diversify teaching methods and cater to today's learning environments (Schuck, 2016). These frameworks are essential for addressing the limitations of traditional mathematics instruction, which may not effectively engage students (Li & Tsai, 2021).

Technological integration is another consideration that shapes the landscape of primary mathematics education. The advent of Augmented Reality (AR) in classroom settings represents a transformative approach to teaching mathematical concepts. Apriza et al. found that AR-based learning media significantly enhances students' understanding of mathematics, suggesting that technology not only makes learning more engaging but also provides novel pathways for delivering complex concepts (Apriza et al., 2024). This technological integration must be balanced with teacher training; educators must be well-prepared to utilize these tools pedagogically, as emphasized by Nwoke regarding the importance of activity-based learning approaches that foster creativity among students (Nwoke, 2021).

Addressing the challenges in primary mathematics education requires a multifaceted approach that considers curriculum design, pedagogical techniques, technological integration, teacher preparedness, and socio-cultural dynamics. Collaborative efforts among educators, policymakers, and researchers are essential to create a supportive infrastructure for effective mathematics education.

One significant issue is the identification and understanding of difficulties in mathematics learning. Alshatri et al. highlight that many primary educators exhibit limited professional knowledge regarding the nature of these difficulties, based on feedback from 918 teachers. This lack of understanding contributes to ineffective teaching of complex mathematical concepts and problem-solving strategies (Alshatri et al., 2019).

The curriculum content itself has also faced criticism for failing to engage students adequately. Rigid mathematics teaching methods often emphasize textbook content exclusively, which can result in a lack of interest and an inability to demonstrate the relevance of mathematics in everyday contexts. This disconnection not only impedes retention of mathematical concepts but also diminishes student motivation, leading to lower achievement in mathematics. While the TCEM aims to cultivate competencies beyond conventional academic skills, findings suggest that teachers are poorly equipped to nurture creativity and critical thinking in mathematics.

Finally, post-pandemic evaluations indicate a substantial shift in educational methodologies, particularly influenced by the transition to remote learning. Stakeholders have expressed concerns regarding assessment methods during remote teaching, advocating for innovative strategies to measure student understanding in mathematics that do not rely on traditional assessment frameworks, which may not translate well to digital environments. This concern resonates globally, as numerous studies call for flexible education models that integrate technological solutions to enhance learning. It is presents a forward-thinking framework for reforming primary education in mathematics, persisting challenges such as teachers' knowledge deficits, ineffective curriculum content, and inadequate assessment methods hinder its successful implementation. Furthermore, continuous teacher training and adaptation to modern pedagogical methods are essential to improving students' mathematical competencies in the evolving educational landscape. Here are some of the challenges and considerations in primary mathematics education.

1. Accessibility of AI in Primary Mathematics Education

The integration of AI in primary mathematics education presents both significant opportunities and challenges in terms of accessibility. To ensure that all students can benefit from these advances, it's crucial to consider the ethical dimensions, the pedagogical implications and the infrastructure needed for effective implementation.

A key challenge is the potential for AI technologies to inadvertently reinforce existing inequalities. Without careful planning and attention to equity, AI can exacerbate inequalities between students, particularly affecting those from marginalised backgrounds (Eden et al., 2024; (Roshanaei et al., 2023). For example, generative AI systems and intelligent tutoring systems can provide personalised learning experiences, which have been shown to increase engagement and improve understanding in subjects such as mathematics (Roshanaei et al., 2023).

In addition, teacher readiness and digital literacy play a critical role in the successful integration of AI in mathematics education. Research highlights that teachers need to be adequately trained not only to understand AI tools, but also to use them effectively in the classroom (Arvin et al., 2023). The presence of AI in education may change the traditional role of teachers, especially with intelligent tutoring systems that can provide real-time feedback to students (Koedinger & Aleven, 2015). However, teachers without sufficient training may struggle to utilise these tools appropriately to enhance student learning. It is therefore essential to invest in professional development programmes that equip teachers with the skills needed to facilitate AI-enhanced learning environments.

The ethical considerations surrounding AI in education cannot be overlooked. Issues such as data privacy and algorithmic bias are paramount, as they may disproportionately affect vulnerable student populations (Akgün & Greenhow, 2021). For example, AI systems that analyse student performance data must adhere to strict data protection standards to ensure that sensitive information is not misused. In addition, the algorithms involved in personalising education could inadvertently favour certain demographic groups and marginalise others if not properly managed (Arvin et al., 2023). Ongoing dialogue among stakeholders, including educators, policymakers, and technologists, is needed to establish ethical guidelines for the use of AI in primary mathematics education (Akgün & Greenhow, 2021).

2. Privacy and Security in Primary Mathematics Education AI

The integration of AI in primary mathematics education requires a strong focus on the privacy and security of students' personal data. The increasing presence of AI-based tools in educational settings is contributing to heightened privacy concerns, particularly with respect to data collected from vulnerable populations such as children. These concerns are compounded by the challenges associated with ensuring the ethical use of AI, as highlighted by various studies (Alrayes et al., 2024). Current technologies can unintentionally perpetuate bias and misleading information, and often lack transparency about how data is processed and used (Alrayes et al.,

2024). This suggests that policy frameworks governing the use of AI must prioritise comprehensive guidelines to protect student data.

Furthermore, basic cybersecurity knowledge among students has been identified as crucial in the context of implementing AI tools in education (Çoklar & Aslan, 2023). Specific measures, including strong data use policies and robust security infrastructures, need to be put in place to adequately protect sensitive information. Effective security strategies could include the implementation of firewalls, data encryption, and proactive monitoring of networks to prevent unauthorised access and ensure the stability of educational processes. As schools increasingly adopt digital and AI systems, the role of cybersecurity education becomes critical in empowering students and teachers alike and enhancing their ability to safely engage in these technologically enhanced environments.

In addition, the design of school environments must include applications that operate outside of easily traceable networks, which can be achieved by establishing filters to protect students from harmful online content (Kamenskih, 2022). Properly implemented cybersecurity measures not only protect students, but also contribute to a conducive learning environment that allows for exploration and innovation using AI tools (Cuellar & Fisher, 2022). By comprehensively addressing these privacy and security concerns, educational institutions can foster an atmosphere of trust that is conducive to effective AI integration in elementary mathematics education, while enhancing students' learning experiences. The intersection of AI integration in education and the critical need for cybersecurity measures underscores the importance of developing and implementing sound privacy policies. As the educational landscape evolves with technology, these principles will form the backbone of creating safe, responsive and ethical educational environments for primary mathematics education.

3. Teacher Competencies in Using AI in Primary School Mathematics Teaching

The integration of AI in primary school mathematics teaching necessitates that teachers possess specific competencies that facilitate both the effective use of AI technologies and the enhancement of pedagogical practices. As educational landscapes evolve, it is crucial for educators to develop technological literacy, pedagogical adaptability, data analysis skills, and awareness of ethical considerations related to AI usage.

a. Technological Literacy:

Technological literacy encompasses the skills to effectively use AI-based educational tools while understanding their foundational principles. Research indicates that teachers with a higher level of education demonstrate increased awareness of AI technologies, suggesting that access to continuing education and professional development is vital for enhancing this literacy among teachers (Ferikoğlu & Akgün, 2022). Furthermore, effective integration of AI into teaching strategies relies on teachers receiving practice-oriented training, which fosters positive attitudes and supports increased use of technology in the classroom (Güneyli et al., 2024).

The increasing integration of AI into educational contexts necessitates a comprehensive understanding of technological literacy defined as the ability to effectively utilize technology while also grasping the foundational principles upon which such technologies are built. The successful incorporation of AI-based educational tools relies heavily on the proficiency of educators in leveraging these tools effectively. As the landscape of education continues to evolve, the intersection of technology and pedagogy becomes paramount, directing attention toward the prerequisite skills and knowledge that teachers must possess. Recent research emphasizes the correlation between the level of education attained by teachers and their awareness of emerging AI technologies, pointing to a critical gap that must be bridged through continued professional development.

Effective technological integration in classrooms, particularly in the context of AI, hinges on the professional growth and training that educators receive. The necessity of practice-oriented training cannot be overstated, as it serves to enhance teachers' comfort levels with technology while simultaneously fostering positive attitudes toward its use in pedagogy. Studies have identified that such training not only empowers educators to incorporate AI tools into their teaching methodologies but also significantly influences their willingness to innovate in their instructional practices (Güneyli et al., 2024).

In examining the dimensions of technological literacy pertinent to AI, it is essential to delineate the core competencies educators should develop. Among these are the ability to navigate AI applications, analyze data generated by these applications, and assess their implications for student learning outcomes. Teachers must familiarize themselves with diverse AI tools, including intelligent tutoring systems, automated grading software, and adaptive learning platforms, each presenting unique benefits and challenges. By developing a nuanced understanding of these tools, educators can tailor their instructional strategies to better meet the diverse needs of learners, thereby enriching the educational experience.

However, the mere inclusion of AI tools in the classroom does not guarantee that students will benefit from them; educators must possess the requisite knowledge to utilize these technologies efficiently and effectively. This includes an awareness of the ethical considerations surrounding AI, such as issues of data privacy, algorithmic bias, and the potential for misinformation. Teachers equipped with such knowledge can foster an environment of critical engagement among students, empowering them to discern the efficacy and reliability of AI-generated information, thus cultivating a generation of technologically literate individuals.

The role of ongoing professional development is crucial in dismantling the barriers that may hinder teachers from embracing technological literacy. Current models of teacher training often fail to keep pace with rapid advancements in technology and emerging educational methodologies. Therefore, systemic efforts to provide continuous education tailored to new AI tools and their applications in education are vital. Such initiatives should focus not only on skills acquisition but also on creating a robust theoretical framework that contextualizes the use of AI in educational settings, enabling teachers to understand the underlying principles guiding these technologies. The integration of AI into educational programs must extend beyond mere technical training. It should also encompass the cultivation of critical thinking and problem-solving skills, anchored in an understanding of how these technologies impact learning and teaching practices. By doing so, teachers can foster an educational environment where both they and their students engage deeply with AI, promoting a culture of inquiry and innovation.

The pedagogical implications of AI adoption are also manifold. Teachers need to engage in reflective practices that allow them to evaluate the effectiveness of AI tools in enhancing teaching and learning experiences. This reflective cycle can lead to an iterative process of adaptation and improvement, contributing to a more dynamic and responsive educational landscape. With proper training, educators can become champions of technology, advocating for its responsible use and considering its impact on student engagement, motivation, and achievement.

Equally important is the notion of collaboration among educators, tech developers, and researchers. Partnerships among these stakeholders can facilitate the development of resources and training initiatives that are responsive to educators' needs. For instance, collaborative workshops that bring together teachers and AI specialists can enhance the effectiveness of technological integration by providing real-world scenarios and hands-on experiences. Such opportunities help teachers see the practical applications of AI in their teaching contexts, thereby increasing their confidence and competence in utilizing these tools.

The overall impact of AI in education, according to various studies, suggests a profound shift in the teacher-student dynamic. As AI assumes roles traditionally held by educators—such as providing personalized learning pathways and immediate feedback—teachers are afforded opportunities to focus on higher-order teaching practices. This transition necessitates a redefinition of the teacher's role from dispenser of knowledge to facilitator of learning, where the emphasis is placed on mentorship, guidance, and fostering critical thinking skills.

In conclusion, the journey toward fostering a technologically literate educational environment framed by AI necessitates a multi-faceted approach. Teachers must engage in a rigorous pursuit of knowledge through ongoing professional development and practice-oriented training that reflects the evolving nature of technology in education. It is imperative that educational stakeholders commit to providing the necessary resources, infrastructure, and collaborative opportunities to empower teachers. Only through such dedicated efforts can we cultivate an educational framework that embraces technological advancements while fostering the skills, knowledge, and competencies essential for educators in the 21st century. The successful integration of AI into education holds great promise, but its realization hinges on an informed, skilled, and adaptable teaching workforce equipped to navigate this new landscape.

b. Pedagogical Adaptability:

Pedagogical adaptability involves the ability to tailor AI solutions to meet diverse student needs. This adaptability is crucial as it allows teachers to modify instructional strategies based on individual learner profiles. Developing such competencies necessitates dedicated professional development programs that emphasize hands-on experience with AI technologies and illustrate practical applications within the classroom setting (Aghaziarati et al., 2023). Collaborative approaches, such as teacher study groups and professional learning communities, can also enhance pedagogical adaptability by providing opportunities for peer support and knowledge sharing (Bayram & Bıkmaz, 2021).

The integration of AI into the educational landscape has dramatically altered the traditional teaching paradigm. As educators encounter increasingly diverse student populations, the necessity for pedagogical adaptability becomes paramount. Pedagogical adaptability refers to the ability of educators to adjust instructional strategies to cater to the individual learning profiles of students. This adaptability is essential in a landscape where AI technologies can provide personalized learning experiences, helping to engage students and address their unique educational needs (Aghaziarati et al., 2023). This paper examines the critical role of professional development in enhancing pedagogical adaptability and explores collaborative approaches that can facilitate effective teaching practices.

In an era characterized by rapid technological advancement, educational contexts are evolving at an unprecedented pace. The diversity of student needs is a reflection of various factors including socio-economic status, cultural backgrounds, and varying cognitive abilities. Therefore, educational institutions face the challenge of creating inclusive learning environments that are responsive to these diverse needs. Pedagogical adaptability plays a vital role in equipping teachers with the skills necessary to modify their instructional strategies effectively. By embracing AI solutions, educators can develop personalized learning pathways that resonate with individual learners (Aghaziarati et al., 2023).

As educators recognize the limitations of one-size-fits-all approaches, the need for teaching strategies that can be tailored to individual learning profiles has become increasingly apparent. The qualitative difference provided by adaptable pedagogies can lead to improved student engagement, motivation, and overall academic performance. Various studies have demonstrated that students who experience personalized instruction are more likely to benefit from enhanced learning outcomes compared to those subjected to traditional instructional models.

The development of pedagogical adaptability demands a robust framework for professional development focused on the integration of AI technologies. To cultivate the skills necessary for teachers to tailor their instructional practices effectively, professional development programs should emphasize hands-on experiences with AI tools. These programs must not only train educators on the functionalities of AI applications but also provide them with pedagogical strategies that align with these technologies. By facilitating an understanding of how to leverage AI resources, teachers can come to grips with the potential of these innovations to enrich the learning experience.

Central to effective professional development is the provision of hands-on experience with AI technologies. The theoretical knowledge imparted during training sessions must be complemented by practical applications within the classroom setting. Educators need opportunities to implement AI solutions in real-world situations, allowing them to test, evaluate, and adapt their pedagogies accordingly. This experiential learning approach is instrumental for fostering pedagogical adaptability and enables educators to grapple with the complexities of integrating AI into their curricula.

For instance, professional development workshops could be designed to simulate classroom environments where teachers can utilize AI-driven tools to design lesson plans that meet diverse student needs. By practicing in controlled settings, educators are better equipped to understand the intricacies of personalized learning. Furthermore, collaboration among educators during these exercises can enhance problem-solving skills and provide a supportive network for addressing common challenges associated with AI integration.

Collaborative frameworks also encourage reflective practices among educators. Engaging in discussions with peers about instructional successes and setbacks allows for a deeper understanding of the pedagogical implications of utilizing AI technologies. This reflective practice can yield valuable insights that inform the ongoing development of adaptive teaching strategies. Moreover, collaboration nurtures a culture of innovation, wherein educators feel empowered to experiment with new methodologies without the fear of failure.

Despite the clear advantages of pedagogical adaptability, several barriers may impede educators from fully integrating AI into their teaching practices. Resistance to change is a common challenge faced by many institutions, often rooted in a lack of familiarity with new technologies or fear of inadequacy in harnessing them effectively. Furthermore, limited access to resources and inadequate institutional support can hinder the successful implementation of AI-driven pedagogies.

To overcome these barriers, educational leaders must prioritize the establishment of a supportive infrastructure that facilitates AI integration. This includes providing adequate training, access to resources, and ongoing professional development initiatives. Moreover, fostering a culture of collaboration among educators can mitigate feelings of isolation and uncertainty associated with adopting new teaching strategies. By ensuring that educators feel supported and capable, institutions can cultivate a workforce that is adaptable to the needs of an ever-evolving educational landscape.

c. Data Analysis and Use:

Data analysis and use is increasingly important in the context of AI-supported education. Teachers must be able to analyze student performance data to craft personalized learning strategies. Effective use of AI can facilitate more informed decisions regarding instructional adjustments, allowing for tailored support that enhances student achievement (Zhao et al., 2022). Programs aimed at improving teachers' capabilities in data utilization should be integrated into pre-service and in-service training curricula to ensure comprehensive understanding and application (Eden et al., 2024).

Technology's pervasive influence has permeated various facets of human life, with education being particularly affected in recent years. AI-supported education is increasingly becoming an area of rich exploration, yielding a plethora of tools designed to facilitate learning through data-driven insights. The exponential growth of data availability has endowed educators with unprecedented opportunities to leverage quantitative insights for optimizing student outcomes. However, this potential hinges on teachers' capabilities to proficiently analyze and interpret student performance data. In this context, Zhao et al. (2022) outline the necessity for educators to engage with student data analytically, forming the cornerstone of personalized learning strategies that are pivotal in responding to the varying needs of learners.

As educational institutions increasingly adopt AI-driven interventions, the need to harness data effectively becomes paramount. Data analysis serves as a vehicle through which educators can distill actionable insights from raw data regarding student performance, behaviors, and engagement levels. For instance, by systematically analyzing assessment scores, attendance records, and participation metrics, teachers can discern patterns that might indicate areas of struggle or opportunity for individual students or entire cohorts. This analytical understanding not only informs instructional strategies but also allows for dynamic curricular adjustments that resonate with the needs of learners in real-time.

Integral to the successful deployment of AI in educational endeavors is its capacity to facilitate personalized learning experiences. AI can leverage vast datasets to generate tailored learning pathways, addressing individual student needs based on their unique strengths, weaknesses, and preferences. This is particularly critical in diverse classrooms where a one-size-fits-all approach is often ineffective, leading to variations in student engagement and achievement. Customized learning experiences foster not only improved academic outcomes but also enhance students' motivation, self-efficacy, and overall educational satisfaction.

The ability to make informed instructional adjustments is closely linked to the educator's capability to interpret data meaningfully. In AI-supported educational frameworks, teachers can utilize advanced analytical tools to visualize performance metrics effectively, leading to a clear understanding of the instructional impact on student learning. For instance, real-time data dashboards can display student progress, highlighting areas requiring immediate intervention or modification in pedagogical approaches. Such adjustments not only promote responsive teaching practices but also align curricular content with students' learning trajectories, ultimately fostering an adaptive learning environment.

The evolving landscape of education mandates a significant shift in teacher professional development concerning data literacy. Teacher training programs need to encompass robust curricula focusing on data analysis tools and pedagogical approaches that promote data-informed decision-making. Research highlights the imperative that both pre-service and in-service training should be structured to not only teach theoretical underpinnings of data analysis but also to provide practical hands-on experiences in interpreting and applying data insights effectively. By integrating data utilization training within professional development, educators can cultivate a culture of evidence-based practice that permeates their instructional methodologies.

Embedding data analysis within educational curricula requires a comprehensive approach, ensuring that prospective and current educators are adequately equipped to handle the complexities of AI-supported learning environments. Integrative frameworks should include courses on statistics, data mining, and software applications specifically tailored for educational contexts. Additionally, the creation of collaborative learning opportunities, such as peer-led workshops or mentorship programs, can further strengthen educators' competencies in data analysis. The evolution of technology and its implications for educational data handling necessitate continuous professional enhancement and adaptation.

While the advantages of data-driven education are manifold, numerous challenges persist in effectively harnessing data for instructional purposes. One significant hurdle is the proficiency gap among educators regarding data literacy, where many educators may lack the foundational understanding needed to analyze data autonomously. Furthermore, the ethical considerations surrounding student data privacy and security play a salient role, as educators navigate the murky waters of utilizing sensitive information while ensuring compliance with legal and organizational standards. Overcoming these challenges requires systemic support that promotes data literacy and addresses ethical concerns proactively.

Institutions play a critical role in facilitating teachers' capabilities in data utilization by fostering an organizational culture that values data-driven practices. This can be achieved through the provision of necessary resources, including access to data analysis tools and professional development workshops targeting data literacy. Moreover, establishing collaborative networks among educators allows for shared learning experiences where successful data-driven interventions can be showcased and discussed comprehensively. Institutional support is paramount in ensuring that educators feel empowered and adequately prepared to incorporate data analysis in their teaching methodologies.

Looking forward, the integration of AI within educational ecosystems implies that data analysis will become even more sophisticated and nuanced. Predictive analytics powered by AI can provide deeper insights into student learning patterns, informing educators of potential future trajectories and enabling proactive interventions. Embracing advancements in AI and machine learning technologies will enable educators to optimize their instructional strategies continually, refining educational practices based on data-driven evidence. Additionally, the continuous feedback loop established within AI frameworks encourages an ongoing process of instructional improvement that exponentially benefits student learning.

d. Ethics and Security Awareness:

Lastly, ensuring ethics and security awareness in AI education is essential to protect student data and promote an understanding of the ethical implications of technology use. As AI technologies become more prevalent in education, teachers must be equipped to navigate issues related to data privacy and ethical considerations. Incorporating discussions about ethics into professional development facilitates a holistic understanding of the broader implications of AI technologies in education.

Integrating AI in primary school mathematics teaching offers distinct advantages like adaptive learning opportunities, automated assessments, and continuous monitoring of student progress. To maximize these benefits, it is imperative that professional development programs extend beyond mere technical instruction. By providing educators with comprehensive training that integrates practical examples of how to apply AI pedagogically, educational institutions can effectively support the transition to AI-enhanced learning environments. Successful integration is contingent upon equipping teachers with both the technical and pedagogical skills necessary to foster a more effective, personalized, and student-centered approach to mathematics education.

CONCLUSION

As AI technologies increasingly penetrate educational settings, particularly in primary school mathematics instruction, the necessity for ethical and security awareness has become paramount. This paper discusses the critical role of ethics in the professional development of educators, emphasizing the importance of understanding data privacy, ethical implications, and technical competencies in the context of AI tools. By establishing a comprehensive approach to professional development, we can foster effective and responsible integration of AI in educational practices.

Students' data privacy is a fundamental concern when utilizing AI in educational environments. According to the Family Educational Rights and Privacy Act (FERPA), educational institutions must safeguard the personally identifiable information of students. Consequently, educators must be aware of the potential risks associated with AI implementations that utilize student data for adaptive learning and assessments. This awareness is crucial for preventing data breaches and ensuring compliance with privacy regulations.

Discussion

The integration of AI technologies in educational settings presents both significant advantages and profound ethical challenges. Educators must be sufficiently prepared to navigate the complex ethical landscape that arises from AI implementations in the classroom. One prominent issue is the existence of algorithmic bias within AI systems, which can inadvertently perpetuate existing inequalities, particularly in educational outcomes. This phenomenon underscores the necessity of engaging educators in discussions around ethical AI practices, as studies indicate that biased algorithms can disproportionately affect marginalized communities, leading to significant consequences in educational equity (Morley et al., 2019)

Moreover, the importance of transparency in AI systems cannot be overstated. Educators must be equipped with a comprehensive understanding of how AI systems function to critically assess their implications for teaching and learning. A lack of transparency may hinder educators' ability to evaluate the potential risks and benefits of these systems, thus emphasizing the need for professional development that incorporates training on ethical standards surrounding AI usage (Morley et al., 2019), Brendel et al., 2021). Such training should further include case studies that illuminate both the advantages and pitfalls of AI, providing educators with a nuanced perspective on its role in their practice. Fostering an environment where critical analysis of AI's impacts can occur is essential to preparing educators to advocate for responsible AI practices within their institutions and classrooms (Ayling & Chapman, 2021).

Incorporating practical examples and real-world case studies into professional development curricula can substantially enhance educators' comprehension of AI applications, particularly in specialized fields such as mathematics education (Qin & Ao, 2023). For instance, insights gained from adaptive learning platforms demonstrate how AI can personalize instruction to cater to individual learner needs. This capability not only promotes innovative teaching methods but also aligns educational practices with the ethical imperative of ensuring equitable access to personalized learning experiences (Schmidt & Strassner, 2022).

Nevertheless, it is paramount that educators are not only technically proficient with AI tools but also possess the pedagogical knowledge necessary for their effective application in the classroom. The integration of AI into teaching is contingent upon the development of a sound pedagogical framework that nurtures ethical considerations while leveraging AI's capabilities. Professional development should thus encompass instruction on how to navigate the ethical dilemmas posed by AI, enabling educators to uphold ethical standards while personalizing learning (Jobin et al., 2019).

In summary, the implementation of AI in education poses complex ethical dilemmas, particularly concerning algorithmic bias and transparency. To navigate these challenges, it is imperative that professional development for educators includes a robust focus on ethical AI practices. By integrating practical examples and fostering robust discussions, educators can cultivate the critical thinking skills necessary to advocate for ethical implementations of AI technology in their classrooms.

Limitations of the Study and Practical Suggestions

Limitations: The article focuses primarily on the professional development and ethical awareness of educators. The effects of AI applications on other important stakeholders, such as students, parents, school administrators, and policymakers, and the roles of these stakeholders are discussed in less detail. Although it is generally limited to the context of elementary school mathematics, it does not sufficiently take into account the differences in technology access and application capacities among schools of different socioeconomic levels. This may limit the generalizability of the recommendations to all educational environments.

Practical Suggestions: Schools and school districts should establish clear procurement protocols that prioritize transparency, accountability, and fairness when selecting AI tools. Information should be requested from vendors about how the algorithms of the procured AI systems work and how they are tested for potential biases. Within educational institutions, committees composed of teachers, parents, technology experts, and ethics experts can be established to oversee the selection, implementation, and impact of AI tools. These committees should be tasked with ensuring compliance with ethical standards and finding solutions to emerging issues. Before integrating an AI tool into their lessons, teachers should critically evaluate not only the pedagogical value of the tool, but also its potential biases, data collection practices, and impact on student privacy. Technology should not take precedence over pedagogy. Teachers should view AI as a tool that enriches existing teaching methods and use technology consciously to achieve learning objectives and provide an equitable learning environment for every student.

REFERENCES

Agbong-Coates, I. (2024). Chatgpt integration significantly boosts personalized learning outcomes: A philippine study. *International Journal of Educational Management and Development Studies*, *5*(2), 165–186. DOI: 10.53378/353067

Aghaziarati, A., Nejatifar, S., & Abedi, A. (2023). Artificial intelligence in education: investigating teacher attitudes. *AI and tech in behavioral and social sciences, 1*(1), 35-42. https://doi.org/DOI: 10.61838/kman.aitech.1.1.6

Akçay, A., Karahan, E., & Bozan, M. (2021). The effect of using technology in primary school math teaching on students' academic achievement: A meta-analysis study. *Fire Forum for International Research in Education*, *7*(2), 1–21. DOI: 10.32865/fire202172231

Akgün, S., & Greenhow, C. (2021). Artificial intelligence in education: Addressing ethical challenges in k-12 settings. *AI and Ethics*, *2*(3), 431–440. DOI: 10.1007/s43681-021-00096-7 PMID: 34790956

Alrayes, A., Henari, T., & Ahmed, D. (2024). Chatgpt in education – understanding the bahraini academics perspective. *Electronic Journal of e-Learning*, *22*(2), 112–134. DOI: 10.34190/ejel.22.2.3250

Alshatri, S., Wakil, K., & Bakhtyar, R. (2019). The difficulties of theoretical and applied learning for mathematics subject in primary schools. *International E-Journal of Educational Studies*, *3*(6), 141–149. DOI: 10.31458/iejes.591997

Apriza, B., Suprapto, I., & Mahendra, Y. (2024). The influence of augmented reality-based learning media on the understanding of mathematical concepts in elementary school children. *West Science Interdisciplinary Studies*, *2*(3), 502–508. DOI: 10.58812/wsis.v2i03.694

Arvin, N., Hoseinabady, M., Bayat, B., & Zahmatkesh, E. (2023). Teacher experiences with ai-based educational tools. *AI and tech in behavioral and social sciences, 1*(2), 26-32. https://doi.org/DOI: 10.61838/kman.aitech.1.2.5

Ayling, J., & Chapman, A. (2021). Putting ai ethics to work: Are the tools fit for purpose? *AI and Ethics*, *2*(3), 405–429. DOI: 10.1007/s43681-021-00084-x

Brendel, A., Mirbabaie, M., Lembcke, T., & Hofeditz, L. (2021). Ethical management of artificial intelligence. *Sustainability*, *13*(4), 1974. DOI: 10.3390/su13041974

Capinding, A. (2023). Revolutionizing pre-calculus education: photomath's ai-powered mathematics tutorship. *Problems of Education in the 21st Century, 81*(6), 758-775. https://doi.org/DOI: 10.33225/pec/23.81.758

Çoklar, A., & Aslan, S. (2023). Determination of cyber security knowledge level of vocational high school students in the field of information technologies. *Social Mentality and Researcher Thinkers Journal*, *9*(78), 5207–5213. DOI: 10.29228/smryj.73684

Cuellar, M., & Fisher, B. (2022). Securing schools? examining the longitudinal relationships between student behavior and engagement with security measures in urban school systems. *Journal of Interpersonal Violence*, *37*(9), 5857–5886. DOI: 10.1177/08862605221079275 PMID: 35311408

Eden, C., Chisom, O., & Adeniyi, I. (2024). Integrating ai in education: opportunities, challenges, and ethical considerations. M*agna Scientia Advanced Research and Reviews, 10*(2), 006-013. https://doi.org/DOI: 10.30574/msarr.2024.10.2.0039

Ferikoğlu, D., & Akgün, E. (2022). An investigation of teachers' artificial intelligence awareness: A scale development study. *Malaysian Online Journal of Educational Technology*, *10*(3), 215–231. DOI: 10.52380/mojet.2022.10.3.407

Gadanidis, G. (2017). Artificial intelligence, computational thinking, and mathematics education. *International Journal of Information and Learning Technology*, *34*(2), 133–139. DOI: 10.1108/ijilt-09-2016-0048

Güneyli, A., Burgul, N., Dericioğlu, S., Cenkova, N., Becan, S., Şimşek, Ş., & Güneralp, H. (2024). Exploring teacher awareness of artificial intelligence in education: A case study from northern cyprus. *European Journal of Investigation in Health, Psychology and Education*, *14*(8), 2358–2376. DOI: 10.3390/ejihpe14080156 PMID: 39194950

Gürefe, N., & Aktaş, G., & ÖKSÜZ, H. (2024). Investigating the impact of the ai-supported 5e (ai-s5e) instructional model on spatial ability. *Behavioral Sciences (Basel, Switzerland)*, *14*(8), 682. DOI: 10.3390/bs14080682 PMID: 39199078

Gürkan, S. (2018). The effect of feedback on instructional behaviours of pre-service teacher education. Universal. *The Journal of Educational Research*, *6*(5), 1084–1093. DOI: 10.13189/ujer.2018.060530

Hai, H., Hoang, T., Do, H., Dang, T., & Nguyen, T. (2023). A review of studies on math teaching methods. J*ournal for Educators. Teachers and Trainers*, *14*(2). Advance online publication. DOI: 10.47750/jett.2023.14.02.042

Han, F. (2019). Self-concept and achievement in math among australian primary students: Gender and culture issues. *Frontiers in Psychology*, *10*(2). Advance online publication. DOI: 10.3389/fpsyg.2019.00603 PMID: 30971976

Hidayat, R., Mohamed, M., Suhaizi, N., Sabri, N., Mahmud, M., & Baharuddin, S. (2022). Artificial intelligence in mathematics education: A systematic literature review. *International Electronic Journal of Mathematics Education*, *17*(3), em0694. Advance online publication. DOI: 10.29333/iejme/12132

Hwang, S. (2022). Examining the effects of artificial intelligence on elementary students' mathematics achievement: A meta-analysis. *Sustainability*, *14*(20), 13185. DOI: 10.3390/su142013185

Jauhiainen, J., & Guerra, A. (2023). Generative ai and chatgpt in school children's education: Evidence from a school lesson. *Sustainability*, *15*(18), 14025. DOI: 10.3390/su151814025

Jehlička, V., & Rejsek, O. (2018). A multidisciplinary approach to teaching mathematics and information and communication technology. *Eurasia Journal of Mathematics, Science and Technology Education*, *14*(5), 1705–1718. DOI: 10.29333/ejmste/85109

Jobin, A., Ienca, M., & Vayena, E. (2019). The global landscape of ai ethics guidelines. *Nature Machine Intelligence*, *1*(9), 389–399. DOI: 10.1038/s42256-019-0088-2

Kamenskih, A. (2022). The analysis of security and privacy risks in smart education environments. *Journal of Smart Cities and Society*, *1*(1), 17–29. DOI: 10.3233/scs-210114

Ke, F., Dai, C., & West, L. (2024). Mathematical experience in game-based problem-solving. *Journal of Computer Assisted Learning*, *40*(3), 1083–1097. DOI: 10.1111/jcal.12938

Koedinger, K., & Aleven, V. (2015). An interview reflection on intelligent tutoring goes to school in the big city. *International Journal of Artificial Intelligence in Education*, *26*(1), 13–24. DOI: 10.1007/s40593-015-0082-8

Li, H., & Tsai, T. (2021). Education for sustainable development in mathematics education: What could it look like? *International Journal of Mathematical Education in Science and Technology*, *53*(9), 2532–2542. DOI: 10.1080/0020739x.2021.1941361

Liu, Q. (2023). Gamification in primary school mathematics teaching. *Journal of Education Humanities and Social Sciences*, *22*(2), 428–433. DOI: 10.54097/ehss.v22i.12493

Maity, S., & Deroy, A. (2024). Generative AI and Its Impact on Personalized Intelligent Tutoring Systems. *Open Journal of Social Sciences, 13*(4), 1–13. DOI: 10.48550/arXiv.2410.10650

Mínguez, R., Tarín-Ibáñez, J., & Lacruz-Pérez, I. (2021). Analysis of word problems in primary education mathematics textbooks in Spain. *Mathematics, 9*(17), 2123. DOI: 10.3390/math9172123

Morley, J., Floridi, L., Kinsey, L., & Elhalal, A. (2019). From what to how: An initial review of publicly available ai ethics tools, methods and research to translate principles into practices. *Science and Engineering Ethics, 26*(4), 2141–2168. DOI: 10.1007/s11948-019-00165-5 PMID: 31828533

Noguchi, Y., Kogure, S., Konishi, T., & Itoh, Y. (2015). Practice supporting system with related problem set generator based on targeted educational effects. *Research and Practice in Technology Enhanced Learning, 10*(1). Advance online publication. DOI: 10.1007/s41039-015-0004-2 PMID: 30613215

Nurhayati, F., & Rasyid, H. (2019). Implementation of outdoor games to improve 4-5 year old childrens number sense. *Jurnal Obsesi Jurnal Pendidikan Anak Usia Dini, 3*(1), 10. DOI: 10.31004/obsesi.v3i1.133

Nwoke, B. (2021). Enhancing primary school pupils' mathematics creative ability through activity based learning approach. *Malikussaleh Journal of Mathematics Learning, 4*(2), 70. DOI: 10.29103/mjml.v4i2.5707

Outhwaite, L., Faulder, M., Gulliford, A., & Pitchford, N. (2019). Raising early achievement in math with interactive apps: A randomized control trial. *Journal of Educational Psychology, 111*(2), 284–298. DOI: 10.1037/edu0000286 PMID: 30774149

Qin, Q., & Ao, L. (2023). *A new world of open space - reflections and perspectives of chinese scholars on the digital transformation of education and future education research*. MCET., DOI: 10.55162/mcet.05.153

Ramirez, G., Hooper, S., Kersting, N., Ferguson, R., & Yeager, D. (2018). Teacher math anxiety relates to adolescent students' math achievement. *AERA Open, 4*(1). Advance online publication. DOI: 10.1177/2332858418756052 PMID: 31069247

Roshanaei, M., Olivares, H., & Lopez, R. (2023). Harnessing ai to foster equity in education: Opportunities, challenges, and emerging strategies. *Journal of Intelligent Learning Systems and Applications, 15*(4), 123–143. DOI: 10.4236/jilsa.2023.154009

Saenz, M., Nandakumar, V., & Adamuti-Trache, M. (2023). A comparative study of high school students' math achievement and attitudes: Do math teacher qualifications matter? *International Journal of Education in Mathematics Science and Technology*, *11*(2), 304–322. DOI: 10.46328/ijemst.2528

Salminen, J., Koponen, T., Leskinen, M., Poikkeus, A., & Aro, M. (2015). Individual variance in responsiveness to early computerized mathematics intervention. *Learning and Individual Differences*, *43*, 124–131. DOI: 10.1016/j.lindif.2015.09.002

Santos, G., & Jorge, J. (2013). Interoperable intelligent tutoring systems as open educational resources. *IEEE Transactions on Learning Technologies*, *6*(3), 271–282. DOI: 10.1109/tlt.2013.17

Schmidt, T., & Strassner, T. (2022). Artificial intelligence in foreign language learning and teaching. *Anglistik*, *33*(1), 165–184. DOI: 10.33675/angl/2022/1/14

Schuck, S. (2016). Enhancing teacher education in primary mathematics with mobile technologies. *The Australian Journal of Teacher Education*, *41*(3), 126–139. DOI: 10.14221/ajte.2016v41n3.8

Setiawan, A., & Fitria, H. (2024). Analysis of learning results of students in the application of gamification quizizz on mathematics lessons. *Progres Pendidikan*, *5*(2), 193–197. DOI: 10.29303/prospek.v5i2.728

Sperling, K., Stenliden, L., Nissen, J., & Heintz, F. (2022). Still w(ai)ting for the automation of teaching: An exploration of machine learning in swedish primary education using actor-network theory. *European Journal of Education*, *57*(4), 584–600. DOI: 10.1111/ejed.12526

Sundari, S., & Hertuti, A. (2022). Fun learning by applying competition and cooperation strategies through mathematical games. *Tekno-Pedagogi. Jur. Tek. Pend*, *12*(1), 34–41. DOI: 10.22437/teknopedagogi.v12i1.32509

Tashtoush, M., Wardat, Y., AlAli, R., & Saleh, S. (2024). Artificial intelligence in education: Mathematics teachers' perspectives, practices and challenges. *Iraqi Journal for Computer Science and Mathematics*, *5*(1). Advance online publication. DOI: 10.52866/ijcsm.2024.05.01.004

Wardat, Y., Belbase, S., & Tairab, H. (2022). Mathematics teachers' perceptions of trends in international mathematics and science study (timss)-related practices in abu dhabi emirate schools. *Sustainability*, *14*(9), 5436. DOI: 10.3390/su14095436

Zhao, L., Wu, X., & Luo, H. (2022). Developing ai literacy for primary and middle school teachers in china: Based on a structural equation modeling analysis. *Sustainability*, *14*(21), 14549. DOI: 10.3390/su142114549

ADDITIONAL READING

Hwang, G.-J., & Tu, Y.-F. (2022). Artificial intelligence in mathematics education: A systematic review. *Computers & Education*, *28*(1), 1–17. DOI: 10.15359/ru.38-1.20

Li, M., & Manzari, E. (2025). AI utilization in primary mathematics education: A case study from a southwestern Chinese city. *Education and Information Technologies*, •••, 1–34. DOI: 10.1007/s10639-025-13315-z

Nguyen, A., Ngo, H. N., Hong, Y., Dang, B., & Nguyen, B. T. (2022). Ethical principles for artificial intelligence in education. *Education and Information Technologies*, *28*(4), 4221–4241. DOI: 10.1007/s10639-022-11316-w PMID: 36254344

Xu, Y., & Warschauer, M. (2023). Chatbots as tutors in primary school mathematics: Exploring student engagement. *Journal of Educational Technology & Society*, *26*(1), 45–60. DOI: 10.46245/ijorer.v4i2.331

KEY TERMS AND DEFINITIONS

Artificial Intelligence: Artificial Intelligence (AI) refers to computer systems designed to perform tasks that typically require human cognition, such as learning from data, recognizing patterns, solving complex problems, and making autonomous decisions. AI enables machines to mimic human-like thinking by processing large amounts of data, adapting through algorithms, and improving performance over time without explicit programming.

Education: Education is a holistic and lifelong process that equips children, youth, and adults with the knowledge, skills, values, and competencies needed to thrive as individuals and contribute meaningfully to society.

Mathematics teaching: Mathematics teaching is a systematic process designed to help learners acquire mathematical concepts, skills, and problem-solving strategies. It involves structured methods to make abstract ideas accessible and applicable. Topics include teaching the reasoning behind mathematical rules (e.g. place value and fractions), using concrete tools such as blocks and counters before moving on to abstract symbols, and developing speed and accuracy in basic operations such as addition and multiplication.

Primary School Mathematics Teaching: Primary school mathematics teaching involves introducing foundational mathematical concepts—such as numbers, arithmetic, geometry, and problem-solving to young learners (typically ages 6–11) in an engaging, age-appropriate manner.

Primary School: A state-authorised institution, operating for a minimum of four years, was established for the purpose of providing basic education for boys and girls of a school-going age.

Compilation of References

Abhulimen, A., & Ejike, O. (2024). Ethical considerations in AI use for SMEs and supply chains: Current challenges and future directions. *International Journal of Applied Research in Social Sciences*. https://doi.org/DOI: 10.51594/ijarss.v6i8.1391

Abimbola, C., Eden, C., Chisom, O., & Adeniyi, I. (2024). *Integrating AI in education: Opportunities, challenges, and ethical considerations*. Magna Scientia Advanced Research and Reviews., DOI: 10.30574/msarr.2024.10.2.0039

Acharya, A. S., Prakash, A., Saxena, P., & Nigam, A. (2013). Sampling: Why and how of it. *Indian Journal of Medical Specialties*, *4*(2), 330–333. DOI: 10.7713/ijms.2013.0032

Acut, D. P., Gamusa, E. V., Pernaa, J., Yuenyong, C., Pantaleon, A. T., Espina, R. C., & Garcia, M. B. (2025). AI Shaming Among Teacher Education Students: A Reflection on Acceptance and Identity in the Age of Generative Tools. In *Pitfalls of AI Integration in Education: Skill Obsolescence, Misuse, and Bias*. IGI Global., DOI: 10.4018/979-8-3373-0122-8.ch005

ADB. (2023). *Cambodia education sector assessment: Strategy and road map*. Asian Development Bank. https://www.adb.org/publications/cambodia-education-sector-assessment

Adeniyi, I., Edeni, C., & Adeleye, O. (2024). *The role of AI-enhanced tools in overcoming socioeconomic barriers in education: A conceptual analysis*. World Journal of Advanced Research and Reviews., DOI: 10.30574/wjarr.2024.21.3.0780

Adesoga, T., Ojo, C., Obani, O., Nwafor, K., & Rasul, O. (2024). *AI integration in business development: Ethical considerations and practical solutions*. GSC Advanced Research and Reviews., DOI: 10.30574/gscarr.2024.20.1.0282

Agbong-Coates, I. (2024). Chatgpt integration significantly boosts personalized learning outcomes: A philippine study. *International Journal of Educational Management and Development Studies*, *5*(2), 165–186. DOI: 10.53378/353067

Aghaziarati, A., Nejatifar, S., & Abedi, A. (2023). Artificial intelligence in education: investigating teacher attitudes. *AI and tech in behavioral and social sciences, 1*(1), 35-42. https://doi.org/DOI: 10.61838/kman.aitech.1.1.6

Akçay, A., Karahan, E., & Bozan, M. (2021). The effect of using technology in primary school math teaching on students' academic achievement: A meta-analysis study. *Fire Forum for International Research in Education, 7*(2), 1–21. DOI: 10.32865/fire202172231

Akgün, S., & Greenhow, C. (2022). Artificial intelligence in education: Addressing ethical challenges in K-12 settings. *AI and Ethics, 2*, 431–440. DOI: 10.1007/s43681-021-00096-7 PMID: 34790956

Akolekar, H., Jhamnani, P., Kumar, V., Tailor, V., Pote, A., Meena, A., Kumar, K., Challa, J. S., & Kumar, D. (2025). The role of generative AI tools in shaping mechanical engineering education from an undergraduate perspective. *Scientific Reports, 15*(1), 9214. DOI: 10.1038/s41598-025-93871-z PMID: 40097637

Alam, A., & Mohanty, A. (2024). Integrated constructive robotics in education (ICRE) model: A paradigmatic framework for transformative learning in educational ecosystem. *Cogent Education, 11*(1), 2324487. Advance online publication. DOI: 10.1080/2331186X.2024.2324487

Albahli, S. (2025). Advancing sustainable educational practices through AI-driven prediction of academic outcomes. *Sustainability, 17*(3), 1087. DOI: 10.3390/su17031087

Ali, O., Murray, P., Momin, M., & Al-Anzi, F. (2023). The knowledge and innovation challenges of ChatGPT: A scoping review. *Technology in Society, 75*(102402).

Almusaed, A., Almssad, A., Yitmen, I., & Homod, R. Z. (2023). Enhancing Student Engagement: Harnessing "AIED"'s Power in Hybrid Education—A Review Analysis. *Education Sciences, 13*(7), 1–24. DOI: 10.3390/educsci13070632

Alrayes, A., Henari, T., & Ahmed, D. (2024). Chatgpt in education – understanding the bahraini academics perspective. *Electronic Journal of e-Learning, 22*(2), 112–134. DOI: 10.34190/ejel.22.2.3250

Alshatri, S., Wakil, K., & Bakhtyar, R. (2019). The difficulties of theoretical and applied learning for mathematics subject in primary schools. *International E-Journal of Educational Studies, 3*(6), 141–149. DOI: 10.31458/iejes.591997

Alshiha, A. A., & Ghaleb, M. M. (2023). Empowering self-management: Unveiling the impact of artificial intelligence in learning on student self-efficacy and self-monitoring. [EJER]. *Eurasian Journal of Educational Research, 107*, 1–17.

Alt, D. (2023). Assessing the Benefits of Gamification in Mathematics for Student Gameful Experience and Gaming Motivation. *Computers & Education*, *200*, 1–15. DOI: 10.1016/j.compedu.2023.104806

Anderson, R., Belova, T., & Kim, H. (2023). The role of AI in personalized learning environments. *Educational Technology Journal*, *25*(2), 85–102.

Angrosino, M. (2007). *Doing ethnographic and observational research.* SAGE Publications., DOI: 10.4135/9781849208932

Anselmi, J., Gaujal, B., & Rebuffi, L. S. (2024). Learning optimal admission control in partially observable queueing networks. Queueing Systems, 108(1), 31-79. arXiv. https://arxiv.org/abs/2308.02391

Apriza, B., Suprapto, I., & Mahendra, Y. (2024). The influence of augmented reality-based learning media on the understanding of mathematical concepts in elementary school children. *West Science Interdisciplinary Studies*, *2*(3), 502–508. DOI: 10.58812/wsis.v2i03.694

Arif, Y. M., Nugroho, F., Aini, Q., Fauzan, A. C., & Garcia, M. B. (2025). A Systematic Literature Review of Serious Games for Physical Education: Technologies, Implementations, and Evaluations. In *Global Innovations in Physical Education and Health*. IGI Global., DOI: 10.4018/979-8-3693-3952-7.ch001

Arif, Y. M., & Nurhayati, H. (2022). Learning Material Selection for Metaverse-Based Mathematics Pedagogy Media Using Multi-Criteria Recommender System. *International Journal of Intelligent Engineering and Systems*, *15*(6), 541–551. DOI: 10.22266/ijies2022.1231.48

Armani, F., Daly, I., Vernitski, A., Gillmeister, H., & Scherer, R. (2023). Maths Anxiety and Cognitive State Monitoring for Neuroadaptive Learning Systems Using Electroencephalography. *2023 IEEE International Conference on Metrology for eXtended Reality, Artificial Intelligence and Neural Engineering (MetroXRAINE)*. https://doi.org/DOI: 10.1109/MetroXRAINE58569.2023.10405694

Arvin, N., Hoseinabady, M., Bayat, B., & Zahmatkesh, E. (2023). Teacher experiences with ai-based educational tools. *AI and tech in behavioral and social sciences, 1*(2), 26-32. https://doi.org/DOI: 10.61838/kman.aitech.1.2.5

Asy'ari, M., & Sharov, S. (2024). Transforming education with ChatGPT: Advancing personalized learning, accessibility, and ethical AI integration. *International Journal (Toronto, Ont.)*, *3*(2), 119–134.

Atahan, Ş. (2025). *Vygotsky'nin bilişsel kuramı bağlamında ARCS motivasyon öğretim tasarımı modeli ile matematik öğretimi*. Balıkesir Üniversitesi, Fen Bilimleri Enstitüsü.

Avinash, G., Pachori, H., Sharma, A., & Mishra, S. (2025). Time series forecasting of bed occupancy in mental health facilities in India using machine learning. *Scientific Reports, 15*, 86418. DOI: 10.1038/s41598-025-86418-9 PMID: 39837951

Ayling, J., & Chapman, A. (2021). Putting ai ethics to work: Are the tools fit for purpose? *AI and Ethics*, *2*(3), 405–429. DOI: 10.1007/s43681-021-00084-x

Azaria, A., Azoulay, R., & Reches, S. (2024). ChatGPT is a remarkable tool: For experts. *Data Intelligence*, *6*(1), 240–296. DOI: 10.1162/dint_a_00235

Babur, M. N. (2025). AI in education: A luxury or a necessity for developing nations? *Journal of Biological and Allied Health Sciences*, *5*(1), 1–2. DOI: 10.56536/jbahs.v5i1.111

Bagheri, M. M. (2015). Intelligent and adaptive tutoring systems: How to integrate learners. *International Journal of Education*, *7*(2), 1–16.

Baker, T., & Smith, L. (2019). *Educ-AI-tion rebooted? Exploring the future of artificial intelligence in schools and colleges*. Nesta. https://www.nesta.org.uk/report/education-rebooted/

Baker, R. S., & Yacef, K. (2009). The state of educational data mining in 2009: A review and future visions. *Journal of Educational Data Mining*, *1*(1), 3–17.

Barocas, S., Hardt, M., & Narayanan, A. (2023). *Fairness and Machine Learning: Limitations and Opportunities*. The MIT Press.

Barrett, L., & Stephens, M. (2024). Ethical considerations of AI in classrooms: A critical review. *Journal of Educational Ethics*, *12*(1), 45–61.

Basri, W. S. (2024). Effectiveness of AI-powered tutoring systems in enhancing learning outcomes. [EJER]. *Eurasian Journal of Educational Research, 110*, 25–40.

Bekdemir, Y. (2024). The urgency of AI integration in teacher training: Shaping the future of education. *Journal of Research in Didactical Sciences*. https://doi.org/DOI: 10.51853/jorids/15485

Benzer, R., Benzer, S., & Doğan, T. (2025). Assessing science teachers' digital literacy with survey-based machine learning. *Information Development*. Advance online publication. DOI: 10.1177/02666669251350669

Berson, I. R., Berson, M. J., Luo, W., & He, H. (2023). Intelligence Augmentation in Early Childhood Education: A Multimodal Creative Inquiry Approach. In *Communications in Computer and Information Science* (pp. 756-763). Springer Nature Switzerland. https://doi.org/DOI: 10.1007/978-3-031-36336-8_116

Bertrand, M. G., Sezer, H. B., & Namukasa, I. K. (2024). Exploring AR and VR Tools in Mathematics Education Through Culturally Responsive Pedagogies. *Digital Experiences in Mathematics Education, 10*(3), 462–486. DOI: 10.1007/s40751-024-00152-x PMID: 39497730

Bishop, C. M. (1995). *Neural networks for pattern recognition*. Oxford University Press.

Bishop, M. (2006). *Pattern recognition and machine learning*. Springer.

Biton, Y., & Segal, R. (2025). Learning to craft and critically evaluate prompts: The role of generative AI (ChatGPT) in enhancing pre-service mathematics teachers' TPACK and problem-posing skills. [IJEMST]. *International Journal of Education in Mathematics, Science, and Technology, 13*(1), 202–223.

Boddington, P. (2017). *Towards a Code of Ethics for Artificial Intelligence*. Springer International Publishing., DOI: 10.1007/978-3-319-60648-4

Bonotto, C., & Santo, D. L. (2015). On the relationship between problem posing, problem solving, and creativity in the primary school. In Singer, F. M., Ellerton, N. F., & Cai, J. (Eds.), *Mathematical problem posing: From research into effective practice* (pp. 103–123). Springer.

Boutilier, C. (2000). Decision Making under Uncertainty: Operations Research Meets AI (Again). National Conference on Artificial Intelligence, 1145–1150. https://www.aaai.org/Papers/AAAI/2000/AAAI00-208.pdf

Bower, M. (2019). *Design of technology-enhanced learning: Integrating research and practice*. Emerald Publishing Limited.

Bozkurt, A., Xiao, J., Farrow, R., Bai, J. Y. H., Nerantzi, C., Moore, S., & Asino, T. I. (2024). The Manifesto for Teaching and Learning in a Time of Generative AI: A Critical Collective Stance to Better Navigate the Future. *Open Praxis, 16*(4), 487–513. DOI: 10.55982/openpraxis.16.4.777

Braun, V., & Clarke, V. (2006). Using thematic analysis in psychology. *Qualitative Research in Psychology, 3*(2), 77–101. DOI: 10.1191/1478088706qp063oa

Brendel, A., Mirbabaie, M., Lembcke, T., & Hofeditz, L. (2021). Ethical management of artificial intelligence. *Sustainability, 13*(4), 1974. DOI: 10.3390/su13041974

Breuer, L., & Baum, D. (2005). An introduction to queueing theory and matrix-analytic methods. Springer. https://link.springer.com/book/10.1007/1-4020-3631-0

Broutin, M. S. T. (2024). Exploring Mathematics Teacher Candidates' Instrumentation Process of Generative Artificial Intelligence for Developing Lesson Plans. *Yükseköğretim Dergisi*, *14*(1), 165–176.

Brown, T. (2008, June). Design Thinking. *Harvard Business Review*. https://hbr.org/2008/06/design-thinking

Brown, S. I., & Walter, M. I. (1983). *The art of problem posing*. Franklin Institute Pres.

Brown, S. R. (1980). *Political subjectivity: Applications of Q methodology in political science*. Yale University Press.

Bruner, J. S. (1961). The act of discovery. *Harvard Educational Review*, *31*, 21–32.

Bryman, A. (2016). *Social research methods* (5th ed.). Oxford University Press.

Buckingham Shum, S., & Ferguson, R. (2012). Social learning analytics. *Journal of Educational Technology & Society*, *15*(3), 3–26.

Bulut, N., Cevikbas, M., & Kaiser, G. (2024). Teaching Mathematics Through Augmented, Virtual, and Mixed Reality: An Analysis of Recent Advancements. In F. Dilling & I. Witzke (Eds.), *Augmented and Virtual Reality in Mathematics Education: International Symposium on Augmented and Virtual Reality 2022* (pp. 11-35). Springer Fachmedien Wiesbaden. https://doi.org/DOI: 10.1007/978-3-658-45271-1_2

Bulut, O., & Wongvorachan, T. (2022). *Feedback generation through artificial intelligence*. The Open/Technology in Education, Society, and Scholarship Association Conference., DOI: 10.18357/otessac.2022.2.1.125

Burgstahler, S. (2015). *Universal Design in Higher Education* (2nd ed.). Harvard Education Press. https://hep.gse.harvard.edu/9781612508160/universal-design-in-higher-education-second-edition/

Burrell, J. (2016). How the machine 'thinks': Understanding opacity in machine learning algorithms. *Big Data & Society*, *3*(1). DOI: 10.1177/2053951715622512

Bushuyev, S. D., Bushuyev, S. D., Igbal, A. B., & Elams, C. (2024). The AI revolution in IT education: Революция искусственного интеллекта в ИТ-образовании. *International Journal of Information and Communication Technology*, *5*(2[18]), 8–22. DOI: 10.54309/IJICT.2024.18.2.001

Busuttil, L., & Calleja, J. (2025). Teachers' Beliefs and Practices About the Potential of ChatGPT in Teaching Mathematics in Secondary Schools. *Digital Experiences in Mathematics Education*, *11*(1), 140–166. DOI: 10.1007/s40751-024-00168-3

Busuttil, L., & Calleja, J. (2025). Teachers' beliefs and practices about the potential of ChatGPT in teaching Mathematics in secondary schools. *Digital Experiences in Mathematics Education*, *11*, 140–166.

Cai, J., & Hwang, S. (2002). Generalized and generative thinking in US and Chinese students' mathematical problem solving and problem posing. *The Journal of Mathematical Behavior*, *21*(4), 401–421. DOI: 10.1016/S0732-3123(02)00142-6

Cai, J., & Hwang, S. (2020). Learning to teach through mathematical problem posing: Theoretical considerations, methodology, and directions for future research. *International Journal of Educational Research*, *102*, 101391.

Cai, J., Hwang, S., Jiang, C., & Silber, S. (2015). Problem-posing research in mathematics education: Some answered and unanswered questions. In Cai, J., Ellerton, N., & Singer, F. M. (Eds.), *Mathematical problem posing: From research to effective practice* (pp. 3–34). Springer.

Cai, J., Moyer, J. C., Wang, N., Hwang, S., Nie, B., & Garber, T. (2013). Mathematical problem posing as a measure of curricular effect on students' learning. *Educational Studies in Mathematics*, *83*(1), 57–69. DOI: 10.1007/s10649-012-9429-3

Cai, J., Ran, H., Hwang, S., Ma, Y., Han, J., & Muirhead, F. (2023). Impact of prompts on students' mathematical problem posing. *The Journal of Mathematical Behavior*, *72*, 101087.

Cai, J., & Rott, B. (2024). On understanding mathematical problem-posing processes. *ZDM Mathematics Education*, *56*(1), 61–71.

Canonigo, A. (2024). Levering AI to enhance students' conceptual understanding and confidence in mathematics. *Journal of Computer Assisted Learning*, *40*, 3215–3229. DOI: 10.1111/jcal.13065

Capinding, A. (2023). Revolutionizing pre-calculus education: photomath's ai-powered mathematics tutorship. *Problems of Education in the 21st Century, 81*(6), 758-775. https://doi.org/DOI: 10.33225/pec/23.81.758

Carter, J., & McCarthy, M. (2019). Artificial intelligence in education: Potential and challenges. *Journal of Educational Technology*, *15*(3), 45–58.

CAST. (2018). Universal design for learning guidelines version 2.2. CAST. http://udlguidelines.cast.org

Celik, I. (2023). Exploring the determinants of artificial intelligence (AI) literacy: Digital divide, computational thinking, cognitive absorption. *Telematics and Informatics*, *83*. Advance online publication. DOI: 10.1016/j.tele.2023.102026

Celik, I., Dindar, M., Muukkonen, H., & Järvelä, S. (2022). The promises and challenges of artifcial intelligence for teachers: A systematic review of research. *TechTrends*, *66*(4), 616–630.

Chaiarwut, S., Srikoon, S., Siritaratiwat, A., & Kwangmuang, P. (2025). Enhancing Executive Mathematics Problem-Solving Through a Constructivist Digital Learning Platform: Design, Development and Evaluation. *Social Sciences & Humanities Open*, *11*, 1–15. DOI: 10.1016/j.ssaho.2025.101338

Chan, C. K. Y. (2023). *A Comprehensive AI Policy Education Framework for University Teaching and Learning* (No. arXiv:2305.00280). arXiv. /arXiv.2305.00280DOI: 10.48550

Chaudhary, H., Sharma, G., Nishad, D. K., & Khalid, S. (2025). Advanced queueing and scheduling techniques in cloud computing using AI-based model order reduction. *Computing*, *28*, 75.

Chea, P., Bo, C., & Minami, R. (2022). Cambodian Secondary School Teachers' Readiness for Online Teaching During the Covid-19 Pandemic (CDRI Working Paper Series No. 134). Cambodia Development Research Institute. https://doi.org/ DOI: 10.64202/wp.134.202205

Chen, H., Park, H. W., & Breazeal, C. (2020). Teaching and learning with children: Impact of reciprocal peer learning with a social robot on children's learning and emotive engagement. *Computers & Education*, *150*, 103836. DOI: 10.1016/j.compedu.2020.103836

Chen, L., Chen, P., & Lin, Z. (2020). Artificial intelligence in education: A review. *IEEE Access : Practical Innovations, Open Solutions*, *8*, 75264–75278. DOI: 10.1109/ACCESS.2020.2988510

Chen, M.-F., Chen, Y.-C., Zuo, P.-Y., & Hou, H.-T. (2023). Design and Evaluation of a Remote Synchronous Gamified Mathematics Teaching Activity That Integrates Multi-Representational Scaffolding and a Mind Tool for Gamified Learning. *Education and Information Technologies*, *28*(10), 13207–13233. DOI: 10.1007/s10639-023-11708-6 PMID: 37361748

Chen, T., & Cai, J. (2020). An elementary mathematics teacher learning to teach using problem posing: A case of the distributive property of multiplication over addition. *International Journal of Educational Research*, *102*, 101420.

Chen, W., & Adler, J. L. (2019). Assessment of screen exposure in young children, 1997 to 2014. *JAMA Pediatrics*, *173*(4), 391–393. DOI: 10.1001/jamapediatrics.2018.5546 PMID: 30776061

Chen, X., Xie, H., Zou, D., & Hwang, G.-J. (2020). Application and theory gaps during the rise of artificial intelligence in education. *Computers and Education: Artificial Intelligence*, *1*, 100002. DOI: 10.1016/j.caeai.2020.100002

Chen, X., & Zhou, Y. (2020). The impact of AI tools on reading comprehension. *Reading & Writing Quarterly*, *36*(2), 175–188.

Choi, I. (2022). *Exploring teaching and learning methods using artificial intelligence (AI) in the mathematics classroom: Focusing on the development of middle school statistic scenarios*. Korean School Mathematics Society., DOI: 10.30807/ksms.2022.25.2.003

Choustoulakis, E. (2024). The impact of AI-driven gamified learning of mathematical economics on higher-education student motivation and achievement: An empirical survey in sport management undergraduate students in Greece. In *ICERI2024 Proceedings* (pp. 2095–2103). IATED.

Christ, B. R., Kropko, J., & Hartvigsen, T. (2024). MATHWELL: Generating Educational Math Word Problems Using Teacher Annotations. *Findings of the Association for Computational Linguistics*.

Christakis, D. A., & Zimmerman, F. J. (2009). Young children and media: Limitations of current knowledge and future directions for research. *The American Behavioral Scientist*, *52*(8), 1177–1185. DOI: 10.1177/0002764209331540

Christou, C., Pitta-Pantazi, D., & Chimoni, M. (2024). Teachers' mathematical problem posing: The role of processes and complexity levels in posing problems on the fraction part-whole concept. *The Journal of Mathematical Behavior*, *73*, 101134.

Çiftçi, S., Taşkaya, S. M., & Alemdar, M. (2013). The opinions of classroom teachers about the FATIH project. *Elementary Education Online*, *12*(1), 227–240.

Clark-Wilson, A., Robutti, O., & Thomas, M. (2020). Teaching with digital technology. *ZDM Mathematics Education*, *52*, 1223–1242. DOI: 10.1007/s11858-020-01196-0 PMID: 33133297

Coelho, L., & Reis, S. (2021). Ethical Issues of Gamification in Healthcare: The Need to be Involved. In *Handbook of Research on Solving Modern Healthcare Challenges With Gamification*. IGI Global. DOI: 10.4018/978-1-7998-7472-0.ch001

Coelho, L., & Reis, S. S. (2023). Enhancing learning experiences through artificial intelligence: Classroom 5.0. In *Fostering pedagogy through micro and adaptive learning in higher education: Trends, tools, and applications* (pp. 169–191). IGI Global. https://www.igi-global.com/chapter/enhancing-learning-experiences-through-artificial-intelligence/328747

Çoklar, A., & Aslan, S. (2023). Determination of cyber security knowledge level of vocational high school students in the field of information technologies. *Social Mentality and Researcher Thinkers Journal*, *9*(78), 5207–5213. DOI: 10.29228/smryj.73684

Crespo, S. (2003). Learning to pose mathematical problems: Exploring changes in preservice teachers' practices. *Educational Studies in Mathematics*, *52*, 243–270.

Crespo, S., & Sinclair, N. (2008). What makes a problem mathematically interesting? Inviting prospective teachers to pose better problems. *Journal of Mathematics Teacher Education*, *11*, 395–415.

Creswell, J. W., & Plano Clark, V. L. (2018). *Designing and conducting mixed methods research* (3rd ed.). SAGE Publications.

Creswell, J. W., & Poth, C. N. (2018). *Qualitative inquiry and research design: Choosing among five approaches* (4th ed.). SAGE Publications.

Crompton, H., & Burke, D. (2023). Artificial intelligence in higher education: The state of the field. *International Journal of Educational Technology in Higher Education*, *20*(1), 22. DOI: 10.1186/s41239-023-00392-8

Cuellar, M., & Fisher, B. (2022). Securing schools? examining the longitudinal relationships between student behavior and engagement with security measures in urban school systems. *Journal of Interpersonal Violence*, *37*(9), 5857–5886. DOI: 10.1177/08862605221079275 PMID: 35311408

Damaševičius, R., & Sidekerskienė, T. (2023a). Designing Gamified Augmented Reality-Based Escape Rooms. *International Workshop on Gamification and Motivational Technologies.*

Damaševičius, R., & Sidekerskienė, T. (2023b). Designing Metaverse Escape Rooms for Microlearning in STEM Education. In Queirós, R., Cruz, M., Pinto, C., & Mascarenhas, D. (Eds.), *Fostering Pedagogy Through Micro and Adaptive Learning in Higher Education: Trends, Tools, and Applications* (pp. 192–211). IGI Global., DOI: 10.4018/978-1-6684-8656-6.ch009

de Treville, S., & van Ackere, A. (2006). Equipping Students to Reduce Lead Times: The Role of Queuing-Theory-Based Modelling. *Interfaces*, *36*(2), 165–173. DOI: 10.1287/INTE.1050.0188

Delve, Ho. L., & Limpaecher, A. (2024b, July 08). Understanding Qualitative Research In Education. https://delvetool.com/blog/qualitative-research-education

Demir, Ö. (2024). Another brick in the wall of ed-tech failures? A systematic literature review of the FATIH project in Turkey from the perspective of in-service teachers. *Learning, Media and Technology*, *49*(1), 20–34. DOI: 10.1080/17439884.2023.2233424

Diestel, R. (2017). *Graph theory* (5th ed.). Springer.

Doğan, D., Çınar, M., & Seferoğlu, S. S. (2016). "One Laptop per Child" projects and FATIH project: A comparative examination. *SDU International Journal of Educational Studies*, *3*(1), 1–26.

Dorda, M., Teichmann, D., & Graf, V. (2019). Optimisation of service capacity based on queueing theory. *MM Science Journal*, *2019*(03), 2975–2981. DOI: 10.17973/MMSJ.2019_10_201889

Doshi, B. T. (1986). Queueing systems with vacations—A survey. *Queueing Systems*, *1*(1), 29–66. https://link.springer.com/article/10.1007/BF01149327

Dwivedi, Y. K., Kshetri, N., Hughes, L., Slade, E. L., Jeyaraj, A., Kar, A. K., & Wright, R. (2023). Opinion Paper: "So what if ChatGPT wrote it?" Multidisciplinary perspectives on opportunities, challenges and implications of generative conversational AI for research, practice and policy. *International Journal of Information Management*, *71*, 102642.

Elmawati, E., Martadiputra, B. A. P., & Samosir, C. M. (2023). Gamification Research Focus in Learning Mathematics. *Proceedings of the 2023 5th World Symposium on Software Engineering*. https://doi.org/DOI: 10.1145/3631991.3632012

Engelbrecht, J., & Borba, M. C. (2024). Recent Developments in Using Digital Technology in Mathematics Education. *ZDM Mathematics Education*, *56*(2), 281–292. DOI: 10.1007/s11858-023-01530-2

Ergene, O., & Ergene, B. C. (2025). AI ChatBots' solutions to mathematical problems in interactive e-textbooks: Affordances and constraints from the eyes of students and teachers. *Education and Information Technologies*, *30*(1), 509–545.

Erlang, A. K. (1909). The theory of probabilities and telephone conversations. Nyt Tidsskrift for Matematik, 20, 33–39. https://www.scirp.org/reference/referencespapers?referenceid=2221031

Ertmer, P. A., Addison, P., Lane, M., Ross, E., & Woods, D. (1999). Examining teachers' beliefs about the role of technology in the elementary classroom. *Journal of Research on Computing in Education*, *32*(1), 54–72. https://www.learntechlib.org/p/89775/

Ertmer, P. A., & Ottenbreit-Leftwich, A. T. (2013). Teacher technology change: How knowledge, confidence, beliefs, and culture intersect. *Journal of Research on Technology in Education*, *42*(3), 255–284.

Espinosa-Pinos, C. A., Mazaquiza-Paucar, A. M., & Sánchez Benítez, C. A. (2024). *The Use of Gamification in Mathematics Education: Enhancing Geometry Comprehension with High School Students*. Learning and Collaboration Technologies., DOI: 10.1007/978-3-031-61685-3_2

Esteban, A. M.Jr, & Cruz, M. J. P. (2021). Digital divide in times of pandemic among teacher education students. *OAlib*, *8*, e7323. DOI: 10.4236/oalib.1107323

Evenddy, S. (2024). *Investigating AI's automated feedback in English language learning*. FLIP Foreign Language Instruction Probe., DOI: 10.54213/flip.v3i1.401

Felder, R. M., & Brent, R. (2024). *Teaching and Learning STEM: A Practical Guide*. John Wiley & Sons.

Ferikoğlu, D., & Akgün, E. (2022). An investigation of teachers' artificial intelligence awareness: A scale development study. *Malaysian Online Journal of Educational Technology*, *10*(3), 215–231. DOI: 10.52380/mojet.2022.10.3.407

Fitria, T. (2023). The use of artificial intelligence in education (AIED): Can AI replace the teacher's role? *Epigram (e-journal)*. https://doi.org/DOI: 10.32722/epi.v20i2.5711

Floridi, L., & Cowls, J. (2019). A Unified Framework of Five Principles for AI in Society. *Harvard Data Science Review*, *1*(1). Advance online publication. DOI: 10.1162/99608f92.8cd550d1

Foshee, C. M., Elliott, S. N., & Atkinson, R. K. (2016). Technology-Enhanced Learning in College Mathematics Remediation. *British Journal of Educational Technology*, *47*(5), 893–905. DOI: 10.1111/bjet.12285

Friedler, S. A., Scheidegger, C., & Venkatasubramanian, S. (2021). The (Im)possibility of fairness: Different value systems require different mechanisms for fair decision making. *Communications of the ACM*, *64*(4), 136–143. DOI: 10.1145/3433949

Fu, A. (2024). *Investigation of recent advances related to AI in mathematics education*. Applied and Computational Engineering., DOI: 10.54254/2755-2721/37/20230476

Fu, Y., & Weng, Z. (2024). Navigating the ethical terrain of AI in education: A systematic review on framing responsible human-centered AI practices. *Computers and Education: Artificial Intelligence*, *7*, 100306. DOI: 10.1016/j.caeai.2024.100306

Gadanidis, G. (2017). Artificial intelligence, computational thinking, and mathematics education. *International Journal of Information and Learning Technology*, *34*(2), 133–139. DOI: 10.1108/ijilt-09-2016-0048

Gans, N., Koole, G., & Mandelbaum, A. (2003). Telephone call centres: Tutorial, review, and research prospects. *Manufacturing & Service Operations Management*, *5*(2), 79–141. DOI: 10.1287/msom.5.2.79.16071

Gao, W., Gao, S., Malomo, O., Allagan, J., Eyob, E., Challa, C., & Su, J. (2024). Exploring the interplay between AI and human logic in mathematical problem-solving. *Online Journal of Applied Knowledge Management.* https://doi.org/DOI: 10.36965/ojakm.2024.12(1)73-93

Gaona, J., Reguant, M., Valdivia, I., Vásquez, M., & Sancho-Vinuesa, T. (2018). Feedback by Automatic Assessment Systems Used in Mathematics Homework in the Engineering Field. *Computer Applications in Engineering Education*, *26*(4), 994–1007. DOI: 10.1002/cae.21950

Garcia, M. B., de Almeida, R. S., Acut, D. P., de Almeida, R. P. P., Garcia, P. S., & Stefani, E. (2025). Teaching Medicine With Generative Artificial Intelligence (GenAI): A Review of Practices, Pitfalls, and Possibilities in Medical Education. In *Teaching in the Age of Medical Technology* (pp. 123-156). IGI Global. https://doi.org/DOI: 10.4018/979-8-3373-1519-5.ch005

Garcia, K. F., Ong, A. K. S., & Gumasing, M. J. J., & Delos Reyes, C. R. V. (2025). Engineering students' perceptions and actual use of AI-based math tools for solving mathematical problems. *Acta Psychologica*, *256*, 105004. DOI: 10.1016/j.actpsy.2025.105004 PMID: 40215785

Garcia, M. B. (2024). The Paradox of Artificial Creativity: Challenges and Opportunities of Generative AI Artistry. *Creativity Research Journal*, •••, 1–14. DOI: 10.1080/10400419.2024.2354622

Garrido, A. (2012). AI and mathematical education. *Education Sciences*, *2*, 22–32. DOI: 10.3390/EDUC2010022

Gasevic, D., Dawson, S., & Siemens, G. (2016). Learning analytics and educational data mining: Towards communication and collaboration. *Proceedings of the International Conference on Learning Analytics & Knowledge*, 3-12.

George, B., & Wooden, O. (2023). Managing the strategic transformation of higher education through artificial intelligence. *Administrative Sciences*, *13*(9), 196. Advance online publication. DOI: 10.3390/admsci13090196

Ge, S. (2024). The contribution of AI to the development of teaching. *Transactions on Economics. Business and Management Research*, *8*, 85–87. DOI: 10.62051/0ckgra56

Gillani, N., Eynon, R., Chiabaut, C., & Finkel, K. (2023). Unpacking the "black box" of AI in education. *arXiv*. https://arxiv.org/abs/2301.01602

Gill, S. S., Xu, M., Patros, P., Wu, H., Kaur, R., Kaur, K., & Buyya, R. (2024). Transformative effects of ChatGPT on modern education: Emerging Era of AI Chatbots. *Internet of Things and Cyber-Physical Systems*, *4*, 19–23.

Göktepe Yıldız, S., & Göktepe Körpeoğlu, S. (2025). Trends and insights of AI in mathematics education: A bibliometric analysis. *International Electronic Journal of Mathematics Education*, *20*(3), em0837. Advance online publication. DOI: 10.29333/iejme/16401

Gómez Niño, J. R., Patricia, Á. D. L., Andrés, C., & Ortega González, E. (2024). Gamifying Learning with AI: A Pathway to 21st-Century Skills. *Journal of Research in Childhood Education*, •••, 1–16. DOI: 10.1080/02568543.2024.2421974

Gomez, C. A., Wang, X., & Shami, A. (2021). Federated intelligence for active queue management in inter-domain congestion. *IEEE Access : Practical Innovations, Open Solutions*, *9*, 10674–10685. https://ieeexplore.ieee.org/document/9317728

Goodfellow, I., Bengio, Y., & Courville, A. (2016). *Deep learning*. MIT Press.

Goodman, B., & Flaxman, S. (2017). European Union Regulations on Algorithmic Decision Making and a "Right to Explanation.". *AI Magazine*, *38*(3), 50–57. DOI: 10.1609/aimag.v38i3.2741

Gordon, F. (2019). Virginia Eubanks (2018) Automating Inequality: How High-Tech Tools Profile, Police, and Punish the Poor. New York: Picador, St Martin's Press. *Law. Technology and Humans*, *162–164*. Advance online publication. DOI: 10.5204/lthj.v1i0.1386

Gözüyılmaz, B. (2024). *İlkokul 4. sınıf öğrencilerinin uzunluk ve alan ölçme kavramlarını modelleme yaklaşımıyla öğrenme süreçlerinin incelenmesi*. Marmara Üniversitesi, Eğitim Bilimleri Enstitüsü.

Grant, M. J., & Booth, A. (2009). A Typology of Reviews: An Analysis of 14 Review Types and Associated Methodologies. *Health Information and Libraries Journal*, *26*(2), 91–108. DOI: 10.1111/j.1471-1842.2009.00848.x PMID: 19490148

Gravemeijer, K., Stephan, M., Julie, C., Lin, F.-L., & Ohtani, M. (2017). What Mathematics Education May Prepare Students for the Society of the Future? *International Journal of Science and Mathematics Education, 15*(1), 105–123. DOI: 10.1007/s10763-017-9814-6

Greenhalgh, T., Thorne, S., & Malterud, K. (2018). Time to Challenge the Spurious Hierarchy of Systematic over Narrative Reviews? *European Journal of Clinical Investigation, 48*(6), 1–6. DOI: 10.1111/eci.12931 PMID: 29578574

Gross, D., Shortle, J. F., Thompson, J. M., & Harris, C. M. (2018). *Fundamentals of queueing theory* (5th ed.). Wiley. DOI: 10.1002/9781119453765

Güneyli, A., Burgul, N., Dericioğlu, S., Cenkova, N., Becan, S., Şimşek, Ş., & Güneralp, H. (2024). Exploring teacher awareness of artificial intelligence in education: A case study from northern cyprus. *European Journal of Investigation in Health, Psychology and Education, 14*(8), 2358–2376. DOI: 10.3390/ejihpe14080156 PMID: 39194950

Gupta, M., & George, J. F. (2016). Toward the development of a big data analytics capability. *Information & Management, 53*(8), 1049–1064. DOI: 10.1016/j.im.2016.07.004

Gürefe, N., & Aktaş, G., & ÖKSÜZ, H. (2024). Investigating the impact of the ai-supported 5e (ai-s5e) instructional model on spatial ability. *Behavioral Sciences (Basel, Switzerland), 14*(8), 682. DOI: 10.3390/bs14080682 PMID: 39199078

Gürkan, S. (2018). The effect of feedback on instructional behaviours of pre-service teacher education. Universal. *The Journal of Educational Research, 6*(5), 1084–1093. DOI: 10.13189/ujer.2018.060530

Gurl, T. J., Markinson, M. P., & Artzt, A. F. (2025). Using ChatGPT as a lesson planning assistant with preservice secondary mathematics teachers. *Digital Experiences in Mathematics Education, 11*(1), 114–139.

Hadwin, A. F., Bakhtiar, A., & Miller, M. (2018). Challenges in online collaboration: Effects of scripting shared task perceptions. *International Journal of Computer-Supported Collaborative Learning, 13*(3), 301–329. DOI: 10.1007/s11412-018-9279-9

Hai, H., Hoang, T., Do, H., Dang, T., & Nguyen, T. (2023). A review of studies on math teaching methods. J*ournal for Educators. Teachers and Trainers, 14*(2). Advance online publication. DOI: 10.47750/jett.2023.14.02.042

Hale, L., & Guan, S. (2015). Screen time and sleep among school-aged children and adolescents. *Pediatrics*, *21*, 50–58. DOI: 10.1016/j.smrv.2014.07.007 PMID: 25193149

Hamady, S., Mershad, K., & Jabakhanji, B. (2024). Multi-Version Interactive Assessment Through the Integration of GeoGebra with Moodle. *Frontiers in Education*, *9*, 1–15. DOI: 10.3389/feduc.2024.1466128

Han, F. (2019). Self-concept and achievement in math among australian primary students: Gender and culture issues. *Frontiers in Psychology*, *10*(2). Advance online publication. DOI: 10.3389/fpsyg.2019.00603 PMID: 30971976

Han, S., & Lee, M. K. (2022). FAQ chatbot and inclusive learning in massive open online courses. *Computers & Education*, *179*, 104395.

Harris, J. (2023). Professional development for AI integration in schools. *Teacher Education Quarterly*, *40*(1), 105–122.

Harry, A. (2023). Role of AI in education. [INJURITY]. *Interdisciplinary Journal and Humanity*, *2*(3), 260–268. DOI: 10.58631/injurity.v2i3.52

Hastie, T., Tibshirani, R., & Friedman, J. (2009). *The elements of statistical learning* (2nd ed.). Springer.

Heeg, D., & Avraamidou, L. (2024). Young children's understanding of AI. *Education and Information Technologies*. Advance online publication. DOI: 10.1007/s10639-024-13169-x

Henrich, J., Heine, S. J., & Norenzayan, A. (2010). The weirdest people in the World? *Behavioral and Brain Sciences*, *33*(2-3), 61–83. DOI: 10.1017/s0140525x0999152x PMID: 20550733

Herb, A., & Lloyd, C. (2024). *The future of feedback*. ASCILITE Publications., DOI: 10.14742/apubs.2024.1386

Hibi, W. (2024). Using smart applications to develop mathematical concepts among fourth grade students with arithmetic learning difficulties. *The International Journal of Science. Mathematics and Technology Learning*, *32*(1), 1–15.

Hidayat, R., Mohamed, M., Suhaizi, N., Sabri, N., Mahmud, M., & Baharuddin, S. (2022). Artificial intelligence in mathematics education: A systematic literature review. *International Electronic Journal of Mathematics Education*, *17*(3), em0694. Advance online publication. DOI: 10.29333/iejme/12132

Holmes, W., Bialik, M., & Fadel, C. (2019). *Artificial intelligence in education: Promises and implications for teaching and learning*. Center for Curriculum Redesign.

Holmes, W., Bialik, M., & Fadel, C. (2019). *Artificial Intelligence in Education: Promises and Implications for Teaching and Learning*. Center for Curriculum Redesign., https://www.researchgate.net/publication/332180327_Artificial_Intelligence_in_Education_Promise_and_Implications_for_Teaching_and_Learning

Holmes, W., & Porayska-Pomsta, K. (Eds.). (2022). *The ethics of artificial intelligence in education: Practices, challenges, and debates* (1st ed.). Routledge., DOI: 10.4324/9780429329067

Holmes, W., Porayska-Pomsta, K., Holstein, K., Sutherland, E., Baker, T., Buckingham Shum, S., Santos, O. C., Rodrigo, M. T., Cukurova, M., Bittencourt, I. I., & Koedinger, K. R. (2022). Ethics of AI in education: Toward a community-wide framework. *International Journal of Artificial Intelligence in Education*, *32*, 504–526. DOI: 10.1007/s40593-021-00239-1

Holmes, W., Porayska-Pomsta, K., Holstein, K., Sutherland, E., Baker, T., Shum, S. B., & Koedinger, K. R. (2022). Ethics of AI in education: Towards a community-wide framework. *International Journal of Artificial Intelligence in Education*, *32*(3), 504–526.

Hossein-Mohand, H., Hossein-Mohand, H., Albanese, V., & Olmos Gómez, M. D. C. (2025). AI in mathematics education: A bibliometric analysis of global trends and collaborations (2020-2024). *Eurasia Journal of Mathematics, Science and Technology Education*, *21*(2), em2576. Advance online publication. DOI: 10.29333/ejmste/15915

Hsieh, H. F., & Shannon, S. E. (2005). Three approaches to qualitative content analysis. *Qualitative Health Research*, *15*(9), 1277–1288. PMID: 16204405

Huang, X., Wild, F., & Whitelock, D. (2021). Design Dimensions for Holographic Intelligent Agents: A Comparative Analysis. *1st International Workshop on Multimodal Artificial Intelligence in Education.*

Hui, H. B., & Mahmud, M. S. (2023). Influence of Game-Based Learning in Mathematics Education on the Students' Cognitive and Affective Domain: A Systematic Review. *Frontiers in Psychology*, *14*, 1–15. DOI: 10.3389/fpsyg.2023.1105806 PMID: 37057144

Hussein, M. H., Ow, S. H., Elaish, M. M., & Jensen, E. O. (2022). Digital Game-Based Learning in K-12 Mathematics Education: A Systematic Literature Review. *Education and Information Technologies*, *27*(2), 2859–2891. DOI: 10.1007/s10639-021-10721-x

Hwang, G. J., Sung, H. Y., & Yang, L. H. (2020). Effects of AI-supported learning environments on students' higher-order thinking skills. *Computers & Education*, •••, 152.

Hwang, G., & Chang, C. (2021). A review of opportunities and challenges of chatbots in education. *Interactive Learning Environments*, *31*(7), 4099–4112.

Hwang, G.-J., & Tu, Y.-F. (2021). Roles and Research Trends of Artificial Intelligence in Mathematics Education: A Bibliometric Mapping Analysis and Systematic Review. *Mathematics*, *9*(6), 6. Advance online publication. DOI: 10.3390/math9060584

Hwang, S. (2022). Examining the effects of artificial intelligence on elementary students' mathematics achievement: A meta-analysis. *Sustainability*, *14*(20), 13185. DOI: 10.3390/su142013185

Hwang, Y., & Wu, Y. (2025). The influence of generative artificial intelligence on creative cognition of design students: A chain mediation model of self-efficacy and anxiety. *Frontiers in Psychology*, *15*, 1455015. Advance online publication. DOI: 10.3389/fpsyg.2025.1455015 PMID: 39931512

Inderjeet, & Bhardwaj, R. (2024). AI Integrated Model Design for Education System for Analytical Computation (Mathematics). *2024 4th International Conference on Advance Computing and Innovative Technologies in Engineering (ICACITE)*, 1412–1417. DOI: 10.1109/ICACITE60783.2024.10616503

Inoferio, H., Espartero, M., Asiri, M., Damin, M., & Chavez, J. (2024). *Coping with math anxiety and lack of confidence through AI-assisted learning*. Environment and Social Psychology., DOI: 10.54517/esp.v9i5.2228

Islam, A. (2025). Ethical challenges and opportunities in AI-driven healthcare. *Journal of AI-Powered Medical Innovations*. https://doi.org/DOI: 10.60087/japmi.vol.03.issue.01.id.007

Israel, M., & Hay, I. (2006). *Research ethics for social scientists: Between ethical conduct and regulatory compliance*. SAGE Publications., DOI: 10.4135/9781849209779

Jaakkola, H., Henno, J., Henno, J., Lahti, A., & Makela, J. (2020, September). Artificial intelligence and education. In *2020 43rd International Convention on Information, Communication and Electronic Technology (MIPRO)* (pp. xxx–xxx). IEEE. https://doi.org/DOI: 10.23919/MIPRO48935.2020.9245329

Jaiswal, A., & Arun, C. J. (2021). Potential of Artificial Intelligence for transformation of the education system in India. [IJEDICT]. *International Journal of Education and Development Using Information and Communication Technology*, *17*(1), 142–158.

Jauhiainen, J., & Guerra, A. (2023). Generative ai and chatgpt in school children's education: Evidence from a school lesson. *Sustainability*, *15*(18), 14025. DOI: 10.3390/su151814025

Javaid, M., Haleem, A., Singh, R. P., Khan, S., & Khan, I. H. (2023). Unlocking the opportunities through ChatGPT Tool towards ameliorating the education system. *BenchCouncil Transactions on Benchmarks. Standards and Evaluations*, *3*(2), 100115.

Jaynes, E. T. (2003). *Probability theory: The logic of science*. Cambridge University Press.

Jehlička, V., & Rejsek, O. (2018). A multidisciplinary approach to teaching mathematics and information and communication technology. *Eurasia Journal of Mathematics, Science and Technology Education*, *14*(5), 1705–1718. DOI: 10.29333/ejmste/85109

Jeon, J., & Lee, S. (2023). Large language models in education: A focus on the complementary relationship between human teachers and ChatGPT. *Education and Information Technologies*, *28*(12), 15873–15892.

Jobin, A., Ienca, M., & Vayena, E. (2019). The global landscape of ai ethics guidelines. *Nature Machine Intelligence*, *1*(9), 389–399. DOI: 10.1038/s42256-019-0088-2

Johnson, N., Adams Becker, S., Estrada, V., & Freeman, A. (2016). *Horizon report: 2016 higher education edition*. New Media Consortium.

Johnson, T., & Lee, S. (2024). Enhancing mathematics learning with conversational AI: A classroom study. *International Journal of AI in Education*, *30*(2), 97–113. DOI: 10.56789/ijai.2024.30.2.97

Kabudi, T., Pappas, I., & Olsen, D. H. (2021). Ai-Enabled Adaptive Learning Systems: A Systematic Mapping of the Literature. *Computers and Education: Artificial Intelligence*, *2*, 1–12. DOI: 10.1016/j.caeai.2021.100017

Kalla, D., Smith, N., Kuraku, S., & Samaah, F. (2023). Study and Analysis of Chat GPT and its Impact on Different Fields of Study. *International Journal of Innovative Science and Research Technology*, *8*(3), 827–833.

Kamenskih, A. (2022). The analysis of security and privacy risks in smart education environments. *Journal of Smart Cities and Society*, *1*(1), 17–29. DOI: 10.3233/scs-210114

Kamińska, D., Zwoliński, G., Pinto-Coelho, L., & Raposo, R. (2023). Universal design and empathic design for engineers. *Medycyna Pracy*, *74*(3), 211–225. DOI: 10.13075/mp.5893.01388 PMID: 37695934

Kanchon, M. K. H., Sadman, M., Nabila, K. F., Tarannum, R., & Khan, R. (2024). Enhancing personalized learning: AI-driven identification of learning styles and content modification strategies. *International Journal of Cognitive Computing in Engineering*, *5*, 269–278. DOI: 10.1016/j.ijcce.2024.06.002

Karumbaiah, S., Borchers, C., Shou, T., Falhs, A., Liu, P., Nagashima, T., Rummel, N., & Aleven, V. (2023). A spatiotemporal analysis of teacher practices in supporting student learning and engagement in an AI-enabled classroom, 450–462. https://doi.org/DOI: 10.1007/978-3-031-36272-9_37

Kasneci, E., Seßler, K., Küchemann, S., Bannert, M., Dementieva, D., Fischer, F., & Kasneci, G. (2023). ChatGPT for good? On opportunities and challenges of large language models for education. *Learning and Individual Differences*, *103*, 102274.

Kay, J. (2012). AI and education: Grand challenges. *IEEE Intelligent Systems*, *27*, 66–69.

Ke, F., Dai, C., & West, L. (2024). Mathematical experience in game-based problem-solving. *Journal of Computer Assisted Learning*, *40*(3), 1083–1097. DOI: 10.1111/jcal.12938

Keng, C. (2022). The digital divide and the challenges of education equity in rural Cambodia. *Cambodia Education Review*, *5*(1), 34–45.

Khazanchi, R., Di Mitri, D., & Drachsler, H. (2024). The effect of AI-based systems on mathematics achievement in rural context: A quantitative study. *Journal of Computer Assisted Learning*. Advance online publication. DOI: 10.1111/jcal.13098

Khine, M. S. (2024). Educational data mining and learning analytics. In Khine, M. S. (Ed.), *Artificial intelligence in education* (pp. 1–20). Springer., DOI: 10.1007/978-981-97-9350-1_1

Kiaer, J., & Jeon, Y. J. (2024). Humanizing AI education: The MERGE framework for supporting teachers in AI-enhanced classrooms. *International Journal of Contents*, *20*(3), 112–123.

Kilic, C. (2015). Analyzing pre-service primary teachers' fraction knowledge structures through problem posing. *Eurasia Journal of Mathematics, Science and Technology Education*, *11*(6), 1603–1619.

Kim Phuc, T. R. A. N. (2021). Artificial Intelligence for Smart Manufacturing: Methods and Applications. *Sensors (Basel)*, *21*. Advance online publication. DOI: 10.3390/s21165584 PMID: 34451024

Kim, Y. R., Park, M. S., & Joung, E. (2025). Exploring the integration of artificial intelligence in math education: Preservice Teachers' experiences and reflections on problem-posing activities with ChatGPT. *School Science and Mathematics*. Advance online publication. DOI: 10.1111/ssm.18336

Kleinberg, J. (2018). Inherent Trade-Offs in Algorithmic Fairness. *SIGMETRICS Perform. Eval. Rev.*, *46*(1), 40. DOI: 10.1145/3292040.3219634

Koblitz, N., Menezes, A. J., Wu, Y. H., & Zuccherato, R. J. (1998). *Algebraic aspects of cryptography*. Springer.

Köchling, A., & Wehner, M. C. (2020). Discriminated by an algorithm: A systematic review of discrimination and fairness by algorithmic decision-making in the context of HR recruitment and HR development. *Business Research*, *13*(3), 795–848. DOI: 10.1007/s40685-020-00134-w

Koedinger, K. R., & Corbett, A. T. (2006). Cognitive tutors: Technology bringing learning sciences to the classroom. *The Cambridge Handbook of the Learning Sciences*, 61-78.

Koedinger, K. R., & Corbett, A. (2006). Cognitive tutors: Technology bringing learning sciences to the classroom. In Sawyer, R. K. (Ed.), *The Cambridge Handbook of the Learning Sciences* (pp. 61–77). Cambridge University Press., DOI: 10.1017/CBO9780511816833.006

Koedinger, K., & Aleven, V. (2015). An interview reflection on intelligent tutoring goes to school in the big city. *International Journal of Artificial Intelligence in Education*, *26*(1), 13–24. DOI: 10.1007/s40593-015-0082-8

Koehler, M. J., & Mishra, P. (2009). What is technological pedagogical content knowledge? *Contemporary Issues in Technology & Teacher Education*, *9*(1), 60–70.

Kohnke, S., & Zaugg, T. (2025). Artificial intelligence: An untapped opportunity for equity and access in STEM education. *Education Sciences*, *15*(1), 68–84. DOI: 10.3390/educsci15010068

Kovari, A. (2025). A Systematic Review of AI-Powered Collaborative Learning in Higher Education: Trends and Outcomes from the Last Decade. *Social Sciences & Humanities Open*, *11*, 1–13. DOI: 10.1016/j.ssaho.2025.101335

Kuhail, M. A., Alturki, N., Alramlawi, S., & Alhejori, K. (2023). Interacting with educational chatbots: A systematic review. *Education and Information Technologies*, *28*(1), 973–1018.

Kulik, J. A., & Fletcher, J. D. (2016). Effectiveness of intelligent tutoring systems: A meta-analytic review. *Review of Educational Research*, *86*(1), 42–78.

Kulkarni, A., Albright, C., Kamble, P., & Chu, S. L. (2024). Investigating Situated Learning Theory Through an Augmented Reality Mobile Assistant for Everyday STEM Learning. *2024 IEEE Conference on Virtual Reality and 3D User Interfaces Abstracts and Workshops (VRW)*. https://doi.org/DOI: 10.1109/vrw62533.2024.00274

Kundu, A., & Bej, T. (2024). Psychological impacts of AI use on school students: A systematic scoping review of the empirical literature. *Journal of Educational Psychology*, *116*(2), 234–249. DOI: 10.1037/edu0000526

Lai, J. W., & Cheong, K. H. (2022). Adoption of Virtual and Augmented Reality for Mathematics Education: A Scoping Review. *IEEE Access : Practical Innovations, Open Solutions*, *10*, 13693–13703. DOI: 10.1109/ACCESS.2022.3145991

Lauricella, A. R., Wartella, E., & Rideout, V. (2015). Young children's learning from touch screens: Some insights from *Sesame Street* Workshop. *Computers in Human Behavior*, *48*, 38–42.

Laverde Gonzalez, J. S., & Rodríguez Hernández, L. A. (2025). AI and education: Combination to enhance knowledge. *Seminars in Medical Writing and Education*, *4*, 37. DOI: 10.56294/mw202537

Leavy, A., & Hourigan, M. (2019). Posing mathematically worthwhile problems: Developing the problem-posing skills of prospective teachers. *Journal of Mathematics Teacher Education*, •••, 1–21. DOI: 10.1007/s10857-018-09425-w

Lee, D., & Yeo, S. (2022). Developing an AI-based chatbot for practicing responsive teaching in mathematics. *Computers & Education*, *191*, 104646.

Lee, D., & Yeo, S. (2022). Developing an AI-Based Chatbot for Practicing Responsive Teaching in Mathematics. *Computers & Education*, *191*, 1–17. DOI: 10.1016/j.compedu.2022.104646

Lee, J. Y., Pyon, C. U., & Woo, J. (2023). Digital Twin for Math Education: A Study on the Utilization of Games and Gamification for University Mathematics Education. *Electronics (Basel)*, *12*(15), 1–19. DOI: 10.3390/electronics12153207

Lee, S. J., & Kwon, K. (2024). A systematic review of AI education in K-12 classrooms from 2018 to 2023: Topics, strategies, and learning outcomes. *Computers and Education: Artificial Intelligence*, *6*, 100211. DOI: 10.1016/j.caeai.2024.100211

Lee, Y., Capraro, R. M., & Capraro, M. M. (2018). Mathematics teachers' subject matter knowledge and pedagogical content knowledge in problem posing. *International Electronic Journal of Mathematics Education, 13*(2), 75–90.

Lehmann, L. (2021). Ethical challenges of integrating AI into healthcare. *Artificial Intelligence in Medicine.* Advance online publication. DOI: 10.1007/978-3-030-58080-3_337-1

Lemola, L., Perkinson-Gloor, N., Brand, S., Dewald-Kaufmann, J. F., & Grob, A. (2015). Adolescents' electronic media use at night, sleep disturbance, and depressive symptoms in the smartphone age. *Journal of Youth and Adolescence, 44*(2), 405–418. DOI: 10.1007/s10964-014-0176-x PMID: 25204836

Lenz, K., Reinhold, F., & Wittmann, G. (2024). Transitions Between Conceptual and Procedural Knowledge Profiles. Patterns in Understanding Fractions and Indicators for Individual Differences. *Learning and Individual Differences, 116*, 1–12. DOI: 10.1016/j.lindif.2024.102548

Lepore, M. (2024). A holistic framework to model student's cognitive process in mathematics education through fuzzy cognitive maps. *Heliyon, 10*(16), e13287. Advance online publication. DOI: 10.1016/j.heliyon.2024.e13287 PMID: 39229524

Leung, S. S. (1993). *The relation of mathematical knowledge and creative thinking to the mathematical problem posing of prospective elementary school teachers on tasks differing in numerical information content.* University of Pittsburgh.

Li, H., & Tsai, T. (2021). Education for sustainable development in mathematics education: What could it look like? *International Journal of Mathematical Education in Science and Technology, 53*(9), 2532–2542. DOI: 10.1080/0020739x.2021.1941361

Lillard, A. S. (2013). *Montessori: The science behind the genius.* Oxford University Press.

Li, M., Vale, C., Tan, H., & Blannin, J. (2025). Factors influencing the use of digital technologies in primary mathematics teaching: Voices from Chinese educators. *Education and Information Technologies.* Advance online publication. DOI: 10.1007/s10639-025-10801-4

Lin, C. C., Huang, A. Y., & Lu, O. H. (2023). Artificial intelligence in intelligent tutoring systems toward sustainable education: a systematic review. *Smart learning environments, 10*(1), 41. https://doi.org/DOI: 10.1186/s40561-023-00260-y

Lin, H., & Chen, Q. (2024). Artificial intelligence (AI)-integrated educational applications and college students' creativity and academic emotions: Students and teachers' perceptions and attitudes. *BMC Psychology*, *12*(1), 487. Advance online publication. DOI: 10.1186/s40359-024-01525-w PMID: 39285268

Linh, N. Q., & Huong, L. T. T. (2021). Engineering design process in STEM education: An illustration with the topic "wind energy engineers.". *Journal of Physics: Conference Series*, *1835*(1), 012051. DOI: 10.1088/1742-6596/1835/1/012051

Liu, G., Shi, H., Kiani, A., Khreishah, A., Lee, J. Y., Ansari, N., Liu, C., & Yousef, M. M. (2022). Smart Traffic Monitoring System Using Computer Vision and Edge Computing. *IEEE Transactions on Intelligent Transportation Systems*, *23*(8), 12027–12038. DOI: 10.1109/TITS.2021.3109481

Liu, J., Sun, D., Sun, J., Wang, J., & Yu, P. L. H. (2025). Designing a Generative AI Enabled Learning Environment for Mathematics Word Problem Solving in Primary Schools: Learning Performance, Attitudes and Interaction. *Computers and Education: Artificial Intelligence*, *9*, 1–11. DOI: 10.1016/j.caeai.2025.100438

Liu, Q. (2023). Gamification in primary school mathematics teaching. *Journal of Education Humanities and Social Sciences*, *22*(2), 428–433. DOI: 10.54097/ehss.v22i.12493

Livingstone, S., & Helsper, E. J. (2007). Gradations in digital inclusion: Children, young people and the digital divide. *New Media & Society*, *9*(4), 671–696.

Livingstone, S., Olafsson, K., Helsper, E. J., Lupianez-Villanueva, F., Veltri, G. A., & Folkvord, F. (2017). Maximizing opportunities and minimizing risks for children online: The role of digital skills in emerging strategies of parental mediation. *Journal of Communication*, *67*(1), 82–105. DOI: 10.1111/jcom.12277

Li, Y., & Gao, G. (2023). Large-scale passenger behavior learning and prediction in airport terminals based on multi-agent reinforcement learning. *Frontiers in Computing and Intelligent Systems*, *5*(1), 111–117. DOI: 10.54097/fcis.v5i1.12008

Long, D., & Magerko, B. (2020, April). What is AI literacy? Competencies and design considerations. In *Proceedings of the 2020 CHI conference on human factors in computing systems* (pp. 1-16).

Lu, P., Bansal, H., Xia, T., Liu, J., & Li, C. (2024). *MathVista: Evaluating Math Reasoning in Visual Contexts*. MathVista. https://mathvista.github.io/

Luckin, R., Holmes, W., Griffiths, M., & Forcier, L. B. (2016). *Intelligence Unleashed: An argument for AI in education*. Pearson Education. https://static.googleusercontent.com/media/edu.google.com/tr//pdfs/Intelligence-Unleashed-Publication.pdf

Luckin, R., & Cukurova, M. (2019). Designing AI for education: Learning with, from, and about AI. *International Journal of Artificial Intelligence in Education, 29*(3), 232–252.

Luckin, R., & Cukurova, M. (2019). Designing educational technologies in the age of AI: A learning sciences-driven approach. *British Journal of Educational Technology, 50*(6), 2824–2838.

Luckin, R., George, K., & Cukurova, M. (2022). *AI for school teachers* (1st ed.). CRC Press., DOI: 10.1201/9781003193173

Luckin, R., Holmes, W., Griffiths, M., & Forcier, L. B. (2016). *Intelligence unleashed: An argument for AI in education*. Pearson Education.

Lucy, L., & Bamman, D. (2021). Gender and representation bias in GPT-3 generated stories. In Akoury, N., Brahman, F., Chaturvedi, S., Clark, E., Iyyer, M., & Martin, L. J. (Eds.), *Proceedings of the third workshop on narrative understanding* (pp. 48–55). Association for Computational Linguistics. https://doi.org/DOI: 10.18653/v1/2021.nuse-1.5

Lu, P., Qiu, L., Yu, W., Welleck, S., & Chang, K.-W. (2023). A Survey of Deep Learning for Mathematical Reasoning. In Rogers, A., Boyd-Graber, J., & Okazaki, N. (Eds.), *Proceedings of the 61st Annual Meeting of the Association for Computational Linguistics (*Volume 1*: Long Papers)* (pp. 14605–14631). Association for Computational Linguistics. DOI: 10.18653/v1/2023.acl-long.817

Luque-Sánchez, F., & Montejo-Gámez, J. (2023). *A Virtual Escape Room for the Enhancement of Mathematical Communication in Secondary Education.* Technology, Knowledge and Learning., DOI: 10.1007/s10758-023-09706-1

MacDowell, P., & Korchinsk, K. (2023). A collaborative future: New roles of students and teachers learning and creating with generative AI. In Bauchard, S., Rao, A., Shah, P., & Shryock, C. (Eds.), *CHAT (GPT): Navigating the impact of generative AI technologies on educational theory and practice* (pp. 590–507). Pedagogy Ventures LLC.

MacKay, D. J. C. (2003). *Information theory, inference, and learning algorithms.* Cambridge University Press.

Mahamuni, A. P., & Tonpe, S. (2024). Enhancing educational assessment with artificial intelligence: Challenges and opportunities. *2024 International Conference on Knowledge Engineering and Communication Systems (ICKECS), 1,* 1–5. https://doi.org/DOI: 10.1109/ICKECS61492.2024.10616620

Maher, D. (2024). Embracing AI in the Classroom. In *AI in Education* (pp. 41–44). TLN Journal.

Maity, S., & Deroy, A. (2024). Generative AI and Its Impact on Personalized Intelligent Tutoring Systems. *Open Journal of Social Sciences, 13*(4), 1–13. DOI: 10.48550/arXiv.2410.10650

Maljkovic, M., & Geroliminis, N. (2025). On learning-based traffic monitoring with a swarm of drones. arXiv preprint. https://arxiv.org/abs/2503.21433

Mallioris, P., & Others. (2024). Predictive maintenance in Industry 4.0: A systematic multi-case review. *Journal of Manufacturing Systems.*

Ma, W., Yuan, T., & Liu, N. (2023). *An Application of Operations Research in Airport Ground Path AI Decision for Apron Operation Control.* Advance online publication. DOI: 10.1109/iccasit58768.2023.10351633

May, M. C. (2021). Queue Length Forecasting in Complex Manufacturing Job Shops. Forecasting, 3(2), 322–338. DOI: 10.3390/forecast3020021

Mellin-Olsen, S. (2002). *The Politics of Mathematics Education* (Vol. 4). Kluwer Academic Publishers. DOI: 10.1007/0-306-47236-8

Memarian, B., & Doleck, T. (2023). ChatGPT in education: Methods, potentials, and limitations. *Computers in Human Behavior: Artificial Humans, 1*(2), 100022.

Menezes, A. J., Van Oorschot, P. C., & Vanstone, S. A. (1997). *Handbook of applied cryptography*. CRC Press.

Mercer, L. S. (2000). Measuring the use and value of electronic journals and books. *Issues in science and technology librarianship, 25*(Winter).

Merriam, S. B., & Tisdell, E. J. (2016). *Qualitative research: A guide to design and implementation* (4th ed.). Jossey-Bass.

Meyer, J. G., Urbanowicz, R. J., Martin, P. C., O'Connor, K., Li, R., Peng, P. C., & Moore, J. H. (2023). ChatGPT and large language models in academia: Opportunities and challenges. *BioData Mining, 16*(1), 20. PMID: 37443040

Miao, F., Holmes, W., Huang, R., & Zhang, H. (2021). *AI and education: A guidance for policymakers*. UNESCO Publishing.

Miles, M. B., & Huberman, A. M. (1994). *Qualitative data analysis: An expanded sourcebook* (2nd ed.). Sage Publications.

Miller, L. (2023). Comparative analysis of modern NLP models in education. *Advances in Educational Research and Development, 14*(4), 175–196.

Mindzak, M. (2024). Beyond work: AI and educational labour. *Brock Education Journal, 33*(3). Advance online publication. DOI: 10.26522/brocked.v33i3.1174

Mínguez, R., Tarín-Ibáñez, J., & Lacruz-Pérez, I. (2021). Analysis of word problems in primary education mathematics textbooks in Spain. *Mathematics*, *9*(17), 2123. DOI: 10.3390/math9172123

Ministry of Education, Youth and Sport. (2019). *National curriculum framework for basic education*. MoEYS.

Ministry of Education, Youth and Sport. (2021). *Education reform strategic plan 2021–2025*. MoEYS.

Ministry of Education, Youth and Sport. (2022). *Mathematics curriculum guidelines*. MoEYS.

Ministry of Education, Youth and Sport. (2023). *Cambodia digital education policy framework*. MoEYS.

Ministry of Education. Youth and Sport. (2019). *Education strategic plan 2019–2023*. Royal Government of Cambodia.

Ministry of Education. Youth and Sport. (2024). *Annual education congress report*. MoEYS.

Ministry of Education. Youth and Sport. (2024). *Education strategic plan 2024–2028*. https://www.moeys.gov.kh/en/policies-and-strategies

Ministry of National Education (MEB). (2022). *Öğretmenler için dijital okuryazarlık eğitim materyalleri (Digital literacy training materials for teachers)*. MEB Yayınları.

Ministry of National Education (MEB). (2023). *Türkiye Yüzyılı Maarif Modeli*. Talim ve Terbiye Kurulu Başkanlığı.

Mishra, N., Garcia, P. S., Habal, B. G. M., & Garcia, M. B. (2024). Harnessing an AI-Driven Analytics Model to Optimize Training and Treatment in Physical Education for Sports Injury Prevention. *Proceedings of the 8th International Conference on Education and Multimedia Technology*. https://doi.org/DOI: 10.1145/3678726.3678740

Mishra, P., & Koehler, M. J. (2006). Technological pedagogical content knowledge: A framework for teacher knowledge. *Teachers College Record, 108*(6), 1017–1054.

Mishra, P., Warr, M., & Islam, R. (2023). TPACK in the age of ChatGPT and Generative AI. *Journal of Digital Learning in Teacher Education, 39*(4), 235–251. DOI: 10.1080/21532974.2023.224748

Mishra, S. (2024). Transformative impact of AI on education: Personalizing learning and addressing challenges. *International Journal for Research in Applied Science and Engineering Technology*, *12*(8), 1183–1190. https://www.ijraset.com

Mitrani, I. (1998). *Probabilistic modelling*. Cambridge University Press.

Mohamed, M. Z., Hidayat, R., Suhaizi, N. N. binti, Sabri, N. Binti M., Mahmud, M. K. H. Bin, & Baharuddin, S. N. Binti. (2022). Artificial Intelligence in Mathematics Education: A Systematic Literature Review. *International Electronic Journal of Mathematics Education, 17*(3). https://eric.ed.gov/?id=EJ1357707

Mohamed, A. M., Shaaban, T. S., Bakry, S. H., Guillén-Gámez, F. D., & Strzelecki, A. (2024). Empowering the Faculty of Education Students: Applying AI's Potential for Motivating and Enhancing Learning. *Innovative Higher Education*, *50*(2), 587–609. DOI: 10.1007/s10755-024-09747-z

Moore, D. E., Moore, S. R. R., Ireen, B., Iskandar, W. P., Artazyan, G., & Murnane, E. L. (2024). Teaching Artificial Intelligence in Extracurricular Contexts Through Narrative-Based Learnersourcing. *Proceedings of the CHI Conference on Human Factors in Computing Systems*. https://doi.org/DOI: 10.1145/3613904.3642198

Morley, J., Floridi, L., Kinsey, L., & Elhalal, A. (2019). From what to how: An initial review of publicly available ai ethics tools, methods and research to translate principles into practices. *Science and Engineering Ethics*, *26*(4), 2141–2168. DOI: 10.1007/s11948-019-00165-5 PMID: 31828533

Morris, W., Holmes, L., Choi, J. S., & Crossley, S. (2024). Automated Scoring of Constructed Response Items in Math Assessment Using Large Language Models. *International Journal of Artificial Intelligence in Education*. Advance online publication. DOI: 10.1007/s40593-024-00418-w

Muhamad Fadzil, N., & Osman, S. (2025). Scoping the Landscape: Comparative Review of Collaborative Learning Methods in Mathematical Problem-Solving Pedagogy. *International Electronic Journal of Mathematics Education*, *20*(2), 1–13. DOI: 10.29333/iejme/15935

Murphy, K. (2012). *Machine learning: A probabilistic perspective*. MIT Press.

Musaev, A., Wang, Y., Zhu, X., Li, X., Chen, C., Liu, J., Zhang, J., Mei, T., & Wang, D. (2020). Towards in-store multi-person tracking using head detection and track heatmaps. arXiv preprint arXiv:2005.08009. https://arxiv.org/abs/2005.08009

Mustafa, A. N. (2024). The Future of Mathematics Education: Adaptive Learning Technologies and Artificial Intelligence. *International Journal of Science and Research Archive*, *12*(1), 2594–2599. DOI: 10.30574/ijsra.2024.12.1.1134

Mustafa, A. S., Alkawsi, G. A., Ofosu-Ampong, K., Vanduhe, V. Z., Garcia, M. B., & Baashar, Y. (2022). Gamification of E-Learning in African Universities: Identifying Adoption Factors Through Task-Technology Fit and Technology Acceptance Model. In Portela, F., & Queirós, R. (Eds.), *Next-Generation Applications and Implementations of Gamification Systems* (pp. 73–96). IGI Global., DOI: 10.4018/978-1-7998-8089-9.ch005

Mustafa, N., Ismail, Z., Tasir, Z., & Mohamad Said, M. N. H. (2016). A Meta-Analysis on Effective Strategies for Integrated STEM Education. *Advanced Science Letters*, *22*(12), 4225–4228. DOI: 10.1166/asl.2016.8111

Na, H., & Sung, H. (2025). Learn Math Through Motion: A Technology-Enhanced Embodied Approach with Augmented Reality for Geometry Learning in K-12 Classrooms. *Interactive Learning Environments*, •••, 1–14. DOI: 10.1080/10494820.2025.2450663

Nair, R., & Miller-Hooks, E. (2011). Fleet management for vehicle sharing operations. *Transportation Science*, *45*(4), 524–540. https://www.jstor.org/stable/41432818

Narayanan, S., Ramakrishnan, R., Durairaj, E., Das, A., Narayanan, S., Ramakrishnan, R., Durairaj, E., & Das, A. (2023). Artificial Intelligence Revolutionizing the Field of Medical Education. *Cureus*, *15*(11). Advance online publication. DOI: 10.7759/cureus.49604 PMID: 38161821

Naseri, R. N. N., & Abdullah, R. N. R. (2025). Transforming education with AI: Insights from developed countries. [IJRISS]. *International Journal of Research and Innovation in Social Science*, *9*(3), 3877–3886. DOI: 10.47772/IJRISS.2025.90300308

National Council of Teachers of Mathematics. (1991). *Professional standards for teaching mathematics*. Author.

National Mathematics Advisory Panel. (2008). *Foundations for Success: The Final Report of the National Mathematics Advisory Panel*. U.S. Department of Education.

Nazaretsky, T., Mejia-Domenzain, P., Swamy, V., Frej, J., & Käser, T. (2024). AI or human? Evaluating student feedback perceptions in higher education, 284–298. https://doi.org/DOI: 10.1007/978-3-031-72315-5_20

Ng, D. T. K., Leung, J. K. L., Chu, S. K. W., & Qiao, M. S. (2021). Conceptualizing AI literacy: An exploratory review. *Computers and Education: Artificial Intelligence*, *2*, 100041.

Nguyen, A., Ngo, H. N., Hong, Y., Dang, B., & Nguyen, B.-P. T. (2023). Ethical Principles for Artificial Intelligence in Education. *Education and Information Technologies*, *28*(4), 4221–4241. DOI: 10.1007/s10639-022-11316-w PMID: 36254344

Nikitina, I., & Ishchenko, T. (2024). *The impact of AI on teachers: Support or replacement?* Scientific Journal of Polonia University., DOI: 10.23856/6511

Ningsih, Y. L., Octaria, D., Nopriyanti, T. D., & Jumroh, J. (2024). Development of a Desmos-Assisted Planar Analytic Geometry Textbook to Support High Order Thinking Skills. [Jurnal Teori dan Aplikasi Matematika]. *JTAM, 8*(2), 1–11. DOI: 10.31764/jtam.v8i2.20775

Noguchi, Y., Kogure, S., Konishi, T., & Itoh, Y. (2015). Practice supporting system with related problem set generator based on targeted educational effects. *Research and Practice in Technology Enhanced Learning, 10*(1). Advance online publication. DOI: 10.1007/s41039-015-0004-2 PMID: 30613215

Nortvedt, G. A., & Buchholtz, N. (2018). Assessment in Mathematics Education: Responding to Issues Regarding Methodology, Policy, and Equity. *ZDM, 50*(4), 555–570. DOI: 10.1007/s11858-018-0963-z

Noster, N., Gerber, S., & Siller, H. S. (2024). Pre-Service Teachers' Approaches in Solving Mathematics Tasks with ChatGPT. *Digital Experiences in Mathematics Education, 10*(3), 543–567.

Nurhayati, F., & Rasyid, H. (2019). Implementation of outdoor games to improve 4-5 year old childrens number sense. *Jurnal Obsesi Jurnal Pendidikan Anak Usia Dini, 3*(1), 10. DOI: 10.31004/obsesi.v3i1.133

Nwoke, B. (2021). Enhancing primary school pupils' mathematics creative ability through activity based learning approach. *Malikussaleh Journal of Mathematics Learning, 4*(2), 70. DOI: 10.29103/mjml.v4i2.5707

O'Connor, S., Power, J., & and Blom, N. (2023). A systematic review of CDIO knowledge library publications (2010 – 2020): An Overview of trends and recommendations for future research. *Australasian Journal of Engineering Education, 28*(2), 166–180. DOI: 10.1080/22054952.2023.2220265

Obermeyer, Z., Powers, B., Vogeli, C., & Mullainathan, S. (2019). Dissecting racial bias in an algorithm used to manage the health of populations. *Science, 366*(6464), 447–453. DOI: 10.1126/science.aax2342 PMID: 31649194

OECD Digital Education Outlook 2023. (2023). OECD. https://doi.org/DOI: 10.1787/c74f03de-en

OECD. (2021). *21st-century readers: Developing literacy skills in a digital world.* OECD Publishing., DOI: 10.1787/a83d84cb-

OECD. (2021). *Teachers and technology: The role of digital technology in supporting teaching*. OECD Publishing., DOI: 10.1787/f5d50f16-

Okewu, E., Adewole, P., Misra, S., Maskeliunas, R., & Damasevicius, R. (2021). Artificial Neural Networks for Educational Data Mining in Higher Education: A Systematic Literature Review. *Applied Artificial Intelligence*, *35*(13), 983–1021. DOI: 10.1080/08839514.2021.1922847

Olivier, J., Bayaga, A., & Jean, G. (2024). Gamification as a Teaching Strategy for Enhancing Math Problem-Solving Skills in AI: A South African Perspective. In Idrissi, A. (Ed.), *Modern Artificial Intelligence and Data Science 2024: Tools, Techniques and Systems* (pp. 295–305). Springer Nature Switzerland. DOI: 10.1007/978-3-031-65038-3_23

Opesemowo, O. A. G., & Adewuyi, H. O. (2024). A systematic review of artificial intelligence in mathematics education: The emergence of 4IR. *Eurasia Journal of Mathematics, Science and Technology Education*, *20*(7), em2478. Advance online publication. DOI: 10.29333/ejmste/14762

Orduño-Osuna, J. H., Hernández, G. T., Mercado, A., & Murrieta-Rico, F. N. (2025). Boosting learning through AI in STEM for socioeconomic development in emerging economies. In *Transformative Approaches to STEAM Integration in Modern Education* (pp. 499–528). IGI Global Scientific Publishing.

Orji, F. A. (2024). *Artificial intelligence and persuasive computing approach for motivating students and enhancing their learning experience* (Doctoral dissertation). University of [Name].

Osasona, F., Amoo, O., Atadoga, A., Abrahams, T., Farayola, O., & Ayinla, B. (2024). *Reviewing the ethical implications of AI in decision making processes*. International Journal of Management & Entrepreneurship Research., DOI: 10.51594/ijmer.v6i2.773

Osman, S., Mohammad, S., & Abu, M. S. (2015). A preliminary study on the integral relationship between critical thinking and mathematical thinking among practicing civil engineers. *AIP Conference Proceedings*, *1660*(1), 070030. DOI: 10.1063/1.4915748

Outhwaite, L., Faulder, M., Gulliford, A., & Pitchford, N. (2019). Raising early achievement in math with interactive apps: A randomized control trial. *Journal of Educational Psychology*, *111*(2), 284–298. DOI: 10.1037/edu0000286 PMID: 30774149

Owoc, M. L., Sawicka, A., & Weichbroth, P. (2021). *Artificial Intelligence Technologies in Education: Benefits* (Vol. 599). Challenges and Strategies of Implementation. DOI: 10.1007/978-3-030-85001-2_4

Owusu, R., Bonyah, E., & Arthur, Y. D. (2023). The Effect of GeoGebra on University Students' Understanding of Polar Coordinates. *Cogent Education, 10*(1), 1–16. DOI: 10.1080/2331186x.2023.2177050

Palinkas, L. A., Horwitz, S. M., Green, C. A., Wisdom, J. P., Duan, N., & Hoagwood, K. (2015). Purposeful sampling for qualitative data collection and analysis in mixed method implementation research. *Administration and Policy in Mental Health, 42*(5), 533–544. DOI: 10.1007/s10488-013-0528-y PMID: 24193818

Palm, T., & Burman, L. (2002). Reality in mathematics assessment–an analysis of task-reality concordance in Finnish and Swedish national assessments.

Panqueban, D., Huincahue, J., Panqueban, D., & Huincahue, J. (2024). Artificial Intelligence in Mathematics Education: A Systematic Review. *Uniciencia, 38*(1), 357–373. DOI: 10.15359/ru.38-1.20

Papadimitriou, C. H., & Steiglitz, K. (1998). Combinatorial optimisation: Algorithms and complexity. Dover Publications. https://store.doverpublications.com/products/9780486402581

Papert, S. (1980). *Mindstorms: Children, computers, and powerful ideas*. Basic Books.

Pardo, A., & Siemens, G. (2014). Ethical considerations in learning analytics. *Proceedings of the International Conference on Learning Analytics & Knowledge, 45*(3), 1-10.

Park, M., & Lim, W. (2023). AI-integrated mathematics education: A review of literature in the Korean context. *The Korean Society of Educational Studies in Mathematics – Journal of Educational Research in Mathematics.* https://doi.org/ DOI: 10.29275/jerm.2023.33.3.771

Park, J., & Li, X. (2023). Addressing digital disparities in AI-assisted learning environments. *Educational Equity Journal, 16*(1), 121–138.

Pataranutaporn, P., Danry, V., Leong, J., Punpongsanon, P., Novy, D., Maes, P., & Sra, M. (2021). AI-generated characters for supporting personalized learning and well-being. *Nature Machine Intelligence, 3*(12), 1013–1022. DOI: 10.1038/s42256-021-00417-9

Patel, A., & Nguyen, H. (2023). Teacher perspectives on integrating AI tools in mathematics classrooms. *Teaching Innovations Quarterly, 12*(1), 33–49.

Patrick, J. (2008). Reducing wait times through operations research: Optimising the use of surge capacity. *Healthcare Quarterly*, *11*(3), 77–83. DOI: 10.12927/HCQ.2013.19844 PMID: 18536537

Pelton, T., & Pelton, L. F. (2023, March). Adapting ChatGPT to support teacher education in mathematics. In *Society for Information Technology & Teacher Education International Conference* (pp. 1662-1670). Association for the Advancement of Computing in Education (AACE).

Pen, S., & Morrell, P. D. (2024). Perceptions and challenges of technological use in teaching among late-career teachers: A case study in Cambodia. *Discover Education*, *3*(1), 211. DOI: 10.1007/s44217-024-00265-w

Pepin, B., Buchholtz, N., & Salinas-Hernández, U. (2025). A scoping survey of ChatGPT in mathematics education. *Digital Experiences in Mathematics Education*, •••, 1–33.

Pepin, B., Buchholtz, N., & Salinas-Hernández, U. (2025). A Scoping Survey of ChatGPT in Mathematics Education. *Digital Experiences in Mathematics Education*, *11*(1), 9–41. DOI: 10.1007/s40751-025-00172-1

Piaget, J. (1954). *The construction of reality in the child* (Cook, M., Trans.). Basic Books.

Pinto, C. M. A., Nikolopoulos, C., Cruz, M., Queirós, R., & Petridis, K. (2024). Empowering Engineering Students' Math Literacy with Digital Escape Rooms. *2024 IEEE World Engineering Education Conference (EDUNINE)*. https://doi.org/DOI: 10.1109/EDUNINE60625.2024.10500542

Ponnusamy, S., Chourasia, H., Rathod, S. B., & Patil, D. (2024). Ai-driven traffic management systems: Reducing congestion and improving safety in smart cities. In *Smart cities* (pp. 96–121). CRC Press.

Pope, D. (2022). Using Desmos and GeoGebra to Engage Students and Develop Conceptual Understanding of Mathematics. In *Advances in Educational Technologies and Instructional Design* (pp. 104-129). IGI Global. https://doi.org/DOI: 10.4018/978-1-6684-5920-1.ch006

Pouezevara, L., Dincer, G., Kipp, S., & Sener, U. (2013). *Turkey's FATIH Project: A plan to conquer the digital divide or a technological leap of faith?* RTI International.

Prajapati, S. (2025). *Ethical considerations in AI design and deployment.* World Journal of Advanced Research and Reviews., DOI: 10.30574/wjarr.2025.25.1.0270

Prasad, A. (2025, February). Role of AI in modern education. In *Transforming Knowledge: A Multidisciplinary Research on Integrative Learning Across Disciplines* (pp. xxx–xxx). https://doi.org/DOI: 10.51767/ic250459

Prinsloo, P., & Slade, S. (2017). An integrated framework for student learning data in higher education. *The Internet and Higher Education, 33*, 26–36.

Pum, M., & Sok, S. (2024). Leveraging AI in education in Cambodia: A review of perceived concerns and associated benefits. *Asian Journal of Distance Education, 19*(2). https://asianjde.com/ojs/index.php/AsianJDE/article/view/794

Purwanto, A., Fauzan, M., Widya, T., & Azzaky, N. (2024). Ethical implications and challenges of AI implementation in business operations. *TechComp Innovations. Journal of Computer Science and Technology*. Advance online publication. DOI: 10.70063/techcompinnovations.v1i2.52

Putra, P. D. A., & Sulaeman, N. F., Supeno, & Wahyuni, S. (2023). Exploring Students' Critical Thinking Skills Using the Engineering Design Process in a Physics Classroom. *The Asia-Pacific Education Researcher, 32*(1), 141–149. DOI: 10.1007/s40299-021-00640-3

Qin, Q., & Ao, L. (2023). *A new world of open space - reflections and perspectives of chinese scholars on the digital transformation of education and future education research*. MCET., DOI: 10.55162/mcet.05.153

Rahman, M. M., & Watanobe, Y. (2023). ChatGPT for education and research: Opportunities, threats, and strategies. *Applied Sciences (Basel, Switzerland), 13*(9), 5783.

Raimi, L., Bamiro, N. B., & Lim, S. A. (2024). Two facets of AI-driven applications for sustainable learning and development: A systematic review of tech-entrepreneurial benefits and threats to creative learning. In *Social Responsibility, Technology and AI* (pp. 223–248). IGI Global.

Ramakrishnan, S., Bishnoi, M., Joghee, S., Jijitha, S., & Kumar, A. (2024). Social engineering: Role of teachers in cohabitation of AI with education. *2024 2nd International Conference on Cyber Resilience (ICCR)*, 1–6. https://doi.org/DOI: 10.1109/ICCR61006.2024.10532897

Ramirez, G., Hooper, S., Kersting, N., Ferguson, R., & Yeager, D. (2018). Teacher math anxiety relates to adolescent students' math achievement. *AERA Open, 4*(1). Advance online publication. DOI: 10.1177/2332858418756052 PMID: 31069247

Rasul, T., Nair, S., Kalendra, D., Robin, M., de Oliveira Santini, F., Ladeira, W. J., & Heathcote, L. (2023). The role of ChatGPT in higher education: Benefits, challenges, and future research directions. *Journal of Applied Learning and Teaching, 6*(1), 41–56.

Rathakrishnan, T., Kumar, T. B. J., Tsen, M. K., Leong, M. K., & Yaacob, A. (2024). AI tools: Anxiety to achievement—Unveiling the psychological dynamics of technology adoption. In *Transdisciplinary Teaching and Technological Integration for Improved Learning: Case Studies and Practical Approaches* (pp. 42–65). IGI Global.

Rehman, N., Huang, X., Mahmood, A., Zafeer, H. M. I., & Mohammad, N. K. (2025). Emerging trends and effective strategies in STEM teacher professional development: A systematic review. *Humanities & Social Sciences Communications*, *12*(1), 1–23. DOI: 10.1057/s41599-024-04272-y

Reis, S., Coelho, L., Sarmet, M., Araújo, J., & Corchado, J. M. (2023). The Importance of Ethical Reasoning in Next Generation Tech Education. *2023 5th International Conference of the Portuguese Society for Engineering Education (CISPEE)*, 1–10. DOI: 10.1109/CISPEE58593.2023.10227651

Reis, S., Guimarães, P., Coelho, F., Nogueira, E., & Coelho, L. (2018). A framework for simulation systems and technologies for medical training. *2018 Global Medical Engineering Physics Exchanges/Pan American Health Care Exchanges (GMEPE/PAHCE)*, 1–4. DOI: 10.1109/GMEPE-PAHCE.2018.8400757

Reiser, R. A., Carr-Chellman, A. A., & Dempsey, J. V. (2017). *Trends and issues in instructional design and technology*. Routledge.

Reis, S., Coelho, F., & Coelho, L. (2020). Success Factors in Students' Motivation with Project Based Learning: From Theory to Reality. *International Journal of Online and Biomedical Engineering*, *16*(12), 12. Advance online publication. DOI: 10.3991/ijoe.v16i12.16001

Remoto, J. P. (2024). ChatGPT and other AIs: Personal relief and limitations among mathematics-oriented learners. *Environment and Social Psychology*, *9*(1), 1–13.

Richard, P. R., Vélez, M. P., & Van Vaerenbergh, S. (Eds.). (2022). *Mathematics Education in the Age of Artificial Intelligence: How Artificial Intelligence can Serve Mathematical Human Learning* (Vol. 17). Springer International Publishing. DOI: 10.1007/978-3-030-86909-0

Roe, J., Perkins, M., Singapore, D., Vietnam, B., & V., V. (2024). Understanding student and academic staff perceptions of AI use in assessment and feedback. *arXiv*. https://doi.org/DOI: 10.70770/rzzz6y35

Romero, C., & Ventura, S. (2010). Educational data mining: A review of the state of the art. *IEEE Transactions on Systems, Man, and Cybernetics. Part C, Applications and Reviews*, *40*(6), 601–618.

Rosé, C., Wang, Y. C., Cui, Y., Arguello, J., Stegmann, K., Weinberger, A., & Fischer, F. (2008). Analyzing collaborative learning processes automatically: Exploiting the advances of computational linguistics in computer-supported collaborative learning. *International Journal of Computer-Supported Collaborative Learning, 3*(3), 237–271.

Roselainy, A., Rahman, R., Yusof, Y., Ismail, Z., Kashefi, H., & Firouzian, S. (2013, July 5). A New Direction in Engineering Mathematics: Integrating Mathematical Thinking and Engineering Thinking. *Research in Engineering Education Symposium, REES 2013*. Research in Engineering Education Symposium, Kuala Lumpur.

Rosenshine, B., Meister, C., & Chapman, S. (1996). Teaching students to generate questions: A review of the intervention studies. *Review of Educational Research, 66*(2), 181–221.

Roshanaei, M., Olivares, H., & Lopez, R. (2023). Harnessing ai to foster equity in education: Opportunities, challenges, and emerging strategies. *Journal of Intelligent Learning Systems and Applications, 15*(4), 123–143. DOI: 10.4236/jilsa.2023.154009

Rospigliosi, P. A. (2023). Artificial intelligence in teaching and learning: What questions should we ask of ChatGPT? *Interactive Learning Environments, 31*(1), 1–3.

Rozgonjuk, D., Kraav, T., Mikkor, K., Orav-Puurand, K., & Täht, K. (2020). Mathematics Anxiety Among STEM and Social Sciences Students: The Roles of Mathematics Self-Efficacy, and Deep and Surface Approach to Learning. *International Journal of STEM Education, 7*(1), 1–11. DOI: 10.1186/s40594-020-00246-z

Run, N., Tep, P., Mot, N., & Phuong, C. (2025). Reviewing challenges of curriculum implementation in Cambodian teacher education and possibilities for improvement. *Journal of Multidisciplinary Research, 4*(1). Advance online publication. DOI: 10.56943/jmr.v4i1.735

Russell, S., & Norvig, P. (2020). *Artificial intelligence: A modern approach* (4th ed.). Pearson.

Saad, M. (2024). Optimizing multi-objective task scheduling in fog computing: A hybrid genetic algorithm–particle swarm optimization approach. *Sensors (Basel), 24*(2), 556. DOI: 10.3390/s24020556 PMID: 38257649

Saborío-Taylor, S., & Rojas-Ramírez, F. (2024). Universal Design for Learning and Artificial Intelligence in the Digital Era: Fostering Inclusion and Autonomous Learning. *International Journal of Professional Development. Learners and Learning, 6*(2), 1–8. DOI: 10.30935/ijpdll/14694

Sadak, M., Incikabi, L., Ulusoy, F., & Pektas, M. (2022). Investigating mathematical creativity through the connection between creative abilities in problem posing and problem solving. *Thinking Skills and Creativity*, *45*, 101108.

Saenz, M., Nandakumar, V., & Adamuti-Trache, M. (2023). A comparative study of high school students' math achievement and attitudes: Do math teacher qualifications matter? *International Journal of Education in Mathematics Science and Technology*, *11*(2), 304–322. DOI: 10.46328/ijemst.2528

Saing, C. H., Chea, P., & Song, S. (2023). *Assessing technology readiness of students and teachers in Cambodian higher education during COVID-19: Implications for digital learning* [Working paper]. Cambodia Development Research Institute., DOI: 10.64202/wp.143.202311

Salameh, W. (2025). *Exploring the impact of AI-driven real-time feedback systems on learner engagement and adaptive content delivery in education*. International Journal of Science and Research Archive., DOI: 10.30574/ijsra.2025.14.2.0299

Salminen, J., Koponen, T., Leskinen, M., Poikkeus, A., & Aro, M. (2015). Individual variance in responsiveness to early computerized mathematics intervention. *Learning and Individual Differences*, *43*, 124–131. DOI: 10.1016/j.lindif.2015.09.002

Sam, R., Li, X., Sok, K., Tieng, M., & Yoeng, H. (2025). Effective Turnaround Leadership Practices in Cambodia: Perspectives from School Principals. In Liu, P., & Thien, L. M. (Eds.), *Turnaround Leadership in Southeast Asian Countries*. Springer., DOI: 10.1007/978-981-96-7894-5_5

Sam, R., Sok, K., Tieng, M., Yoeng, H., Chiv, S., Thay, S., & Saorann, S. (2025). Examining principal leadership in Cambodian high schools: A case study approach. *European Journal of Educational Management*, *8*(1), 13–29. DOI: 10.12973/eu-jem.8.1.13

Sam, R., Tieng, M., Yoeng, H., Chiv, S., Thay, S., & Saing, S. (2025). Exploring school principal leadership: A case study of upper secondary school in Northwestern Cambodia. *Multidisciplinary Reviews*, *8*(10), 2025311. DOI: 10.31893/multirev.2025311

Sánchez-Ruiz, L. M., Moll-López, S., Nuñez-Pérez, A., Moraño-Fernández, J. A., & Vega-Fleitas, E. (2023). ChatGPT challenges blended learning methodologies in engineering education: A case study in mathematics. *Applied Sciences (Basel, Switzerland)*, *13*(10), 6039.

Sangwin, C. J., & Köcher, N. (2016). Automation of Mathematics Examinations. *Computers & Education*, *94*, 215–227. DOI: 10.1016/j.compedu.2015.11.014

Santos, G., & Jorge, J. (2013). Interoperable intelligent tutoring systems as open educational resources. *IEEE Transactions on Learning Technologies, 6*(3), 271–282. DOI: 10.1109/tlt.2013.17

Santos, W. D. M. Q. D., Peretti, A., Teixeira, J. M. X. N., Peres, F. F. F., Mauricio, C. R. M., & Silva, M. M. O. D. (2025). Mixed Reality as a Tool to Enhance Mathematics Education in Elementary School. *2025 IEEE Conference on Virtual Reality and 3D User Interfaces Abstracts and Workshops (VRW).* https://doi.org/DOI: 10.1109/VRW66409.2025.00055

Saputra, I., Kurniawan, A., Yanita, M., Putri, E., & Mahniza, M. (2024). *The evolution of educational assessment: How artificial intelligence is shaping the trends and future of learning evaluation.* The Indonesian Journal of Computer Science., DOI: 10.33022/ijcs.v13i6.4465

Saranya, K., & Sankaradass, V. (2023). Hyperpersonalization of Educational Content Through Multimodal Deep Learning and Gamification. *2023 International Conference on Data Science, Agents & Artificial Intelligence (ICDSAAI).* https://doi.org/DOI: 10.1109/icdsaai59313.2023.10452428

Sarkar, S., & Bhatia, G. (2021). Writing and Appraising Narrative Reviews. *Journal of Clinical and Scientific Research, 10*(3), 169–172.

Savaş, S. (2021). Yapay zekâ ve eğitimde yenilikçi uygulamalar: Türkiye örneği. *Journal of Information Systems and Management Research, 1*(1), 1–13.

Sawant, L., & Patil, S. A. (2020). Cryptography and image processing by matrices. *International Research Journal of Engineering and Technology, 7*(8), 4327–4330.

Scherer, R., Siddiq, F., & Tondeur, J. (2021). Teacher's attitudes toward the use of artificial intelligence (AI) applications in education. *Computers in Human Behavior, 115*, 106612. DOI: 10.1016/j.chb.2020.106612

Scherer, R., Tondeur, J., & Siddiq, F. (2019). The importance of attitudes toward technology for preservice teachers' technological, pedagogical, and content knowledge. *Computers & Education, 137*, 1–12. DOI: 10.1016/j.compedu.2019.04.002

Schmidt, T., & Strassner, T. (2022). Artificial intelligence in foreign language learning and teaching. *Anglistik, 33*(1), 165–184. DOI: 10.33675/angl/2022/1/14

Schmolck, P. (2014). *PQMethod (Version 2.35) [Computer software].* http://schmolck.org/qmethod

Schuck, S. (2016). Enhancing teacher education in primary mathematics with mobile technologies. *The Australian Journal of Teacher Education, 41*(3), 126–139. DOI: 10.14221/ajte.2016v41n3.8

Schukajlow, S., Rakoczy, K., & Pekrun, R. (2023). Emotions and Motivation in Mathematics Education: Where We Are Today and Where We Need to Go. *ZDM Mathematics Education, 55*(2), 249–267. DOI: 10.1007/s11858-022-01463-2 PMID: 36684477

Sebastian, G. (2023). Privacy and Data Protection in ChatGPT and Other AI Chatbots: Strategies for Securing User Information. *International Journal of Security and Privacy in Pervasive Computing, 15*(1), 1–14.

Selwyn, N. (2016). *Is technology good for education?* John Wiley & Sons.

Selwyn, N. (2019). *Should robots replace teachers? AI and the future of education.* Polity Press.

Selwyn, N. (2021). Rethinking education in the age of AI: Critical perspectives on artificial intelligence in schools. *Educational Futures Journal, 18*(3), 97–114.

Selwyn, N. (2022). *Education and technology: Key issues and debates* (3rd ed.). Bloomsbury.

Setiawan, A., & Fitria, H. (2024). Analysis of learning results of students in the application of gamification quizizz on mathematics lessons. *Progres Pendidikan, 5*(2), 193–197. DOI: 10.29303/prospek.v5i2.728

Shah, K., Joshi, H., & Joshi, H. (2025). Integrating moral values in AI: Addressing ethical challenges for fair and responsible technology. *Journal of Informatics and Web Engineering*. https://doi.org/DOI: 10.33093/jiwe.2026.4.1.16

Shahriari, K., & Shahriari, M. (2017). IEEE standard review — Ethically aligned design: A vision for prioritizing human wellbeing with artificial intelligence and autonomous systems. *2017 IEEE Canada International Humanitarian Technology Conference (IHTC)*, 197–201. DOI: 10.1109/IHTC.2017.8058187

Sharma, P. (2024). *Revolutionizing math education: The power of personalized learning*. Online Submission.

Shen, L., & Su, A. (2020). The changing roles of teachers with AI. In *Revolutionizing Education in the Age of AI and Machine Learning*. https://doi.org/DOI: 10.4018/978-1-5225-7793-5.ch001

Shimizu, Y., & Vithal, R. (2023). *Mathematics Curriculum Reforms Around the World: The 24th ICMI Study*. Springer Cham., DOI: 10.1007/978-3-031-13548-4

Shukla, S. (2024). Principles governing ethical development and deployment of AI. *International Journal of Engineering Business Management*. Advance online publication. DOI: 10.22161/ijebm.8.2.5

Sidekerskienė, T., & Damaševičius, R. (2023). Out-of-the-Box Learning: Digital Escape Rooms as a Metaphor for Breaking Down Barriers in STEM Education. *Sustainability*, *15*(9), 1–33. DOI: 10.3390/su15097393

Silver, E. A. (1994). On mathematical problem posing. *For the Learning of Mathematics*, *14*(1), 19–28.

Silver, E. A., & Cai, J. (1996). An analysis of arithmetic problem posing by middle school students. *Journal for Research in Mathematics Education*, *27*(5), 521–539.

Simms, V. (2016). [Review of the book *Mathematical mindsets: Unleashing students' potential through creative math, inspiring messages and innovative teaching*, by J. Boaler]. *Research in Mathematics Education*, *18*(3), 317–320. DOI: 10.1080/14794802.2016.1237374

Simpson, A. (2017). The surprising persistence of Biglan's classification scheme. *Studies in Higher Education*, *42*(8), 1520–1531. DOI: 10.1080/03075079.2015.1111323

Singh, V., Gupta, P., & Jain, S. (2025). A novel CNN-GRU-LSTM based deep learning model for accurate traffic prediction. *Neural Computing & Applications*. Advance online publication. DOI: 10.1007/s10791-025-09526-0

Smith, A., & Jones, B. (2020). Teachers' perceptions of AI-enhanced learning tools. *Educational Research Review*, *25*(4), 123–136.

Snell, J., Swersky, K., & Zemel, R. (2017). Prototypical networks for few-shot learning. *Advances in Neural Information Processing Systems*, •••, 30.

Soares, M. N., Pontes, A., Lima, M., Moreira, S., Machado, F., Ferreira, J., & Coelho, V. (2024). Creative education and psychology: Connecting minds and technologies for educational success. In *Creativity and Learning: Navigating Transformative Perspectives for Complex and Contemporary Environments* (pp. 15–43). Springer Nature Switzerland.

Sok, S., Heng, K., & Pum, M. (2025). Investigating high school students' attitudes toward the use of AI in education: Evidence from Cambodia. *SAGE Open*, *15*(3). Advance online publication. DOI: 10.1177/21582440251353575

Sperling, K., Stenberg, C.-J., McGrath, C., Åkerfeldt, A., Heintz, F., & Stenliden, L. (2024). In Search of Artificial Intelligence (AI) Literacy in Teacher Education: A Scoping Review. *Computers and Education Open*, *6*, 1–13. https://doi.org/https://doi.org/10.1016/j.caeo.2024.100169

Sperling, K., Stenliden, L., Nissen, J., & Heintz, F. (2022). Still w(ai)ting for the automation of teaching: An exploration of machine learning in swedish primary education using actor-network theory. *European Journal of Education*, *57*(4), 584–600. DOI: 10.1111/ejed.12526

Srivastav, M. K., & Nath, A. (2015). Study on mathematical modeling of social networks. *International Journal of Emerging Technology and Advanced Engineering*, *5*(3), 611–618.

Stephenson, W. (1953). *The study of behavior: Q-technique and its methodology*. University of Chicago Press.

Stickles, P. R. (2011). An analysis of secondary and middle school teachers' mathematical problem posing. *Investigations in Mathematics Learning*, *3*(2), 1–34.

Stinson, C. (2022). Algorithms are not neutral. *AI and Ethics*, *2*(4), 763–770. DOI: 10.1007/s43681-022-00136-w PMID: 35128540

Stohlmann, M. S. (2023). Mathematical Digital Escape Rooms. *School Science and Mathematics*, *123*(1), 26–30. DOI: 10.1111/ssm.12564

Stoyanova, E., & Ellerton, N. F. (1996). A framework for research into students' problem posing in school mathematics. In Clarkson, P. (Ed.), *Technology in mathematics education* (pp. 518–525). MERGA.

Straker, L., Zabatiero, J., Danby, S., Thorpe, K., & Edwards, S. (2018). Conflicting guidelines on young children's screen time and use of digital technology create policy and practice dilemmas. *The Journal of Pediatrics*, *202*, 300–303. DOI: 10.1016/j.jpeds.2018.07.019 PMID: 30139534

Strang, G. (2016). *Linear algebra and its applications* (5th ed.). Cengage Learning.

Strielkowski, W., Grebennikova, V., Lisovskiy, A., Rakhimova, G., & Vasileva, T. (2024). AI-driven adaptive learning for sustainable educational transformation. *Sustainable Development*, *32*(1), 62–72. DOI: 10.1002/sd.2290

Sukhera, J. (2022). Narrative Reviews: Flexible, Rigorous, and Practical. *Journal of Graduate Medical Education*, *14*(4), 414–417. DOI: 10.4300/jgme-d-22-00480.1 PMID: 35991099

Sundari, S., & Hertuti, A. (2022). Fun learning by applying competition and co-operation strategies through mathematical games. *Tekno-Pedagogi. Jur. Tek. Pend, 12*(1), 34–41. DOI: 10.22437/teknopedagogi.v12i1.32509

Sun, H., Chen, W., & Ge, Z. (2021). Preparing teachers for AI integration in education. *Educational Technology Research and Development, 69*(1), 105–121.

Suresh Babu, S., & Dhakshina Moorthy, A. (2024). Application of artificial intelligence in adaptation of gamification in education: A literature review. *Computer Applications in Engineering Education, 32*(1), e22683. DOI: 10.1002/cae.22683

Sutton, R. S., & Barto, A. G. (2018). *Reinforcement learning: An introduction* (2nd ed.). MIT Press.

Syifa, A. (2024). *Ethics in the age of AI: Principles and guidelines for responsible implementation in workplace.* International Journal of Advanced Technology and Social Sciences., DOI: 10.59890/ijatss.v2i2.1398

Taha, H. A. (2017). *Operations research: An introduction* (10th ed.). Pearson.

Tamilmani, K., Rana, N. P., Wamba, S. F., & Dwivedi, R. (2021). The extended Unified Theory of Acceptance and Use of Technology (UTAUT2): A systematic literature review and theory evaluation. *International Journal of Information Management, 57*, 102269. DOI: 10.1016/j.ijinfomgt.2020.102269

Tan, C. (2007). Education reforms in Cambodia: Issues and concerns. *Educational Research for Policy and Practice, 6*(1), 15–24. DOI: 10.1007/s10671-007-9020-3

Tan, D. Y., & Cheah, C. W. (2021). Developing a Gamified Ai-Enabled Online Learning Application to Improve Students' Perception of University Physics. *Computers and Education: Artificial Intelligence, 2*, 1–10. DOI: 10.1016/j.caeai.2021.100032

Tang, K. Y., & Chen, H. Y. (2021). Language learning with AI: Benefits and challenges. *International Journal of Artificial Intelligence in Education, 31*(3), 219–239.

Tan, P. L. (2010). Toward a culturally sensitive and deeper understanding of "rote learning" and memorization of adult learners. *Journal of Studies in International Education, 15*(2), 124–145. DOI: 10.1177/1028315309357940

Tan, S., & Huang, W. (2023). AI integration in education: Ethical implications and policy directions. *International Journal of Educational Technology, 31*(3), 55–73.

Tan, X., Cheng, G., & Ling, M. H. (2025). Artificial Intelligence in Teaching and Teacher Professional Development: A Systematic Review. *Computers and Education: Artificial Intelligence, 8*, 1–19. DOI: 10.1016/j.caeai.2024.100355

Tariq, M. U. (2024). Generative AI in Curriculum Development in Higher Education. In Fields, Z. (Ed.), *Impacts of Generative AI on Creativity in Higher Education* (pp. 227–258). IGI Global., DOI: 10.4018/979-8-3693-2418-9.ch009

Tariq, M. U. (2025). AI-Driven Research Methodologies: Revolutionizing Data-Driven Discoveries in Engineering and Physical Sciences. In Basha, J., Alade, T., Al Khazimi, M., Vasudevan, R., & Khan, J. (Eds.), *Optimizing Research Techniques and Learning Strategies With Digital Technologies* (pp. 97–122). IGI Global Scientific Publishing., DOI: 10.4018/979-8-3693-7863-2.ch004

Tariq, M. U. (2025). Integrating Theory and Practice: Transformative Approaches in Practice-Led Research for Professional Development. In Kwok, S., Yu, P., & Le Corre, J. (Eds.), *Exploring Practice-Led Research for Professional Development* (pp. 419–436). IGI Global Scientific Publishing., DOI: 10.4018/979-8-3693-6376-8.ch016

Tariq, M. U. (2025). Leveraging Libraries and Information Centers for Startup Innovation and Growth. In Gupta, V., & Gupta, C. (Eds.), *Navigating Strategic Partnerships for Sustainable Startup Growth* (pp. 1–28). IGI Global Scientific Publishing., DOI: 10.4018/979-8-3693-4066-0.ch001

Tariq, M. U. (2025). Navigating Public Administration 5.0: Embracing AI for Smarter Governance. In Wongmahesak, K., Ahmad, J., & Mustanir, A. (Eds.), *Public Governance Practices in the Age of AI* (pp. 167–186). IGI Global Scientific Publishing., DOI: 10.4018/979-8-3693-9286-7.ch008

Tashtoush, M., Wardat, Y., AlAli, R., & Saleh, S. (2024). Artificial intelligence in education: Mathematics teachers' perspectives, practices and challenges. *Iraqi Journal for Computer Science and Mathematics*, *5*(1). Advance online publication. DOI: 10.52866/ijcsm.2024.05.01.004

Taufikin, M., S., Azifah, N., Nikmah, F., Kuanr, J., & P., P. (2024). The impact of AI on teacher roles and pedagogy in the 21st century classroom. *2024 International Conference on Knowledge Engineering and Communication Systems (ICKECS), 1,* 1–5. https://doi.org/DOI: 10.1109/ICKECS61492.2024.10617236

Thakre, P., Niveditha, P., Jain, P., Soni, D., & Vishwakarma, M. (2023). *Exploring the ethical dimensions of AI in decision-making processes*. International Journal of Innovative Research in Computer and Communication Engineering., DOI: 10.15680/ijircce.2023.1110048

Thompson, A., & Mishra, P. (2007–2008). Breaking news: TPCK becomes TPACK! *Journal of Computing in Teacher Education*, *24*(2), 38–64.

Tlili, A., Shehata, B., Adarkwah, M. A., Bozkurt, A., Hickey, D. T., Huang, R., & Agyemang, B. (2023). What if the devil is my guardian angel: ChatGPT as a case study of using chatbots in education. *Smart Learning Environments, 10*(1), 15.

Torres-Peña, R., Peña-González, D., Chacuto-López, E., Ariza, E., & Vergara, D. (2024). Updating calculus teaching with AI: A classroom experience. *Education Sciences*. Advance online publication. DOI: 10.3390/educsci14091019

Tran, T. T., Terekhov, D., Down, D. G., & Beck, J. C. (n.d.). Hybrid Queueing Theory and Scheduling Models for Dynamic Environments with Sequence-Dependent Setup Times. DOI: 10.1609/icaps.v23i1.13552

Trigka, M., Dritsas, E., & Mylonas, P. (2024). New Perspectives in e-Learning: EEG-Based Modelling of Human Cognition Individual Differences. *IFIP Advances in Information and Communication Technology*. Advance online publication. DOI: 10.1007/978-3-031-63227-3_20

Trindade, M. A. M., Edirisinghe, G. S., & Luo, L. (2025). Teaching Mathematical Concepts in Management with Generative Artificial Intelligence: The Power of Human Oversight in AI-Driven Learning. *International Journal of Management Education, 23*(2), 1–18. DOI: 10.1016/j.ijme.2024.101104

Trivedi, N. B. (2023). AI in education—a transformative force. *2023 1st DMIHER International Conference on Artificial Intelligence in Education and Industry 4.0 (IDICAIEI).*

Truong, U. (2024). Writing classes in the AI era: Redefining English teachers' roles. *2024 6th International Workshop on Artificial Intelligence and Education (WAIE),* 50–55. https://doi.org/DOI: 10.1109/WAIE63876.2024.00016

TÜBİTAK. (2022). *Yapay zekâ destekli öğrenme ortamlarının geliştirilmesi ve pilot uygulaması: Matematik derslerinde işbirliğine dayalı öğrenme örnekleri (Development and pilot application of artificial intelligence-supported learning environments: Examples of collaborative learning in mathematics lessons).* TÜBİTAK Proje Raporu.

Tunç, M. P. (2024). Examining Pre-service Mathematics Teachers' Purposes of Using ChatGPT in Lesson Plan Development. *Sakarya University Journal of Education, 14*(2), 391–406.

Tuomi, I. (2018). The Impact of Artificial Intelligence on Learning, Teaching, and Education: Policies for the Future. *European Commission Report*. https://doi.org/. https://publications.jrc.ec.europa.eu/repository/handle/JRC113226DOI: 10.2766/16182

Ucar, A., Karakose, M., & Kırımça, N. (2024). Artificial Intelligence for Predictive Maintenance Applications: Key Components, Trustworthiness, and Future Trends. *Applied Sciences (Basel, Switzerland), 14*(2), 898. DOI: 10.3390/app14020898

Uddin, A. S. M. A. (2023). The Era of AI: Upholding Ethical Leadership. *Open Journal of Leadership, 12*(4), 4. Advance online publication. DOI: 10.4236/ojl.2023.124019

Ulusoy, F. (2023). Middle Level Mathematics Teachers' Problems on Linear Relationships in a Semi-Structured Problem Posing Situation. *RMLE Online: Research in Middle Level Education, 46*(10), 1–19.

Ulusoy, F. (2025). Using general-mathematical and content-specific elements to assess the quality of prospective mathematics teachers' problems in a problem-posing context. *Journal of Mathematics Teacher Education*, •••, 1–33. DOI: 10.1007/s10857-025-09697-z

Ulusoy, F., & Kepceoğlu, İ. (2018). İlköğretim matematik öğretmen adaylarının yarıyapılandırılmış problem kurma bağlamında oluşturdukları problemlerin bağlamsal ve bilişsel yapısı. *Kırşehir Eğitim Fakültesi Dergisi, 19*(3), 1910–1936.

Ulusoy, F., Sadak, M., Incikabi, L., & Pektas, M. (2025). Exploring Gender Differences in Mathematical Creativity: Linking Problem Posing and Problem Solving. *Psychology in the Schools*. Advance online publication. DOI: 10.1002/pits.70060

Umamaheswari, P. (2025). A comprehensive approach to the integration of intelligent systems in the didactic of social and cognitive studies. In *Utilizing ICT for Didactics of Social and Experimental Sciences* (pp. 95–112). IGI Global.

UNESCO. (2020). *Cambodia education sector snapshot*. https://unesdoc.unesco.org

UNESCO. (2021). *AI and education: Guidance for policy-makers*. UNESCO. https://unesdoc.unesco.org/ark:/48223/pf0000376704

UNESCO. (2022). *Digital learning for all in Cambodia*. UNESCO., DOI: 10.54675/UNES2022.KH

UNESCO. (2022). *Education transformation in Cambodia*. UNESCO., DOI: 10.54675/UNES2022.CAM

UNESCO. (2022). *Reimagining our futures together: A new social contract for education*. Paris: UNESCO. https://unesdoc.unesco.org/ark:/48223/pf0000379707.locale=en

UNESCO. (2023). *AI and education in the Global South*. UNESCO., DOI: 10.54675/UNES2023.AIED

UNESCO. (2023). *AI for equitable education.* UNESCO. https://doi.org/DOI: 10.7890/unesco-ai-2023

UNESCO. (2023). ChatGPT and artificial intelligence in higher education: quick start guide. UNESCO International Institute for Higher Education in Latin America and the Caribbean. https://unesdoc.unesco.org/ark:/48223/pf0000385146

UNESCO. (2023). *Global education monitoring report: Cambodia country profile.* https://www.unesco.org/gem-report/cambodia

Valderama, A. M. C., Tuazon, J. B. D., & Garcia, M. B. (2022). Promoting Student Thinking and Engagement Through Question-Based and Gamified Learning. *2022 IEEE 14th International Conference on Humanoid, Nanotechnology, Information Technology, Communication and Control, Environment and Management (HNICEM).* https://doi.org/DOI: 10.1109/HNICEM57413.2022.10109470

Vallor, S. (2016). *Technology and the Virtues: A Philosophical Guide to a Future Worth Wanting*. Oxford University Press.

Van Harpen, X. Y., & Sriraman, B. (2013). Creativity and mathematical problem posing: An analysis of high school students' mathematical problem posing in China and the USA. *Educational Studies in Mathematics*, *82*(2), 201–221.

VanLehn, K. (2011). The relative effectiveness of human tutoring, intelligent tutoring systems, and other tutoring systems. *Educational Psychologist*, *46*(4), 197–221.

VanLehn, K. (2022). Intelligent tutoring systems for STEM education. *AI Magazine*, *43*(1), 34–50. DOI: 10.1609/aimag.v43i1.19118

Velastegui, D., Pérez, M. L. R., & Garcés, L. F. S. (2023). Impact of artificial intelligence on learning behaviors and psychological well-being of college students. *Salud. Ciencia y Tecnologia-Serie de Conferencias*, *2*, 343–358.

Veletsianos, G., & Russell, G. S. (2014). Designing and integrating immersive technologies in educational systems. *Journal of Educational Technology & Society*, *17*(1), 21–30.

Venkatesh, V., & Davis, F. D. (2000). A theoretical extension of the technology acceptance model: Four longitudinal field studies. *Management Science*, *46*(2), 186–204. DOI: 10.1287/mnsc.46.2.186.11926

Venkatesh, V., Morris, M. G., Davis, G. B., & Davis, F. D. (2003). User acceptance of information technology: Toward a unified view. *Management Information Systems Quarterly*, *27*(3), 425–478. DOI: 10.2307/30036540

Vicente, S., & Manchado, E. (2017). Dominios de contenido y autenticidad: Un análisis de los problemas aritméticos verbales incluidos en los libros de texto españoles. *PNA. Revista de Investigación en Didáctica de la Matemática, 11*(4), 253–279.

Vieriu, A. M., & Petrea, G. (2025). The Impact of Artificial Intelligence (AI) on Students' Academic Development. *Education Sciences, 15*(3), 3. Advance online publication. DOI: 10.3390/educsci15030343

Villegas-Ch, W., Buenano-Fernandez, D., Navarro, A. M., & Mera-Navarrete, A. (2025). Adaptive intelligent tutoring systems for STEM education: Analysis of the learning impact and effectiveness of personalized feedback. *Smart Learning Environments, 12*(1), 1–31. DOI: 10.1186/s40561-025-00389-y

Vintere, A., Safiulina, E., & Panova, O. (2024). AI-Based Mathematics Learning Platforms in Undergraduate Engineering Studies: Analyses of User Experiences. *Engineering for Rural Development, 23*, 1042–1047. DOI: 10.22616/ERDev.2024.23.TF216

von Glasersfeld, E. (1995). *Radical constructivism: A way of knowing and learning*. Falmer Press.

Vygotsky, L. S. (1978). *Mind in society: The development of higher psychological processes*. Harvard University Press.

Waghmare, S., & Mali, U. (2020). Development of matrix for cryptography. *Journal of Emerging Technologies and Innovative Research, 7*(4), 112–118.

Walter, Y. (2024). Embracing the Future of Artificial Intelligence in the Classroom: The Relevance of AI Literacy, Prompt Engineering, and Critical Thinking in Modern Education. *International Journal of Educational Technology in Higher Education, 21*(1), 1–29. DOI: 10.1186/s41239-024-00448-3

Wang, X., Li, L., Tan, S. C., Yang, L., & Lei, J. (2023). Preparing for AI-enhanced education: Conceptualizing and empirically examining teachers' AI readiness. *Computers in Human ehavior, 146*. 107798. https://doi.org/DOI: 10.1016/j.chb.2023.107798

Wang, P., Zhang, Q., Zhang, W., & Sun, J. (2024). The application of ChatGPT in nursing: A bibliometric and visualized analysis. *Frontiers in Medicine, 11*, 1521712. PMID: 39744533

Wang, Y. (2024). Ethical considerations of AI in financial decision. *Computers and Artificial Intelligence*. Advance online publication. DOI: 10.59400/cai.v2i1.1290

Wardat, Y., Tashtoush, M., AlAli, R., & Jarrah, A. (2023). ChatGPT: A revolutionary tool for teaching and learning mathematics. *Eurasia Journal of Mathematics, Science and Technology Education, 19*(7), (#2286). https://doi.org/DOI: 10.29333/ejmste/13272

Wardat, Y., Belbase, S., & Tairab, H. (2022). Mathematics teachers' perceptions of trends in international mathematics and science study (timss)-related practices in abu dhabi emirate schools. *Sustainability, 14*(9), 5436. DOI: 10.3390/su14095436

Wartelle, A., Mourad-Chehade, F., Yalaoui, F., Laplanche, D., & Sanchez, S. (2022). Analysis of saturation in the emergency department: A data-driven queuing model using machine learning. *Health Systems (Basingstoke, England), 11*(2), 95–118. DOI: 10.1080/20476965.2022.2074659 PMID: 35612022

Watts, S., & Stenner, P. (2012). Doing Q methodological research: Theory, method and interpretation. *Sage (Atlanta, Ga.)*.

Weintrop, D., Beheshti, E., Horn, M., Orton, K., Jona, K., Trouille, L., & Wilensky, U. (2016). Defining computational thinking for mathematics and science classrooms. *Journal of Science Education and Technology, 25*(1), 127–147. DOI: 10.1007/s10956-015-9581-5

Wei, X. (2025). *Artificial Intelligence in Mathematics Education*. Springer Singapore.

Whitt, W. (1993). Approximations for the GI/G/m queue. *Production and Operations Management, 2*(2), 114–161.

Williamson, B., & Eynon, R. (2020). Historical threads, missing links, and future directions in AI in education. *Learning, Media and Technology, 45*(3), 223–235. DOI: 10.1080/17439884.2020.1798995

Winkler, R., & Söllner, M. (2018, July). Unleashing the potential of chatbots in education: A state-of-the-art analysis. In *Academy of management proceedings* (Vol. 2018, No. 1, p. 15903). Briarcliff Manor, NY 10510: Academy of Management.

Wolfram, S. (1986). *Cryptography with cellular automata in advances in cryptology* (Vol. 218). Lecture Notes in Computer Science. Springer-Verlag.

Woolf, B. (2015). AI and education: Celebrating 30 years of marriage.

World Bank. (2018). *Higher education in Cambodia: Vision and roadmap 2030*. World Bank. https://www.worldbank.org

World Bank. (2023). *Cambodia digital human capital development report*. World Bank. https://doi.org/DOI: 10.1596/978-1-4648-1987-6

World Bank. (2023). *Cambodia higher education expansion and employability*. World Bank. https://www.worldbank.org/en/country/cambodia/publication/higher-education-expansion

World Bank. (2023). *Education technology in Southeast Asia*. World Bank., DOI: 10.1596/wb-edtech-2023

Xiao, J., Bozkurt, A., Nichols, M., Pazurek, A., Stracke, C. M., Bai, J. Y. H., & Themeli, C. (2025). Venturing into the Unknown: Critical Insights into Grey Areas and Pioneering Future Directions in Educational Generative AI Research. *TechTrends*, •••, 1–16. DOI: 10.1007/s11528-025-01060-6

Xia, Q., Weng, X., Ouyang, F., Lin, T. J., & Chiu, T. K. F. (2024). A Scoping Review on How Generative Artificial Intelligence Transforms Assessment in Higher Education. *International Journal of Educational Technology in Higher Education*, *21*(1), 1–22. DOI: 10.1186/s41239-024-00468-z

Xu, W., & Ouyang, F. (2022). The application of AI technologies in STEM education: A systematic review from 2011 to 2021. *International Journal of STEM Education*, *9*(1), 59. DOI: 10.1186/s40594-022-00377-5

Yadav, D. S. (2024). Transformative trends in education with advanced technologies: Exploring the intersection of IoT and AI. In *Applications of Artificial Intelligence in the Internet of Things: Today's and Tomorrow's World* (pp. 316–336). IGI Global.

Yadav, S. (2025). Transformative learning with advanced technologies: Harnessing VR and AR for immersive educational experiences. In *Revolutionizing Pedagogy Through Smart Education* (pp. 139–156). IGI Global Scientific Publishing.

Yakkala, K. (2024). *AI-powered assessment tools for e-learning: Enhancing feedback and grading systems*. World Journal of Advanced Engineering Technology and Sciences., DOI: 10.30574/wjaets.2024.13.1.0497

Yang, H., Xiong, Z., Zhao, J., Niyato, D., Xiao, L., & Wu, Q. (2021). Deep reinforcement learning-based intelligent reflecting surface for secure wireless communications. *IEEE Transactions on Wireless Communications*, *20*(1), 375–388. DOI: 10.1109/TWC.2020.3024860

Yem, B. (2025). From social disparities to educational disparities: An academic reflection and discussion in the Cambodian education system. *Studies in Empowering Education*, *6*(1), 1–8. DOI: 10.3943/siee.77

Yeo, S., Moon, J., & Kim, D. (2024). Transforming Mathematics Education with AI: Innovations, Implementations, and Insights. *The Mathematics Educator*, *63*(2), 386–392. DOI: 10.7468/mathedu.2024.63.2.387

Yi, L., Liu, D., Jiang, T., & Xian, Y. (2025). The effectiveness of AI on K-12 students' mathematics learning: A systematic review and meta-analysis. *International Journal of Science and Mathematics Education, 23*, 1105–1126. DOI: 10.1007/s10763-024-10499-7

Yıldırım, A., & Şimşek, H. (2021). *Sosyal bilimlerde nitel araştırma yöntemleri (12. baskı)*. Seçkin Yayıncılık.

Yim, I. H. Y., & Su, J. (2024). Artificial intelligence (AI) learning tools in K-12 education: A scoping review. *Journal of Computers in Education, 12*, 93–131. DOI: 10.1007/s40692-023-00304-9

Youn, C., Salam, A., & Rahman, A. (2025). *AI-driven tools in providing feedback on students' writing*. International Journal of Research and Innovation in Social Science., DOI: 10.47772/ijriss.2025.903sedu0006

Young, J., Young, J., & Edosomwan, K. (2025). The Intersection of Race, Data, and Learning: Applying QuantCrit to Mathematics Education Research. *Journal of Urban Mathematics Education, 17*(2), 2. Advance online publication. DOI: 10.21423/jume-v17i2a730

Yu, S., & Lu, Y. (2021). Frontiers of AI in education. In *An Introduction to Artificial Intelligence in Education.*

Yuan, X., & Sriraman, B. (2011). An exploratory study of relationships between students' creativity and mathematical problem-posing abilities. *The elements of creativity and giftedness in mathematics*, 5-28.

Yünkül, E., & Güneş, A. M. (2022). The relationship between prospective teachers' digital literacy skills, attitude towards the teaching profession and academic motivations. *Educational Policy Analysis and Strategic Research., 13*(3), 140–163.

Zakaria, R., Herwanis, D., Wahyuni, S., Abadi, A. S., Umar, A., Mandasari, L., Agama, I., & Takengon, I. (2024). *AI in English and math education: Bridging the gap between theory and practice*. Communications on Applied Nonlinear Analysis., DOI: 10.52783/cana.v31.1101

Zakariya, Y. F. (2022). Improving Students' Mathematics Self-Efficacy: A Systematic Review of Intervention Studies. *Frontiers in Psychology, 13*, 1–13. DOI: 10.3389/fpsyg.2022.986622 PMID: 36225698

Zawacki-Richter, O., Marín, V. I., Bond, M., & Gouverneur, F. (2019). Systematic review of research on artificial intelligence applications in higher education – Where are the educators? *International Journal of Educational Technology in Higher Education, 16*(1), 39. DOI: 10.1186/s41239-019-0171-0

Zeeshan, K., Hämäläinen, T., & Neittaanmäki, P. (2024). Computational thinking and AI coding for kids to develop digital literacy. *International Journal of Education, 12*(3), 55–74. DOI: 10.5121/ije2024.12305

Zhai, C., Wibowo, S., & Li, L. D. (2024). The effects of over-reliance on AI dialogue systems on students' cognitive abilities: A systematic review. *Smart Learning Environments, 11*(1), 28. DOI: 10.1186/s40561-024-00316-7

Zhang, J., & Zhang, Z. (2024). AI in teacher education: Unlocking new dimensions in teaching support, inclusive learning, and digital literacy. *Journal of Computer Assisted Learning, 40*, 1871–1885. DOI: 10.1111/jcal.12988

Zhang, L., Stylianides, G. J., & Stylianides, A. J. (2024). Enhancing mathematical problem posing competence: A meta-analysis of intervention studies. *International Journal of STEM Education, 11*, 48.

Zhang, Q. (2023). Harnessing the power of technology: A systematic analysis of challenges, theoretical frameworks, and recommendations for K–12 online learning. *SN Social Sciences, 3*(9), 164. Advance online publication. DOI: 10.1007/s43545-023-00111-1

Zhang, Q., & Wong, M. (2023). Systematic review of AI tools in enhancing personalized learning environments in higher education. *Journal of Educational Technology, 44*(6), 1031–1052.

Zhang, R., & Sun, L. (2023). Strategies for integrating AI into education policy. *Journal of Educational Technology & Society, 31*(2), 145–162.

Zhang, R., Zou, D., & Cheng, G. (2023). Chatbot-based learning of logical fallacies in EFL writing: Perceived effectiveness in improving target knowledge and learner motivation. *Interactive Learning Environments*. Advance online publication. DOI: 10.1080/10494820.2023.2220374

Zhao, L., Wu, X., & Luo, H. (2022). Developing ai literacy for primary and middle school teachers in china: Based on a structural equation modeling analysis. *Sustainability, 14*(21), 14549. DOI: 10.3390/su142114549

Zhou, Y., Zheng, B., & Wang, Y. (2020). Enhancing student engagement using conversational agents in online learning. *Journal of Educational Technology Development and Exchange, 13*(1), 25–38.

Zou, Y., Kuek, F., Feng, W., & Cheng, X. (2025). Digital learning in the 21st century: Trends, challenges, and innovations in technology integration. *Frontiers in Education, 10*, 1562391. DOI: 10.3389/feduc.2025.1562391

Zreik, M. (2024). Redefining Mathematics Education in the Age of Artificial Intelligence: Challenges and Opportunities. In Njurai, E., & Uworwabayeho, A. (Eds.), *Impacts of Globalization and Innovation in Mathematics Education* (pp. 19–40). IGI Global Scientific Publishing., DOI: 10.4018/979-8-3693-2873-6.ch002

Zuo, F., & Chan, E. (2024). Cognitive modeling in math education using AI. *International Journal of Artificial Intelligence in Education*, *26*(2), 155–170. DOI: 10.1007/s40593-024-00274-x

Zwoliński, G., Kamińska, D., Haamer, R. E., Pinto-Coelho, L., & Anbarjafari, G. (2023). Enhancing empathy through virtual reality: Developing a universal design training application for students. *Medycyna Pracy*, *74*(3), 199–210. DOI: 10.13075/mp.5893.01407 PMID: 37695933

About the Contributors

Ali Mazı was born in Hatay in 1992. They completed their primary and secondary education in Hatay. They entered Kahramamaraş Sutcu Imam University in 2010. They studied in the department of elementary mathematics teaching. After completing my education, I graduated in 2014. In 2018, they completed their master's degree at Kahramanmaraş Sütçü İmam University's Department of Educational Management, Inspection, Planning and Economics. They have been working as a mathematics teacher at the Ministry of National Education since 2014. They completed their Ph.D. in 2023 at Hacettepe University Primary Education Department. Their fields of study are primary education, mathematics education and inclusive education.

***

Dharel P. Acut is a licensed professional teacher and a Science Education Instructor at Cebu Technological University, Cebu City, Philippines. He holds a Bachelor's degree in Secondary Education, majoring in General Science, from MSU-Iligan Institute of Technology, and is currently completing his Master's degree in Science Education at Cebu Normal University. As an Associate Member of the National Research Council of the Philippines (DOST-NRCP), his research interests include science education, STEM education, systematic literature reviews, education for sustainable development, science instrumentation, and educational technology. His ongoing research projects focus on investigating scientific creativity and creative thinking in STEM education, aiming to enhance instructional strategies and foster innovative problem-solving skills.

Ahmet Oğuz Akçay, is an associate professor of primary education at Eskisehir Osmangazi University, Eskisehir, Türkiye. He received his B.A. in primary education from Selcuk University, Konya, Türkiye. He was awarded a full scholarship by the Turkish Ministry of National Education to pursue a master's and doctorate in Primary Education in the United States. He completed his Master's in Curriculum Instruction at the University of Texas at San Antonio in the USA. Dr. Akçay earned his doctorate at Duquesne University, USA, in 2016. Throughout his time in graduate school, he actively engaged in various projects and worked as a researcher primarily focused on teacher professional development of mathematics teaching. His research focuses on mathematics education, primary school educatiobn, STEM education, technology integration, teacher preparation, and teacher education.

Jogymol Alex is an Assistant Professor of Mathematics Education at the College of Education in the United Arab Emirates University (UAEU) in UAE. She joined UAEU in January 2024 from Walter Sisulu University, South Africa, where she was a full Professor in Mathematics Education and Head of the Department of Mathematics and Sciences Education. Her research interests concern how mathematics pre-service and in-service teachers and school learners can be empowered through teaching, research, and community projects with local, national, and international partnerships. This has earned her numerous awards in teaching and learning and community engagement.

Yunifa Miftachul Arif is an Associate Professor at the Department of Informatics Engineering and Department of Electrical Engineering, Universitas Islam Negeri Maulana Malik Ibrahim, Malang, Indonesia. His research interests include game technology, artificial intelligence, recommender systems, blockchain, and IoT.

Yonca Arkalı is an English teacher in Türkiye, working for the Ministry of National Education. She has a bachelor’s degree in English Language Teaching from Marmara University and a master’s degree in Curriculum and Instruction from Van Yüzüncü Yıl University. Her research interests focus on designing early childhood curriculums, creating effective learning environments, and using technology in teaching. She has published several articles in academic journals. Some of her recent publications include: • Evaluation of 2nd Grade English Language Curriculum According to Stufflebeam’s Context-Input- Process-Product (CIPP) Model • Challenges Encountered by English Teachers Working in Primary Schools in Teaching Foreign Languages at Early Ages • The Relationship between Teachers’ Readiness for Authentic Learning and Their Competencies to Gain Problem Solving Skills

Pisith Chin is the executive director of the National University of Cheasim Kamchaymear (NUCK), Kampong Cham Campus. Demonstrating a natural aptitude for leadership, he has effectively cultivated widespread appeal for NUCK among the student body. Through adept management and strategic vision, he has positioned NUCK as a highly sought-after institution, drawing interest and admiration from numerous students. His innate leadership abilities have significantly contributed to NUCK's heightened visibility and desirability within the academic community. With 20 years of experience in the educational sector, Mr. CHIN Pisith has traversed various roles from teaching to assuming leadership positions within NUCK. His extensive tenure underscores a rich understanding of the nuances inherent in academia, providing him with a robust foundation to navigate the complexities of educational leadership effectively. Through his diverse professional journey, Mr. CHIN Pisith brings a wealth of expertise to his current leadership role, poised to drive NUCK's continued growth and success. Mr. CHIN Pisith's academic trajectory underscores a commitment to scholarly pursuit and professional advancement within the educational domain. Currently immersed in his doctoral studies, pursuing a Doctor of Philosophy (PhD) in Educational Science at NUCK, Mr. CHIN Pisith's academic journey began with the attainment of a Master's Degree in Business Administration from NUCK in 2009. Before this, he laid the groundwork for his educational prowess by earning a Bachelor's Degree in Management from the esteemed National Institute of Management in 2003. Further enhancing his pedagogical acumen, Mr. CHIN Pisith underwent specialized training as a higher education instructor, focusing on Economics and Geography from 2003 to 2004 at the National Institute of Education (NIE). Leveraging his academic rigor and experiential insights, Mr. CHIN Pisith has contributed significantly to the scholarly discourse, with approximately 10 articles published and co-authored in reputable educational journals. His scholarly impact extends to the digital realm, with his work accessible through platforms such as Google Scholar and ResearchGate, exemplifying his dedication to advancing knowledge and fostering academic dialogue in the educational sphere.

Thomas Chiu is a researcher of AI and STEM education at the Department of Curriculum and Instruction at The Chinese University of Hong Kong. He has a strong academic background in software development and mathematics. He is an associate director of the Centre for University and School Partnership and Centre for Learning Sciences and Technologies.

Emel Çilingir Altıner is a faculty member at Çukurova University, where she serves as an Associate Professor in the field of Elementary Mathematics Education. Her academic expertise lies in mathematics teaching and learning at the primary school level, with a special focus on curriculum development, measurement and estimation strategies, number sense, and the integration of digital and sustainable approaches in mathematics education. She has contributed extensively to teacher education and has been actively involved in the design and evaluation of curriculum innovations aligned with the Türkiye Yüzyılı Maarif Modeli. Dr. Çilingir Altıner's research encompasses both theoretical and practice-based studies, including the use of concept cartoons, realistic mathematics education, AI-supported learning environments, and enrichment and support strategies for diverse learners. Her scholarly work is informed by a commitment to equity, values education, and the holistic development of students. She has authored and co-authored numerous academic publications, conference papers, and educational resources, and has also taken part in national education reform initiatives and interdisciplinary projects. With a strong background in both research and classroom practice, Dr. Çilingir Altıner is dedicated to preparing future educators and contributing to the advancement of mathematics education in Turkey and beyond.

Luis Coelho is an associate professor at the Engineering School of Polytechnic Institute of Porto. He is a PhD in Telecommunications and Signal Processing since 2012, and a MsC in Electronics Engineering, since 2005. As a researcher he has published several scientific articles in conferences and journals. He actively collaborates with the scientific community as participant, reviewer, organizer of scientific conferences or as journal editor. His main research interests are on image and signal processing, human-machine interaction and management, all topics with a special focus on the healthcare area.

Vutha Da is a PhD student specializing in educational management at the National University of Battambang. I also serve as the acting director of the Research and Development Center at the National University of Battambang. I have completed a master's degree in accounting and finance, as well as a bachelor's degree in fisheries science.

Robertas Damaševičius received the B.Sc. degree in informatics, the M.Sc. degree (cum laude), and the Ph.D. degree from the Faculty of Informatics, Kaunas University of Technology (KTU), Kaunas, Lithuania, in 1999, 2001, and 2005, respectively. He is currently a Professor with the Software Engineering Department, KTU, where he lectures the robot programming and software maintenance courses. He has authored or co-authored over 100 papers and a monograph published by Springer. His research interests include brain–computer interface, bioinformatics, data mining, and machine learning.

Adem Doğan received his bachelor's, master's and doctoral degrees at Gazi University with studies on mathematics teaching. He worked as a Mathematics teacher at the Ministry of National Education for 20 years. Half of this time was spent providing mathematics and project consultancy to gifted students. He works in areas such as mathematics education, gifted students, basic education, classroom education, inclusive education, problem solving and mathematics stories. Currently, He teaches mathematics at Kahramanmaraş Sütçü İmam University, Faculty of Education, Department of Basic Education, Classroom Education.

Em Sereyrath is a Cambodian government teacher of English, a university lecturer, and an educational researcher with 18 years of experience in teaching, instructing, and lecturing. He currently serves as an Editor at the Cambodian Journal of Educational Research (CJER) and is the Founder and Editor-in-Chief of the Cambodian Journal of Educational and Social Sciences (CJESS). He also serves as a reviewer for many well-known journals and publishers such as Cogent Education, Frontiers, MDPI, Taylor & Francis, and Palgrave Macmillan, among other Scopus-indexed outlets. Dr. EM Sereyrath began his professional career as a private English teacher in 2007 and as a secondary school teacher of English and the Khmer language in 2012. Academically, he holds multiple advanced degrees, including an MA in TESOL from Human Resource University (2017), an MA in Educational Administration from the National Institute of Education (2019) supported by the Cambodia International Education Support Foundation (CIESF), and an MBA from the National Institute of Entrepreneurship and Innovation (2023). Then he earned a Ph.D. in Educational Science from Khemarak University in late 2023, followed by a second Ph.D. in Educational Administration from the University of Cambodia in 2025. Committed to continuous professional development, Dr. EM Sereyrath completed specialized training courses such as lower-secondary school teacher training in 2012, higher education teacher training in 2018, in Cambodia, and teaching the four macro language skills at the Regional Language Center (RELC), Singapore, between 2020 and 2021. Additionally, he participated in over 50 national and international workshops and seminars as a guest speaker and an attendee. He also participated in a seminar on Green Energy Development for Cambodia in Beijing, China (September 2023), and served as a Cambodian delegate to Guizhou Medical University, China (August 2024). Besides, he has additional experience of study visits and interpretation work in Thailand, Hungary, the Arab Emirates, Vietnam, and Laos. Dr. EM Sereyrath has authored and co-authored around 110 scholarly articles published in national and international journals, including those indexed by Scopus and Web of Science, and his Scopus ID is 58000264900 and WoS ID is AGB-4629-2022. His research interests include English language teaching, teaching methodology, educational management and science, educational leadership, learning and teaching motivation, and educational challenges. Currently, he is a lecturer of the School of Foreign Languages at the University of Cambodia and a Ph.D. candidate in Cooperative Education at the Institute of Social Technology, Suranaree University of Technology, Nakhon Ratchasima, Thailand.

Manuel B. Garcia is a professor of information technology and the founding director of the Educational Innovation and Technology Hub (EdITH) at FEU Institute of Technology, Manila, Philippines. He holds a Doctor of Information Technology degree from the University of the East and is currently pursuing a Doctor of Philosophy in Education at the University of the Philippines. His interdisciplinary research interests include topics that, individually or collectively, span the disciplines of education and information technology. He is a licensed professional teacher and a proud member of the National Research Council of the Philippines – an attached agency to the country's Department of Science and Technology (DOST-NRCP). Dr. Garcia is the first-ever recipient of the Ramon Dimacali Award for Information Technology, conferred by the Philippine Association for the Advancement of Science and Technology, and has been recognized as one of the World's Top 2% Scientists for three consecutive years (2023-2025) by Elsevier.

Sinoeurn Kheuy is a PhD Student in the science of Educational Management at the National University of Battambang, Cambodia (since 2022), And he is a senior lecturer in education since 2019 and also an advisor to the Royal Government of Cambodia (politician), working at the office of council Ministers since 2022. He graduated the Master's degree in Business Administrations and the Bachelor's Degree in English Arts Language Teaching. In 2017, He was a Vice-President of Provincial Election Committee and a vice-dean of UME (2014-2015).

Damian Maher brings with him to UTS a wealth of knowledge after working in primary and secondary schools for a period of 20 years in various states and territories around Australia. As a university lecturer, Damian worked at UTS from 2000 onward as a casual tutor, teaching ICT to prospective primary school teachers. During this period he also taught at UWS teaching ICT and action research to prospective primary school teachers and at the Australian Institute of Music teaching ICT to budding musicians. During 2008 he worked as a full time lecturer at Macquarie University in the Primary Education Program teaching Creative Arts. Damian is focusing on the use of digital technologies in both primary and secondary schools and on teaching and learning in the tertiary sector with his research. The use of spaces to support learning, both physical and online and the ethical implications of this are areas Damian is investigating. He is also interested in project-based learning and how this is being implemented in schools. His current research is situated around a STEM focus. He is also interested in examining pre-service teacher learning. In looking at both of these fields, the impact of AI is also a teaching and research focus.

Regan Murugesan is an Associate Professor in the Mathematics Department at Vel Tech Rangarajan Dr. Sagunthala R& D Institute of Science and Technology,

Avadi, Chennai, Tamil Nadu, India. His research focuses on innovative applications of mathematics, and he has published in top-tier journals. He supervises doctoral students and contributes to the academic community through his expertise. Through his work, continues to make significant contributions to the field of mathematics, advancing knowledge and inspiring future generations of researchers

Sinath No currently serves as the Head of the Civil Engineering Department in the Faculty of Science and Technology, (NUBB). Prior to higher education, completed an Intensive English Academic Purpose program at the Pannasastra Institute of Foreign Languages in Cambodia (2005-2006), which prepared for international academic pursuits. Have begun higher education journey in Russia, where earned a Bachelor of Technics and Technology in the field of Construction from Voronezh State University of Architecture and Civil Engineering in 2010. Following bachelor's degree, pursued a graduate master's degree in Civil and Industrial Engineering, specializing in "Effective and Economy Composite Structures" at the same university, which completed in late 2012.In 2018, has successfully defended Professional Engineer certification (No. 0005343PE/Bldg.) and was honored with the title and decoration of Gold Medal by the Asian Engineering Register (AER). The professional excellence was further recognized in 2019 when was conferred the honorary title of a member of the Asian Federation of Engineering Organizations. In the journey of civil engineering is marked by continuously pursuit of knowledge and professional growth has received a certificate of design from the Ministry of Land Management, Urban Planning, and Construction in Cambodia, underscoring of expertise in engineering design. With a career spanning over a decade, continues to inspire future engineers and contribute to the development of sustainable and effective construction practices in Cambodia through role at NUBB. This expertise, coupled with commitment to education and professional development, makes a prominent figure in the field of civil engineering in Cambodia. Tel: (+855) 12543334 E-Mail: no.sinath@nubb.edu.kh

Sara Reis is an MSc in Clinical Process Optimization. PhD in Bioethics / Biomedical Engineering. Polytechnic Higher Education Teacher with the category of Prof. Adjunct. Interest in the area of Biomedical Engineering, namely in the areas of Innovation and Health Management.

Balveer Saini is a Senior Research Fellow Department of Mathematics MS Brij University Bharatpur Rajasthan India.

Sam Rany is the Vice-Rector of the National University of Battambang (NUBB), a public university in northwest Cambodia, which he joined in 2008. He has been the Cambodian Director of the Confucius Institute at the National University of

Battambang since 2019. He is a member of the Southeast Asia Research Academy (SEARA). He received his PhD in Education from the School of Educational Studies at the University of Science Malaysia (USM) in 2016. In 2017 and 2022, he graduated from the Royal School of Administration in Cambodia with diplomas in public administration, leadership, and innovation programs. He graduated with a Bachelor's and Master's Degrees in Law (LL.B & LL.M) at the Royal University of Law and Economics (RULE), Cambodia, in 2004 and 2007, respectively. For his key achievement, he has published 50 academic papers and book chapters; he is also a project coordinator in various projects, including 10 Erasmus+ Capacity Building in Higher Education, 1 Korean ODA, 1 USAID, and 1 World Bank-funded Higher Education Improvement Project (HEIP). Legal Studies, Public Policy and Administration, Educational History and Cooperation, Educational Leadership and Management, and other types of social research were all things he was interested in. His email address is samrany82@gmail.com/sam.rany@nubb.edu.kh, and his mobile phone number is +855 (92) 646-680/(0)10-646-680.

Sarith Chiv is a PhD student at the National Institute of Education, Cambodia, and a vice-rector of the National Meanchey University, Cambodia.

Muhammad Usman Tariq has more than 16+ year's experience in industry and academia. He has authored more than 200+ research articles, 110+ case studies, 130+ book chapters and several books other than 4 patents. He is founder and CEO of The Case HQ, a unique repository for courses, narrative and video case studies. He has been working as a consultant and trainer for industries representing six sigma, quality, health and safety, environmental systems, project management, and information security standards. His work has encompassed sectors in aviation, manufacturing, food, hospitality, education, finance, research, software and transportation. He has diverse and significant experience working with accreditation agencies of ABET, ACBSP, AACSB, WASC, CAA, EFQM and NCEAC. Additionally, Dr. Tariq has operational experience in incubators, research labs, government research projects, private sector startups, program creation and management at various industrial and academic levels. He is Certified Higher Education Teacher from Harvard University, USA, Certified Online Educator from HMBSU, Certified Six Sigma Master Black Belt and has been awarded PFHEA, SFSEDA, SMIEEE, and CMBE.

Thol Ngorntheng is a government official who has worked at the Ministry of Education, Youth, and Sport from 2015 until now in Cambodia. He has served as the Vice Dean at the University of Battambang since 2012, at the faculty of Art, Humanity, and Language (Internal Position). He has been a Ph.D. candidate in Educational Science at the National University of Chea Sim Komchaymear since 2022 in Cambodia. He graduated with Bachelor's and Master's Degrees in Khmer Literature at the Khemarak University (KU), Cambodia, in 2008 and 2010, respectively. In 2004 and 2006, he graduated with a Diploma in English-Khmer Teaching Skills for Secondary school at the Phnom Penh Regional Teacher Training Center (PRTTC) in Cambodia. He is also actively teaching at some universities in Cambodia. His email address is ngornthengubb@gmail.com /thol.gnorntheng@outlook.com, and his mobile phone number is +855 (78) 772-296/+855 (12) 293-980.

Tith Kamrang, with over 20 years of experience in the financial sector, has held diverse roles ranging from a Credit Officer to a member of top management in both microfinance institutions and banks. Simultaneously, he has dedicated over 20 years to educating future generations as a teacher at primary schools, secondary schools, and as a lecturer at universities. His passion for financial literacy led him to become a Master Trainer and Curriculum Specialist in this field. Notably, he holds the prestigious title of Master Trainer in Financial Literacy awarded by World Education Australia. In Cambodia, he is also recognized as a Financial Literacy Thought Leader. Mr. Kamrang's commitment extends beyond education. He founded and leads Rithipul Co., Ltd, the first financial education firm in Cambodia. Additionally, he spearheads the development of the Kotluy App, a Personal Finance Management Platform. Through his tireless efforts, Mr. Tith Kamrang has positively impacted the lives of over 500,000 individuals across Cambodia, empowering them to make informed financial decisions.

Fadime Ulusoy is a Lecturer in the Department of Mathematics and Science Education at Kastamonu University, Turkey. She received her Ph.D. in Mathematics Education from Middle East Technical University in 2016. She has been awarded the "METU 2017 Thesis of Award" with her doctorate thesis entitled "Developing prospective mathematics teachers' knowledge for teaching quadrilaterals through a video case- based learning environment". Her research interests are elementary mathematics education, video cases and teacher education. She specifically interested in: the use of video cases in teacher education; active learning techniques; covariational reasoning, teaching and learning of geometry, multiple representations in teaching and learning of mathematics; subject matter knowledge and pedagogical content knowledge; noticing theory.

Yousef Wardat is an Assistant Professor in the Department of Curriculum and Instruction, Faculty of Mathematics Education, Higher Colleges of Technology, UAE. He received his Ph.D. in Mathematics Education from United Arab Emirates

University, UAE, in 2022. His research interest includes a range of interdisciplinary areas, Data analysis, Quantitative methods, SPSS analysis, mathematical modeling, mathematics education, He has published several peer-reviewed articles in different journals.

Deniz Yağmur is a specialist teacher and school principal working in the Ministry of National Education in Türkiye. She holds a BA degree in Preschool Teaching from Muğla University. Specializing in educational sciences, she conducts studies on artificial intelligence and music integration, sustainability and digital transformation.

Hak Yoeng is currently the Dean of the Faculty of Arts, Humanities, and Education at the National University of Battambang, Cambodia. He is also a PhD student specializing in educational management at the National University of Battambang in Cambodia.

Index

A

C

D

E

F

G

I

M

O

P

R

S

T

www.ingramcontent.com/pod-product-compliance
Lightning Source LLC
LaVergne TN
LVHW060007031026
849161LV00025B/1552